P9-DDM-219

Minnie and The Mick

Minnie and The Mick

The Go-Go White Sox Challenge the Fabled Yankee Dynasty, 1951 to 1964

BOB VANDERBERG

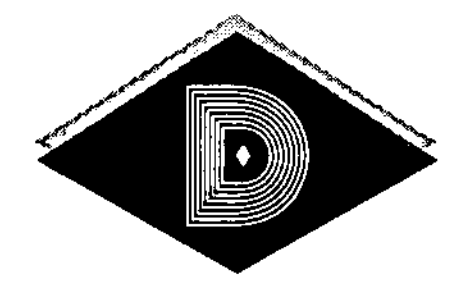

Diamond Communications, Inc.
South Bend, Indiana
1996

Minnie and The Mick
The Go-Go White Sox Challenge
the Fabled Yankee Dynasty, 1951-1964

10 9 8 7 6 5 4 3 2 1

Manufactured in the United States of America

Diamond Communications, Inc.
Post Office Box 88
South Bend, Indiana 46624-0088
Editorial: (219) 299-9278
Orders Only: (800) 480-3717
FAX (219) 299-9296

Library of Congress Cataloging-in-Publication Data

Vanderberg, Bob, 1948–
Minnie and the Mick : the go-go White Sox challenge the fabled Yankee dynasty, 1951–1964 / Bob Vanderberg.
p. cm.
Includes bibliographical references (p.).
ISBN 1-888698-02-0
1. Chicago White Sox (Baseball team)--History. 2. New York Yankees (Baseball team)--History. 3. Mantle, Mickey, 1931– . 4. Minoso, Minnie, 1922– . I. Title.
GV875.C58V35 1996
796.357'64'0977311--dc20 96-30426
CIP

Contents

Author's Note

During the writing of this book, four figures in the narrative have passed from our midst—former Yankees Mickey Mantle and Allie Reynolds and ex-White Sox Ray Moore and Saul Rogovin, the latter of whom graciously provided me with an hour's worth of memories and insisted I call him when the book was completed. Sadly, I was never able to tell him.

Acknowledgments

Putting together a book such as this one requires the cooperation of many, many people. Fortunately, I received exactly that, in particular from the former Yankees and White Sox I have interviewed over the years. For their time and their recollections, I thank, from the Yankees, Hank Bauer, Jerry Coleman, Bob Cerv, Art Ditmar, Bob Grim, Tony Kubek, Johnny Kucks, Hector Lopez, Bobby Richardson, Bobby Shantz, Charlie Silvera, Ralph Terry, Tom Tresh, Bob Turley and, last but not least, Gil McDougald—with whom I corresponded by mail before he underwent what I can happily report was successful surgery to restore his hearing. From the White Sox, I thank Earl Battey, Ray Berres, Johnny Buzhardt, Chico Carrasquel, Phil Cavarretta, Larry Doby, Dick Donovan, Walt Dropo, Sam Esposito, Ferris Fain, Warren Hacker, Jack Harshman, Fred Hatfield, Joe Horlen, Deacon Jones, Jim Landis, Al Lopez, Marty Marion, Sam Mele, Minnie Minoso, Dave Philley, Billy Pierce, Juan Pizarro, Jim Rivera, Herb Score, Bob Shaw, Roy Sievers, Al Smith, Gerry Staley, Chuck Stobbs, Virgil Trucks, Pete Ward, and Al Weis. And, finally, thanks to these men who played for both clubs: Tommy Byrne, Andy Carey, Eddie Robinson and Chicago's own Bill "Moose" Skowron.

Only one person, of all those contacted, wished not to be interviewed, and that, to my disappointment, was Whitey Ford.

Thanks, too, to fellow *Chicago Tribune* staffers Jim Binkley and Rich LaSusa for their editing suggestions and to Steve Marino of the *Tribune*'s Information Center for his help with microfilm, reference books, and photographs.

Foreword

More than 30 years have passed since the era of baseball that this book covers, and yet to so many people—myself included—that era is still vivid in our minds. People today still come up to me and say how much they remember the big series with the Yankees or my pitching matchups with Whitey Ford. They might not remember the final score, but they'll remember the big Friday night crowds, the big Sunday doubleheader crowds.

The '50s was such an exciting time for the Chicago baseball fan. You have to remember that the White Sox had been down for 20 or 30 years. Their fans had had almost nothing to cheer about for decades. But the Yankee rivalry revived everything. I think the excitement started with the fans and carried over to the ballplayers. We might not have finished in second place every one of those years, but when we were playing the Yankees, in our minds we were fighting for the pennant.

Playing against a Hall-of-Famer in center field, a Hall-of-Famer at catcher, a Hall-of-Famer at shortstop, a Hall-of-Famer on the mound—it was an exciting time. And playing in Yankee Stadium at that time was special. New York was a big tourist town, of course, so we'd have as many people cheering for us as for the Yankees. And then you had Giants fans and Dodger fans in New York, too. And when they came out to Yankee Stadium in those days, they cheered for whomever was playing the Yankees. So it was funny—we had lots of people on our side when we played at Yankee Stadium. And really, Yankee Stadium was the Taj Mahal of baseball in that period. It will be a sad day when they tear that place down, just like it was sad to watch them tear down old Comiskey Park.

Nobody can tear down our memories, though, and this book brings back a lot of them, like that night in New York when the rain wiped out our ninth-inning rally and cost us a big ballgame. There was the day at Yankee Stadium when

Paul Richards put me at first base for a couple of batters in the ninth inning, the day Enos Slaughter made the mistake of taking on big Walt Dropo at Comiskey Park, the night Casey Stengel and the boys used sparklers to poke fun at Bill Veeck and our new exploding scoreboard.

There was the night I was in the shower, figuring I had a win, when Mickey Mantle hit a grand slam in the ninth to beat us, and the day Bill Skowron hit a grand slam in the ninth to beat us. Then there was the afternoon in New York when Tommy Byrne hit a grand slam in the ninth to beat *them*. And, of course, I'll never forget the homer Minnie Minoso hit off Vic Raschi in his first time up for us.

The book also reminded me of things I had forgotten, like that game that Minnie hit his first White Sox home run was also the game in which Mantle hit his first major-league homer. As a matter of fact, I thought we had won that game. It turns out we didn't. And I knew that I had given up a home run on a 3-0 pitch once to Joe DiMaggio, but I couldn't remember when. It's here in the book.

I just enjoyed reading about all the fellows I played with and against during all those years. And I'm sure that anyone who was a baseball fan—especially a White Sox fan—during the '50s and '60s will find many enjoyable memories when reading this book.

—Billy Pierce

Introduction

Casey Stengel, the wily "Ol' Perfessor" who managed the New York Yankees through their glory decade of the 1950s, put it this way when someone asked him about the No. 1 contender for his team's crown:

"You ain't goin' to no picnics when you tangle up with them Chicagos."

Remembered Bill Skowron, Stengel's muscular first baseman: "That was the team we had to beat—the White Sox. And, also, Detroit and Cleveland. But we were more worried about the Sox, because they had great pitching. And we were always up for them games."

Through the 1950s and up through the mid-1960s, the almost total domination of the American League by the Yankees was tested by several teams. The Boston Red Sox threat, a leftover from the postwar years, ended before the '50s were three years old. The Cleveland Indians, strong early because of solid pitching and their readiness to sign black talent, began fading by mid-decade.

With the advent of the 1960s, Baltimore, Detroit, and Minnesota made sporadic, threatening noises. But only one team consistently carried the fight to the Yankees, and that team was the Chicago White Sox. The White Sox were talented, well managed, well schooled in fundamental baseball, well prepared, proud of their pitching, speed, and defense, but—when it mattered most—seemed utterly unable to beat the Yankees.

To quote Brendan C. Boyd and Fred C. Harris in their wonderfully irreverent *The Great American Baseball Card Flipping, Trading and Bubble Gum Book*: "If the Yankees were the bullying big brothers of the American League of the '50s and the Red Sox the pesky little brothers, and if the Tigers were the kindly, elderly uncles and the Indians the nervous, bumbling fathers, if the Browns were the stupid distant cousins and the Athletics the annoying brothers-in-law and the Senators the obnoxious little nephews, then the White Sox were the fussy, fretting aunts. The White Sox had great pitching, great speed, great defense, great hustle and the most anemic and ineffectual hitting this side of the Pioneer League. For this reason, most of their games were decided by one run, and they always came in second in the American League."

Second to the Yankees, of course. First place belonged to the Yankees every year from 1949 through 1953. Cleveland—with Al Lopez managing, Early Wynn, Bob Lemon, and Mike Garcia pitching and Al Rosen, Larry Doby, and Bobby Avila hitting—won 111 games and the pennant in 1954. Then the Yankees finished first nine of the next 10 seasons. The one year they failed to win, 1959, the White Sox did, with a team that finished sixth in the league in batting and dead last in home runs—but, as was usually the case during this period, first in pitching, first in fielding, and first in stolen bases.

It was a style of baseball that appealed to many—including, oddly enough, a big first baseman named Walt Dropo, who was a Fenway Park masher with the Red Sox before winding up in a Chicago uniform—and it was a style of baseball unimpressive to many others—among them the late Bill Veeck, who purchased the Sox in December 1958 and whose team, despite all his predictions of doom, won the AL championship his first year in operation.

Said Dropo: "I actually enjoyed my stay in Chicago as well as anywhere. And you'll say, 'Why?' Well, because, at Fenway, we won some games 29-4, 15-12. I mean, those games are not baseball games. But in Chicago, every game we played seemed to be a close game. And I liked that, because every play meant something. Every pitch meant something."

Countered Veeck: "Teams like the White Sox that depend upon speed and defense delight the hearts of all old-timers and generally finish in the second division."

The White Sox, however, always finished in the first division—every year from 1951 through 1967. To be sure, their success against the Yankees was less than rousing—indeed, New York was a deceptively one-sided 174-118 against the Sox from '51 through '64. But there was sufficient reason for that.

Just ponder, for a moment, what the White Sox were up against when the decade of the '50s began.

At Phoenix in 1951, before they started the regular phase of spring training, the Yankees held a special camp for the prize youngsters in their system. Among them were outfielders Jackie Jensen, 23, Bob Cerv, 24, and Skowron, then 20 and not yet a first baseman; infielders Gil McDougald, 23, Andy Carey, 20, and Billy Martin, 22; and pitchers Tom Morgan, 21, and Tom Sturdivant, 21. Oh, and there was a 19-year-old switch-hitting shortstop who had played just one year of organized ball, at Class C Joplin, Missouri—a kid by the name of Mickey Mantle.

Most of them were so impressive that Stengel, starting his third year as Yankee manager, asked them to remain and train with the regulars, who already included such established, younger players as Gene Woodling, Hank Bauer and Joe Collins, all 28; Jerry Coleman, 26; Yogi Berra, 25; and Ed "Whitey" Ford, 22. Then there was the old guard, the other veterans of two straight World Series championship clubs: Joe DiMaggio, Phil Rizzuto, Johnny Mize, Bobby Brown, Billy Johnson, Vic Raschi, Allie Reynolds, Eddie Lopat, and Tommy Byrne.

Meanwhile, over in Pasadena, California, the only good-looking rookie prospects in the White Sox camp were Jim Busby, a 23-year-old center fielder, and Bob Boyd, a 24-year-old first baseman who had been purchased from the Memphis Red Sox of the old Negro leagues. And there were three youngsters—pitcher Billy Pierce, 24, and shortstop Chico Carrasquel and second baseman Nellie Fox, both 23—who had just finished their first full year together with the Sox. The lack of young prospects was frightening, but not surprising. The club's farm system, begun only a couple of years earlier, consisted of just eight clubs, compared to the Yankees' 18.

So the bulk of the team that went to camp that spring in Chicago uniforms was made up of veterans—position players like Eddie Robinson, Gus Zernial, Dave Philley, Al Zarilla, Phil Masi, Gus Niarhos, Hank Majeski, and Floyd Baker and pitchers like

Joe Dobson, Randy Gumpert, Howie Judson, Lou Kretlow, Harry Dorish, Luis Aloma, and Ken Holcombe.

It was not until much, much later that the Sox could quit depending on general manager Frank Lane's trades, minor-league purchases, and waiver acquisitions and begin reaping production from their farm system, which in the latter half of the decade began turning out prospects like Luis Aparicio, Jim Landis, Earl Battey, Johnny Romano, Norm Cash, Jim McAnany, Barry Latman, and Johnny Callison. But, of course, by then, the Yankee system had reloaded and was producing Tony Kubek, Bobby Richardson, Norm Siebern, Jerry Lumpe, Johnny Kucks, Ralph Terry, Jim Coates, and many, many more.

Also, the Yankees had been winning for years, drawing 70,000 people a game for World Series after World Series and using all that resulting money to scout and sign players for their vast minor-league organization. The White Sox had been losing for years, drawing little more than flies while firmly establishing themselves as the No. 2 baseball team in Chicago, well behind the Cubs in money and popularity. There had been a brief flurry of competence in the years 1936-40 under Jimmy Dykes, but the Sox hadn't had a winning season since 1943, when most of the good major-league ballplayers were off fighting Germans or Japanese—or boredom in stateside military posts. Losing seasons begat empty seats, which begat empty bank accounts, which meant the Sox could spend precious little on the procurement and development of young talent.

This was the situation into which 42-year-old Paul Richards, brought in by Lane, was walking as he took over the White Sox in spring training at Pasadena in 1951. How could this franchise compete with the mighty Yankees, let alone established first-division clubs like Cleveland, Boston, and Detroit? Well, before many months would go by, the White Sox were competing, and successfully, with all the clubs in the American League—even, at times, the Yankees.

And, as the years progressed, the White Sox would establish themselves as masters of all they surveyed in the American League, except for the Yankees. But that does not mean they didn't battle the Yankees and make it exciting. Because they did. And they generally did it in front of gigantic crowds, both at old Comiskey Park and at Yankee Stadium. This was before the giveaway days, before Bat Days and Helmet Nights and Sun Visor Days and Floppy Hat Nights. You didn't have to give away free tankards or posters or caps or postgame fireworks to get 45,000 for a White Sox-Yankee night game at Comiskey Park or 60,000 for a Sox-Yankee doubleheader at Yankee Stadium. The draw, plain and simple, was the promise of exciting baseball, pennant race baseball, games so often decided by one run—and in the final inning or two.

"Those games," recalled Walt Dropo, "were clinics. Every game was a World Series game."

Indeed, for generations of White Sox fans, those games were the closest they would get to a World Series atmosphere—except for the miracle year of 1959. And even then, the White Sox's opponents in the Series, the Los Angeles Dodgers, did not strike anywhere near the same kind of fear into Sox fans' hearts as did the dreaded Yankees, with their terrific defense, underrated pitching, and game-breaking, heart-wrenching ninth-inning home runs.

The excitement of those days is what this book attempts to recapture, to bring back to life. In the pages ahead, the memories await.

The Cast of Characters

NEW YORK

Some of the big names that will pop up often in the pages ahead:

Mickey Mantle: Played in all 14 years covered by this book...American League Most Valuable Player in 1956, '57, and '62. Won Triple Crown in '56 with 52 home runs, 130 runs batted in, and a .353 batting average. Hit .365 in '57, but Ted Williams beat him out with .388. Spectacular center fielder, dangerous switch hitter. Led league in walks five years and in strikeouts a like number. His 18 World Series homers are a record, as are his 40 Series RBIs. Hall of Fame, 1974.

Yogi Berra: 14 years...League MVP in '51, '54, and '55. Hit 30 homers in '52 and '56, drove in 100 or more runs five times. Particularly dangerous in late innings. Lifetime .285 hitter, All-Star catcher 13 years. Tops all-time list with 75 World Series games played. Managed Yankees to pennant in '64. Hall of Fame, 1971.

Whitey Ford: 12 years...Club's big winner throughout '50s and '60s, ended 236-106 for .690 winning percentage, third best of all time. Led AL three times in wins (18 in '55, 25 in '61, 24 in '63) and twice in ERA (2.47 in '56 and 2.01 in '58). Little lefty (5-10, 178), an All-Star pick eight years, baffled White Sox hitters all through his career. Hall of Fame, 1974.

Elston Howard: 10 years...League MVP in 1963, when he led Yankees, who were weakened by injuries to Mantle and Roger Maris, to the pennant with 28 HR, 85 RBIs, and .287 average. Catcher-outfielder hit .348 in '61. Broke in in '55 as first black to play for Yankees. Caught superbly, played the outfield well, and, in 1959 after Bill Skowron broke his wrist, filled in expertly at first base. Hit over .300 three times. Nine-time All-Star.

Gil McDougald: 10 years...Voted AL Rookie of the Year in '51 by Baseball Writers Association of America after hitting .306 with 14 HR and 14 steals. Clutch player, drove in 78 runs in '52 and 83 in '53. Five-time All-Star, played third base, second and shortstop capably. Hit career-high .311 in '56, tailed off final three seasons (.250, .251, .258) after his line drive hit Cleveland's Herb Score in the eye in May '57.

Hank Bauer: Nine years...Solid all-around outfielder, ran bases with ferocity, no surprise in that he was a former U.S. Marine. Consistent hitter (.320, .296, .293, .304, .294 in successive seasons). Hit 20 HR in '55, career-best 26 in '56. Often a leadoff man, nonetheless reached 84 RBIs in '56. All-Star pick three years.

Bill Skowron: Nine years...Went from Chicago's Weber High to Purdue University to Yankee Stadium. Broke into majors in '54, hitting .340 as part-timer; became regular first baseman in '56, hitting .308 with 23 HR and 90 RBIs. "Moose" had best year in 1960 (26, 91, .309) after missing second half of '59 with broken wrist. Five-time All-Star. Finally came home to White Sox in '64.

Tony Kubek: Nine years...Won BBWAA's and *Sporting News*' AL Rookie of the Year Award in '57 after coming up from Denver, where he had been a .331-hitting shortstop the year before. At age 20 and playing mostly left in '57 rather than his normal position, he hit .297. Took over as club's No. 1 shortstop in '58. Best year probably 1960, when he hit .273 with 14 HR and 62 RBIs. Three-time All-Star, had 38 doubles in '61. Retired at age 28 after '65 season.

Bobby Richardson: Eight years...Came up to stay in '57 after teaming with close friend Kubek to form American Association's best double-play combination. He'd hit .328 at Denver in '56, reached .301 in '59, and .302 in '62, when he led AL in hits with 209. Seven-time All-Star known best for his splendid defense, his record 12 RBIs in the '60 World Series, his evangelical Christian beliefs and his willingness to share them with youth groups around the country.

Bob Turley: Eight years...Was AL strikeout king in '54 with Baltimore, after which Yankees traded for him. Big right-hander (6-2, 215) from downstate Illinois then fanned 210 in '55 but was surpassed by Cleveland rookie Herb Score's 245. Won 17 in '55, slumped to eight in '56, then went 13-6 in '57 and 21-7 with six shutouts in '58, when he won the Cy Young Award. Also had six shutouts in '55. Generally ineffective after '60.

Joe Collins: Seven years...Often platooned during his career, all of it with the Yankees. Excellent defensive first baseman, had best year with bat in '52, when he hit 18 homers with .280 average in 428 at-bats, the most he ever had. Most proficient in the clutch. Low-ball hitter who perfected the art of lofting homers over the close-in right-field fence in Yankee Stadium.

Roger Maris: Five years...League MVP in 1960 and '61. Caught Yankees' attention in '58, when he was hitting 28 HR at Kansas City with 80 RBIs. Yanks traded Bauer, Norm Siebern, Don Larsen, and Marv Throneberry to get him in December 1959, and he promptly hit .283 with 39 homers and 112 RBIs in '60, then, incredibly, 61 HR with 142 RBIs in '61. Followed with 33, 23, and 26 homers next three years. Superb defensive rightfielder as well.

Eddie Lopat: Five years...A Yankee for seven and a half years after his trade February 24, 1948 from the White Sox for catcher Aaron Robinson and young pitchers Bill Wight and Fred Bradley. Became Yankee mainstay, fooling hitters with slow-slower-slowest repertoire. Lefty had seasons of 17-11, 15-10, 18-8, 16-4, and 12-4. His best was '51, when he was 21-9 with a 2.91 ERA and five shutouts. His 2.42 ERA led league in '53.

Art Ditmar: Five years...After winning 12 games two straight seasons with lowly Kansas City, went to Yankees in February 1957 in 11-player deal. Continued his mastery of the White Sox over next five seasons, going 10-2 against them. Became top righthander on New York staff in '59 and '60, winning 13 and 15 games those two years. Known, too, for the brushback pitch that ignited the Sox-Yankee brawl in June of '57 at Comiskey Park.

Allie Reynolds: Four years...A Yankee as the result of a Bill Veeck deal that sent Joe Gordon to Cleveland. Acquired at age 32 in 1947, "the Chief" went 19-8, 16-7, 17-6, 16-12, 17-8, 20-8, 13-7, and 13-4 in a New York uniform and led the AL in ERA, shutouts (six), and strikeouts in 1952 as a 37-year-old. Also led in shutouts (five) in '51. Threw at least 213 innings six straight years, until Casey Stengel began using him more in relief in '53. Retired after '54 season.

The Cast of Characters

CHICAGO

Some more names that will be prominent in the pages ahead:

Nellie Fox: Played for the White Sox in 13 of the 14 years covered by this book...Came to Chicago for an obscure catcher named Joe Tipton after 1949 season. Became American League's dominant second baseman (12 All-Star selections, three Gold Gloves, six fielding titles) and was MVP in '59, the year the Sox won the pennant. Led AL in hits (with 201) in '54 and in '52, '57, and '58. Topped .300 six times during '51-'59. Missed Hall of Fame by two votes in 1985, 10 years after he had died of cancer.

Sherm Lollar: 12 years...No. 2 catcher in AL, behind Yogi Berra, through much of the '50s but established himself as No. 1 in '58 and '59, when, coupled with his usual outstanding defense, he hit 20 and 22 homers with 84 RBIs each year. Best year for average was '56, when he hit .293 with 75 RBIs. Six-time All-Star became Sox regular in '52 after trade from St. Louis Browns. Like Fox, died of cancer, in 1977.

Billy Pierce: 11 years...Ranked with Whitey Ford as AL's premier lefty throughout the '50s; actually was 8-6 in head-to-head competition (9-6 including '62 World Series victory when Billy was with the Giants). Started All-Star Game in '53, '55, and '56. Led AL in strikeouts in '53, ERA in '55, complete games in '56, '57, and '58, and wins in '57. Twenty-game winner in '56 and '57 and was named *Sporting News'* Pitcher of the Year both those years. Career record 211-169 with 3.27 ERA, 1,999 strikeouts to 1,178 walks, but never close to Hall-of-Fame election.

Minnie Minoso: 10 years...No. 3 hitter, almost invariably, in Chicago lineup from the day he arrived from Cleveland, April 30, 1951, through '57 season. After two years with Indians, "Cuban Comet" returned in '60 at age 37 to hit .311 with 20 HR and 105 RBIs and lead AL in hits (184). Eight-time All-Star hit .300 or better eight years. Drove in 100-plus runs and scored 100 or more four times; three times led AL in steals and triples. In best year, '54, hit .320 with 18 triples, 19 homers, 116 RBIs. *Sporting News'* AL Rookie of the Year in '51.

Jim Rivera: Nine years...Came to Chicago in 1952 and became an outfield mainstay for the rest of the decade. A crowd favorite because of his speed and hustle, stole 20 bases or more five times, always with his patented head-first slides. Severe hitch at plate helped keep his career average at .256. "Jungle Jim" led AL in triples with 16 in '53 and in outfield assists with 22 in '55.

Jim Landis: Eight years...Five-time Gold Glove winner, rated by most as better defensive center fielder than Mickey Mantle. Never known for his bat, nonetheless developed into solid hitter in '58, second year in majors, with 15 HR and .277 average, then hit .272 in '59 in No. 3 hole in lineup. In '61, hit .283 with 22 HR and 85 RBIs. In successive seasons, stole 18, 20, 23, and 19 bases.

Luis Aparicio: Seven years...Venezuelan speedster was given shortstop job in spring '56 after trade of his countryman, Chico Carrasquel, to Cleveland and began 18-year career culminated by Hall-of-Fame election in 1984. Led AL shortstops in assists six straight years and in fielding percentage seven straight. Led league in stolen bases nine years in a row ('56-'64), tying then-Sox record of 56 in '59. Followed that by stealing 51 and 53 bases the next two years. With Sox, an All-Star six times.

Dick Donovan: Six years...Broke in with 15-9 record in '55, followed with 12-10 in '56 and 16-6 (2.77 ERA) in '57, when he shared AL percentage title with the Yankees' Tom Sturdivant. Won 15 games in '58 despite a 3-10 start. A right-handed workhorse known for exceptional control (45 walks in 220 $\frac{2}{3}$ innings in '57 typical of his career) and a left-handed hitter known for his power (three homers each in '56 and '57). One of a very few to own winning record against Yankees.

Chico Carrasquel: Five years...Aparicio's predecessor, was an All-Star four years with Chicago, missing in '52 when sidelined two months by a broken finger. Acquired from Dodger system, broke in by batting .282 in '50 and fielding sensationally but lost out to Boston's Walt Dropo in Rookie-of-the-Year voting. Led AL shortstops in fielding percentage in '51, '53, and '54. Hit career-high 12 HR in '54, when he scored career-high 106 runs.

Al Smith: Five years...Solid outfielder for Cleveland for four years, came to Chicago in '58 with Early Wynn for Minoso and Fred Hatfield. Played on bad ankle first two years, hitting just .237 in pennant year but winning several games with his arm and late-inning home runs. Came all the way back in '60, hitting .315, second best in AL. Had 28 HR with 93 RBIs in '61, then .292 with 82 RBIs in '62 before dealt to Baltimore.

Floyd Robinson: Five years...Broke in during August 1960 stretch drive, established himself as regular in Sox outfield in '61, when he hit .310. Set club record, since broken, with 45 doubles in '62, when he hit .312 with 109 RBIs. Slipped to .283 in '63, bounced back to .301 in '64. Decent outfielder, solid left-handed hitter, Sox's biggest threat in clutch in early '60s.

Early Wynn: Five years...Thought to be finished when he went 14-16 in '58, his first year in Chicago, but came back to go 22-10 in '59 with 3.17 ERA to win Cy Young Award and *Sporting News*' Pitcher of the Year honor. Big righthander led AL in strikeouts in '58 at age 38 and in shutouts with four in 1960 at age 40. Went 0-6 vs. Yankees in '58, then beat them three of five in pennant year of '59. The 300-game winner entered Hall of Fame in 1971.

Juan Pizarro: Four years...Acquired in three-team deal with Reds and Braves after '60 season, became regular starter in June '61 and went 14-7 (2-1 vs. Yankees). Followed 12-14 off-year in '62 with 16-8 (2.39 ERA) in '63 and 19-8 (2.56) in '64. Hard-throwing lefty fanned 188 in 194⅔ innings in '61. Like Donovan, a dangerous left-handed hitter; batted .246 in '61, .211 with three homers in '64. Was 8-8 vs. New York in '61-'64.

John Buzhardt: Three years...Came to White Sox from Phillies with third baseman Charlie Smith for Roy Sievers in November 1961. Worked mostly as spot starter for next three seasons, going 8-12, 9-4, 10-8, but established himself as a Yankee-killer, going 5-0, with two shutouts, against them. Best season was '65 (13-8, 3.01 in 32 games, 30 of them starts). Was off to 9-4, 2.42 start in '63—with three shutouts—before arm trouble ended his season.

Pete Ward: Two years...Came to Chicago in January 1963 in six-player deal that sent Aparicio and Smith to Baltimore. Sox regular for seven seasons, best of which were his first two: Hit .295 with 34 doubles, six triples, 22 homers, and 84 RBIs in '63 to win *Sporting News*' AL Rookie Player of the Year Award, then hit .282 with 23 HR and 94 RBIs in '64. Particularly effective against New York, with whom he concluded his career in 1970.

1951

Setting the Stage

This was the year the Chicago-New York rivalry, flourishing for decades on so many other fronts, found its way into a new arena—American League baseball. New manager Paul Richards, with the help of general manager Frank Lane's deal-a-week pace, transformed a torpid 60-94 disaster that had drawn 781,330 fans the year before and stolen all of 19 bases into an exciting contender that led the league into July, finished 81-73, drew 1,328,234, and stole 99 bases—an unheard-of total in those days.

Lane's additions that winter had included right fielder Al Zarilla and pitchers Joe Dobson from Boston for pitchers Ray Scarborough and Bill Wight—the Red Sox have always been looking for pitching—and outfielder Eddie Stewart from Washington for another outfielder, Mike McCormick. Fresh arrivals from what passed for a farm system were center fielder Jim Busby and pitcher Marv Rotblatt. During the season's early weeks, Lane landed pitcher Saul Rogovin from Detroit for lefty Bob Cain, and third baseman Bob Dillinger on waivers from Pittsburgh. Lane later picked up outfielder Don Lenhardt, author of 22 home runs the year before as a rookie, in a three-team deal with the St. Louis Browns and Philadelphia A's.

But the whopper of them all came on April 30, when "Frantic Frank"—as Richards and the sportswriters called him—completed a three-team blockbuster with Cleveland and Philadelphia. To the A's went outfielders Gus Zernial and Dave Philley (from Chicago) and catcher Ray Murray and pitcher Sam Zoldak (from Cleveland), to Cleveland went much-coveted lefty Lou Brissie and to Chicago (from the A's) came outfielder Paul Lehner and (from the Indians) Orestes Minoso, called Minnie. Ever since he'd been hired the previous fall, Richards had been badgering Lane to get Minoso, who—with his bat and legs, but not his glove—had torn up the Pacific Coast League in 1950 at San Diego while Paul was managing against him at Seattle. "But he can't play anything," Lane protested—remember, these were the pre-DH days. "Don't you worry about him playing anything. I'll find a place for him," countered Richards. "We'll just let him hit and run."

Which is exactly what the White Sox's first black player did, hitting .326 and stealing a league-leading 31 bases. He teamed with the swift Busby to cause such a commotion on the basepaths that Comiskey Park crowds—embarrassingly small before but routinely now in excess of 30,000—began chanting "Go! Go! Go!" whenever one of the Sox, regardless of his speed, reached base. Thus began the era of the Go-Go Sox.

While all this was transpiring, the country's attention was focused on the Korean War and the firing by President Harry Truman of his top commander, Gen. Douglas MacArthur, who had demanded permission, which was not forthcoming, to bomb Chinese Communist bases in Manchuria. MacArthur returned home to ticker-tape parades, but the soldiers he left behind fought on and on. Armistice negotiations, begun that July, would drag on for two years.

This was also the year in which Julius and Ethel Rosenberg were sentenced to death for passing atomic secrets to the Soviets and in which Estes Kefauver's Senate committee conducted an investigation into organized crime. In 1951, too, J.D. Salinger wrote *Catcher in the Rye*, fellow novelist Sinclair Lewis died, and color television was born. Humphrey Bogart won the Oscar for best actor with his performance in *African Queen*, Vivian Leigh (*A Streetcar Named Desire*) was voted best actress, and *An American in Paris* best picture.

Meanwhile, in Chicago that May, the White Sox returned from an 11-0 road trip to discover they had chased the Korean War off the front page. They won three more games to extend the streak to 14, lost two, then ran off six more victories in a row to put their AL-best record at 32-11. On the day the Minoso deal was made, they were 6-4. They lost Minnie's first two games—to the Yankees, of course—then went 26-5, a pace that forced even the Yankees to take notice. But it could not and would not last. New York, with 21-game winners Vic Raschi and Eddie Lopat, ended up battling Cleveland, not Chicago, down the stretch, the Yankees finally beating out rookie manager Al Lopez's Indians by five games. Brissie had helped Cleveland, especially in relief, but add Minoso's bat and speed to Luke Easter (27 home runs), Al Rosen (24), Larry Doby (20), Bobby Avila (.304 average), and Dale Mitchell (.290), plus 20-game winners Bob Feller, Early Wynn, and Mike Garcia, and it might not have been an all-New York World Series. But, thanks in part to the persistence of Richards and Lane, it was.

Rosters

Lists position players who appeared in 20 or more games, pitchers who appeared in 10 or more games, plus regulars who may have been traded/sold or acquired during the season.

1951 YANKEES

PITCHERS
Tommy Byrne, Tom Ferrick, Bob Hogue, Jack Kramer, Bob Kuzava, Eddie Lopat, Tom Morgan, Joe Ostrowski, Stubby Overmire, Vic Raschi, Allie Reynolds, Johnny Sain, Jack Sanford, Art Schallock, Frank Shea

CATCHERS
Yogi Berra, Charlie Silvera

INFIELDERS
Bobby Brown, Jerry Coleman, Joe Collins, Johnny Hopp, Billy Johnson, Billy Martin, Johnny Mize, Gil McDougald, Phil Rizzuto

OUTFIELDERS
Hank Bauer, Joe DiMaggio, Jackie Jensen, Mickey Mantle, Cliff Mapes, Gene Woodling

1951 WHITE SOX

PITCHERS
Luis Aloma, Bob Cain, Joe Dobson, Harry Dorish, Randy Gumpert, Ken Holcombe, Howie Judson, Lou Kretlow, Billy Pierce, Saul Rogovin, Marv Rotblatt

CATCHERS
Phil Masi, Gus Niarhos, Bud Sheely

INFIELDERS
Floyd Baker, Chico Carrasquel, Joe DeMaestri, Bob Dillinger, Nellie Fox, Bert Haas, Hank Majeski, Eddie Robinson

OUTFIELDERS
Jim Busby, Ray Coleman, Paul Lehner, Don Lenhardt, Minnie Minoso, Dave Philley, Eddie Stewart, Al Zarilla, Gus Zernial

1951

Most Glorious Victory
Tuesday Night, July 17

At Comiskey Park
Attendance: 45,580

The race had tightened. Again. And the White Sox were going back to work. Again. A grueling stretch of baseball had ended for them two days earlier with a doubleheader defeat at the hands of the seventh-place Philadelphia A's. The Athletics had taken advantage of a weary bunch of Chicago players, who were just getting over the effects of a twi-night doubleheader loss to the Red Sox on July 12—the second game of which had gone 17 innings—and a dramatic 5-4, 12-inning victory over the same club the following evening. Now the mighty Yankees were in town for a three-game series, with the standings reading as follows:

Boston	51-32	–
Chicago	51-34	1
New York	48-32	1½
Cleveland	48-34	2½

Saul Rogovin, who had gone the entire distance in that 17-inning loss to Boston, was set to oppose the Yankees' Allie Reynolds this night. Rogovin, who would go on to lead the American League in earned-run average in 1951, had already faced the Yankees twice this season, losing 2-1 at home on June 10 and winning 5-2 just 11 days later in New York. He would beat them twice more and lose to them twice more in '51, and each game would be a taut one. He relished the prospect.

"I think I pitched better against the Yankees than I did against any other club," Rogovin had said from his home in New York City, before his death in 1994. "I guess, first of all, there's a little extra incentive when you're playing against the Yankees because they're so good, you know they're the team to beat, and actually you hate them—you know, competitively—because they're always winning. So you're trying to knock them off all the time. That's the way I felt about it. So I bore down a little extra hard, I concentrated more, when I pitched against them. Looking back, I wish I could've zoned in every time I walked out there like I did against the Yankees. I think I would've been a better pitcher."

He could not have been much better than he was through the first six innings on this night. The Yankees were without a run and had managed just three hits. But Reynolds likewise had the Sox handcuffed. This was hardly unusual for Rogovin, he recalled: "When I was going good, like in '51, I pitched a lot of games that were 0-0 going into the sixth, 0-0 going into the seventh."

With two out and Gil McDougald on base in this seventh, Hank Bauer, with one hit in his last 25 times up, drilled a Rogovin pitch into the lower deck in left for a 2-0 Yankee lead. But the Sox struck back against Reynolds with three in the eighth, tying the score on RBI singles by Eddie Stewart and Minnie Minoso and going ahead when Stewart came home from third while second baseman Jerry Coleman was making a diving stop to throw out Eddie Robinson. So out went Rogovin for the ninth, ahead 3-2 and full of confidence.

"All that year, and the next, in the last three innings, I found an extra speed on my pitches. I found a second wind. And I was able to step it up a little bit in the last three innings and really shut the door on somebody when I had 'em beat."

But not always. True, he retired Yogi Berra on a flyball to center fielder Jim Busby to start the ninth, one dangerous man out of the way. But then Joe Collins walked on a 3-2 pitch, and Bobby Brown—much, much later the president of the American League—batted for McDougald and looped an opposite-field double down the third-base line, Collins making it to third. That brought up Bauer again, and manager Paul Richards, in a no-brainer, called for an intentional walk to set up the double play.

Johnny Hopp batted for Coleman and hit the necessary groundball, only it was hit to the wrong spot—past Robinson at first and forcing Nellie Fox to range far to his left to make the pickup. His only play was to first, to retire Hopp, but Collins scored to even things at 3-3. Rogovin then induced another pinch swinger, Cliff Mapes, to ground to Fox to end the inning, stranding runners at second and third.

The Sox failed in the home ninth against reliever Stubby Overmire, and things looked dark when young Jackie Jensen, subbing in center field for the injured Joe DiMaggio, singled toward left-center leading off the 10th and set sail for second in an attempt for two bases. Busby, however, hustled over for the ball and fired to shortstop Chico Carrasquel, who tagged Jensen for the first out of the inning. Chico then leaped high for a one-handed grab of Phil Rizzuto's line shot, and Rogovin wrapped things up by getting Gene Woodling on a fly to Busby.

There was one gone in the Sox 10th when Stewart dumped a blooper in front of Jensen in short-center and hustled it into a double. That brought up Minoso, who was given an intentional pass, putting runners at first and second. Not only had first base been open, but Yankee manager Casey Stengel preferred to have Overmire, a lefty, pitch to the left-handed-hitting Robinson, not the right-handed-hitting Minoso. Robinson didn't care one way or the other.

"No, not at all," said Eddie from his Ft. Worth home. "I hit as well against lefthanders as I did against righthanders. I didn't hit for the same power as I did against righthanders, but I hit 'em just as well for average."

That's what he did here. Robinson smoked a line single to center, Stewart came home with the winning run, Rogovin had a much-deserved "W," and the Sox were back in a virtual tie for the AL lead with Boston, which had lost to Cleveland and Bob Feller an hour or so before. The winning hit by Robinson was just one of many big ones he delivered against the Yankees that season and the next.

"I hit good against the Yankees," said Robinson, who indeed hit five of his team-high 29 home runs that year against New York. "I hit good against all the good clubs. In fact, it might have been that same year, I hit .300 against every club but Philadelphia and Washington.

"We really wanted to beat the Yankees. We thought we had a pretty good club. In fact, we did. They were too good for us, though. We weren't that deep. Paul Richards had done a hell of a job with the team. He was getting top production from everybody, but we didn't have, really, that many great players. I mean, Rogovin was pitching like hell, and other guys too. They were not all that good, except they did good for Richards. Richards knew how to get it out of them."

And on this July evening, Robinson and Rogovin had served notice that they knew how to get the best of the Yankees.

1951

Most Devastating Defeat

Friday Night, July 27

At Yankee Stadium
Attendance: 50,125

Decades later, the scars remain.

"That one just killed us," said Billy Pierce.

"That was the hardest loss to the Yankees I can remember," said Eddie Robinson.

The White Sox defeat to which they referred was inflicted upon them more by the umpires and the elements than it was by the Yankees.

The evening began with Nellie Fox singling off Yankee rookie Tom Morgan, taking third on Al Zarilla's base hit, and scoring when Minnie Minoso grounded into a forceout.

It ended with White Sox manager Paul Richards screaming at the umpires, with Sox players staring sullenly into their locker stalls and with the Yankee clubhouse "the scene of wild celebration," as one account put it.

Here is what happened in between:

With two out in the bottom of the third, Pierce made a pitch too good to Gene Woodling. Woodling lined it over the right-field fence to tie the game, 1-1. In the sixth, Jerry Coleman lined a hit to left, moved up on Morgan's sacrifice bunt, and scored on a bouncing single to right by Woodling.

Meanwhile, the Sox—who had been swept four straight at home the weekend before by the lowly Washington Senators and thus had entered this game in fourth place, three and a half games behind the league-leading Yankees—were doing nothing with Morgan, a 21-year-old righthander. After seven and a half innings, it was still 2-1 New York. Then, in the eighth, again with two out, the Yankees struck. Pierce went to 3-0 on Joe DiMaggio, and Joe "D" hit the next pitch 420 feet into the seats in left-center. Now the Yankees led by two.

But then, suddenly, the Sox awoke. Robinson singled to center to start the ninth, and Joe DeMaestri, a rookie infielder, went in to run for him. Now, from the skies, which had been threatening all evening, came the rain. Eddie Stewart walked. It was pouring now. Floyd "the Blotter" Baker, better known for his glove, instead grabbed his bat and went up to hit for Jim Busby. With the count 2-2, and the rain's intensity not letting up at all, third baseman Gil McDougald called time and went to the mound to visit with Morgan. Most everyone figured McDougald, then a rookie, did so under orders from his manager, Casey Stengel, to stall for time. Not so, claimed McDougald, more than 40 years afterward.

"All of a sudden the heavens opened up and the rain really started coming down," he recalled. "And the third-base umpire asked me to run over and tell Tom Morgan to put the resin bag in his pocket. At this point, Bill McGowan, the dean of American League umpires, came over from his first-base umpiring spot, waving his arms to throw me out of the game. He wouldn't listen to my explanation, and then Casey started to argue. And it was like monsoon season, with water everywhere." Finally, McDougald remembered, he was sent away, with Stengel sloshing along behind, Casey however having managed to avoid ejection. With order restored, but with the rain still descending, play resumed and Baker came through with a hit to right to score DeMaestri. It was 3-2 but, more importantly, it was getting wetter. Plate umpire Hank Soar called for the grounds crew, which was painfully slow, as far as the White Sox were concerned, in getting the field covered.

When the game resumed after a delay of 26 minutes, lefty Joe Ostrowski had replaced Morgan, and Bob Dillinger, a right-handed hitter, replaced lefty Bud Sheely at the plate. Dillinger tried to bunt the runners along, but he bunted too hard and the lead man, Stewart, was out at third, the first out of the inning. Don Lenhardt, a right-handed long-ball threat, was sent up to hit for

Chico Carrasquel. Stengel waved in Frank "Spec" Shea, a righthander, and waved out Ostrowski. Lenhardt walked, filling the bases. Almost on signal, the rain began anew.

The due batter was Pierce, so Richards sent up a right-handed hitter, Bert Haas, to swing for him. And Stengel, even though a righthander was already pitching, brought in another one, Jack Kramer, to face Haas. Whoever was pitching, it looked like a mismatch. Berthold John Haas, age 37, a native of Naperville, Illinois —and a veteran of National League wars as a member of the Dodgers, Reds, Phillies, and Giants—had gone to bat just 30 times since his purchase from the Oakland Oaks of the Pacific Coast League in June and had collected all of three hits. Here, however, he lined a two-run single to left, and the Sox had a 4-3 lead.

Next, Fox singled off second baseman Coleman's glove, and the bases were reloaded. At this point, Soar, deciding it was raining too hard to continue play, again motioned the grounds crew into action. Also springing into action was Richards, who came flying out of the dugout to demand assurances from Soar and his colleagues. Richards, a couple of years before he passed away in 1986, related what happened next.

"The umpires told me they'd hold it for three or four hours and try to get it in. And then they waited exactly 30 minutes and they called it."

Actually, the official wait was one hour 10 minutes, at which time—12:32 A.M.—the downpour had tailed off to a slight mist. And, 10 minutes later, it had stopped raining altogether. Regardless, the score reverted to the last completed inning, the eighth. So the Sox, instead of being ahead 4-3 and threatening to score more—after all, the bases were loaded with just one out—were 3-1 losers. Angry 3-1 losers. What especially angered Richards, in addition to the umpires' breaking their word, was Soar's failure to inspect the field to determine whether or not it was playable.

"I charged into the umpires' dressing room," Richards recalled. Then he stopped, laughing to himself. "Actually, the first place I went was into Stengel's office—I got it mixed up with the umpires' room. But I finally made it to the umpires' room and gave 'em hell. But they didn't do anything. By the time we left the Stadium, the moon was out and the skies were clear."

And the Sox were four and a half games out of first instead of two and a half. (The deficit would become six and a half before the understandably dispirited Chicagoans left New York two days later.) Richards and general manager Frank Lane immediately filed a formal protest, calling for the game to be resumed at the point it had been called. Weeks later, American League President Will Harridge tossed out the protest. But in the days intervening, Richards seldom let up on the umpires.

"All they had to do," he said the day after the debacle, "was take the tarp off. Ten minutes after they called it off, it stopped raining. Since when are they in such a hurry? What's the big rush? They told us we could play until morning. There's no curfew—there's no time limit."

Here Richards had paused, thinking back to a twi-nighter against the Red Sox in Chicago two weeks before. The second game had gone 17 innings, the White Sox finally losing 5-4 at 12:47 A.M. The umpiring crew that night had included one Mr. Hank Soar. With that thought in mind, Richards related what Soar had told him in defense of his decision to call the game at Yankee Stadium. "Soar says to me, 'We don't want to keep these people out too late.' But it was all right to keep 'em out until one in the morning at Chicago, wasn't it? If they want a time limit, let the league put it on. Not the umpires."

Indeed, a night-game curfew finally was established by the American League a decade or so later. By that time, that rainy Friday night in Yankee Stadium had been all but forgotten—except by Paul Richards, Billy Pierce, Eddie Robinson, and a couple dozen other folks who were wearing Chicago uniforms that evening.

1952

Setting the Stage

As the Korean War dragged on, the summer and fall were enlivened by the campaign for president between Democrat Adlai Stevenson, governor of Illinois, and the eventual winner, Republican Dwight D. Eisenhower, former supreme commander of Allied forces in World War II.

In the Caribbean, Fulgencio Batista returned to power in Cuba. In the Pacific, the U.S. exploded the first hydrogen bomb. Acclaimed new books included Ernest Hemingway's *The Old Man and the Sea* and John Steinbeck's *East of Eden*. The Oscar for best actor went to Gary Cooper (*High Noon*), the award for best picture to *The Greatest Show on Earth*.

For the Yankees, even with the off-season retirement of the great Joe DiMaggio and the loss to the service of second baseman Jerry Coleman, it was business as usual. Cleveland, however, with AL home-run champion Larry Doby (32), RBI champ Al Rosen (105), and pitchers Early Wynn (23-12) and Bob Lemon and Mike Garcia (both 22-11), made it even closer than it had been in '51, this time falling two games short. The Yankees' 20-year-old Mickey Mantle, in his second season, showed his superstar potential (23 homers, 87 RBIs, .311 average). Yogi Berra filled the power vacuum left by DiMaggio and hit 30 home runs; and Allie Reynolds won 20 games with a league-best 2.06 earned-run average.

Over the winter, the White Sox had added pitchers Chuck Stobbs and Marv Grissom, catcher Sherm Lollar, and third baseman Hector Rodriguez, like Minnie Minoso a black Cuban. Minnie, though a bit short on English himself, immediately became Hector's interpreter, which, as could be imagined, didn't always work out so well. Once, Minoso co-signed a loan for Rodriguez so Hector could purchase a car. When the season ended, Rodriguez was sold to Toronto of the International League, where he had spent 1951. So Hector was out of the country. Some time later, loan company representatives sought out Minoso, demanding payment. All of a sudden, Minnie couldn't understand a word of English. Eventually, they wore him down, and Minoso finally spoke: "Minnie sign paper saying Hector nice fellow. Minnie no sign saying Minnie pay."

The Rodriguez acquisition was met with more approval by Paul Richards than another of Frank Lane's 1952 deals, the one in early May that sent Jim Busby to Washington for Sam Mele. "Over my violent protests," Richards recalled, several years later. "I was violently opposed to that deal. I didn't think we were getting enough back, and I knew you needed a strong center fielder in Chicago."

But Lane was attempting to strengthen an offense that had started the season in a slumber. Mele's addition, however, woke up very few Sox bats. The club's hitters, in one stretch, went to bat 99 straight times without so much as one extra-base hit. It did not help, either, to lose shortstop Chico Carrasquel for two months because of a broken finger—although that mishap set in motion the Chicago-to-St. Louis express that brought back to Comiskey Park shortstop Willie Miranda on June 28, just 13 days after Lane had traded him to Bill Veeck's Browns. Willie was dealt back to the Browns, by the way, less than five months later. Another Sox-Browns deal, this one on July 28, brought to the South Side one "Jungle Jim" Rivera, who stepped right into the White Sox outfield, where he would remain a fixture for the rest of the decade, delighting fans with his circus catches and belly-buster, head-first slides.

Despite the injury to Carrasquel and the offensive falloff from 1951, the White Sox moved up to third place, their best finish since 1941. But then again, they just barely beat out Philadelphia, Washington and Boston to finish that high—and the Red Sox's dive could be traced to the departure, in early

May, of Marine pilot Ted Williams for Korea. No, the White Sox would need more offense to go with pitchers Billy Pierce, Saul Rogovin, Joe Dobson, Harry Dorish, and Grissom if they were going to close the gap between themselves and the Yankees. Only Eddie Robinson (22 homers, 104 RBIs, .296) and Nellie Fox had come close to their production of the season before. Changes, Lane and Richards knew, would have to be made.

The only significant change for the Yankees this fall was their World Series opponent. This time it was the Brooklyn Dodgers rather than the New York Giants. The Series went seven games, instead of six as it had in '51, but the Yankees, who hit 10 home runs—three by Johnny Mize—won for the fourth straight year.

Rosters

Lists position players who appeared in 20 or more games, pitchers who appeared in 10 or more games, plus regulars who may have been traded/sold or acquired during the season.

1952 YANKEES

PITCHERS
Ewell Blackwell, Tom Gorman, Bob Hogue, Bob Kuzava, Eddie Lopat, Bill Miller, Tom Morgan, Jim McDonald, Joe Ostrowski, Vic Raschi, Allie Reynolds, Johnny Sain, Ray Scarborough, Johnny Schmitz

CATCHERS
Yogi Berra, Charlie Silvera

INFIELDERS
Jim Brideweser, Bobby Brown, Joe Collins, Billy Martin, Johnny Mize, Gil McDougald, Phil Rizzuto

OUTFIELDERS
Hank Bauer, Bob Cerv, Jackie Jensen, Mickey Mantle, Irv Noren, Gene Woodling

1952 WHITE SOX

PITCHERS
Luis Aloma, Skinny Brown, Joe Dobson, Harry Dorish, Marv Grissom, Ken Holcombe, Howie Judson, Bill Kennedy, Lou Kretlow, Billy Pierce, Saul Rogovin, Chuck Stobbs

CATCHERS
Darrell Johnson, Sherm Lollar, Phil Masi, Bud Sheely

INFIELDERS
Chico Carrasquel, Sam Dente, Nellie Fox, Rocky Krsnich, Willie Miranda, Eddie Robinson, Hector Rodriguez

OUTFIELDERS
Jim Busby, Ray Coleman, Hank Edwards, Sam Mele, Minnie Minoso, Jim Rivera, Eddie Stewart, Tom Wright, Al Zarilla

1952

Most Glorious Victory

Friday Night, June 20

At Comiskey Park
Attendance: 39,444

The White Sox, losers of all seven of their games to date in this particular year against the Yankees, were three outs away from making it an unsightly 0 for 8. Sox-killer Vic Raschi was on the mound, the Yankees led, 5-1, and many of the 39,444 fans began departing, in search of more pleasurable pursuits.

But hold everything. Eddie Stewart opened the ninth by singling to center. Leo Thomas, with the Sox less than a week, drew a walk. After Phil Masi forced Thomas at second, Ray Coleman, swinging for Chico Carrasquel, lined a hit to right to score Stewart. It was 5-2.

Next, Sherm Lollar, benched because his batting average had plummeted to .216, came up to hit for pitcher Luis Aloma. He singled to left to load the bases. That was all for Raschi. In came lefty Joe Ostrowski to face Nellie Fox. Base hit, left field, a run in—5-3, bases still loaded.

Out came Ostrowski, in came Bob Hogue, a righthander, to face Minnie Minoso. Minnie grounded a hit to left for two runs, and the game was tied. Fox and Minoso moved up on a wild pitch, effectively taking the bat out of the hands of Sabath Anthony Mele, who took his nickname from the initials of his full name. Sam, only a week removed from having driven in six runs in one inning in a game at Philadelphia, was given an intentional walk, loading the bases for Eddie Robinson, a noted clutch hitter. Not this time. Eddie smacked the first pitch on two hops to second baseman Billy Martin, who started a 4-6-3 double play that sent the game into extra innings.

Nothing of note occurred until the bottom of the 11th, when Fox opened against Hogue with a double to right. Casey Stengel, seeing first base open and remembering Minoso's two-run single off Hogue in his last at-bat, ordered an intentional walk. That brought up Mele, the No. 3 hitter in the lineup. But the Sox being the Sox, the No. 3 hitter was flashed the sacrifice-bunt sign by third-base coach Luman Harris, who had received the signal from Paul Richards, hiding in the dugout runway. (Richards had been given the heave-ho earlier in the evening by umpire Larry Napp, Paul's fifth ejection of the year—and third in games against the Yankees.)

A good soldier, Mele willingly accepted his instructions and prepared to lay one down, even though he had been acquired six weeks before from Washington for Jim Busby with the idea of providing the Sox with a solid run producer.

From his Quincy, Massachusetts, home, he recalled the details.

"I tell you one thing about that trade to Chicago. Frank Lane called me from New York, where the White Sox were—I was in Washington—and he said, 'I'd like to have you here right away.' And I says, 'Geez, yeah, as soon as I get all my stuff together.'

"He says, 'Listen, you get right up here right now and I'll buy you a new $200 suit.'

"And I got there right away and he said, 'Well, I promised you the suit.' And I says, 'You know, I'd rather have the cash.' And he did give me the cash."

Now Mele was about to cash in big. First, however, was the matter of the bunt.

"We had a problem sacrificing guys over against the Yankees," he recalled, " 'cause when you were bunting against the Yankees, they're charging hard. You couldn't get a bunt down. First baseman's charging right down your throat, third baseman's charging right down your throat.

"And Paul Richards had said, 'If they're doin' that, and you feel like you want to swing away, go ahead. You have my OK.' You know, 'cause if I bunt, they're gonna get the guy at third, and maybe get a double play, 'cause I didn't run all that well.

"So I come to bat, and Bobby Hogue, a little righthander, is pitching. I get the bunt sign, and I square around. Ball one. And they're right down my throat. Geez, I don't know how the hell I'm gonna bunt it. Next pitch. Ball two. And they're right down my throat again."

Mele called time and went up the line to chat with Harris. "I says, 'Luman, didn't Richards say that if they're running right down your throat, you can go ahead and swing away?' He said, 'That's exactly right.' "

Sam strolled back to the batter's box. You can guess what happened next.

"Goddamn if I don't hit the next pitch into the left-field stands to win the ballgame," Mele said, chuckling. "And when I got into the clubhouse, Paul Richards came over to me and said, 'You had the option, and you did it.'

"And I'll never forget it."

The 8-5 victory ignited, if only briefly, the Sox, who went on to take the series three games to one and close to within two games of the league leaders. But that would be as close as the Sox would come in 1952.

"The Yankees had a better ballclub than we did," Mele admitted, "but dammit, we always fought 'em tough. And I'll tell ya, they knew that we played tough against them, too. They knew that. And Paul Richards was one of the big reasons. Of course, we had a pretty good club, with Minnie, Billy Pierce, Nellie, Sherm Lollar, Eddie Robinson. But Richards was an absolute stickler for fundamentals, and he made you execute them well."

Unless, of course, you were Sam Mele and you were being asked to bunt against the Yankees.

1952

Most Devastating Defeat

Tuesday Night, July 29

At Comiskey Park
Attendance: 38,967

The White Sox were struggling, just three games over .500 and in fifth place, seven games back of the Yankees and even one and a half back of the surprising, fourth-place Washington Senators. The Sox, two games out of the lead on June 23, had begun their slide two days later, when Chico Carrasquel broke his finger. He was to miss two months. The Sox would finish a distant third. Forty years later, another Sox team with pennant aspirations lost another Venezuelan shortstop, Ozzie Guillen, for a whole season. The team finished a distant third. Losing All-Star-caliber shortstops for lengthy periods is not advised when you are trying to win pennants.

But now, there were still two months left in the season, time enough to get back in the race. And finally, for the first time in 1952, Billy Pierce was going to beat the Yankees. He took an 11-7 record into this night, but he was 0-5 against the Yankees. Incredibly, his teammates had pounded New York pitching for a grand total of seven runs in those five defeats. This time, it appeared, the results would be different.

The Sox built a 7-0 lead over the first six innings, Eddie Robinson driving in all but one of the runs. Jim McDonald was touched for one run almost immediately. Nellie Fox started the first inning with a single and moved up on another, this one by the newest member of the ballclub, outfielder Jungle Jim Rivera, acquired the day before from the St. Louis Browns. Minnie Minoso forced Rivera at second, but Minnie promptly stole second, putting Sox at second and third for Robinson, who lined a hit to right for the first two of his RBIs.

Two innings later, Rivera doubled and scored on Sam Mele's two-out single. It was 3-0. With two out in the fifth, Rivera drew a walk and went to second when McDonald, who a few years later was to wear a White Sox uniform, nailed Minoso, his future teammate, with a pitch on the left elbow. Two pitches later, Robinson whacked a drive into the lower deck in right, good for three runs and a 6-0 lead.

Robby's 70th RBI of the year, tops in the American League, came on a single following Minoso's sixth-inning triple, making it 7-0. Pierce, breathing easy, gave up a three-spot in the seventh after having stopped the Yanks on two hits through six. Then he was excused, in favor of Harry Dorish, which had been the plan.

"I had pitched with two days' rest, " Billy recalled, "and Paul Richards said, 'Bill, go seven innings and we'll let Harry mop up.' So Harry came in and, in the eighth inning, he got 'em out. Ninth inning, I'm in there taking a shower, feeling good, listening to the game on the clubhouse radio. Then there were a couple of walks and a hit, and an easy groundball was hit to Hector Rodriguez at third, and he booted it. And that set the stage for everything else."

The groundball, coming with two outs and runners at first and third, was hit by rookie Jim Brideweser, who had replaced Phil Rizzuto at shortstop when, as far as manager Casey Stengel was concerned, the game's outcome had been decided. The error by Rodriguez, a 32-year-old Cuban rookie generally regarded as a competent glove man, allowed Yogi Berra to score with the run that made it 7-5. Those among the crowd of 38,967 who had started for the exits—after all, it was past 11:30 — slowed up a bit in the aisles.

Dorish was lifted and, because the next two Yankee batters—Joe Collins and Irv Noren—swung left-handed, manager Richards summoned lefthander Chuck Stobbs from the center-field bullpen. Stobbs, in a starting role, had six-hit the Yankees and Eddie Lopat 5-1 on June 21 in Comiskey Park, but by now was finding himself shifted between starting and relieving. Life with the White Sox had become somewhat unsettled for him.

"Richards did a lot of funny things—Richards and I didn't get along too well, anyway," Stobbs said from his home in Sarasota, Florida, only a mile or so from the Sox's spring-training headquarters. "I used to throw across my body before, and he didn't like that, so he tried to change me all around, change my delivery and everything. And I lost my curveball that way.

"Then, you know, you'd start a game, and before you knew it, he'd have guys warming up in the bullpen. Well, if he was gonna do that, why start me in the first place? These things didn't go over too well with me."

Of course, what was about to happen wasn't going to go over too well with Richards. Stobbs started off by walking Collins to fill the bases. "Then," Pierce said, "I remember Irv Noren fouling off about 10 pitches before finally drawing a walk."

That forced in a run, making it a 7-6 ballgame. Up stepped switch hitter Mickey Mantle, the 20-year-old wunderkind who, just three days before, in Detroit, had hit his first major-league grand slam. Stobbs—minus his curveball, remember—tried to spot his fastball. The fastball was last spotted disappearing into the left-field upper deck. "The most thrilling homer I ever hit in my life," Mantle, for many years, called it.

The Yankees led 10-7. That's how the score remained.

"Frank Lane," Billy Pierce recalled, "was so mad, Rodriguez never played another game for us."

"I'll never forget Mantle hittin' that home run," Eddie Robinson said, 41 years later. "It just disappeared into the darkness."

Chuck Stobbs soon disappeared, too, to Washington, in a December deal for Mike Fornieles. Four games into the 1953 season, Stobbs faced Mantle once again, at Griffith Stadium. And Mantle got the best of the duel again, clobbering a home run 565 feet—at least, that was what Yankee publicity man Red Patterson measured what the baseball world quickly accepted as the longest home run ever hit. In any event, it was the longest home run ever hit in Griffith Stadium.

"People used to call a lot," said Stobbs, "and ask about the long one I gave up to Mantle in Washington, and you get tired of that after a while. I'll tell ya, I haven't been to a game in eight years. So that should tell you how much interest I have in it.

"But honestly, I don't remember the game I beat Lopat and I don't remember the grand slam Mantle hit. And I'd tell you if I did. But I guess maybe that's about when my Alzheimer's must have started setting in, right?"

❖ ❖ ❖

A footnote on Hector Rodriguez, the poor soul whose misplay made Stobbs' saddest Sox moment possible: Pierce's memory is slightly faulty. Rodriguez did indeed play another game with the Sox, in fact several. But, yes, Frank Lane was mad—so much so that, the very next day, 24-year-old third baseman Rocco Peter Krsnich, called "Rocky," was flown in from Seattle of the Pacific Coast League. Soon Krsnich was appearing in boxscores more often than Rodriguez, who in 1953 found himself back in the International League, from whence he had come.

1953

Setting the Stage

This was an abundantly eventful year around the globe. An armistice finally brought an end to the Korean War, Soviet dictator Josef Stalin died, Dag Hammerskjold became secretary-general of the United Nations, Queen Elizabeth II was coronated, Edmund Hillary reached the top of Mount Everest, the Rosenbergs were executed at Sing Sing and, in August, Moscow announced that it, too, had exploded a hydrogen bomb, thereby making everyone watching the developments in the Cold War even a little more nervous. And nervous people abounded in the U.S., where Sen. Joseph McCarthy continued his "witch hunt" for Communists in high places.

The world was changing, and so were the White Sox. Frank Lane, in January, dealt Eddie Robinson, his only legitimate longball hitter, to the Philadelphia A's with two young players—infielder Joe DeMaestri and outfielder Eddie McGhee—for the American League's two-time defending batting champion, Ferris Fain. Fain, known also for his fancy glove and his combative style, on and off the field, had hit .344 and .327 in successive seasons. For Chicago, he spent most of '53 around .280, broke his hand in a saloon slugfest in early August, and wound up at .256. "That was another deal Lane shoved down my throat," Paul Richards, an admirer of Robinson, his fellow Texan, recalled long afterwards. " 'Cause again we gave up too much, and Fain came over and was a washout for us."

Two weeks after pulling the trigger on the Fain trade, Lane packed up three pitchers—Marv Grissom, Hector "Skinny"

Brown and Bill Kennedy—and shipped them to Boston for the rapidly fading, and rapidly expanding, Vern "Junior" Stephens, of whom Brendan C. Boyd and Fred C. Harris wrote: "Vern Stephens hit popups. High popups. Neck-straining popups. Vern Stephens, it has often been said, could have played his entire career in a stovepipe—if they could have found one wide enough to hold him." Stephens, "the answer" at third base, was hitting .186 when he was released in July.

But no matter who played first or third base for the White Sox this year, it wasn't going to matter, because the Yankees—perhaps sparked by Mickey Mantle's 565-foot home run in Washington during the first week of the season—started spectacularly and did not cool off until an 18-game winning streak ended in mid-June. And by that time, the White Sox and Cleveland were both more than 10 games behind—as if the year's top film, *From Here to Eternity*, had been released with the American League contenders' plight in mind. But after a June 13 trade with the Browns brought them pitcher Virgil Trucks and yet another veteran third baseman, Bob Elliott, the Sox got hot and managed to close the gap on New York. They inched to within four games by July 19, only to lose a pair to the Yankees before 54,215 at Comiskey Park, and were still in shouting range—five games—by August 7, when they opened a four-game series in New York. The Yankees won three of four, including a doubleheader sweep in front of 68,000-plus on August 8.

Thereafter, the Sox faded to third place and the Yankees made it five straight pennants—beating out Cleveland by seven games, Chicago by 10—and five straight World Series crowns, downing Brooklyn in six games. When the year was over, the White Sox could point, with some pride, to the fact they had enjoyed their winningest season since 1920, the offensive feats of Minnie Minoso (.313 average, 104 RBIs, a league-high 25 steals) and the one-two pitching punch of 20-game winner Trucks and AL strikeout champ Billy Pierce (18-12, 2.72 ERA). But chasing the Yankees was becoming frustrating, and the Yankees did not appear to be slowing down.

Rosters

Lists position players who appeared in 20 or more games, pitchers who appeared in 10 or more games, plus regulars who may have been traded/sold or acquired during the season.

1953 YANKEES

PITCHERS
Ewell Blackwell, Whitey Ford, Tom Gorman, Bob Kuzava, Eddie Lopat, Bill Miller, Jim McDonald, Vic Raschi, Allie Reynolds, Johnny Sain, Ray Scarborough

CATCHERS
Yogi Berra, Charlie Silvera

INFIELDERS
Don Bollweg, Andy Carey, Joe Collins, Billy Martin, Willie Miranda, Johnny Mize, Gil McDougald, Phil Rizzuto

OUTFIELDERS
Hank Bauer, Mickey Mantle, Irv Noren, Bill Renna, Gene Woodling

1953 WHITE SOX

PITCHERS
Luis Aloma, Gene Bearden, Tommy Byrne, Sandy Consuegra, Joe Dobson, Harry Dorish, Mike Fornieles, Connie Johnson, Bob Keegan, Lou Kretlow, Billy Pierce, Saul Rogovin, Virgil Trucks

CATCHERS
Sherm Lollar, Bud Sheely, Red Wilson

INFIELDERS
Bob Boyd, Chico Carrasquel, Bob Elliott, Ferris Fain, Nellie Fox, Rocky Krsnich, Freddie Marsh, Connie Ryan, Vern Stephens

OUTFIELDERS
Sam Mele, Minnie Minoso, Jim Rivera, Eddie Stewart, Tom Wright

1953

Most Glorious Victory

Saturday, May 16

At Yankee Stadium
Attendance: 24,966

The luckless Billy Pierce drew Vic Raschi, 7-2 against the White Sox since the opening of the 1951 season, as his mound opponent this day. And it surely looked like Raschi would make it 8-2 as the Sox came to bat in the top of the ninth inning. For Raschi had them shut out on just two hits and was leading, 3-0. But then came a most unusual role reversal in the Sox-Yankee rivalry.

Bud Sheely, pinch-hitting for Luis Aloma, who'd relieved Pierce in the eighth, led off the Sox ninth with a base hit, and Freddie Marsh went in to run for him. Marsh took second on Nellie Fox's infield out and stayed there as Ferris Fain drew a walk. Minnie Minoso hit into a force play, on which Marsh went to third. Tom Wright singled to, of course, right, scoring Marsh, and Raschi walked Jim Rivera to fill the bases.

That was all Casey Stengel wished to see of Raschi, even though he still led 3-1 and two were out. Stengel instead waved in Ewell Blackwell, a veteran, sidearming righthander who had once won 22 games with the Cincinnati Reds and still could be extremely tough on right-handed hitters—one of which, Vern Stephens, was coming up next.

But Sox manager Paul Richards had other ideas. He called to the bullpen for Tommy Byrne, who had been KO'd as the starting pitcher in the series' opener two days before. Richards knew Byrne could swing the bat. The wild lefthander coudn't find the plate with his pitches, but he could reach the seats with his power. He would end up with 14 home runs in his career, and Richards already had seen Byrne hit two others in exhibition games as a member of the Sox—once in a game at Memphis and another in the final spring contest, against the Cubs and Warren Hacker in Wrigley Field. Now Richards was hoping for another one.

Byrne, from his hometown of Wake Forest, North Carolina, where after retiring from baseball he served two terms as mayor, recalled the game as if it had been played last week:

"I didn't know what the hell Richards wanted me for. I guess he didn't know—and I didn't, either—that Stephens had hit that many grand slams. He'd hit 10 of 'em. Anyway, Richards says, 'Have you ever hit against this fella?' I said, 'Yeah, 11 years ago. I was at Newark and he was at Syracuse.' And I said I got two for four, a double and a single, and I played left field. So he says, 'Well, how 'bout goin' up there and hittin' one out of here?' I said, 'Well, he throws a sinker, and he's got a good one, and occasionally he comes in on you, as a left-handed hitter. But I'll see what I can do.'

"And then I'm loosenin' up and swingin' the bat, and Ferris Fain comes runnin' up and says, 'Don't let him hit you on the fists with that slider of his—he's got a pretty good slider.' So I decided to take a pitch or two. And the first one was a ball and the second was a strike. Next one was a ball, next one a called strike — and it was that sinker, and I thought it was gonna hit me in the knee. I thought it was inside, but Scotty Robb, the umpire, said, 'That ball was good enough to hit.' And I said, 'Let's see that ball.' Blackwell throws the ball in, and Scotty Robb looked at it and said, 'There's nothing wrong with that ball.' I just wanted to collect my thoughts, you know?

"And the next pitch comes in, and I just swung and let that bat fly, and that damned thing went into the right-field seats. Oh, it was a line drive, went up in there about 25 rows. Isn't that somethin'?"

Indeed it was. The Sox had a 5-3 lead, and Harry Dorish's relief work in the bottom of the ninth ensured that it would be a 5-3 victory. Byrne's grand slam had given the Sox a sweep of the two-game series and put them just a half game behind first-place New York. "Everyone went crazy," said Byrne. "I remember Minoso jumpin' up in my lap and kissin' me when I crossed homeplate. Everybody went crazy—including Casey."

Stengel had managed Byrne with the Yankees before and would do so again before the next season had run its course. It was then that Byrne learned a bit more about the effect his one shining moment with the White Sox had had on his old boss.

"The guys on the Yankees told me later, when I got back, that Casey had jumped straight up when I hit that ball. And when he did, he hit his head on the top of the dugout. And that little metal button—on the top of the cap?—it cut into his head, and knocked him back down. Then he stuck his head out to see where the ball was going—of course, it went up in the seats—and then he reached up and grabbed his head, and the blood was on his hand. And the guys got a big kick out of that. He wasn't hurt real bad, but he was so damned mad he forgot he had hurt himself. I don't think he ever let Blackwell pitch another game for the Yankees."

As for Byrne, who had struggled with his control in the three starts he'd made for the Sox, he got into only two more games in a Chicago uniform. Richards, who had begged general manager Frank Lane to get Byrne—and Lane did, giving Willie Miranda and Hank Edwards to the St. Louis Browns in exchange for Byrne and Joe DeMaestri the previous October—finally grew weary of trying to teach Byrne control. Tommy was sold to the Washington Senators almost before he could finish enjoying his game-winning blow in New York.

"That win put us half a game out of first place. And when I was traded from the Yankees to the Browns [in '51], I went from first place to last place. Now, after that game, I've gone from last place practically to first place. Then I find out I'm going to Washington, and Washington at that time was in last place. So I'm going from first place to last place again."

But he got the last laugh. He ended up back with the Yankees, winning 16 games for them in 1955 and cashing World Series checks that year, the next, and the one after that. And he would hit seven more home runs, one of them a memorable shot in Comiskey Park. But more on that later.

1953

Most Devastating Defeat
Saturday, August 8

At Yankee Stadium
Attendance: 68,529

This was the series the White Sox had to either sweep or win three games to one, because they had entered it five games behind the world champions. The day before, the Yankees had taken the opener, 6-1, ending the Sox's remarkable Yankee Stadium winning streak at nine games. Their old nemesis, Eddie Lopat, had rendered their bats silent once again, so now, before the major leagues' biggest crowd of 1953, a sweep was definitely in order, if indeed the Sox were serious about their pennant dreams. There was a sweep, all right, but the wrong team brandished the broom.

In Game 1, Whitey Ford, who would soon replace Lopat as both the Yankee ace lefthander and as chief Sox tormentor, opposed little Sandy Consuegra, the Cuban righthander who spent his non-pitching hours breaking up teammates with his many impersonations, ranging from Sox pitcher Dick Donovan all the way to Adolf Hitler. There were no laughs this day. Consuegra matched Ford zero for zero through eight innings. In the ninth, Minnie Minoso chased left fielder Gene Woodling back some 420 feet from homeplate to haul down his long drive. And then, after Ford struck out Bob Elliott, Sam Mele lined what looked potentially like the go-ahead home run toward the left-field corner, where the fence was only 301 feet away. No such luck. The ball hit the top of the fence and bounded right to Woodling, who fired back in to gun down Mele at second base to end the inning.

Sure enough, Woodling, who'd made the big play to end the previous half-inning, led off the next. He drew a walk and moved to second, thanks to a sacrifice bunt by Billy Martin. With first base open, Sox manager Paul Richards ordered a walk to Phil Rizzuto, forcing Casey Stengel to remove Ford from the game for a pinch hitter. That was all right as far as Casey was concerned. He simply called on 40-year-old Johnny Mize, the hulking, lefty-swinging former National League home run champ who'd already helped the Yankees win four straight World Series since his arrival from the New York Giants late in 1949 and was soon to make it five.

Richards, unwilling to entrust this situation to his only lefty reliever, Gene Bearden, left Consuegra in to face Mize, who quickly got ahead in the count, 3-1. Mize lined the next pitch into left field to score Woodling with the game's only run.

Game 2 was more of the same, only worse. Lefty Bob Kuzava, like Lopat a former Comiskey employee, was even tougher than Ford had been. He not only held the Sox scoreless through the first eight innings, he held them hitless. In the meantime, his teammates had grabbed a 3-0 lead over Virgil Trucks, due mostly to Hank Bauer, who drove in two of the runs with a home run and sacrifice fly. Trucks had entered with a 9-1 record since coming to the Sox with Elliott in a June 13 deal with Bill Veeck's St. Louis Browns. Even Virgil could sense he was about to be handed loss No. 2: After all, the Sox had scored all of one run in the series' first 26 innings. The 27th held only the suspense of whether or not Kuzava would get his no-hitter.

Elliott batted for Trucks to start the ninth and fouled out to catcher Yogi Berra. Up stepped rookie first baseman Bob Boyd, playing only because the regular, Ferris Fain, was sidelined by a broken left hand, the result of some barroom fisticuffs the weekend before at a roadhouse in Colmar Manor, Maryland, just outside the District of Columbia line. Boyd, the third black to play for the Sox—following Minoso and Sam Hairston—hit Kuzava's first pitch, a fastball, on a line into right-center for a double to bust up the no-hit bid and draw the noisy wrath of the assembled throng. Moments later, the Yankee fans were cheering again, Nellie Fox and Minoso having gone out quietly to enable Kuzava to finish with a one-hitter, giving the Yanks a sweep of the doubleheader and an eight-game lead over the second-place Chicagoans.

Then came an even crueler fate for the Sox players, courtesy of Richards, who had proclaimed on the eve of this series that he had discerned a weakness in the Yankees and was about to exploit it. To which Stengel, noting the Sox's frustrating inability to dominate Jimmy Dykes' lowly Athletics, retorted: "If he's so smart, how come he can't beat Philadelphia?" Now, three games, one run, and three defeats later, Richards was fit to be tied. Watching his club pound out six hits in four hours 41 minutes of baseball was the crowning blow. Chico Carrasquel recalled the moment.

"We were in the clubhouse, nobody saying a word. Then in comes Luman Harris [Sox coach and Richards' top lieutenant]. He tell us, 'Leave your uniforms on. We're gonna have a workout.' We all look at each other: 'What's happening?' But you know what they did? Richards [or Reechards, as Chico pronounced it] asked Stengel if he could use the field. Stengel say, 'No, we got another game tomorrow here.' "

Richards, thinking fast, called the Polo Grounds offices of the New York Giants, who were in St. Louis playing the Cardinals. Bingo!

Carrasquel: "Here's what happen. We all get in taxis, with our uniforms on, about five of us to a cab. They drive us over the bridge across the Harlem River to the Polo Grounds. And we had batting practice and worked out for about two hours. Two hours! And this was after we have been at the ballpark since, I dunno, about 9:30 that morning? And we've played two games—a hot, muggy day. Oh, we're all grumbling, 'Reechards, you S.O.B.'...He was tough—a tough manager."

But, at times, there was a method to his madness. The next day, the weary Sox returned to Yankee Stadium and, with Billy Pierce pitching, blanked the Yanks, 5-0, and totaled 10 hits, three of them by Boyd, who opened the game with a home run off Vic Raschi. Richards-bashing ceased, for the time being, among his finally victorious athletes.

1954

Setting the Stage

The Supreme Court, in *Brown vs. Board of Education* of Topeka, unanimously banned segregation in the nation's public schools, setting the tone for a year of breakthroughs on a host of fronts. Dr. Jonas Salk announced discovery of a vaccine to fight the crippling ravages of polio, and the U.S.S. *Nautilus*, the first nuclear-powered submarine, was launched.

Half a world away, in a place called Dienbienphu, Communist rebels under the leadership of a tiny man named Ho Chi Minh defeated French forces after a brutal, two-month battle, and that is how many Americans learned for the first time about Vietnam.

On the society front, the story of the year was the marriage, albeit short-lived, of Joe DiMaggio and Marilyn Monroe. William Golding's *Lord of the Flies* was big in the bookstores, and Tennessee Williams' *Cat on a Hot Tin Roof* won rave reviews among the theater crowd. *On the Waterfront* dominated the Oscars, winning for best picture, best director (Elia Kazan), best actor (Marlon Brando), and best supporting actress (Eva Marie Saint).

Speaking of dominance, the Cleveland Indians scored an American League record 111 victories and beat out the Yankees by eight games. They defeated Washington 20 out of 22 times and toyed with the lowly (54-100) Baltimore Orioles—the transplanted St. Louis Browns—and the even lowlier (51-103) Philadelphia A's—soon to be transplanted to Kansas City. The Indians did not dominate the White Sox, however. The teams broke even over 22 games, leaving some to wonder if this, had it not been for injuries, could have been a White Sox year. The Sox had traded Sam Mele to Baltimore for Chicagoan Johnny Groth to play center field, moving Jim Rivera to right. They had added infield depth with Cass Michaels, a regular previously with the A's, Senators, and, before that, the Sox. For power off the bench, they had added a former National League slugger, Willard Marshall, from Cincinnati at the cost of Saul Rogovin and infielders Rocky Krsnich and Connie Ryan.

And, in May, with the Sox playing well and Ferris Fain resembling again the Ferris Fain of '51 and '52, Frank Lane added more reserve strength by signing the old Cub hero, Phil Cavarretta, then sent Grady Hatton and $125,000—big money in those days—to Boston for third baseman George Kell, thus rounding out an All-Star caliber infield. Virgil Trucks, second-year man Bob Keegan, 1953 pickup Sandy Consuegra, and rookie lefty Jack Harshman were pitching well, and Harry Dorish and Morrie Martin did superb work out of the bullpen. But Billy Pierce, after coming up with a sore arm at the club's new spring camp in Tampa, never did get untracked. Fain, hitting .302 and having already driven in 51 runs, tore up a knee on June 27 in a homeplate collision with Red Sox catcher Sammy White and was lost for the season. Then Kell injured one of his knees July 2 and was sidelined for more than a month.

These injuries were simply too much to overcome, despite career years from Minnie Minoso (.320 average, 29 doubles, 18 triples, 19 homers, 116 RBIs), Nellie Fox (201 hits, .319, 16 steals), Keegan (16-9, 3.09), and Consuegra (16-3, 2.69).

As for the Yankees, they had lost sparkplug second baseman Billy Martin to the Army, but back from the service were Jerry Coleman and pitcher Tom Morgan, a rookie standout in 1951. They sold holdout pitcher Vic Raschi to the Cardinals and, days later, traded three farmhands—including center fielder Bill Virdon—to the same club for the old warhorse, Enos Slaughter. A 22-year-old named Andy Carey laid claim to the third-base job, and new faces up from the farms included pitcher Bob Grim—who would go on to win 20 games that year—and first baseman Bill Skowron, a Chicago boy from the Northwest Side.

New York, in addition, had made a big off-season deal with the A's. To Philadelphia went such top prospects as Jim Finigan, Bill Renna, and Don Bollweg—plus the prize catch, a flashy, black rookie first baseman/outfielder named Victor Pellot Power. (The smug Yankee hierarchy, which complained, among other things, about Power's preference for white women, was not quite ready to use a black player: "Our box-holders from Westchester County would be offended to have to sit with that kind," said GM George Weiss.) To New York went pitcher Harry Byrd and the former South Side favorite, Eddie Robinson.

Thus well-stocked, the Yankees went out and won more games than they ever would under Casey Stengel. It wasn't enough.

Rosters

Lists position players who appeared in 20 or more games, pitchers who appeared in 10 or more games, plus regulars who may have been traded/sold or acquired during the season.

1954 YANKEES

PITCHERS
Harry Byrd, Whitey Ford, Tom Gorman, Bob Grim, Jim Konstanty, Bob Kuzava, Eddie Lopat, Tom Morgan, Jim McDonald, Allie Reynolds, Johnny Sain, Marlin Stuart

CATCHERS
Yogi Berra, Charlie Silvera

INFIELDERS
Bobby Brown, Andy Carey, Jerry Coleman, Joe Collins, Willie Miranda, Gil McDougald, Phil Rizzuto, Eddie Robinson, Bill Skowron

OUTFIELDERS
Hank Bauer, Bob Cerv, Mickey Mantle, Irv Noren, Enos Slaughter, Gene Woodling

1954 WHITE SOX

PITCHERS
Sandy Consuegra, Harry Dorish, Mike Fornieles, Jack Harshman, Don Johnson, Bob Keegan, Morrie Martin, Billy Pierce, Al Sima, Virgil Trucks

CATCHERS
Matt Batts, Sherm Lollar, Carl Sawatski, Red Wilson

INFIELDERS
Bob Boyd, Chico Carrasquel, Phil Cavarretta, Ferris Fain, Grady Hatton, Ron Jackson, George Kell, Freddie Marsh, Cass Michaels

OUTFIELDERS
Johnny Groth, Willard Marshall, Minnie Minoso, Eddie McGhee, Jim Rivera, Bill Wilson

1954

Most Glorious Victory

Tuesday Night, July 27

At Comiskey Park
Attendance: 53,067

Tuesday night. Warm, humid summer evening. The Yankees in town to open a three-game series. The Sox within shouting distance of the league lead. You knew there'd be a big crowd. But this big?

Remember, these were the days before Team Poster Night, Mug Night, Growth Chart Night, Helmet Day, Cap Day, and post-game fireworks displays. Just baseball, White Sox-Yankee baseball, and who cared if it was a weeknight? Or that the game wasn't scheduled to start until 8:30, that the game wouldn't be over 'til maybe 11, or that folks wouldn't get home 'til after midnight? (There were no expressways back then, either.)

Hordes of people kept coming and coming to 35th and Shields this night. When all the tickets were counted, the crowd totaled 53,067. Only three times before had more people attended a game at Comiskey Park. One of those was the doubleheader loss to the Yankees on July 19 of the previous summer. Another was a Friday night loss to the same club on June 8, 1951. This time, the result was different, due in large part to the contributions of two grand baseball veterans, Virgil Trucks and Phil Cavarretta.

Trucks, a chunky righthander and one of the game's hardest throwers, was going for his 14th victory of the year, tops in the American League. That it could come against the Yankees only served to whet his ample appetite.

"They were my favorite team to pitch against. They were the best, and if you can beat the best, you're doing OK, as far as I'm concerned. And I learned that from an old pitcher, Dazzy Vance. Dazzy told me, 'You know, I've known it to be a real fact that pitchers will sometimes skip a turn to keep from pitching against a good ballclub.' And he said, 'If you get beat by the good ballclub, nobody will ever say anything about it.' That stuck in my mind from then on. So I always loved to pitch against the Yankees, because if they beat me, I got beat by the best, not the worst."

As a member of the last-place Detroit Tigers in June of 1952, he had beaten the Yankees with a no-hitter at Yankee Stadium, his second no-hitter of that season, a season in which, despite those two gems, he ended up with a won-lost record of 5-19. He started '53 with the St. Louis Browns, from whom he was rescued on June 13 by Frank Lane at a time the pitcher was 5-4. Trucks would finish 20-10 with a 2.93 ERA, his best year since '49, when he was 19-11 with Detroit. Now, going into this match with the Yankees, he was already 13-5.

With the huge crowd whooping it up, Trucks fired heat at Yankee batters, allowing just five singles in nine innings. After the fifth, his uniform jersey No. 23 soaked through with perspiration, he went into the clubhouse, tossed aside the wet top, put on an unused No. 11 shirt, and went back out and continued retiring Yankees until he walked off the mound with a 4-0 shutout victory. On a hot night in Chicago, Virgil "Fire" Trucks had lived up to his nickname.

"We didn't have those new, fancy radar guns that they all have now," he said, "but even then, we had the Army gun, and I was clocked at 105 miles an hour on that thing. And Ted Williams always gave me credit, said that for consistency, for throwing hard over the whole nine innings, I was always at high velocity.

"Of course, I was strictly a fastball pitcher, anyway. I never really had a great curveball. I had a decent slider and, under Paul Richards, I developed a pretty good change of pace. And that helped extend my career a few years."

Richards also helped Cavarretta extend his career. Both had gone into 1954 as managers, "Cavvy," the longtime Cub hero, as skipper on the North Side. That lasted until the final week of spring training, when Cavarretta, not sharing the usual optimism of Cub fans and his boss, P.K. Wrigley, told the owner in no uncertain terms what he thought of the '54 Cubs. For his trouble, he was shown the door.

"Just before we broke camp, I went in and talked to Mr. Wrigley, like I'd do every year, to go over the club and what we needed and what he could expect. Well, I went in there and told him what we needed and what he could expect, and I guess he didn't like what I told him. And the board of directors didn't like what I told him. And they let me go.

"So I was sitting at home, in Dallas, and Paul Richards called me up and said, 'You think you can still play?' And I said I feel good, 'cause I worked hard and I was in pretty good shape—I'd been player-manager, you know. So he said, 'Well, come on up. We'll work you out, you can take some batting practice, and we'll see what happens.' Well, they liked what they saw, and I signed with them."

Soon, the former All-Star first baseman was playing for them. A month after Cavvy signed on, regular first baseman Ferris Fain severely injured his knee in a collision at homeplate and was lost for the year. Into the breach went Cavarretta, who at age 38 began playing as if he were 28. When the Yankees arrived in town, he was batting .338 in 80 at-bats. In the first inning on this night, after Minnie Minoso had ignited the throng by drilling a two-out, ground-rule double over the bullpen fence in center, Cavarretta came up to face Yankee pitcher Harry Byrd. "Byrd. I remember him," said Cavarretta. "Righthander. Pretty good sinkerball."

Not good enough this time. Cavarretta lined one of them into center field for a base hit. Minoso rounded third, Mickey Mantle came up throwing but Minoso won the race. Cavarretta, seeing Mantle's throw go through to the plate, took off for second and slid in safely, just beating catcher Yogi Berra's peg. Jim Rivera followed with another single to center, and Cavarretta beat another Mantle throw home. That made it 2-0, and the place was up for grabs. Later, Cavarretta opened the sixth inning with his second hit, went to second on Rivera's second single and to third on Sherm Lollar's infield hit, a topped roller toward short. Cavvy scored when Byrd walked Cass Michaels to force in a run. The Sox and Trucks went on to win, and Cavarretta had been a major catalyst.

"I enjoyed that year so much. I was gonna fill in for 'em, pinch-hit a little, and back up Ferris Fain, who was a very good first baseman. Then he tore up his knee sliding into home, and I got to play quite a bit, and did pretty well. You know, you're 38 years old, you're just trying to go out and help the club any way you can. And I was able to do that."

And he was able to do it all while wearing that old, familiar No. 44 on his back. Coach Ray Berres, who had worn No. 44 since 1949, gladly gave it up to the Cub legend and took No. 37 instead. "Which I thought was great, 'cause I had worn it for so many years, and I was always the superstitious type, anyway. So, to me, forty-four was my number."

And for that one night, anyway, Cavvy, Trucks, and the Sox had the Yankees' number.

1954

Most Devastating Defeat

Wednesday, July 28

At Comiskey Park
Attendance: 38,056

Ignoring the threatening skies and forecasts of rain, the largest weekday crowd in the history of Comiskey Park showed up this day to see if Billy Pierce could repeat the brilliance of Virgil Trucks' shutout pitching the night before.

For six innings, he did. And, remarkably, the Sox even knocked out Sox-killer Eddie Lopat in the process of giving Pierce a 5-1 lead. It should have been greater, because the Sox had the bases filled with none out and a run in when Lopat was replaced by Tom Morgan in the second. But Chico Carrasquel hit into a forceout at the plate, and Nellie Fox grounded into a double play.

The Sox also left men in scoring position in the third and fifth before coming up with two runs in the sixth—Jim Rivera scored on a single to center by Phil Cavarretta (Yogi Berra dropped Mickey Mantle's perfect throw) and Carrasquel singled home Cass Michaels. Chico's hit came moments after Carl Sawatski, the rotund former Cub, had to bat for Pierce, who had torn a nail on his pitching hand and was forced to retire for the afternoon.

With Pierce gone, the white sedan used to bring in Sox pitchers from the bullpen began to pile up the mileage. Before the afternoon was over, the car would be in need of an oil change. Bob Keegan was the passenger for the seventh inning. The rain, which had fallen lightly through much of the game, began falling more heavily. Jerry Coleman greeted Keegan with a single, and Enos Slaughter, batting for Willie Miranda, also singled. When lefty-swinging Gene Woodling was announced as a pinch hitter for Morgan, Paul Richards called for the white sedan again. This time, lefty Morrie Martin emerged. Martin retired Woodling and Irv Noren easily. The rain increased in intensity. The next hitter was Bill Skowron, who batted right-handed. Richards again summoned the white sedan, and this time it carried Sandy Consuegra, the next afternoon's scheduled starter.

Casey Stengel, of course, countered that move by sending up Joe Collins, the lefty, to hit for Skowron. And Consuegra—after the umpires had halted play for 31 minutes to get the field covered—managed to get out of the jam.

Consuegra was not as fortunate in the eighth. Mantle dragged a bunt toward Fox, who charged in and threw the ball into the Yankee dugout, enabling Mantle to reach second base. Again, the rain fell, but the umpires made no move. Berra followed with his fourth hit of the day, a double, scoring Mantle and making it a 5-2 game. Hank Bauer then launched one toward the wall in right-center for a triple. Now it was 5-3. The rain began falling harder. Andy Carey singled, and it was 5-4, with nobody out.

The bullpen gates parted, the white sedan reappeared, and Harry Dorish was dropped off in front of the Sox's dugout. Dorish, after Coleman had bunted Carey to second, retired Bob Cerv and Gil McDougald, and the Sox could breathe a bit easier. Bob Grim took over the Yankee pitching duties, and Rivera, sensing the need for more runs, tripled. But, with the infield drawn in, Sherm Lollar popped to Berra. Cavarretta drew a walk, but Willard Marshall, hitting for Dorish, struck out while Cavarretta was stealing second. With men at second and third, and the rain really coming down now, Carrasquel grounded out.

Once again, the grounds crew was waved into action. One hour and eight minutes later, play resumed on what by now had become a wretched playing surface. Lefthander Jack Harshman, the sixth Sox pitcher of the day, was on the mound. Three days before, in Fenway Park, he had struck out 16 Red Sox to set a White Sox club record that still stands. There would be no such glory this day. The ninth opened with Noren drawing a walk. The crowd sensed disaster just around the corner. Harshman, from his home in San Diego, remembered the gory, and muddy, details.

"The next batter, Collins, hit a groundball that took one hop and, under normal circumstances, would have been a perfect first-to-second-to-first double play. But when Phil Cavarretta went to go after the ball, he fell flat on his face, it was so wet out there. And the ball trickled into right field. And so help me God, the ball was floating when Rivera picked it up."

The Yankees always went from first to third on a single, even, apparently, on a sloppy track. "Noren went skatin' around second," Harshman remembered, "trying to go to third. And Freddie Marsh was playing third for us. And when Jim threw the ball to Fred, Freddie tagged Noren going by. And when he slid, he slid all the way into the coaching box. And Freddie tagged him again before he got back. And Red Flaherty, the umpire, called him safe both times."

Marsh jumped about 10 feet in the air. Richards stormed out of the dugout. Flaherty was surrounded by screaming Sox, including Harshman. "I went over to him," Jack related, "and called him every thing I could think of. He was so absolutely inept, it was incredible. I saw him make two of the worst calls in umpiring history, and that was one of them."

Now Harshman had to face Mantle.

"I think I tried to throw him a curveball, but the mound had gotten so wet, that the footing was very, very slippery. And when you come down on your forward foot, if your heel slips at all, everything tends to go up. And it just doesn't have any velocity. You just lose everything."

Except the ball. That's what Mantle lost—way, way into the center-field bullpen for a 7-5 Yankee lead. "Not that Mantle wasn't capable of hitting one off me or anybody else," said Harshman. "But the way I recall it, the ball just kinda flopped up there, didn't have anything on it. And I'd have been surprised if he hadn't hit the ball out."

Fox and Minnie Minoso managed to get on in the last of the ninth, thanks to the awful conditions. Both hit flyballs toward left-center, and on each occasion, neither Mantle nor Noren, plodding through the water, could make the play. Nellie and Minnie, however, simply became the 13th and 14th runners stranded by the Sox for the day.

"But the fact is," argued Harshman, "we should never ever have had to play that game to the finish. It should've been called long before that. But the umpires figured—because they were the Yankees, they were gonna win the pennant, that sort of thing—'By God, we're gonna finish the game and give them every chance to win.'

"And that's what they did. No question about it."

Interestingly, two of the umpires on this day—Bill McKinley and Jim Honochick—were part of the crew that did *not* allow the completion of that Sox-Yankee game in New York on July 27, 1951, when rain turned a 4-3 Sox lead in the ninth into a 3-1, eight-inning Yankee victory.

Interesting.

1955

Setting the Stage

The word "summit" became part of the lexicon during this year as the leaders of the United States, Britain, France, and the Soviet Union met in July in Geneva, Switzerland, for high-level discussions that, typically, produced no agreements. Fraught with implications for the future were two occurrences from 1955: The U.S. agreed to train the South Vietnamese army, and Rosa Parks, a black woman, refused to give up her seat to a white man on a bus in Montgomery, Alabama, setting in motion a black boycott—led by a preacher named Martin Luther King, Jr.—of the city's bus system and the eventual overturning of Montgomery's bus segregation ordinance.

Meanwhile, Walt Disney unveiled a new theme park, Disneyland, in Anaheim, California, Fess Parker played "Davy Crockett" on Disney's made-for-TV movies, and soon every kid under 10 had to have his own coonskin hat.

In Britain, Winston Churchill resigned as prime minister and was replaced by Anthony Eden. In the USSR, more forcibly, Nikolai Bulganin replaced Georgi Malenkov as premier, and, in Argentina, an uprising resulted in the overthrow and exile of the fascist dictator Juan Peron.

Chicago, meanwhile, had a new mayor, Richard J. Daley of Bridgeport, and the White Sox had a new manager, Marty Marion of St. Louis, Paul Richards having decided to grab Baltimore's offer of big bucks to serve as both field manager and general manager. Marion and Frank Lane moved quickly to add more depth to the club, trading Ferris Fain and a pair of minor leaguers to Detroit for first baseman Walt Dropo, outfielder Bob Nieman, and pitcher Ted Gray, and then, on the same December day, sending catcher Matt Batts, infielder Freddie Marsh, pitcher Don Johnson and another minor leaguer to Richards' Orioles for catcher Clint Courtney, infielder Jim Brideweser, and reliever Bob Chakales.

The Yankees moved even more bodies around. Concerned about the aging process's effect on their shortstop (Phil Rizzuto had slumped to .195 in '54) and pitching staff (Allie Reynolds had retired and Eddie Lopat was on his last legs), general manager George Weiss went into conference with Richards and emerged, hours—perhaps days—later, with announcement of an 18-player blockbuster that sent, among others, pitchers Harry Byrd, Jim McDonald, and Bill Miller, young catchers Hal Smith and Gus Triandos, outfielder Gene Woodling, and shortstop Willie Miranda to Baltimore. Off to New York went, principally, '54 AL strikeout king Bob Turley, 24; righthander Don Larsen, 25; and shortstop Billy Hunter, 26.

Lane immediately told Marion that the Yankees were, once again, the team to beat. Marion, perhaps because he had managed Turley, Larsen, and Hunter in 1953 when they all were wearing St. Louis Browns uniforms, told Lane that Cleveland, which had added Ralph Kiner's home-run bat, would be the No. 1 obstacle to a White Sox title bid. In the end, Lane was proven correct, but all three clubs—plus the surprising Red Sox—were participants in a wild pennant race before it was all over. The White Sox, finally, fought the Yankees on even terms, thrilling Comiskey Park crowds—which often included Mayor Daley and his family—with exciting games against the hated New Yorkers. The Sox were 6-5 in Chicago against the Yankees, 5-6 against them in New York, the first time since 1925 the Sox hadn't lost a season series to their age-old tormentors.

Largely because of their new-found success against New York, the White Sox stayed in the race into September and actually led the league as the Labor Day weekend began—this despite a dull year from Minnie Minoso (.254 at the All-Star break with just two homers before finishing at .288 with 10) and a decline in production from such as Virgil Trucks, Sandy Consuegra, Bob Keegan, Chico Carrasquel, and Jim Busby, reacquired in June from Washington. Heroes included George Kell (club leader in average, .312, and RBIs, 81); league ERA champ Billy Pierce (15-10, 1.97); rookie righthander Dick Donovan (15-9, though slowed the last two months as he recovered from an appendectomy); Dropo, who topped the Sox in home runs and destroyed Yankee pitching; lanky righthander Connie Johnson, recalled from Toronto at midseason and winner of six of his first seven decisions; 35-year-old South Side native Bob Kennedy, who, back with his original team after an absence of seven years, won game after game with his clutch hitting; and Millard Fillmore "Dixie" Howell, also 35, who was rescued from Memphis in June and proceeded to win eight games in relief and save nine others.

They all helped make it sort of a "Year of Marty," not just for 1955's Academy Award-winning film starring Oscar winner Ernest Borgnine, but for Marion as well. He had lifted the White Sox closer to a pennant than had his much glorified predecessor, and for his efforts he was rewarded with a contract extension through 1957. He would have preferred a pennant, but that, once again, went to the Yankees, who trailed the Indians by one and a half games with two weeks to play but, helped by the unexpected early release from the Army of Billy Martin, pulled ahead the next-to-last weekend with a three-game sweep of the Red Sox at Yankee Stadium. The key game was the series opener. The Yankees trailed, 4-3, in the ninth; Bill Skowron, in a rage after striking out, had broken his toe with a savage kick of the water color; and Mickey Mantle had torn a thigh muscle while beating out a drag bunt. But first Hank Bauer and then Yogi Berra homered off Ellis Kinder, and the Yankees were home free. They ended up 96-58, the Indians 93-61, the White Sox 91-63.

Rosters

Lists position players who appeared in 20 or more games, pitchers who appeared in 10 or more games, plus regulars who may have been traded/sold or acquired during the season.

1955 YANKEES

PITCHERS
Tommy Byrne, Rip Coleman, Whitey Ford, Bob Grim, Jim Konstanty, Johnny Kucks, Don Larsen, Eddie Lopat, Tom Morgan, Tom Sturdivant, Bob Turley, Bob Wiesler

CATCHERS
Yogi Berra, Elston Howard

INFIELDERS
Andy Carey, Jerry Coleman, Joe Collins, Billy Hunter, Billy Martin, Gil McDougald, Phil Rizzuto, Eddie Robinson, Bill Skowron

OUTFIELDERS
Hank Bauer, Bob Cerv, Mickey Mantle, Irv Noren, Enos Slaughter

1955 WHITE SOX

PITCHERS
Harry Byrd, Bob Chakales, Sandy Consuegra, Dick Donovan, Harry Dorish, Mike Fornieles, Jack Harshman, Dixie Howell, Connie Johnson, Bob Keegan, Morrie Martin, Billy Pierce, Virgil Trucks

CATCHERS
Clint Courtney, Sherm Lollar, Les Moss

INFIELDERS
Bobby Adams, Jim Brideweser, Chico Carrasquel, Walt Dropo, Nellie Fox, Ron Jackson, George Kell, Bob Kennedy, Vern Stephens

OUTFIELDERS
Jim Busby, Gil Coan, Johnny Groth, Willard Marshall, Minnie Minoso, Eddie McGhee, Bob Nieman, Jim Rivera

1955

Most Devastating Defeat

Friday, September 9

At Yankee Stadium
Attendance: 18,158

The White Sox were on their final eastern swing of the season, and they were in trouble. Only six days before, after winning the opener of a four-game weekend series in Cleveland, they were in first place, albeit barely, ahead of the Yankees and Indians.

Then the Sox dropped the final three games of the Cleveland series, split a Labor Day doubleheader in Detroit, and then, after a day off, won the opener of a two-game set in Washington before letting the finale get away from them, 5-4, in front of a sickly afternoon turnout of some 2,000 people at Griffith Stadium.

Now they had arrived in New York for another two-game series, with their survival in the race at stake. With 16 games to go, the Sox trailed the Indians by two and a half games and the Yankees by two. A sweep in Yankee Stadium was in order. A split would be acceptable, but Chicago would still be behind two clubs with just 14 games remaining—only two of those games against the other contenders.

For the series' opener, manager Marty Marion had rookie Dick Donovan ready and reasonably rested: He had pitched, and lost, the previous Sunday in Cleveland, but he was still showing the effects of an emergency appendectomy performed July 31, at a time his record was 13-4.

"We were sailin' along real high," Marion, now living in St.

Louis, recalled, "and the thing I remember most was Tricky Dick, my buddy, having to have that appendicitis operation. And we went downhill from there. We were struggling right at the end there, because we couldn't get our pitching going."

They couldn't get Donovan going, in particular.

"Three weeks, exactly, after my appendectomy," Donovan said from his home in Cohasset, Massachusetts, "I remember beating Detroit, 8-2, in Comiskey Park on a Sunday [Aug. 21]. That was my 14th win. And I ended up winning 15—and that was with me taking my regular turn."

It was his turn again this afternoon against Don Larsen, soon to be a Yankee legend. Actually, his after-hours adventures were already legend. "The only thing Don fears," said his former manager, Jimmy Dykes, "is sleep."

If anyone was asleep this day, Joe Collins' bat woke him up.

"Joe Collins was a good ballplayer, not a great one certainly," Donovan said, remembering the late Yankee first baseman. "Probably had a lifetime batting average of .235, .240 [actually .256]. But he was a nice hitter for that ballpark. He could pull the ball, and he was a good clutch hitter."

On this afternoon, Collins did both. His single in the second inning was the only hit Donovan had given up when the Yankees came up in the fourth. Gil McDougald's bunt caught Donovan and third baseman Bob Kennedy by surprise, and the result was a baserunner. After Yogi Berra walked on four pitches, Donovan disposed of Mickey Mantle. Up came Collins, hitting just .218 at the moment with only nine homers and 34 runs batted in. Collins swung at Donovan's 3-2 pitch, a sinking fastball, and lofted it into the seats in right, just beyond the 344-foot marker. The Yankees and Larsen were up, 3-0.

Two innings later, Collins came up again, this time with the bases empty and the score still 3-0. And this time, Marion wanted Donovan to take a different approach. He dispatched coach George Myatt to the mound with orders for his pitcher. Marty's explanation, from the *Chicago Tribune*'s account:

"Donovan is a low-ball pitcher. Unfortunately, Collins is a low-ball hitter. The single and first homer Collins hit came on low pitches. When Collins came up in the sixth, I sent George out with instructions: 'Tell Dick to pitch high, even if he walks Collins.' "

Donovan got two strikes on Collins with letter-high fastballs and missed the corner with a curve. The next pitch was low. Collins got under it and skied it toward the right-field corner, where the foul pole was a ridiculous 296 feet from the plate. Jim Rivera drifted back, certain he could make the catch. Years afterwards, sitting in his restaurant in Crooked Lake, Indiana, he remembered the details.

"I go back, put my hand on the rail and vault myself up. I'm gonna catch it. As I'm on my way up, I feel a shove, right in my back. It pushed me forward. The ball goes just over my glove. Home run. Cheap, but a home run. I turn around, and there's a New York cop standin' there. The cop was the guy who shoved me. Can you believe that?"

Indeed, photos—and Rivera's 1956 Topps baseball card—appear to verify Jungle Jim's claim. Photos or not, however, the Sox were down 4-0. And Marion, thereafter, seldom would tell his pitchers what to throw. Almost 40 years later, he told why: "Because they'll pitch the way you told 'em to, but they'll do it halfheartedly. They'll show you up. I'm not sayin' ol' Tricky Dick did that, but I've had that happen a number of times.

"I'd say, 'Pitch this guy high and tight. He couldn't hit *me* if I pitched him high and tight.' Well, the guy will say, 'I think I should pitch him low.' Well, he's gonna prove to you that you're wrong. He doesn't care what happens, as long as he can outsmart the manager."

It was getting a bit late, but the White Sox started to outsmart Larsen in the seventh. With one out, Sherm Lollar walked and, after "Round Ron" Northey flied out for Jim Busby, Donovan sent Lollar to third with a looping single to left. Chico Carrasquel doubled home Lollar, and Nellie Fox's line single to right scored two to make it 4-3. That was it for Larsen. In came the 38-year-old Jim Konstanty, who walked Minnie Minoso. Rivera, however, ended the rally by grounding to Collins.

The Yankees got one of the runs back in their half when Phil Rizzuto blooped a single to center, took second on Hank Bauer's bunt and scored on Berra's double, which got past Minoso in left for an error and let Yogi reach third. Donovan departed, and 35-year-old rookie Dixie Howell made his 31st relief appearance since his June 8 purchase from Memphis. Reliable as usual, Dixie retired Mickey Mantle on a bouncer to first.

In the eighth, the Sox showed again they hadn't learned how to hit in Yankee Stadium. With two out, Lollar walked and Northey came up again. The roly-poly lefthander, who'd faced Konstanty often in the National League, pulled a vicious drive high and deep to right. The ball smacked off the railing below the third deck—about two feet foul. Had Northey simply popped one up 300 feet down the line, as Collins had, the Sox would have tied the game.

One pitch later, Northey settled for a single to right, and Bob Nieman, batting for Howell, also singled to drive in Lollar and drive out Konstanty. Bob Grim took over and retired Carrasquel on an infield roller.

Down 5-4 now in the ninth, the Sox still showed signs of life. Fox opened with a single, and, after Minoso flied out and Rivera struck out, Kennedy lined a hit to center. It was up to Walt Dropo. "The Moose" failed, however, his groundball to Billy Martin at second forcing out Kennedy. The Sox were now three and a half games out, because the Indians, in Boston, also had won.

The Sox would finish five games out, but Dick Donovan maintains to this day they would have been 1955 American League champions had it not been for that appendicitis attack.

"I just didn't have the resiliency after that," he said. "And normally in my career, I was a very strong finisher. If I had pitched halfway well, like I usually did toward the end, I think the White Sox would've won the pennant—Joe Collins or no Joe Collins."

1955

Most Glorious Victory

Saturday, September 10

At Yankee Stadium
Attendance: 31,486

If ever there was a game the White Sox absolutely had to have, this one was it. Another loss in New York would drop them four and a half games behind the first-place Indians and four behind the Yankees. That is exactly what appeared in store, too, after the Yankees scored six times in the second inning off Billy Pierce, the Sox's very best, to go ahead 6-1. The White Sox were out of it. They had fought the good fight; they had stayed in the race until the final two weeks; they had given their fans a season to remember.

Not so fast. The Yankees, it turned out, did not have this one sewn up. Casey Stengel wound up using 21 players, Marty Marion 20, before it was all over. And when it was, after three hours 59 minutes, the Yankees were on their sixth pitcher and third catcher—Hank Bauer, who hadn't caught since his minor-league days. And the Sox were on their fifth pitcher and third catcher—20-year-old Earl Battey, a September callup making his first big-league appearance.

This was a game with more twists than a Chubby Checker nostalgia tour, more turns than a Monopoly marathon, more ups and downs than the old "Bobs" at Riverview.

The heroes were many: relievers Harry Byrd (two and two-thirds scoreless innings), Sandy Consuegra (one run in three innings), Al Papai (a recent arrival who worked a scoreless eighth), and Dixie Howell, the eventual winner; Bob Kennedy, who went 4 for 5, singled in a run in the first and again in the third, then homered with a man on in the seventh to get the Sox to within 7-5; and finally Walt Dropo, who hadn't even started the game because he had gone one for his last 15. But on this day, Dropo rose to the occasion, as he so often did against the Yankees in 1955. In competition versus New York that year, the big (6-5, 220) first baseman hit .385 (25 for 65) with six of his 19 home runs and 18 of his 79 RBIs.

"The Yankees," he said from his home in Boston, "were my personal vendetta. You know, I finished second to them five-six times, with different clubs. We were always in contention, but we never won it. So whenever we played the Yankees, I always had a personal goal to do the very best I could. They were always a rival of mine, personally."

He had grown up in Connecticut, in a town called Moosup, which is about 65 miles from Boston and some 150 from New York City. "We were right in the middle of the Red Sox-Yankee rivalry there, but my affinity was more with the Red Sox. [And that's the team with whom he signed and for whom, in 1950, he hit 34 home runs and drove in 144 runs as the American League's Rookie of the Year.] I liked Williams' style. He had charisma. He had a certain flair."

The 1955 White Sox did not have Ted Williams but they had displayed, all season long, a flair for the dramatic. They did so again this particular afternoon, with Dropo supplying the key blow. Chicago entered the ninth inning still trailing 7-5, with Bob Grim—he had relieved Jim Konstanty after Kennedy's two-run homer—having retired the last six Sox batters in order. He made it seven straight when Minnie Minoso popped out and eight when Bob Nieman flied out. Kennedy walked, but the game surely was over when catcher Les Moss (Sherm Lollar had long since been lifted for a pinch hitter, Ron Northey) grounded to Andy Carey at third.

But Carey bobbled the ball, and the Sox were still alive. Bobby Adams went in to run for Moss, prompting speculation among only the most foolishly optimistic Chicago fans as to who might be the next Sox catcher should this ballgame require a last half of the ninth.

When Chico Carrasquel singled to center to score Kennedy to make it 7-6, Battey, the kid catching prospect from Los Angeles, started loosening up in earnest in the bullpen. Who could say? He might end up playing in the biggest game of the year, after all.

"I was so nervous," said Battey, who now calls Ocala, Florida, home. "I was so nervous it was a shame. That was a packed house, or it seemed like it, and it looked like all the fans were on the field."

Jim Rivera worked Grim for a walk, and now the bases were loaded, with two out, for Dropo, who had batted, unsuccessfully, for Consuegra in the seventh against Grim. So now Walt was one for his last 16, and that, plus the late-afternoon shadows and Grim's 90 M.P.H.-plus fastball, did not bode well for the White Sox.

"Grim was tough," remembered Dropo. "He wasn't Allie Reynolds or Vic Raschi, in that category, but he was just a cut below them as far as toughness—on right-handed hitters, particularly. You had to bear down on him. And Yankee Stadium, particularly in September, with the shadows, was tough to hit in."

Despite all that, Dropo saw enough of Grim's first pitch to notice it was one he could handle. He swung and lined the ball past Grim's head and on into center field. In came Adams from third and Carrasquel from second, and the White Sox, improbably, had an 8-7 lead. But this game and its improbabilities were far from over.

Grim was replaced by his roommate, Johnny Kucks, and Nellie Fox, even though first base was occupied, was given an intentional walk to refill the bases, because the pitcher, Papai, was due up. Marion called to the bullpen for Battey.

"When they told me I was goin' into the game," Battey related, "I said to myself, 'I thought they were trying to win this game.' I struck out on three pitches. And I don't think I ever swung the bat."

Indeed, the All-Star-to-be took a called third strike for the final out, then went to the dugout, strapped on his equipment, and went out to catch the man he had been warming up, Howell. This would not be an uneventful half inning.

After Eddie Robinson, the old South Side hero, batted for catcher Charlie Silvera (Yogi Berra had been excused earlier because of illness) and was retired by Howell; Mickey Mantle, hitless so far on the day, drilled a smash that caromed off Dropo's leg for a double. The tying run was on base, but Joe Collins, for once, failed in the clutch against the White Sox, grounding to Fox at second, Mantle moving to third. Up stepped Hank Bauer, who sent a flyball toward left-center. Minoso caught up to it but, unfathomably, dropped the ball. The game was tied.

Fortunately for Minoso, he soon had a chance to do something positive. Leading off the Sox 10th, he drew a walk from Kucks, who drew a hook from Stengel. In from the distant bullpen trudged Tom Morgan to face Nieman, who put down the obligatory sacrifice bunt that advanced Minnie into scoring position. Thus far, all had gone well behind the plate for Bauer, who at inning's start had volunteered to catch. But Morgan's first pitch to Kennedy deflected off Bauer's glove and rolled a few feet away. Minoso took off for third, Bauer retrieved the ball and fired a strike to Carey—but not in time to nail Minnie, the Yankees' angry protests notwithstanding.

Now, with the go-ahead run at third and the infield in close, Kennedy did what has come so naturally to White Sox batters in similar spots over the years: He tapped a grounder back to the mound. Two out. Howell, a decent left-handed hitter, batted for himself and sent a groundball to Phil Rizzuto. The diminutive shortstop grabbed it and fired to Robinson at first, but now it was the Yankees' turn to play giveaway. Robinson, with umpire Bill Summers poised to call Howell out, simply dropped the ball. And Minoso was home with the go-ahead run.

But this one still wasn't over. Howell, apparently determined to make it exciting, walked Rizzuto to open the Yankee 10th. The 21st Yankee to be used, a rookie named Bobby Richardson, bunted "the Scooter" to second. Irv Noren was next, but all he could manage was a tap back to Howell. Rizzuto was still at second. The next batter, Gil McDougald, lifted a high flyball to shallow left. Carrasquel went back. Minoso came in. Minnie called for the ball and, this time, caught it.

Finally, the White Sox had their 9-8 victory—and new life. No one was happier than Dropo, who had done this day exactly what he had been acquired the previous winter to do.

"I didn't put up the numbers in Chicago that I did in Fenway," he said, "but they didn't expect that. When I got there, Frank Lane said to me, 'Lookit, I'm not interested in anything else. You deliver in the clutch.' The seventh inning on, I was always a threat. They knew that I was able to deliver in those situations. That's really what they got me for—not to hit 30 or 40 home runs. I was no Frank Thomas or Richie Allen. They wanted someone to drive those runs in late in a ballgame. And I know I led the club in '55 in late-inning RBIs. Those are important hits."

None was more important than the one he whistled past Bob

Grim's ear that September afternoon in Yankee Stadium, even though it came in a pennant quest that fell just short.

Recalled Dropo: "Frank Lane had said, when he got me, 'We want you, because we think we can win the pennant with you.'

"And we almost did."

1956

Setting the Stage

It was an election year, although it wasn't much of a race. Democrats, convening in Chicago, again chose Adlai Stevenson to run against President Eisenhower, and again Ike won—big. It was a year of conflict around the world, with first the Suez crisis and then the Hungarian revolt giving rise to fears that we were on the brink of World War III.

Back home, *My Fair Lady* played to sellouts on Broadway, and movie-goers packed theaters to see Yul Brynner in *The King and I*, Ingrid Bergman in *Anastasia* and Rock Hudson, Elizabeth Taylor, and James Dean in *Giant*. Or, folks just turned on the old black-and-white and watched "The Honeymooners," "Dragnet," "You Bet Your Life," and, on Sunday nights, "The Ed Sullivan Show," where one occasionally could get a look at the nation's newest singing sensation, Elvis Presley.

In Chicago, White Sox fans, buoyed by the near-miss of 1955, were thinking that this could be the year for their favorites. True, Frank Lane, weary of feuding with Chuck Comiskey, had fled to St. Louis to wheel and deal for the Cardinals, but Comiskey and his brother-in-law, John Rigney, had made a shrewd deal with Cleveland, sending Chico Carrasquel and Jim Busby to the Tribe for Larry Doby, the left-handed power hitter the Sox so sorely had been lacking. Doby took over for Busby in center field, and Luis Aparicio, a speedy, 22-year-old Venezuelan, came up from Memphis and replaced his countryman, Carrasquel, who had taken up residence in Marty Marion's doghouse. Aparicio was spectacular from the start. Marveled Casey Stengel after seeing him perform in spring training:

"Your new feller gets to balls your old feller never coulda reached, and your old feller was the best in the league."

But all the optimism faded after a month. The pitching was inconsistent; Doby, in and out of the lineup with various maladies, was struggling — indeed, he didn't hit his first White Sox home run until June 13; and George Kell was finding it difficult to play two games in succession. Marion, Comiskey, and Rigney agreed something had to be done. Talk of a big trade with the Yankees, of all people, began to make the rounds. Names tossed about included Dick Donovan, Andy Carey, Johnny Kucks, and a Yankee outfield prospect, Chicagoan Lou Skizas, who had hit .348 at Denver in '55 with 21 homers and 99 RBIs in 112 games. But Marion wanted a veteran starting pitcher, and, on May 21, with the Sox a game under .500, Kell, Bob Nieman, and pitchers Connie Johnson and Mike Fornieles went to Baltimore for Jim Wilson, 34-year-old pipe-smoking righthander, and Dave Philley, 36, a Sox regular during 1946-50 but missing from the Chicago scene since the Minnie Minoso trade of April 1951.

This deal seemed one-sided, and fans lit up the phone lines to newspapers and TV and radio stations to voice their displeasure. But Wilson and Philley had inflicted great damage upon the White Sox in '55, and Marion wanted them on his side. Wilson won six of his first seven decisions in a Sox uniform, and Philley, having arrived in Chicago with a .205 batting average, was placed at first base and, as he later recalled, "started driving in runs like a storm."

The Sox began rising in the standings, reaching second place, but still trailed the Yankees by five games when the champs checked into town June 22 to begin a weekend series. The Yanks, on a pace that would net them a league-record 190 home runs, had already clubbed 88. Mickey Mantle had 27, Yogi Berra another 17. The entire White Sox team had hit 33. But over this miraculous weekend, the Sox were the ones with the big bats. As 125,000-plus looked on, the Sox swept all four games, outscored the Yankees 27-9, outhit them 46-26, and outhomered them 5-0, with Doby getting three of the long ones. The Sox were only a game back, and Mayor Daley predicted there would be a World Series in Comiskey Park come autumn.

He was wrong. The Sox soon swooned, an 11-game losing

streak in July knocking them out of contention. In fact, they had to rally late just to end up third, 12 games out of first and three games behind Cleveland. The Yankees finished 97-57, getting a Triple Crown season from Mantle (52 homers, 130 RBIs, .353 average), 30 homers from Berra, 26 from Hank Bauer, and 23 from Bill Skowron. Gil McDougald, who had played well in past seasons at third base and second, stepped in expertly at shortstop and hit .311. Whitey Ford went 19-6, second-year men Kucks and Tom Sturdivant were 18-9 and 16-8, respectively, and Don Larsen finished 11-5. They kept right on rolling through the World Series, boosted by Larsen's "perfecto" in Game 5 against the Dodgers. The Yankees were looking more unbeatable than ever.

Rosters

Lists position players who appeared in 20 or more games, pitchers who appeared in 10 or more games, plus regulars who may have been traded/sold or acquired during the season.

1956 YANKEES

PITCHERS
Tommy Byrne, Rip Coleman, Whitey Ford, Bob Grim, Johnny Kucks, Don Larsen, Tom Morgan, Mickey McDermott, Tom Sturdivant, Bob Turley

CATCHERS
Yogi Berra, Elston Howard

INFIELDERS
Andy Carey, Tommy Carroll, Jerry Coleman, Joe Collins, Billy Hunter, Jerry Lumpe, Billy Martin, Gil McDougald, Phil Rizzuto, Eddie Robinson, Bill Skowron

OUTFIELDERS
Hank Bauer, Bob Cerv, Mickey Mantle, Irv Noren, Norm Siebern, Enos Slaughter

1956 WHITE SOX

PITCHERS
Sandy Consuegra, Dick Donovan, Mike Fornieles, Jack Harshman, Dixie Howell, Connie Johnson, Bob Keegan, Ellis Kinder, Paul LaPalme, Morrie Martin, Billy Pierce, Howie Pollet, Gerry Staley, Jim Wilson

CATCHERS
Sherm Lollar, Les Moss

INFIELDERS
Luis Aparicio, Jim Brideweser, Walt Dropo, Sammy Esposito, Nellie Fox, Fred Hatfield, Ron Jackson, George Kell, Bob Kennedy, Dave Philley

OUTFIELDERS
Jim Delsing, Larry Doby, Minnie Minoso, Bob Nieman, Ron Northey, Bubba Phillips, Jim Rivera

1956

Most Glorious Victory

Friday Night, June 22

At Comiskey Park
Attendance: 48,346

The first-place Yankees were in town for the traditional June weekend series, and the second-place White Sox, though five games behind, had won 17 of their last 24 games. But those weren't the only reasons for the standing-room-only crowd that gathered on this warm Friday evening.

No, the biggest reason for the huge turnout was the way the Bronx Bombers were pounding the baseball thus far in the 1956 season. (They were also pounding the Sox, having won seven of the eight meetings to date.) Already, in just 60 games, Mickey Mantle had hammered 27 home runs, well ahead of Babe Ruth's record 60-homer pace of 1927. Yogi Berra had hit 17 more. The Yanks' team total was already 88 (compared to the White Sox's puny total of 33).

So the fans were at Comiskey Park to see the Yankees hit a home run or two or three. And, yes, they were there hoping against hope that their heroes could perhaps get off on the right foot in the series, of which the Sox had to win, at the least, three games in order to stay within shouting distance of the league leaders, who came to Chicago riding a seven-game winning streak.

What the fans got was one for the memories. They got a great pitching performance, a heart-wrenching, late-inning Yankee rally, a terrific clutch effort by someone who was always in the lineup but supposedly couldn't hit this night, plus a terrific clutch effort by someone who was seldom in the lineup and supposedly couldn't hit any night.

In short, what they got was the game labeled by the *Chicago Tribune* in 1990—the last season of old Comiskey Park—as the greatest game ever played in the ballpark's 80-year history.

The Yankees sent second-year man Tom Sturdivant, on his way to a 16-win season, against the Sox's Dick Donovan, who was well aware he would have to be at his best this night. Decades later, he remembered the circumstances—and the Yankees.

"They were always the best, so you thought about it a little more, prepared a little more. Those were the big games, the big series. You knew they had the hitting, but they also had exceptional defense—I felt it was comparable to ours—and they had really good pitching. So if you gave up more than two or three runs, you had an awfully good chance of losing."

With that thought in mind, Donovan went out and pitched seven innings of no-hit ball against baseball's greatest offensive lineup. As the eighth inning began, he and the White Sox were ahead 2-0, the runs coming on Dave Philley's two-out RBI single in the third and Larry Doby's home run in the fifth. But now came the late-inning Yankee magic. Chicago native Sammy Esposito, then a Sox rookie and now the just-retired associate athletic director at North Carolina State—where for many years he was head baseball coach—was already cognizant of that late-inning Yankee magic.

"At that time," he said, "they dominated so much that it seemed like you'd get into the late innings with them and they always expected to win and the other team was always waiting to get beat. They had that mystique. You always had that feeling that you were playing the great Yankee ballclub. And it seemed like they'd always end up beating you."

Sure enough, Donovan's no-hitter disappeared in the eighth, Billy Martin's double, the first hit, driving in the first Yankee run. Donovan's lead disappeared in the ninth, Mantle's single driving in Gil McDougald with the tying run. Donovan worked into the 11th, when the Yankees loaded the bases with one out. He got Berra to pop to Sherm Lollar for the second out, but Joe Collins, always a thorn in the side of the Sox—and, often, of Donovan—

singled to right for two runs. The Yankees were ahead, 4-2, and some among the throng began to head for the exits.

More fans began to depart when Yankee reliever Rip Coleman retired Lollar to open the Sox 11th. But Walt Dropo slowed them down by singling to left. Jim Delsing, a former Yankee, went in to run for him. Bubba Phillips struck out, and again the exits beckoned. Manager Marty Marion, desperate for a game-tying homer, called back Luis Aparicio and sent up Minnie Minoso, who went hobbling up to the plate wearing a right shoe cut out at the toe, the better to relieve pressure on a bone broken two days before by a pitch from Baltimore's Don Ferrarese. Most people had expected Minnie to miss the entire series and then some. Not Minnie.

"They say, 'Can you play?' " he recalled. "And I say, 'Well, look, I think I be able to play.' They say, 'No, I don't think you can play.' I say, 'Look, I play, but you gotta buy me two pair new shoes.' It used to cost maybe $25. And they say, 'All right.' So I cut out my shoe, you know, and I play."

Minoso lashed a liner to left that skipped away from Elston Howard far enough to enable Delsing to race to third and Minnie to reach second with a double, broken toe and all. Billy Pierce went in to run for him, and Minnie received a standing ovation as he limped off the field. Now the tying runs were on with two out, and Marion needed another right-handed hitter. Casey Stengel was staying with the lefty, Coleman, rather than bring in a righthander to face a left-handed hitter like the batter due, Donovan (who already had launched a 410-foot double), or the roly-poly pinch hitter deluxe, Ron Northey, whose homer had helped beat Stengel the week before in New York. Marion's options were reserve catcher Les Moss and Esposito, the kid from Fenger High School and Indiana University who, in sporadic opportunities, was hitting .191 with all of six runs batted in and was finding that playing in front of the home folks wasn't as easy as he had felt it would be when he had left Indiana to sign with the White Sox in 1952.

"Playing in Chicago was a lot more difficult for me than for the ordinary ballplayer," he said. "Being a hometown boy, with us playing good ball and drawing real well, there was a lot of pressure on me. I felt it."

Soon, he would really feel it. Marion was walking his way.

"The only reason I pinch hit that night," Esposito remembered, "was that practically everybody else had been used. I sure wasn't known for my hitting. But Marion looked down at me and said, 'Kid, get a bat and go up there and hit.' " Sammy followed Marion's orders. "I hit a liner down the right-field line—I hit it late—and it tied the game."

The double also sent the crowd into a frenzy and sent those fans who had been waiting in the aisles scurrying back to their seats. Jim Rivera followed with an infield hit and Nellie Fox with a bases-filling walk, but Coleman got Doby to ground out, and the game moved to the 12th. Sandy Consuegra, the new Sox pitcher, quickly retired the Yankees in their half, but Philley opened the home half with a single to left. That was all for Coleman. Stengel called upon Tom Morgan, whose first pitch drilled Lollar in the back. Here Marion called for a sacrifice bunt, but Delsing bunted too hard, and Philley was forced out at third. Now it was Phillips' turn, and, as he had in the 11th, Bubba struck out. Out from the Sox dugout, swinging a couple bats, came Northey to bat for Consuegra. Even with first base occupied, however, Stengel wanted no part of the 36-year-old former National League slugger. "I've looked at that guy before," said Casey, "and I know one thing: They don't carry him to do anything but hit."

So Northey was given an intentional walk, bringing up Esposito, who had remained in the game to play shortstop. Stengel, like everyone else, was figuring Sammy couldn't deliver a second time with two outs. They were wrong. Esposito swung and looped one to short left-center, just out of the reach of shortstop Phil Rizzuto, for the game-winning hit precisely at 11:55 P.M. There was bedlam in the stands—and in the clubhouse, where teammates mobbed the local kid with the very rookie-like uniform number of 48 on his back.

"I remember a lot of excitement in our dressing room afterwards—you know, these after all were guys who had been in pro ball for a number of years," said Esposito. "It was still fairly early in the season, so it was quite a celebration for just one ballgame."

The Chicago papers celebrated the moment, as well. The banner headline on page one of the next morning's *Tribune* read: "Rookie Beats Yanks in 12th." The *American* carried on its front page a picture of Esposito outside his folks' home on the far South Side. There was his proud mother planting a kiss on her son's cheek. Little did they know what their son had started. The White Sox went on to sweep the four-game series and close to within a game of the league lead.

"That Yankee game was exciting," Esposito said. "They were still the tops then. All those names, their great record. To have played a part in beating them—especially as a rookie—was a great feeling for me. But what made me feel just as good was the fact that I played darn well in the other games [3 for 9 and several dazzling plays as leadoff man and third baseman in Sunday's doubleheader].

"It was a nice weekend for me. We had tremendous crowds. Those were exciting days."

There would be precious few of them remaining for the White Sox in 1956.

1956

Most Devastating Defeat

Sunday, July 15

At Yankee Stadium
Attendance: 61,351

In just three weeks, the pennant talk coming out of Chicago had been silenced. The Yankees, having shaken off the Comiskey Park debacle of June 22-24, had won 15 out of 17 and their last eight games in a row. While they were doing so, the Sox had lost seven of 11 and had dropped six straight, with the low point seemingly having come the day before in Boston.

There, in Fenway Park, one of the best hitters' parks in baseball, the White Sox had been no-hit by Red Sox lefty Mel Parnell. It could not get any worse than that—or could it? It could. The White Sox now had to go to Yankee Stadium for a doubleheader with the Yankees, who were waiting to deliver the final knockout blow: A New York sweep would leave the Sox 11½ games out. And the Yankees had Whitey Ford (10-4) rested and ready for Game 1. At least Sox manager Marty Marion had Billy Pierce (13-3) and Dick Donovan, his two best pitchers, available to put an end to the losing skid.

With baseball's biggest crowd of 1956 looking on, Pierce and Ford hooked up in one of their classic matchups in the opener. Things began brightly for Chicago when rookie shortstop Luis Aparicio led off with a booming triple over the head of the surprised left fielder, Bob Cerv. Aparicio scored moments later on Minnie Minoso's sacrifice fly, so the Sox had already surpassed their hit total and run output of the previous afternoon. Perhaps this day would be different.

As it happened, however, the only other White Sox who would reach base the rest of the way were Minoso (hit batsman) and Larry Doby and Nellie Fox (singles). Ford fanned seven and did not walk a batter. He had to be that good in order to beat Pierce, who was almost as brilliant (four hits and one walk allowed, plus five strikeouts, in his seven innings). Only in the second inning did he run into difficulty, but that was all it took. He hit Bill Skowron with a pitch, and Hank Bauer surprised him by dropping a beautiful bunt toward third. Pierce charged in, grabbed the ball, and, instead of holding onto it, fired it past first baseman Dave Philley, putting Yankees at second and third. Andy Carey then lined a single to center to score two runs. And Ford made those two runs stand up for a 2-1 victory.

So, with the losing streak at seven, Casey Stengel seemed to take pity on the White Sox by starting lefty Rip Coleman, generally a reliever, and a mediocre one at that, in Game 2. In the lineup at third base for Chicago, lefty or no lefty, was left-handed-hitting Fred Hatfield, acquired from Detroit in May and getting a chance to play regularly.

"At that time," said the former Florida State baseball coach from his home in Tallahassee, "I was playing both ways for Marty [Marion]. I enjoyed playing for Marty. I couldn't understand why he wasn't more popular than he was. Once the game started, he was as good as any manager there was. I had a lot of respect for him. He put it right on the line to me when I got there: 'You're playing third base, until something different happens.' "

Something different surely happened this day. Hatfield, not known for his power, cracked two home runs to go with a single. His three-run shot in the fourth put the Sox ahead, 3-0, and his line drive into the seats just inside the right-field foul pole broke a 4-4 tie in the 10th.

"I hit the three-run homer off a lefthander named Rip Coleman and the other one off Johnny Kucks, a young kid who hadn't been up that long," Hatfield correctly remembered. "See, I was a pull hitter, and Yankee Stadium, if you're a pull hitter, it wasn't like Boston where you almost had to hit it right on the line to get it out. At Yankee Stadium, the first 40-50 feet off the foul line ran out pretty short, compared to a lot of ballparks. If you're not a pull hitter, if you're playing in Yankee Stadium in those days, it would've made a pull hitter out of you."

Being a pull hitter was not to Hatfield's advantage with the White Sox, however. He finished 1956 with seven home runs, hit none in reduced playing time in '57, and was out of the major leagues by '58, having totaled 25 home runs. That's why this Sunday afternoon in New York remains so clear in his memory.

"I'll always remember hittin' 'em that day, 'cause I didn't hit too many home runs in the big leagues—although in the minors [at Birmingham in 1949 and '50] I'd hit my 27-28 home runs and drive in 100 runs. Then I went up to Boston and they told me, 'Just hit your .250 or so and get on base, take a walk or get hit by a pitch, and let the big guys hit you in.' Nowadays, a guy hits .270 with 15 home runs and 60 RBIs in the minors, and he's a big-leaguer."

Hatfield, who like many others had grown weary of the continuous Yankee success ("When I'd see some person wearing a Yankee cap, I'd always say, 'Aw, you front-runner' "), also remembers this day because of the way it turned out. Thanks to his second homer, the Yankees came to bat in the last of the 10th trailing, 5-4. Jim Wilson, who had relieved Donovan in the ninth, now had to face Mickey Mantle, Yogi Berra, and Skowron. He walked the first two, and Skowron, capable of hitting a three-run homer—indeed, he had already hit a two-run shot in this game—did instead what it takes to win, moving the runners along with a sacrifice bunt. With first base open, Wilson gave Joe Collins an intentional walk and then struck out Carey.

Thus, the bases were still loaded but now there were two outs. From the Yankee dugout strode Hank Bauer, 1 for 3 in Game 1 but a spectator in the nightcap, to pinch hit for Phil Rizzuto. If the ball were hit to him, Hatfield knew he had a force at any base. Wilson's first pitch was a strike. Bauer fouled off the second one, and now Wilson was ahead, 0-2. Then came another foul ball, then a pitch that missed the strike zone. Hatfield remembered the next one all too well.

From the late Ed Prell's *Chicago Tribune* account describing Bauer's bounding single that sent Mantle and Berra across with the tying and winning runs:

"Jim Wilson pitched and Bauer stroked a single into left, just out of Fred Hatfield's reach."

The White Sox trudged off the field, their losing streak, one strike away from being broken, having been stretched to eight. It would eventually reach 11.

"Just out of Hatfield's reach," Fred Hatfield repeated, decades afterwards. "That's just enough to make the wound bleed a little bit more."

being, consigned to the bench. Lopez was eager to get started, and so were the Sox: They won 11 of their first 13, then cooled off for a bit, leading to some reshuffling of personnel: Landis wasn't hitting, Doby was having leg problems and Rivera was struggling with his new position but, as usual, giving it all he had. Casey Stengel, a closet Rivera admirer, referred to him as "your feller that plays first base—and not bad—sometimes, and outfield—and darn good—sometimes, and once in a while don't get in the game at all, which I sometimes think is a mistake."

As for Stengel's team, the Yankees were a universal pick to run away and hide from the rest of the American League, the New Yorkers having been strengthened by a bevy of prospects from their Denver farm club and by a winter trade with their own in-league farm club, the Kansas City A's. From Kansas City came pitchers Art Ditmar and Bobby Shantz—both of whom would puzzle White Sox hitters over the next few years—plus the one-time bonus baby, Clete Boyer, destined to be the regular third baseman by 1961. For that package, the Yankees simply unloaded on the A's some of their own disappointments: pitchers Tom Morgan, Mickey McDermott, and Rip Coleman, shortstop Billy Hunter and the gimpy-kneed Irv Noren—as well as minor-league infielder Milt Graff. Up from Denver was that team's entire infield—third baseman Woodie Held (35 homers, 125 RBIs the year before), shortstop Tony Kubek (.331), second baseman Bobby Richardson (.328), and first baseman Marv Throneberry (42 homers, 145 RBIs, .315), plus outfielders Bob Martyn (.314) and Norm Siebern (.300) and pitcher Ralph Terry (13-4). Up from Richmond was another future big-league regular, shortstop Jerry Lumpe (.279). It was the best bunch of kids in a Yankee camp since 1951.

Stengel went north with Kubek, Richardson, Held, and Terry still aboard, and the Yankees broke quickly, with the exception of Whitey Ford, who left a May start against the White Sox with tendinitis in his left shoulder and was sidelined for the better part of two months. With that handicap, plus Chicago's fine play, the Yankees found themselves six games behind the White Sox on June 8. Nonetheless, they caught the Sox before the month was out. The key was a nine-game winning streak that had begun with a memorable free-for-all on June 13 in Comiskey Park and continued despite the trade to Kansas City of Stengel's sparkplug,

Billy Martin. Martin was the designated scapegoat for the "shame" brought upon the organization in the wake of a much-publicized fight involving him and other Yankees at the Copacabana nightclub a month before. The fact that Sherm Lollar had broken his wrist on June 20 in Baltimore and was lost to the Sox for six weeks didn't hurt the Yankees' drive to the top, either.

The race came down to a three-game series in late August in Chicago. The Yankees came to town only three and one half games ahead of the second-place White Sox. They left six and one half ahead. Only the Milwaukee Braves would be able to handle the Yankees in 1957. At least Al Lopez had continued his streak: The Sox had climbed to second after five straight third-place finishes.

Rosters

Lists position players who appeared in 20 or more games, pitchers who appeared in 10 or more games, plus regulars who may have been traded/sold or acquired during the season.

1957 YANKEES

PITCHERS
Tommy Byrne, Al Cicotte, Art Ditmar, Whitey Ford, Bob Grim, Johnny Kucks, Don Larsen, Sal Maglie, Bobby Shantz, Tom Sturdivant, Ralph Terry, Bob Turley

CATCHERS
Yogi Berra, Elston Howard, Darrell Johnson

INFIELDERS
Andy Carey, Jerry Coleman, Joe Collins, Tony Kubek, Jerry Lumpe, Billy Martin, Gil McDougald, Bobby Richardson, Bill Skowron

OUTFIELDERS
Hank Bauer, Mickey Mantle, Harry Simpson, Enos Slaughter

1957 WHITE SOX

PITCHERS
Jim Derrington, Dick Donovan, Bill Fischer, Jack Harshman, Dixie Howell, Bob Keegan, Paul LaPalme, Jim McDonald, Billy Pierce, Gerry Staley, Jim Wilson

CATCHERS
Earl Battey, Sherm Lollar, Les Moss

INFIELDERS
Luis Aparicio, Walt Dropo, Sammy Esposito, Nellie Fox, Fred Hatfield, Bubba Phillips, Earl Torgeson

OUTFIELDERS
Ted Beard, Larry Doby, Jim Landis, Minnie Minoso, Ron Northey, Dave Philley, Jim Rivera

1957

Most Glorious Victory

Sunday, July 14

At Comiskey Park
Attendance: 48,244

After a day and a half of torrential rains, the sun shone brilliantly over Chicago, an indication perhaps of the brilliant day of baseball ahead for the nearly 50,000 that showed up for this day's big doubleheader between the defending world champions (53-27) and the second-place White Sox (50-30), who were three games behind. As had been the case since June 20, the Sox were without catcher Sherm Lollar, who was recovering from a broken wrist and still another two and a half weeks from returning to the lineup. And they were without center fielder Larry Doby, sidelined with a bad leg. Scoring runs, therefore—always a problem for Chicago, anyway—was becoming even more arduous a task.

So it was not surprising that the Sox and their new manager, Al Lopez, utilized the suicide squeeze play as the decisive offensive weapon in Game 1. Here was the situation: The game was tied, 1-1, in the sixth, with Jim Rivera on third, Bubba Phillips on second, and Sammy Esposito on first base with one out. Yankee lefty Bobby Shantz (9-1) was facing his pitching opponent, Billy Pierce (12-6). Lopez was preparing to flash the squeeze sign to his longtime buddy and third-base coach, Tony Cuccinello. Lopez, even after 37 years, was able to recreate the events flawlessly.

"Rivera was on third base, and Tony told him, 'I know Al's gonna put the squeeze on, but I don't know when, so stay alert.' They had Shantz pitching for them, and he was one of the best fielding pitchers I ever saw in the major leagues. And he was taking his windup, and he kept watching Rivera. And the count got to 2-2, and I finally put the squeeze on, and Tony gave Rivera the sign."

From Jungle Jim's reaction, however, he must have thought the sign from Cuccinello was the steal sign.

"As soon as he got the sign," remembered Lopez, chuckling, "he took off for home. And I think Shantz kinda waited to see if he was faking or what, and he waited too long, and now he's gotta throw the ball low. Because if you break too quick, what they do is waste a ball and they got you at the plate. So he throws it low and Billy bunts the ball just as Rivera is sliding in head first into the plate. And we go on to beat 'em, 3-1.

"And it made it look like, you know, I was a genius, but actually, Rivera, by trying to steal home at the same time the squeeze was on, made the play for us."

Pierce, who did not allow a single baserunner after Bobby Richardson's bloop RBI single in the fourth and finished with a five-hitter, striking out seven and walking but one, also found a bit of humor in the recollection of the play.

"I've got the picture of that play," he said. "Jim got such a big jump, he's actually in the picture. As I'm bunting the ball, his head's there—he's coming in head first. If I had taken the pitch, he might've stolen home."

And if Pierce had swung? Well, Rivera's roommate, Esposito, recalled one time when, in almost the same situation, Billy indeed did swing.

"Jim just decided out of the clear blue that he was gonna go. And he always slid head first. You never slide head first into home—you take a chance hurting your head or at least jamming your fingers. But he took off and about the time he slid home, Pierce took one of the best cuts he ever took in his life. But he swung right through the ball—and also missed Jim's head by less than a foot. I don't know how he missed him. And Jim's safe at home, he gets up, dusts himself off and walks into the dugout like nothing happened. And we're all on the floor dying."

On this day, though, thanks to Pierce's pitching and bunting, the White Sox were very much alive, just two games from the lead. A victory in Game 2 would leave them one game away. The pennant was still there for the taking.

1957

Most Devastating Defeat

Sunday, July 14

At Comiskey Park
Attendance: 48,244

The White Sox entered the ninth inning with a 4-0 lead and Dick Donovan with a five-hit shutout. The Sox were three outs away from beating the Yankees twice, defeating old nemesis Whitey Ford and moving to within one game of the league-leading New Yorkers—all in one blissful afternoon.

The singularity of the moment was such that even the normally reserved Bob Elson, broadcasting over WCFL and the Sox radio network, was moved to make a rare bold statement: "The White Sox," he proclaimed, "are about to sweep a doubleheader from the world champion New York Yankees."

In Elson's defense, it had been easy to get carried away. The Sox, after their 3-1 victory in Game 1, had picked up a first-inning run on Luis Aparicio's leadoff triple and Earl Torgeson's sacrifice fly. They added two more runs in the third when rookie third baseman Tony Kubek booted Bubba Phillips' groundball, enabling Nellie Fox to score, and when Les Moss singled home Minnie Minoso.

Two walks and a single by Sammy Esposito had loaded the bases in the fifth and chased Ford, and when reliever Tommy Byrne walked Fox to force in the fourth Chicago run, the celebration was almost ready to begin. And when Donovan zipped through the sixth, seventh, and eighth innings without incident save for sensational fielding plays by Aparicio at short, Esposito at third, and Phillips in center—the celebration, in some parts of the ballpark, did begin.

There remained, however, the rather critical detail of retiring the Yankees in the ninth. Mickey Mantle started things with a base hit, and Yogi Berra followed with another. When Harry "Suitcase" Simpson, late of Kansas City and destined to someday wear a White Sox uniform, delivered an RBI single to center, the score was 4-1. Yankees were on first and second with nobody out and Al Lopez was in a quandary. The Chicago manager had witnessed late-inning failures by such relievers as Paul LaPalme, Gerry Staley, and Dixie Howell. Should he continue with the clearly tired Donovan, go with one of the three above-named rescuers, or turn to someone new? He chose the last option, calling in veteran righthander Jim Wilson, in his first relief appearance of the season after going 9-5 as a starter. Wilson prepared to face Hank Bauer.

"At that time, you held the Yankees in awe," Wilson once recalled. "You had to be careful pitching to those guys. You'd get in the late innings and you had a lead, it was a little harder to protect. The best thing to do was wind up and just hold the ball—not throw it at all."

But he threw it, and Bauer laced a smash toward Esposito at third. Sammy, had he fielded it cleanly, could have stepped on third and fired to first for a double play. Instead, the ball hit the heel of his glove and ricocheted into foul territory. He scrambled after it, grabbed the ball, and dove for third base in an attempt to force Berra. His dive, alas, came up short, and late. Berra, also diving, beat him to the bag. Remembered Lopez: "Esposito had an easy chance, but he booted the ball. And that kept the inning alive. As a rule, Esposito would make that play 99 percent of the time. But he just booted it, and the ball rolled away from him."

Remembered Esposito: "I still had a force play at third, but I just couldn't get up and get to the bag in time."

Bauer was credited with a hit, the bases were loaded, and Elston Howard was the hitter. Wilson bore down and struck him out. One away. Now the due batter was Jerry Coleman, but here Casey Stengel called upon Bill "Moose" Skowron, the native Chicagoan from Weber High School on the Northwest Side who, nursing the usual muscle pull, was sitting out this game after having played in pain and gone hitless in the opener.

"In '57," recalled Tony Kubek, "I roomed with Moose. Moose was so muscle-bound, he was always pulling muscles. Just before we got to Chicago, he had pulled a hamstring, or something in his thigh. Anyway, one morning, Moose is on the john. I hear him calling: 'Tony, c'mere, I need help!' He couldn't get off the john by himself. I had to help pull him off.

"So we get to the ballpark—I think we were in Detroit—and Moose tells Casey he's really hurting. Case says, 'Can you play?' Moose says, 'No, Case, I can't play.' 'Can you pinch-hit?' 'No, Case, I can't swing a bat. Ask Kubek. He'll tell you. He had to help pull me off the john this morning.' And Casey says, 'I'm not asking can you shit. Can you pinch-hit?' "

Now, a few days later, Skowron was indeed able to pinch-hit. But he still was far from 100 percent, and Stengel knew it. Skowron, even though 37 years had gone by, remembered Casey's words to him before he went up to face Wilson.

"Casey says, 'There's one out. If you hit a groundball, just walk into the dugout. Don't even bother to run it out. 'Cause if you hurt that hamstring again, you'll be out six weeks.'

"So the first pitch, Jim Wilson throws a high fastball, and I hit it into the upper deck in left. So see, I didn't have to run it out."

Skowron's grand slam served to put the Yankees ahead by a run, stunned the huge crowd, and so unnerved Wilson that his very next pitch, to Byrne, the Yankee pitcher, was belted into the right-field seats for another home run to make it 6-4. "Our guys didn't even see that one," remembered Byrne, the onetime White Sox grand-slam hero. "They were still celebrating Skowron's slam."

Byrne closed the proceedings by retiring the shell-shocked Sox in order in the home ninth, and New York, with dramatic suddenness, had restored its three-game lead.

"After that one, I didn't sleep for a few nights," Esposito admitted. "That was one of the few times, in the nine or 10 years I was there, where, really, I took part of the blame for the loss.

"But those years, the Yankees were notorious for doing that to all the teams. When the seventh, eighth, ninth inning comes along, and you're winning, you know that they're gonna make a run at you, and they know that, and they usually beat you. They were that good."

And yet, remembered Lopez, "We had 'em that day—ooh, we had 'em. You know, everybody says that we hated the Yankees. We didn't hate the Yankees. They were a great club. And they had a great bunch of guys on their club. And Casey was a great guy. We didn't hate them. We just hated the way they beat us."

Amen.

1958

Setting the Stage

It did not take the U.S. long to make up lost ground in the race to space. On January 31, this country's first earth satellite, Explorer I, was launched into orbit from Cape Canaveral. After a power struggle in the Soviet Union, Nikita Khrushchev emerged as the new premier. Gen. Charles de Gaulle was elected president of France, and, in Cuba, a guerilla leader named Fidel Castro was slowly but surely gaining ground in his quest to overthrow the government of Fulgencio Batista.

Vincente Minnelli's *Gigi* won the Oscar for best picture, the world of literature was graced by the addition of Boris Pasternak's *Doctor Zhivago*, Truman Capote's *Breakfast at Tiffany*'s, and T.H. White's *The Sword in the Stone*; and Henry Mancini's album, *Music from Peter Gunn*, won the first Grammy ever awarded.

In spring training at St. Petersburg, Casey Stengel was saddened by the retirement of three longtime Yankees—Joe Collins, Jerry Coleman, and Tommy Byrne. But ol' Case still had loads of talent, young and old, plus a new, hard-throwing—and equally hard-drinking—relief pitcher who wore incredibly thick glasses to compensate for awful eyesight. He was Ryne Duren, brought into the Yankee chain the previous June in the Billy Martin deal with Kansas City, and he could match even Martin drink for drink. Once, Stengel was leaving the bar at the old Del Prado Hotel in Chicago, well past the players' curfew, and he ran into Duren, who was in a rather inebriated state. "Drunk again!" said Stengel. "Yeah, me too, Casey!" was Duren's reply.

To challenge Stengel's collection of characters and superstars, Al Lopez was drawing a new pennant blueprint. Over the winter, the White Sox had traded their two main power hitters, Minnie Minoso (to Cleveland, causing outcries of anger on the South Side) and Larry Doby (to Baltimore, not causing outcries of anger on the South Side) and in return landed the pitching Lopez believed he needed to combat the Yankees. Early Wynn and Ray Moore joined the staff, and along with them came Al Smith, Billy Goodman, and Tito Francona, hitters who couldn't match Minoso and Doby for power but hopefully would not be all-American outs, either. Explained Lopez at the time: "It wasn't the lack of hitting that cost us a lot of close games last year, but rather the lack of a guy who could stop the opposition in the eighth and ninth innings." Moore, a hard thrower, was to be that guy.

Even Stengel, whose players, almost to a man, called Wynn the toughest pitcher for them to face, voiced concern over the new-look White Sox. He was asked about Lopez's improved pitching staff: "How good is his pitching? Plenty good enough to scare hell outta me. I don't mean we ain't gonna show up at the park on time or anything like that, but any club that can throw Wynn, Donovan, Pierce, and Wilson at you four times in a row is gotta be strong enough to worry you. We had the edge over Chicago 14 games to eight last year, but none of 'em came easy, as I can remember. You ain't goin' to no picnics when you tangle up with them Chicagos."

However, by the time Stengel's club first "tangled up with them Chicagos," on May 20 in Comiskey Park, the Yankees were 19-5, the White Sox 11-16 and in the cellar. Lopez's pennant hopes were shot, and the season was barely a month old. What went wrong? Well, Wynn couldn't win; Smith, playing on a bad ankle, couldn't hit; Dick Donovan couldn't get untracked (he was 3-10 in the first half). The Yankees, meanwhile, won 25 of their first 31. Bob Turley won his first seven decisions, four of them shutouts, while posting an earned-run average of 0.86. The race was over before Memorial Day, and the Yankees went on to regain their world title from the Milwaukee Braves. The Sox, though eventually finishing second, didn't even get over the .500 mark until early August, and they drew only 797,451, failing, for the first time since 1950, to reach the million mark. The fans, crushed by the trade of their beloved Minoso in the winter, retaliated by staying away in the summer.

Nonetheless, the groundwork had been laid for success in 1959, the year the South Side had been waiting for since 1919. Jim Landis established himself as a standout center fielder. Wynn and Smith, heroes-to-be, were already on board, and in June, the Sox had dealt Francona and pitcher Bill Fischer to Detroit for Ray Boone and a young righthander, Bob Shaw, whose rise to stardom in 1959 would surprise the baseball world. Also in June, Walt Dropo was sent to Cincinnati in a waiver deal for ex-Cub reliever Turk Lown, who would team with Gerry Staley to give Lopez a splendid bullpen duo. In September, the farm system delivered outfielders Johnny Callison and Jim McAnany, catcher John Romano, and pitcher Barry Latman.

Not only that, the club's poor showing, on the field and at the gate, expedited the efforts of Dorothy Rigney, Chuck Comiskey's sister, to sell her share, 54 percent, of the ballclub. In December, she found a buyer—Bill Veeck. Baseball in Chicago would never be the same.

Rosters

Lists position players who appeared in 20 or more games, pitchers who appeared in 10 or more games, plus regulars who may have been traded/sold or acquired during the season.

1958 YANKEES

PITCHERS
Murry Dickson, Art Ditmar, Ryne Duren, Whitey Ford, Bob Grim, Johnny Kucks, Don Larsen, Duke Maas, Sal Maglie, Zack Monroe, Bobby Shantz, Tom Sturdivant, Virgil Trucks, Bob Turley

CATCHERS
Yogi Berra, Elston Howard

INFIELDERS
Andy Carey, Tony Kubek, Jerry Lumpe, Gil McDougald, Bobby Richardson, Bill Skowron, Marv Throneberry

OUTFIELDERS
Hank Bauer, Mickey Mantle, Norm Siebern, Harry Simpson, Enos Slaughter

1958 WHITE SOX

PITCHERS
Dick Donovan, Bill Fischer, Bob Keegan, Barry Latman, Turk Lown, Ray Moore, Billy Pierce, Tom Qualters, Bob Shaw, Gerry Staley, Jim Wilson, Early Wynn

CATCHERS
Earl Battey, Sherm Lollar

INFIELDERS
Luis Aparicio, Ray Boone, Walt Dropo, Sammy Esposito, Nellie Fox, Billy Goodman, Ron Jackson, Bubba Phillips, Earl Torgeson

OUTFIELDERS
Tito Francona, Jim Landis, Don Mueller, Jim Rivera, Al Smith

1958

Most Devastating Defeat

Tuesday Night, May 20

At Comiskey Park
Attendance: 36,167

In this most devastatingly uninteresting of seasons, there really was no single devastating loss for the White Sox. There were, however, two devastating months—April and May, during which the Sox, nominated by manager Al Lopez as the team most prepared to dethrone the New York Yankees, managed to remove themselves from contention with their worst start of the decade.

By the time the Yankees arrived in Chicago on this cool May evening, the Sox were mired in last place with an 11-16 record, nine and a half games behind the red-hot (19-5) New Yorkers, who had won six games in a row. Everyone in the American League had always feared there would be a season like this, when the Yankees would run away and hide and, in so doing, declare the pennant race over by the end of May. Now, here it was actually happening, in part because their supposed main challengers, the White Sox, had begun so horribly.

"Those things happen in sports," said Lopez, remembering, and yet trying to forget, that '58 season that went awry. "You know your club is going to hit a rut. And so you always want to get off to a good start, and maybe hit your slump in the middle of the season, rather than late in the season. But we hit ours that year right at the start." There were reasons why that slump hit early. Billy Pierce and Dick Donovan started slowly, as did the newcomer from Cleveland, Early Wynn. Al Smith, the other arrival from Cleveland, was hobbling around on a bad ankle; young first baseman Ron Jackson was trying to find his way as a big-league regular; and the outfielders, as a group (Smith, Jim Landis, Tito Francona, Jim Rivera, Ted Beard, and Don Mueller) were averaging about .190. And, perhaps more importantly, there were the surprising December trades of Minnie Minoso (to Cleveland) and Larry Doby (to Baltimore), deals that had netted badly needed pitchers Wynn and Ray Moore but had left a gaping hole in the middle of the Chicago batting order.

That night's starting pitcher for New York, Johnny Kucks, was well aware of the missing bats. And he was not unhappy about it.

"Anytime you see a couple of guys like that traded from one club, you're gonna feel a little relieved," said Kucks, retired after 20-some years in the steamship business but still living in Hillsdale, New Jersey. "I don't know what it did to that club as far as weakening it, but I'm sure it had some effect."

It certainly did, recalled Sammy Esposito:

"It had a big effect on us scoring runs. We were the kind of team that couldn't score runs, anyway. When you take away the middle of your lineup like that, the potential for the home run here and there, for the big RBI, is gone. And it took us a hell of a long time to get over that and get to .500. You just don't take that out of your middle and keep going."

So the struggling Sox, having dropped any number of 1-0, 2-1, and 3-2 games to lesser teams than New York, now had to face the Yankees for the first time this season. A large crowd, considering the circumstances, was on hand, the fans hoping the Sox were not as bad as their sad record seemed to suggest. Alas, they soon discovered that, in this particular case anyway, the numbers were not lying.

To open the Yankee second, Mickey Mantle looped one to left, but Smith, unable to go full speed, couldn't quite reach the ball, and Mantle wound up at second with a double. One out later, he had scored, thanks to Jerry Lumpe's RBI single. In the fourth, Mantle sent a drive toward left-center that either Smith or Rivera—making a rare start in center field—could have caught easily. Instead, both pulled up and looked at each other as the ball hit the ground and skipped past them to the wall. By the time the ball was retrieved and relayed to the plate, Mantle had sped around the bases with an inside-the-park home run.

Donovan, aware now that even his usually solid defense had deserted him, and that a two-run deficit was nearly insurmountable, the way his teammates had been hitting, was the next to succumb to the listlessness surrounding him. He gave up a leadoff single in the fifth to rookie Marv Throneberry, later a symbol of New York Met ineptitude, and then did the unthinkable. He allowed Kucks, a poor hitter even for a pitcher, to drive the ball into the gap in left-center, Throneberry scoring to make it 3-0. "I got a double to the wall—drove in a run," recalled Kucks, brightening. "Sure, I remember that. It was off Dick Donovan. It was a slider. You always remember the nice hits that you do get, because I was probably about 1 for 92. Oh, I was a lousy hitter. Good bunter, but a lousy hitter."

Kucks had all the runs he would need, but Hank Bauer gave him some insurance in the eighth with a leadoff home run. That was the last inning for Donovan. In came Bill Fischer, and Throneberry welcomed him with his first major-league home run, and it was 5-0. Kucks needed just three more outs for the Yankees' 20th victory and their eighth shutout in their first 25 games. He got the victory, but he missed the shutout when Mueller, picked up during spring training from the San Francisco Giants, batted for Luis Aparicio and singled in the only Chicago run.

For Kucks, who started only 13 games in 1958, five against the White Sox, this was the first of three victories this year over Chicago, all of them at Donovan's expense. In his Yankee career, the righthander would finish 7-4 against the Sox, including three shutouts.

"I didn't realize I had done that well against the White Sox," he admitted. "But see, in 1958, I wasn't a starting pitcher—not a lot, anyway. Why? Probably because I was doin' lousy, and they stuck me in the bullpen, and then they let me work my way out. And then"—he paused to laugh—"I worked my way back in."

As for the White Sox, it would be a while before they could work their way out of the second division. And it would be a while before Sox fans would bother to go out in large numbers to see them try to do it.

1958

Most Glorious Victory

Sunday, August 3

At Comiskey Park
Attendance: 35,695

The White Sox's inglorious 1958 season thankfully was heading into its final eight weeks and, thankfully, the Yankees would be leaving town after this day's doubleheader. New York had already won the first two games of the series, and now the Sox were in a fourth-place tie with Baltimore, 18 games behind the champs.

If that seemed like a lot, and it was, there was comfort in knowing that the second-place Cleveland Indians were 17 games out of first, third-place Boston 17½ behind. There was, however, discomfort in the realization that seventh-place Kansas City was only one and a half games behind the White Sox, that seventh place was far closer than the first-place goal Al Lopez had set for his club back in the happy, naive days of spring training.

Chicago's record stood at 49-52, the first time the Sox had been under .500 in August since 1950. The lack of a pennant race and the attendant lack of excitement had long since guaranteed the Sox would draw far fewer than one million fans, the first time they would miss that mark since, again, 1950. Even so, a decent crowd of 35,000-plus had gathered for this afternoon's matchups of Whitey Ford (13-4) vs. Dick Donovan (7-10) and Johnny Kucks (7-3) vs. Ray Moore (6-3).

Donovan, who had gotten off to a horrendous start (3-10) but had started to turn things around, gave up a solo home run to Bill

Skowron in the second inning. After that, it was all Chicago. In the White Sox second, with two out and nobody on, Earl Battey singled to right-center, Billy Goodman walked and Bubba Phillips—making his first start since breaking his foot back on June 8—singled to center to drive in Battey. Donovan then lined a hit past Ford to bring across Goodman with the go-ahead run. Thereafter, Donovan was in total command, allowing only a double to Skowron and a single to Tony Kubek. He walked only one batter and struck out four. And Chicago, having added an eighth-inning run off the old White Sox hero, Virgil Trucks, with the help of the fourth Yankee error of the game, was a 3-1 winner.

Now came Game 2, with Kucks, a Sox nemesis, against Moore, who along with Goodman (at .331 the American League's leading hitter) was making the big winter trade with Baltimore look splendid. Moore, acquired because Lopez had figured his hard stuff would make him ideal as a late-inning bullpen stopper, instead had won a spot in the starting rotation, thanks largely to his performance against the Yankees. Needing a starter to pitch in a makeup doubleheader in New York on June 5, Lopez had chosen Moore, who responded with a 3-2 victory. Then, in Chicago on the night of June 23, Lopez selected Moore again, this time against Ford, and the result was a 2-0, three-hit triumph.

"It was one of those things," Lopez explained, many years later, "where you just take a chance on a pitcher. You pitch him against a club, and if he has success, you bring him back against that club. Ray had a real good fastball. I think his main problem was once in a while he'd get into a wild streak. But he did a job on the Yankees."

In an attempt to determine why, efforts were made, before his unexpected passing in March 1995, to reach Moore at his home in Upper Marlboro, in Maryland's tobacco-growing region. Like others' efforts had before, they failed.

"No one could get hold of him," said Billy Pierce, who does some community-relations work with the White Sox. "And we tried to contact him for old-timers' games and what have you, and we couldn't get in touch with him. He was either out in the woods or hunting or something, but we just couldn't get in touch with him.

"He had real good stuff. He could throw hard; he had a good curveball. He had the equipment, but he never did seem to stick around too long. 'Old Blue,' they called him."

Warren Brown, the legendary sports columnist of the *Chicago American*, changed it to "Old Blew" after a couple of failed relief jobs by Moore. But no one could make any disparaging remarks about Moore after his performance this particular day in 1958. He blanked the Yankees 4-0 on five hits—three of them, including a triple, by Norm Siebern—and improved his record to 7-3 overall and 3-0 against the Yankees. His teammates had provided all the offense he would need in the very first inning. Nellie Fox, after going 0 for 12 in the series, singled to center and took second when Jim Landis beat out a high infield chopper. After Sherm Lollar flied out for the second out, Earl Torgeson reached Kucks for a single off Skowron's glove to drive in Fox with the first run. Then Don Mueller, the former Giant, singled to center, and Landis was home. And Moore was home free.

"The reason why Ray had success against the Yankees," said Earl Battey, Moore's batterymate and close friend with the Sox and, later, the Senators and Twins, "is because he challenged them. See, I think the guys that tried to finesse the Yankees were the ones that ran into trouble. You know, Ray threw hard and he just went right after them, whereas most pitchers would go against the Yankees and they'd try to pitch to the Yankees' weaknesses instead of pitching to their own strengths. So they were always in a defensive mode. So it was like they were just waiting to get beat, rather than just going after 'em.

"And the Yankees, in those days, were a team that thrived on mistakes. You could have a four-run lead in the ninth inning and you wouldn't feel comfortable with it."

Moore had a four-run lead in the ninth this day and, quite comfortably, made it hold up, handily retiring Skowron and Jerry Lumpe and then firing a called third strike past Marv Throneberry, pinch-hitting for Bobby Richardson. Ray Moore had beaten the Yankees once again.

"Ray was mental toughness," said Battey from his Ocala, Florida, home, "and his thing was, 'If you're gonna beat me, you're gonna beat me on my best pitch.' And that's what he used to tell me all the time. I know, because we became real close and we used to sit together on the bench."

Battey and Moore hit it off real well because Battey's former Sox roommate, pitcher Connie Johnson, had gone to Baltimore in

1956 and become good pals there with Moore. "If you got Connie Johnson and Ray Moore together, you'd hear some of the damnedest lies you'd ever hear about hunting dogs," laughed Battey. "Ray had one named 'Old Blue' and Connie had one named 'Sport.' And their arguments were constantly about who had the best hunting dog.

"So we called Ray 'Old Blue' because that was his dog's name."

Ah, one mystery solved. But one remained. And not even Battey would have been able to help on that one, had Ray Moore lived.

"Nobody could get hold of him," he said, repeating the all too familiar response. "I see his brother every once in a while, because I have relatives in the Upper Marlboro area. But every time I'd try to get in touch with Ray, he was somewhere out in the Chesapeake. He had some charter fishing boats there in Chesapeake Bay."

And the Yankees were likely the farthest thing from his mind.

1959

Setting the Stage

Perhaps to some, 1959 was a slow year when it came to news. Fidel Castro finally overthrew the Batista government in Cuba on New Year's Day; Alaska and Hawaii became the 49th and 50th states of the union; and Nikita Khrushchev visited the U.S. in the fall. Those seemingly were the major news events of 1959.

But for folks in Chicago, this was anything but a ho-hum year.

In April, Richard J. Daley was elected to a second term as mayor, and the St. Lawrence Seaway was opened, and, suddenly, ships from all over the world were docking in Chicago. In July, Queen Elizabeth II, as part of her U.S. tour, stopped off in the Windy City. Chicago was the site, too, of the Pan-American Games in August and September.

However, Chicago's big story of 1959—this memorable year when *Ben Hur* all but swept the Oscars, when Bobby Darin won the Grammy for "Mack the Knife," the Fleetwoods sang "Mr. Blue," and Frankie Avalon petitioned "Venus"—took place at 35th and Shields, where the White Sox finally won a pennant after 40 years of futility. And what made the pennant conquest all the more remarkable was that it was almost completely unexpected.

The world champion Yankees, of course, were overwhelming favorites in the American League, despite their pat hand ("I could get any player in the league for Elston Howard," said Casey Stengel, "but I ain't gonna do it"). And there was far more preseason support for Detroit (Harvey Kuenn, Al Kaline, Charlie Maxwell in the outfield and newly acquired Eddie Yost solidifying the infield at third base) and Cleveland (Jimmy Piersall and Billy Martin added to the already colorful and talented cast of Minnie

Minoso, Rocky Colavito, and Vic Power) than there was for the White Sox, who, off their 1958 performance, were perceived to be on the way down.

At training camp in Tampa, new owner Bill Veeck wasn't exactly overjoyed with the way his ballclub looked. He told Al Lopez he needed more power. Al told him not to worry about it, that he was high on the new kids: Rookie Norm Cash took the first-base job with a late-camp rush, and 20-year-old Johnny Callison was handed left field, with Al Smith moving to right. John Romano, another first-year man, would make the club as a backup catcher, and rookie Barry Latman won a spot in the starting rotation with Billy Pierce, Early Wynn, Dick Donovan, and Ray Moore.

In the bullpen, meanwhile, were Gerry Staley, Turk Lown, young Bob Shaw, and two more rookies—a Cuban lefty named Rodolfo Arias and another lefthander, Don Rudolph, whose wife was a stripper with the stage name of Patti Waggin.

To this group of relievers, Veeck proposed adding Satchel Paige, age 53—according to the more polite record books. When Lopez said he'd leave if Satch arrived, Veeck instead began pursuit of another old friend, Roy Sievers, who had hit 42 and 39 home runs the previous two seasons with the Washington Senators. One of his offers: Moore, Smith, Earl Battey, Bubba Phillips, Jim Rivera, and $250,000 for Sievers and a pitcher, Russ Kemmerer. Years later, Lopez confided: "I wouldn't have given the $250,000, let alone the players."

Whatever, Cal Griffith turned down all of Veeck's advances, so Bill lowered his sights. His first trade, on May 1, was not exactly a blockbuster. He sent the once-glittering Yankee prospect, Lou Skizas, plus Rudolph—and, it is to be assumed, Patti Waggin—to Cincinnati for the once-dangerous Del Ennis. Then, every other day, it seemed, for the rest of the month—in between his special giveaways and nightly fireworks displays— Veeck added one over-the-hill longball hitter after another: first Ennis, then Harry "Suitcase" Simpson (from Kansas City for Ray Boone), then Larry Doby (purchased from Detroit).

Ennis replaced Callison, who had gotten off very slowly—although his single was the only hit the Sox made in a memorable 11-run inning at Kansas City in late April, a night they won, 20-6. Cash, after hitting two home runs in the first week, cooled off and

Earl Torgeson took over at first base. Wynn and Pierce were pitching well, but the same could hardly be said for Donovan, Moore, or Latman. Out of nowhere, however, came Shaw, who, after allowing just three earned runs in 24 innings of relief, was given a start May 13 in Boston and responded with a five-hit shutout. The pitching success story of the season had begun: Shaw would finish 18-6 with a 2.69 ERA.

The Yankees, meanwhile, like the Sox the year before, had stumbled badly out of the gate. Hit fairly hard by injuries (Mickey Mantle, Gil McDougald, Bill Skowron, and Andy Carey all missed time), the Yanks fell to last place on May 20, the first time since May 1940 they'd been that low that late. Cleveland was on top, with the White Sox a close second. In the last week of May, the Yankees turned, as usual, to their Kansas City farm club for aid. To the A's went the disappointing Johnny Kucks, sore-armed Tom Sturdivant, and infielder Jerry Lumpe. In return, the Yankees received the hard-hitting Hector Lopez and young righthander Ralph Terry, "sent down" to Kansas City for "seasoning" two years earlier in the Billy Martin deal.

The Yanks began climbing and came to Chicago on June 26 for a four-game weekend series, just two games out of the lead. Led by Lopez, they tore into Pierce, 8-4, in the Friday game, the same night a large Swede named Ingemar Johansson pummeled Floyd Patterson into submission in the third round at Yankee Stadium to win the heavyweight title. The next day's game turned the Sox's season around: Suitcase Simpson hit a grand slam with two out in the eighth off Bob Turley to beat the Yankees, 5-4. Then came a one-sided Sox sweep (9-2 and 4-2) the next afternoon, behind Wynn and Donovan and a barrage of home runs, and Chicago was off and running (literally, too, with Luis Aparicio racing toward a club-record 56 stolen bases). After the Friday night defeat to New York, the White Sox, getting unexpected production from new right fielder Jim McAnany (who came up from Indianapolis when Callison was sent down), won 26 of their next 34 to take a firm hold on first place, grabbing the lead for good when Pierce, on a home run by Smith, beat the Yankees, 4-3, before 43,829 on the night of July 28 at Comiskey Park.

The Yankees, already plodding along at the .500 mark, suffered their death blow on July 25 in Detroit. Skowron reached into the baserunner's path for a bad throw from third baseman Lopez, whose struggles afield were unmatched in this rivalry until the White Sox landed Gene Freese that winter. The runner could not avoid contact. Skowron's left wrist was broken in two places. "The Moose" was out for the season.

But it is unlikely the Yankees would have won this year even had misfortune not struck Skowron. Once Simpson hit that grand slam off Turley on June 27, the White Sox became convinced that this, finally, was their year. Remembered Al Smith: "It got so that by the end of July and the first of August, we figured we couldn't be beaten. We had a feeling on the bench that we were gonna win. Al Lopez sat down at the end of the bench, and there was a towel next to him. No one sat on that towel. We all said, 'That's where Jesus Christ sits.' "

The Sox ended up beating the Yankees 13 out of 22 games and did even better against their main challenger, Cleveland. The Sox had always played well against the Indians, and they did so again in '59, winning 15 of the teams' 22 meetings. The key series was a four-game weekend set August 28-30 in Cleveland's Municipal Stadium. Tremendous crowds turned out — 70,398 on Friday night, 50,290 Saturday, and 66,586 Sunday. The Sox, bolstered by the waiver pickup of Ted Kluszewski from Pittsburgh earlier that week, won all four games to take a five-and-a-half-game lead. The race was all but over.

The White Sox returned to the same scene on Tuesday night, September 22, needing one victory to clinch. Before 54,293, Gerry Staley relieved with the bases filled and one out in the ninth, his team leading, 4-2. The dangerous Vic Power swung at Staley's first pitch and grounded it to Aparicio, who turned it into a game-ending double play. Chicago had its first American League title in 40 years.

And, in the clubhouse and on the plane back to Chicago, Jim Rivera took great delight in repeatedly hollering, "Whatever happened to the Yankees?" Here's what happened to the Yankees: They finished third, 79-75, 15 games behind the White Sox. And though the Sox went on to lose the World Series to the Dodgers four games to two, they were finally American League champions. A goal that for the first time had seemed attainable eight years before, on the day Minnie Minoso arrived and went up to bat against Vic Raschi, at last had been achieved.

Rosters

Lists position players who appeared in 20 or more games, pitchers who appeared in 10 or more games, plus regulars who may have been traded/sold or acquired during the season.

1959 YANKEES

PITCHERS
Gary Blaylock, Jim Bronstad, Jim Coates, Art Ditmar, Ryne Duren, Whitey Ford, Eli Grba, Johnny Kucks, Don Larsen, Duke Maas, Bobby Shantz, Ralph Terry, Bob Turley

CATCHERS
Yogi Berra, John Blanchard, Elston Howard

INFIELDERS
Clete Boyer, Andy Carey, Tony Kubek, Hector Lopez, Jerry Lumpe, Gil McDougald, Bobby Richardson, Bill Skowron, Marv Throneberry

OUTFIELDERS
Hank Bauer, Mickey Mantle, Norm Siebern, Enos Slaughter

1959 WHITE SOX

PITCHERS
Rodolfo Arias, Dick Donovan, Barry Latman, Turk Lown, Ken McBride, Ray Moore, Billy Pierce, Bob Shaw, Gerry Staley, Early Wynn

CATCHERS
Earl Battey, Sherm Lollar, John Romano

INFIELDERS
Luis Aparicio, Ray Boone, Norm Cash, Sammy Esposito, Nellie Fox, Billy Goodman, Ted Kluszewski, Bubba Phillips, Earl Torgeson

OUTFIELDERS
Johnny Callison, Larry Doby, Del Ennis, Jim Landis, Jim McAnany, Jim Rivera, Harry Simpson, Al Smith

1959

Most Devastating Defeat

Thursday, June 18

At Yankee Stadium
Attendance: 12,217

Before the first-place White Sox had arrived in New York two days earlier, some people had begun writing the 1959 Yankees' obituary. The world champions were far off championship form, lurching along with a 27-29 record, a decidedly un-Yankee-like pace. The early-season injury bug had finally worn off, but even with all the regulars back healthy, the Yankees simply hadn't been able to get untracked. Key pitchers, 1958 Cy Young Award winner Bob Turley among them, were off to slow starts, and few besides Bill Skowron and newcomer Hector Lopez were doing much hitting.

But to the White Sox, if not the rest of the American League, these were still the Yankees, still to be feared, still to be considered the team to beat, no matter that the standings showed that they, the White Sox—and not the Yankees—were leading the pack. The concept that this Chicago team was a potential champion had not yet registered with many of the Sox players, among them Jim Rivera, who had been with the club since 1952 and had seen his share of Sox teams falter in the latter stages of pennant races.

Said "Jungle Jim," years later: "Until we went to Cleveland at the end of August and swept four straight to go up five and a half games, I didn't think we were gonna win it. Oh, no. I never dreamt we were gonna win the pennant. We'd been close before. We'd had better hittin' ballclubs, we'd had better defense, two-three years before that even. And we'd had double the speed: Hey, we had Minnie, Busby, and me in the outfield." So here, in New York for their first real '59 test with the Yankees, the White Sox were doing a splendid job of helping to reconfirm Rivera's doubts. They had fallen meekly before Art Ditmar in the series' opener, and Turley, improving his record to just 6-7, had beaten Ray Moore, 7-3, in the second match. Now, in the finale, young Bob Shaw went up against Yankee rookie Jim Bronstad in an effort to prevent a series' sweep and the Yankees from regaining any lost confidence — although this, despite the sub-.500 record, was a pretty confident bunch. And they were hardly ready to concede defeat in the pennant race.

"The Yankees," said their little lefty, Bobby Shantz, "would have to be down to their last breath before they would give up. I never saw a club with so much confidence. They thought they could beat anybody, and usually they did. But in 1959, we got sidetracked somewhere. I really can't remember what did happen to our club that year, but I know the White Sox were awfully tough."

Except, that is, in this series at New York. True, Chicago led, 4-2, this day, breaking a 2-2 tie in the seventh off reliever Ralph Terry when Shaw doubled, Luis Aparicio walked, and Nellie Fox doubled them both home. However, in the eighth, Yogi Berra's one-out double drove in Norm Siebern, and when Shaw followed that by walking Skowron, Al Lopez arrived at the mound with the hook. In came Turk Lown to face Hector Lopez, who drilled a sharp single to left to bring in Berra with the tying run. Casey Stengel here called upon the lefty-swinging John Blanchard to hit for Bobby Richardson. Al Lopez countered that move by waving in the diminutive Cuban lefthander, Rodolfo Arias. Stengel then switched to Elston Howard, whom Arias walked to fill the bases. The due hitter was Tony Kubek, but Stengel switched to a righthander, Gil McDougald, prompting Lopez to bring in his ace right-handed reliever, Gerry Staley. McDougald lifted a flyball to fairly deep right field, where Rivera made the catch. Skowron tagged up at third and raced home, but the throw from Rivera, who a few seasons earlier had collected the phenomenal total of 22 outfield assists, beat him there.

The game moved to the ninth, and neither team could solve the other's reliever, Shantz for New York and Staley for Chicago.

In the visitors' 10th, Shantz retired the White Sox in order for the third straight inning. It was up to Staley to hold the Yankees in the bottom half of the inning, which would be led off by none other than Mickey Mantle. From his home in Vancouver, Washington, Staley recalled the apprehension inherent in pitching to Mantle, especially when he was swinging left-handed in Yankee Stadium, with its short right-field home run distances.

"Most of the time," Staley said, "I had fairly good luck with him. But he had tremendous power. He could hit 'em out of any park. And Yankee Stadium—well, a guy could stand at home plate and almost spit over the right-field fence out there.

"But with Mantle, I'd try to stick with the sinker and get ahead of him with that and then throw a knuckleball. But most of the time, he was swinging when he left the bench, so I couldn't get ahead of him."

This time, Staley, as usual, opened with his sinkerball, but Mantle judged it a bit too low. The plate umpire, Frank Umont, agreed. Staley fired another sinker, but it did not sink enough. Mantle was ready for it. The ball was last seen settling deep into the right-field bleachers, Mickey's 15th home run of the season. The Yankees had swept the series and, in so doing, had knocked the White Sox out of first place, closed to within three and a half games of the AL lead and served notice that they were back in business. Dick Dozer's lead in the *Chicago Tribune* the next morning said it all:

"The Chicago White Sox Thursday got another convincing demonstration that the New York Yankees are on their way—and that Mickey Mantle is still the world champions' No. 1 hope-wrecker."

And yet, although the Sox left town with the feeling that the Yankees were going to be the same old Yankees, it certainly did not turn out that way. The Yankees would finish 15 games out of first place, just four games above .500. Some blamed injuries—particularly Skowron's broken wrist. Some blamed complacency. Others, like McDougald, pointed to a rare Yankee failure: They were no longer winning the close ones, this game excepted.

"The Yankees," McDougald noted, "were always a good club in winning one-run games, but it became obvious to everyone that we were in trouble in '59, because I think we lost around 31 one-run games that year."

But whereas McDougald and other Yankee veterans were able to see the warning signs early in the season, the younger players, like Richardson, either could not or did not wish to see them. To them, the pennant was like a birthright. "You've got to understand that, starting in '55, my first year, and then '56, '57, and '58, we had won. And then in '59, when the White Sox won, I didn't understand that.

"The only time I gave up—I don't remember exactly when it was—but we went into Boston and lost five in a row. And then I thought, 'Boy, we're not gonna win this year.' And we didn't."

The Yankees went to Boston for that five-game series Thursday through Monday, July 9-13, right after the All-Star break. New York, then 41-39, was in third place, just four and a half games out, with Cleveland on top and the White Sox two games behind. The last-place Red Sox won the opener, 14-5, prevailed Friday night, 8-5, won 8-4 on Saturday on Don Buddin's grand slam off Turley, won again on Sunday, 7-3, and completed the shocking sweep the next day with a 13-3 romp.

The Red Sox, weaklings until this point, had scored 50 runs in five games. The Yankees had fallen to fifth, seven and a half games out. Less than two weeks later, in Detroit, Skowron would break his wrist. Like the Yankees, he would be finished for the year.

1959

Most Glorious Victory

Friday Night, July 17

At Yankee Stadium
Attendance: 42,020

This was a game the White Sox (49-37)—leading Cleveland by one game, Baltimore by four and a half games and the Yankees (44-43) by five and a half—wanted badly in order to get off on the right foot in a four-game series at a place where, in the past, they had had their share of difficulty.

It was a game so dominated by the pitchers—39-year-old Early Wynn of Chicago and 23-year-old Ralph Terry of New York—that all on hand soon realized that one run likely would be all that was needed for either team to win.

It was a game filled with marvelous defensive plays, most of them by the White Sox, including one that Sox broadcaster Bob Elson, whose radio career spanned 40 years, always called one of the two or three greatest catches he ever saw.

And it was, agreed such Yankee Stadium press box regulars as Jimmy Cannon, Dan Daniel, and Bill Corum, the most exciting, most enthralling baseball game in the Bronx since Don Larsen's perfect game against the Dodgers in Game 5 of the 1956 World Series.

When it was over, manager Al Lopez, instead of answering questions, was asking them: "Did you ever see so many spectacular plays in one game?" He hadn't, nor had anyone else. There were two by Nellie Fox, who twice darted back of second base to throw out first Enos Slaughter and then Gil McDougald. There was one by Al Smith, who sped into left-center and made a diving catch on a liner by Slaughter. There were two by Earl Torgeson, one when he reached well into the box seats back of first for a diving catch of a pop foul. Even Billy Goodman, hardly known for his glovework and playing only because Bubba Phillips was hurt, made a terrific stop on Bobby Richardson's smash in the third and threw him out.

But the play of them all, the one Elson would never forget, was turned in by center fielder Jim Landis, who won't forget it, either. Mickey Mantle, leading off the fourth, rocketed a Wynn pitch to straightaway center. The ball was headed for the monuments of past Yankee greats Miller Huggins, Babe Ruth, and Lou Gehrig, nearly 460 feet from homeplate. Landis, getting his usual great jump, raced with his back to the infield and, leaping at the last instant, somehow caught the ball.

"Yeah, that was the 'monument' game," Landis remembered, speaking from his home in Napa, California. "There's no reason for a ball hit that far to be an out.

"You play a guy like Mantle extra deep anyway. Especially in that park, 'cause it was 461 to center and 430 to left-center and 400 to right-center. If he got it between you, it was an inside-the-park homer. It was a gigantic place. If we'd have been in Comiskey Park and he'd hit it that far, it'd be in the bleachers. I wouldn't have had to worry about it.

"Anyway, I just kept running and running. I was about five feet from the monuments when I caught it. You look back and say, 'My God, you hit the ball that far and you don't get anything for it?' If I'd hit a ball that far and somebody had caught it, I think I'd shoot him."

Both teams were shooting blanks, inning after inning, this night, and the game moved into the ninth, tied 0-0. Far more remarkable, however, was that Terry was carrying a no-hitter, Wynn a one-hitter. And even Terry, decades later recalling the evening, was of the opinion that Wynn should still have had a no-hitter going himself. For the lone hit off ol' Gus had been by Terry, who in the sixth, after having grounded a ball to deep short, was ruled safe at first, ostensibly having beaten Luis Aparicio's throw to Torgeson.

"I got the first hit, yeah, but I think I was out on the play," admitted Terry, now living in Larned, Kansas. "I think they had me by about a foot."

So did Torgeson, Wynn, and the rest of the Sox. However, only umpire Ed Rommel's opinion mattered, so Terry alone was bidding for no-hit fame as the ninth inning began. A Chicago rookie named Jim McAnany, a chunky, bespectacled 22-year-old outfielder from Southern Cal who had hit .400 the summer before at Colorado Springs, was leading off. He had been hitting .315 at Indianapolis on June 27 when the White Sox decided to bring him up and send Johnny Callison down. The move was working out: As he stood in against Terry, McAnany was batting .380 and had driven in the winning run in three of the Sox's last five victories. Terry threw a curveball and McAnany lashed it past him into center field for the first Chicago hit.

"Right between my legs," Terry remembered. "It was a good hit. A one-hopper, right over the pitching rubber, and on through."

"That's another reason I remember that game," said Landis. "'Mac' and I were pretty good friends, and, you know, it was good to see him get up to the big leagues, and he was going pretty well at the time, and he got that first hit, which was really good to see."

Next up was Wynn, who bunted the ball in front of the plate. Yogi Berra grabbed the ball and fired to McDougald, covering at second. McAnany, according to umpire John Stevens, anyway, beat the play, and now it was the Yankees' turn to squawk. When calm returned, Aparicio put down another bunt, putting runners at second and third with one out and bringing up Fox, who was hitting .332. Terry needed a strikeout here, and he knew he wouldn't get it from Fox, who never struck out. So an intentional walk, setting up a force anywhere, was the decided course of action.

"I only struck him out once, in all the times I faced him," Terry said of Fox, "and it was a foul tip. Yogi hung onto it, and it stuck in the webbing of his glove. And I can still see Yogi's teeth, grinning through the mask."

A far better candidate for a strikeout was Landis, who was stepping up to the plate. He also was a far better candidate for an out, period. Landis was hitting just .253, and here Terry quickly got ahead of him one ball and two strikes. Landis fouled off two more pitches, then lined the ball into right field for a single that scored McAnany from third and Wynn from second. The White Sox were up, 2-0.

"I hit a fastball," Landis recalled, "and I call it fortunate, because

I'm not a great right-field hitter, but I went with the pitch. I'm proud personally because I thought Ralph made a pretty good pitch on me. But I was fortunate enough to follow the ball real good and go the other way with the ball."

Now it was up to Wynn to hold the lead. Norm Siebern lined a single to center to open the Yankee ninth, finally giving New York a clean hit. Then Mantle ripped one at Torgeson, who made a sparkling pickup, fired to Aparicio at second for one out, and then took the return throw to just beat Mantle for the double play. Mantle screamed, and out of the dugout chugged Casey Stengel to scream as well. There was, apparently, cause for argument. Said Terry: "Let's just say I was more out on my hit than Mickey was in the ninth."

Mantle wound up getting ejected for making contact with umpire Rommel, and Stengel, after getting in his few well-chosen words, returned to the bench just in time to watch Berra pop to Fox for the game's final out. The White Sox were still leading the league, and Wynn had pitched one of the finest games of one of his finest seasons. "I gave 'em a little bit of everything that night," he said. "Fastballs, sliders, curves and about 10 or 12 knucklers."

It was also one of Ralph Terry's finest games. The year before, as a member of the Kansas City A's, he had defeated Camilo Pascual and the Senators, 2-0, in 13 innings in Washington. Later would come a 1-0 victory over the Red Sox in Fenway Park, when he left Carl Yastrzemski stranded at third after a leadoff triple in the ninth. And, of course, there was his 1-0 triumph over the Giants in Game 7 of the 1962 World Series. But the night he nearly no-hit the eventual 1959 American League champions ranks right up there.

Summed up Landis: "That's one game I'll always remember, because it was such a big ballgame, and because both pitchers were so outstanding that night."

And, certainly, so was Jim Landis.

1960

Setting the Stage

This was the year "U-2" became a household word and Francis Gary Powers a household name. Powers' U-2 spy plane was shot down over the Soviet Union on May 1, and an enraged Nikita Khrushchev, after throwing Powers in prison, railed away at President Eisenhower and essentially brought about the collapse of that spring's summit conference in Paris.

In Argentina that same month, Israeli agents captured the notorious Nazi Adolf Eichmann, who was put on trial in Israel for his role in the wartime extermination of millions of Jews and was executed two years later. And in South Vietnam, Communists formed the National Liberation Front, an organization that, in subsequent years, became more familiarly known as the Viet Cong.

In the U.S., Billy Wilder and *The Apartment* were the toast of the movie-going public, Percy Faith won a Grammy for his "Theme from A Summer Place," and Bill Hartack, aboard Venetian Way, won the Kentucky Derby.

A new decade had begun, and change was in the air. Eisenhower was in his final year in office, and his vice president, Richard Nixon, easily won the Republican presidential nomination that July while the Democrats selected the Roman Catholic senator from Massachusetts, John F. Kennedy. The old "I Like Ike" campaign buttons had seen their last days. Soon, a new face would be in the White House.

New faces were already in Yankee and White Sox uniforms—especially White Sox uniforms. Bill Veeck, desperately seeking a repeat pennant, had gone shopping to add some offense to a club that had won in '59 with almost none. Recalled Al Lopez, "Bill said to me, 'You won with no hitting. If we go out and get some hitters, you can repeat.' " Billy Pierce remembered much the same thing: "The statement Bill made was that the '59 team wasn't his team. He wanted to repeat in '60 with his team."

At first, Veeck pursued young boppers from the National League in this, the first winter of interleague trading. But when he failed in efforts to land 25-year-old Bill White from the Cardinals (for catcher Earl Battey and pitcher Ken McBride—both, like White, future All-Stars) or 22-year-old Orlando Cepeda from the slugger-loaded but catcher-less Giants (for Sherm Lollar), he turned at the St. Petersburg winter meetings to a constant trading companion of the past, Cleveland's Frank Lane. To the Indians Veeck sent Bubba Phillips and two '59 rookies, Johnny Romano and Norm Cash. Back to Comiskey Park came South Side legend Minnie Minoso, reportedly 37, plus a trio of players (pitchers Don Ferrarese and Jake Striker and catcher Dick Brown) who wouldn't even be with the club come July.

Two days later, Veeck dealt 20-year-old Johnny Callison, and all that potential, to the Phillies for third baseman Gene Freese, who, though possessing a questionable glove and an untamed throwing arm, had hit 23 homers—four of them grand slams—and driven in 70 runs in '59. Even Casey Stengel professed admiration, although with Case you could never be sure: "The Chicagos came down here needing an outfielder and a third baseman, and they're leaving with both of 'em. First they get Minoso, and now they come up with Freese, who they tell me is another Babe Ruth."

But there was no need to feel sorry for Stengel, because three days after that statement he actually did come up with another Babe Ruth. In the 15th trade the Yankees had made with the A's since they left Philadelphia after the 1954 season, New York shipped Norm Siebern, Marv Throneberry, Don Larsen, and the seemingly eternal Yankee, Hank Bauer, now 37, to Kansas City for two backups—shortstop Joe DeMaestri and first baseman Kent Hadley—and a 25-year-old left-handed pull hitter named Roger Maris, who in 1961 would break Babe Ruth's single-season home-run record. Maris had totaled 44 home runs the previous two years and would be a perfect fit for Yankee Stadium. And Veeck knew it; as he had in the past, he went ballistic about the Kansas City-New York connection:

"This kind of thing comes under the heading of conduct detrimental to baseball. What will this trade do to the Kansas City fan? Just look at that club. Who on that roster didn't come from New York?"

Intoned Cleveland's Lane: "Technically, it's not wrong, but morally it's bad for baseball. The deal comes as no surprise to me, but it's still a shock that there should be so much traffic between two ballclubs."

Yankee GM George Weiss' reply: "We've tried unsuccessfully to trade with other clubs in both leagues. The Yankees and Kansas City have faith in each other."

Veeck now figured he had to add another bat to counter New York's acquisition of Maris. It took a while, but finally, in April, two weeks before the season opened, he at last laid claim to Washington's Roy Sievers, who'd played for Veeck with the old St. Louis Browns in the early '50s. The price on Sievers, who had slumped from 42 and 39 homers in 1957 and '58 to just 21 in '59 (and from .301 and .295 to .242), was still fairly steep: Battey, Don Mincher (a 22-year-old first-base prospect) and $150,000.

So now the White Sox had on their roster Early Wynn, 40; Gerry Staley, 39; Minoso and Jim Rivera, 37; Earl Torgeson and ex-Indian Mike Garcia, 36; Lollar, Ted Kluszewski, and Turk Lown, 35; Billy Goodman, 34; Sievers, Billy Pierce, and Ray Moore, 33; and Nellie Fox, Al Smith, and Dick Donovan, all 32. Future replacements Callison, Cash, Romano, Battey, Mincher, and pitcher Barry Latman—dealt to Cleveland on the eve of the opener for Herb Score—were all elsewhere.

Lane was delighted to point out just how long in the tooth many of the Sox were: "If the White Sox don't win this year, look out. When another season comes around, some of those guys will be eligible for their pensions."

But Veeck was worried only about 1960, and even his critics had to admit that the White Sox appeared to be a most formidable club. They had added punch, they'd retained their speedsters (Luis Aparicio, Jim Landis) and, with newcomer Frank Baumann, a spring-training revelation, seemed to have improved even their pitching—particularly if Score, back under Lopez's eye, could return to his days of brilliance. So the Sox were the choice of most experts to again win the American League pennant, even though the Yankees would be improved with Maris and the return to full health of Bill Skowron. The '59 runners-up from Cleveland didn't appear as fearsome, having dealt off their top winner, Cal McLish, plus Minoso and Rocky Colavito, the league home-run champ who was sent to Detroit two days before the season began for AL batting champion Harvey Kuenn. The Tribe, however, still looked solid enough to contend.

The early-season surprise, however, was Paul Richards' Baltimore club, with rookie pitchers Chuck Estrada and Steve Barber joining other kids like Milt Pappas, Jerry Walker, and Jack Fisher and the grand old knuckleballer, Hoyt Wilhelm. And rookies Ron Hansen and Jim Gentile, plus center fielder Jackie Brandt, a winter acquisition from San Francisco, had given the offense a lift. So it was a four-team, not a three-team, race that raged through early July, when Cleveland began to fade. The Orioles and Yankees took turns at the top until after the All-Star break, when the White Sox—especially Sievers and Score—finally began clicking. The Sox won five straight before heading to New York July 22-24 for a four-game series with the first-place Yankees, who that weekend, in a move that would prove significant, added a journeyman Puerto Rican lefty named Luis Arroyo to their bullpen.

The Sox won the series' first three games to extend their winning streak to eight and pass the Yankees by two games before Eli Grba beat them, 8-2, in the second game of the July 24 doubleheader in front of 60,002. So the Sox, who hadn't led since May 24, left Yankee Stadium with a one-game lead, which was passed among them, the Yankees and Orioles over the next seven and a half weeks until, on September 13, with 17 games left on New York's schedule and 15 on Baltimore's and Chicago's, the Yankees led the Orioles by one game and the White Sox by three. That night, Fox, of all people, hit a two-out home run in the 11th to beat Washington, 6-5, in Chicago after the Yankees and Orioles had both lost. The defending AL champions were now two games back. The next evening, Baltimore won in Detroit and ex-Yankee Andy Carey homered off Art Ditmar in the ninth to give Kansas City a 2-1 victory over New York—but Washington, getting a homer from Battey and superb pitching from Jack Kralick, a former Chicago farmhand, beat the White Sox, 6-1.

Thus, with 13 games left for both Chicago and Baltimore and

15 for New York, the Yankees (82-57) and Orioles (83-58) were tied for first and Chicago (81-60) was two games behind. No one could have dreamed up what transpired thereafter. The Yankees swept a four-game series that weekend from the stage-struck Orioles at Yankee Stadium and never looked back. Their next loss didn't come until the Pittsburgh Pirates beat them in Game 1 of the World Series. And while the Bronx Bombers, who'd ended up getting 40 home runs from Mickey Mantle and 39 more from the newcomer Maris (along with a league-best 112 RBIs), were busy winning their last 15 in a row, the Orioles and White Sox were going 6-7 to finish a misleading eight and 10 games, respectively, behind the new champions.

The Sox had gotten big years, offensively, from their added bats: Minoso (20 homers, 105 RBIs, .311 average and an AL-best 184 hits), Sievers (.295, 28 homers, 93 RBIs) and Freese (.273, 17, 79) all delivered as well as could have been expected. And Al Smith came all the way back, hitting .315, second best in the league to the .320 posted by Boston's Pete Runnels. As for the pitching, another new face, Baumann, went 13-6 and led the league with a 2.67 ERA. Russ Kemmerer, acquired from Washington in mid-May, was 6-3 with a 2.98 ERA in 36 games for Chicago. Also, for a three-week stretch from mid-July through early August, Score, after an agonizingly slow start, pitched almost as brilliantly as he had when he was blowing batters away for Cleveland in '55 and '56.

A case, therefore, can be made that without Veeck's trades, the White Sox never would have been a factor in the 1960 pennant race, particularly when one compares the contributions of the new arrivals with the falloff in production of several holdovers—Landis (.272, 60 RBIs to .253, 49 RBIs), Fox (.306 to .289), Lollar (.265, 22 homers, 84 RBIs to .252, 7, 46), Wynn (22-10, 3.17 to 13-12, 3.49), Shaw (18-6, 2.69 to 13-13, 4.06), and Lown (9-2, 2.89 ERA, 15 saves to 2-3, 3.88, five saves). Lown's slump was more emphatically brought to light in the final six weeks when Staley, overused because of Lown's failure, became less and less a puzzle to opposing hitters. Lopez, in the late going, lost confidence in Staley as well as Lown and began turning to people like Garcia, a trusted hand from the Cleveland days, and Al "Red" Worthington—that is, until the devoutly religious righthander discovered the Sox were stealing signs from the center-field scoreboard and decided to quit the club. It could not have made Lopez any happier to realize that, over in Washington, a closer by the name of Ray Moore, cut loose in the season's early months, was busy compiling a 2.88 ERA and 13 saves—two fewer than Staley and Lown combined.

Thus, despite a record home attendance (1,644,460), Veeck's new exploding scoreboard, the nightly fireworks displays, and a ballclub that led the league in batting average, fielding percentage and stolen bases, was second in runs scored (by five to New York) and in fewest runs allowed, was third in team ERA, and played the Yankees on an equal footing and had their complete respect, the 1960 season was one of disappointment to the White Sox and Al Lopez.

But, in the end, it was one of disappointment to Casey Stengel, as well. For, after his team had pounded the Pirates 16-3, 10-0, and 12-0 only to lose the World Series in seven games because of a bad hop and Bill Mazeroski's home run, Stengel, at age 70, was asked to resign as Yankee manager. After 12 remarkable years, the Ol' Perfessor, the Yankee bosses had decided, was in fact too old. Case's parting words: "I'll never make the mistake of being 70 again."

Rosters

Lists position players who appeared in 20 or more games, pitchers who appeared in 10 or more games, plus regulars who may have been traded/sold or acquired during the season.

1960 YANKEES

PITCHERS
Luis Arroyo, Jim Coates, Art Ditmar, Ryne Duren, Whitey Ford, John Gabler, Eli Grba, Johnny James, Duke Maas, Bobby Shantz, Billy Short, Bill Stafford, Ralph Terry, Bob Turley

CATCHERS
Yogi Berra, John Blanchard, Elston Howard

INFIELDERS
Clete Boyer, Joe DeMaestri, Kent Hadley, Tony Kubek, Dale Long, Gil McDougald, Bobby Richardson, Bill Skowron

OUTFIELDERS
Bob Cerv, Ken Hunt, Hector Lopez, Mickey Mantle, Roger Maris, Jim Pisoni

1960 WHITE SOX

PITCHERS
Frank Baumann, Dick Donovan, Mike Garcia, Russ Kemmerer, Turk Lown, Ray Moore, Billy Pierce, Bob Rush, Herb Score, Bob Shaw, Gerry Staley, Early Wynn

CATCHERS
Sherm Lollar, Joe Ginsberg

INFIELDERS
Luis Aparicio, Sammy Esposito, Nellie Fox, Gene Freese, Billy Goodman, Ted Kluszewski, Roy Sievers, Earl Torgeson

OUTFIELDERS
Joe Hicks, Jim Landis, Minnie Minoso, Jim Rivera, Floyd Robinson, Al Smith

1960

Most Glorious Victory

Saturday, July 23

At Yankee Stadium
Attendance: 37,402

Bob Shaw was languishing, but the White Sox were not. Their winning streak had reached six the night before in the opener of this four-game weekend series, and now they were just .003 behind the first-place Yankees. They were hitting the ball—18 more hits the evening before, giving them 70 in the last five games. And three of their number were in the American League's Top 10 in hitting, an almost unfathomable development in the eyes of most Chicagoans. There was Al Smith, third at .323; Minnie Minoso, fifth at .318; and Roy Sievers, ninth at .304.

Shaw, however, was a different story. After going 18-6 with a 2.69 earned-run average in 1959, here he was, plodding along with an 8-8 record and an ERA slightly above 4.00. Part of the problem, he readily admits now, was of his own making. He simply wasn't pitching well, perhaps because he was still brooding about being offered a $5,000 raise over his '59 salary of $10,000. He held out most of spring training before finally signing for $22,000, but the lack of spring innings set him back. But part of the problem was not of his own making. That was the matter of a weakened White Sox defense, the result of Bill Veeck's off-season deals that had added power (Minoso, first baseman Sievers, and third baseman Gene Freese) at the expense of some good young talent and infield defense. And Shaw, a sinkerball pitcher, missed the everyday glovework of Bubba Phillips at third and Earl Torgeson at first. Shaw, who lives in Jupiter, Florida, and in his real-estate dealings has, many times over, made up for any contract slights he received during his baseball career, told of the ballclub's reaction to the new look during that 1960 season:

"We all knew what Veeck was trying to do, but a lot of the guys didn't think they were very good moves. The deals he made were made to get the new scoreboard to explode, and, in essence, the power wasn't the answer. It hurt the defense. And I was in baseball professionally for 22 years, playing and coaching, and then I stayed in baseball, coaching American Legion and amateur baseball, and the longer you're in the game the more you realize that defense is so, so important."

Shaw will grant that Sievers was a terrific hitter, and that Freese could swing the bat, too. "But Sievers was a poor defensive player, and Gene Freese—see, Freese was a terrible defensive ballplayer. And I can say 'terrible.' He was a bad defensive infielder. He could run a little bit, and he had some pop, but the defensive part of it was not so good."

Not that his defensive shortcomings didn't bother the normally free-spirited Freese. Recalled Bill Sather, a Sox batboy that season: "We were playing Baltimore. We were ahead in the eighth inning, they had people on base. Groundball to Freese, and here's the throw to first: The first baseman didn't even jump. It was way over his head, ball goes into the seats. We end up losing the game.

"And afterwards, Al Lopez—I don't know what he did, but he made a lot of noise in his cubicle, kicking things. He was really hot. And the next day, Freese got to the park real early, at about 10:30, and I was there. And he said, 'You know, last night, I took a case of beer, and I started driving down the expressway. I was goin' 90 miles an hour and I didn't give a shit who was in my way.'"

Yet, even with the defensive deficiencies of some of the 1960 White Sox, here they were, primed to take over the league lead from New York. And Shaw, a local boy, was psyched and ready to pitch in front of family and friends in a game that meant so much.

"I guess I'm one of the few guys who had a winning record against the Yankees in the few years I pitched," said Shaw, who was 4-2 with three no-decisions in nine starts in his nearly two and a half seasons as a Chicago starting pitcher. "And I guess, coming from Garden City, Long Island, I got kind of pumped up and would kind of rise to the occasion against the Yankees. Of course, there were a few teams during my career I didn't rise to the occasion against, Cincinnati being one of them. But I did pitch quite well against New York."

Had he been a Yankee fan growing up?

"No, I was a Dodger fan, and my sister was a Yankee fan. My dad was born and raised on 10th Avenue in Hell's Kitchen in New York, and he was a Giants' fan. My mother, she just stayed out of the way. She just sat and listened."

White Sox fans back in Chicago who were listening to Bob Elson's radio account soon were concerned that Shaw might not be at his best on this steamy afternoon. For, in the very first inning, Hector Lopez singled and came around on Yogi Berra's double over Minoso's head in left. After that, Shaw toughened and waited, hoping —with scant reason to do so, actually—his teammates would do something against Whitey Ford, who blanked the Sox through the first four innings. But in the fifth, Luis Aparicio singled and Nellie Fox walked. Minoso delivered the third of his four straight hits on the day, this one a line single to center field that sent Aparicio home to tie things at 1-1.

Then came the decisive inning, the sixth. Joe Hicks, a rookie playing center field because Jim Landis' hand was swollen, opened by drawing one of the five walks the uncharacteristically wild Ford would allow this afternoon. Shaw bunted Hicks along, and then it was Aparicio's turn to walk. Up came Fox, one hit shy of 2,000 for his career. Nellie sent a grounder to Clete Boyer at shortstop, but Boyer botched the play and the bases were loaded for Minoso. Again, Minnie came through, his line single to left scoring Hicks and Aparicio for a 3-1 Chicago lead.

That was it for Ford. On came Ralph Terry to face Sievers. Terry, too, had trouble with his control, walking Sievers to reload the bases. Sherm Lollar's pop fly dropped into center field for a hit that scored Fox, and when third baseman Gil McDougald, looking for all the world like Gene Freese, fired wide of first base after fielding Freese's easy roller, Minoso checked in to make it 5-1.

But Shaw, given some breathing room, could not breathe easily just yet. In the seventh, Bobby Richardson doubled and McDougald singled him in, and in the eighth, Bill Skowron, who'd already had two hits, ripped a low line drive that hugged the left-field line and just made it over the fence at the 301-foot marker for his 18th home run, a league-best .330 average and a 5-3 ballgame.

Shaw, having allowed 10 hits but, for the second straight outing, zero walks, was excused after the eighth inning and Gerry Staley, just four weeks shy of his 40th birthday, was asked to nail down what would be the White Sox's seventh straight victory. First place was just three outs away. Standing in the path were three pinch hitters—Kent Hadley for Boyer, Elston Howard for Richardson, and, for reliever Bobby Shantz, Mickey Mantle, who had sat this one out because of a sore instep, the result of an unfortunately aimed foul tip the night before.

It took Staley all of six pitches to get the job done. Hadley flied to right field, Howard to left. On the sixth pitch, Mantle swung and hit a sharp grounder to Fox at second. Bob Elson's voice, rising with unusual excitement—for Elson—provided the words across the miles: "And the American League today has a new leader!"

For the first time since May 24, the defending AL champions were back on top. The winning streak was at seven and, suddenly, the idea of a repeat pennant did not seem too improbable anymore—except to some insiders, like, for instance, Bob Shaw. "You're always optimistic," he said, "especially after you've won it the year before. You think positive. But as you look back, when they made those deals, when they took away the defense, the power didn't compensate for the loss of defense."

Which, to Shaw's way of thinking, was going to make defense of the White Sox's 1959 championship difficult. He would be proved correct.

1960

Most Devastating Defeat

Wednesday, August 24

At Yankee Stadium
Attendance: 32,116

With 34 games left on the schedule, the Yankees were leading the American League with a 67-48 record, the White Sox were second at 69-51, and Baltimore third at 68-52. The Sox, behind Early Wynn, had beaten New York, 5-1, the night before to close to within a half game of first place. Now they had a chance to go back into first place this afternoon in a park where they had won six of 10 so far in 1960.

However, they were facing a pitcher against whom they'd had almost no success. That was righthander Art Ditmar, who in 11 starts as a Yankee against Chicago had compiled a 7-0 record with four no-decisions. And even before that, with lamentable Kansas City teams in 1955 and '56, Ditmar had meant trouble for the White Sox, having authored a two-hit shutout in Chicago in '55 and a one-hitter in Kansas City in '56.

"I had confidence when I pitched against them," remembered Ditmar, living in retirement in Myrtle Beach, South Carolina. "I'd started off my career pitching good against them when I was with Kansas City, so when I got to New York [in 1957], they always pitched me against them. New York always pitched you against the teams you did well against."

Opposing Ditmar this day was Herb Score. After sputtering earlier in the year, he had worked closely with Al Lopez on the sidelines, and he had been pitching of late like the smoke-throwing

Score of '55 and '56, when he was among the game's premier lefties, before Gil McDougald's line drive had hit him in the eye and before he had torn a tendon in his pitching elbow. Score was coming off a two-hit shutout of Kansas City, during which he had struck out nine. "Oh, there were flashes, and I'd think I'd found it again," Score, long one of the broadcast voices of the Cleveland Indians, recalled. "But it didn't last. I'd throw a good game here and there, but I just didn't have the consistency and I didn't have that, you know, little extra."

Score was being modest or, perhaps, simply forgetful. Because, in fact, over his previous five starts, four of them complete games, he had worked 43 innings, struck out 40 and walked 19 and had an earned-run average of 1.88.

"But," he said, "I just never felt right. My arm didn't hurt anymore, but the ball was straight. Used to be, the ball would tail or rise. Al would say, 'You're slinging the ball.' They'd take pictures. I'd look at them and say, 'I can see it.' But I couldn't make myself flip it anymore 'cause I'd lost the motion somewhere. I could still throw fairly hard, but it wasn't a live fastball anymore."

And yet, it had been live enough that, exactly two weeks earlier, he had limited the Yankees to one hit, a home run by Bill Skowron, in seven innings, had struck out six and walked no one. He'd allowed two more runs in the eighth before the Yankees broke it open against Chicago relievers to win, 6-0. Score's opponent that day in Comiskey Park had been Ditmar. Now they were paired against each other again, with first place on the line.

The Yankees broke on top almost immediately, with the help of bases on balls, a Score problem even in the mid-'50s, when he was at his most brilliant. Tony Kubek walked with one out and took second on Yogi Berra's opposite-field single. Then, after Mickey Mantle struck out, Skowron walked to fill the bases for Hector Lopez, who singled just over shortstop Luis Aparicio's leap for a 2-0 New York lead.

The way Ditmar zipped through the first three innings—and the way he handled the White Sox generally—those two runs were looming quite large. Ditmar always brightened when he saw those familiar faces in Chicago uniforms.

"I knew Nellie Fox my first year in baseball," Ditmar said. "We were on the same team going to spring training in 1948 with the Philadelphia A's. So I sorta knew how to pitch to Fox, and he was a key man in that lineup. If you kept him off base, him and Aparicio, you were in business. And I knew how to pitch to Aparicio pretty good, too. I mean, there were guys in that lineup that I had confidence I could get 'em out—that if I got a few runs, I could beat 'em."

Sure enough, on this day, leadoff man Aparicio was hitless in three officials trips, Fox in four. Sherm Lollar was 0 for 2, and Minnie Minoso and Al Smith had to wait until the ninth before they could solve Ditmar for base hits. So five men who were at the heart of the Chicago ballclub for years were once again having their usual struggle with Art Ditmar.

"With Fox," Ditmar recalled, "I always started him off with a breaking ball, and he didn't like to swing at the first pitch, anyhow. And once I got ahead of him, I just drove him inside—in and down—and I wouldn't give him the pitch away so he could go the other way. I just kept going down and in on him, and he used to fight it. I mean, he used to talk to himself. I did it that way all the time.

"Aparicio, I used to brush him back and then throw breaking balls. He never liked to be pitched inside. With Minnie, he crowded the plate, so I'd pitch him tight, too. And I kept it down on him, because he liked the ball up.

"They were good ballplayers, but I had the confidence. I'd even get away with bad pitches I'd make against them."

The only Sox hitter who was to give Ditmar any difficulty this day was Roy Sievers—probably because this, after all, was Sievers' first year with Chicago and had not yet had time to fall completely under Ditmar's spell. Sievers, batting in the fourth, drove a home run, his 24th of the season, into the left-field seats against a stiff wind to make it a 2-1 game. He already had walked the first time up and would double the next.

"I had pretty good luck against the Yankees," said Sievers, who still calls his native St. Louis home. "The more people you had in the stands, the more you got pumped up. I enjoyed playing the Yankees and the other top clubs."

He'd been with the bottom clubs, like the Browns and Senators, for too long. Bill Veeck had rescued him from Washington that spring, and now he was delivering as Veeck had anticipated. By this week's end, he would be leading the league in hitting with a mark of .324 and would be among the leaders in home runs with 26. "I was really happy," he remembered. "I always wanted to find out how I would play on a first-division club. I wanted to prove to myself I could play well with a contender."

Kubek, meanwhile, was attempting to prove he could hit home runs off hard-throwing lefties. Tony lofted a Score pitch into the nearby right-field seats with one out in the seventh for a 3-1 Yankee lead. That was the first hit surrendered by Score since the third inning, and the fourth—and last—he would allow overall. But again, he had no offensive support. In his last four starts, his teammates had provided him with a grand total of five runs. Now, Gerry Staley came on to pitch a scoreless eighth inning, and Ditmar took his 3-1 lead into the visitors' ninth.

Fox and rookie Floyd Robinson, still looking for his first major-league hit but batting third in Al Lopez's lineup in this, one of the year's most crucial games, were easy outs. One more and New York's lead would be back to one and a half games. But now, up came Sievers, and there went Ditmar's comfort zone—and the baseball. Sievers cracked homer No. 25 over the fence in left, giving him 81 RBIs on the year (he would drive in just 12 more runs the rest of the season) and giving the Sox renewed hope. Smith followed with a hit to left, and when Minoso did the same, Casey Stengel strolled to the mound, took the ball from Ditmar, and waved in his new bullpen savior, 33-year-old lefty Luis Arroyo, salvaged from the International League junk pile one month earlier. Arroyo's assignment was to retire Gene Freese, a right-handed hitter. Ordinarily, that would seem strange strategy, except that Arroyo's best pitch was a screwball, which would fade away from right-handed batters.

Apparently, Freese had not studied Arroyo too closely when the two were teammates on the pathetic Pirate clubs of 1956 and '57. For there went Freese, chasing a screwball and sending an easy roller to second baseman Bobby Richardson, who fired to Skowron for the final out. Thus, Chicago had lost a precious game in the standings, and Art Ditmar was now 8-0 as a Yankee against the White Sox.

"But that's the way it is," he said. "There are some teams, if you have confidence against them, it seems like you can get 'em out. It seems like things always fall into place."

And the White Sox, so close to first place, were soon going to fall into third.

1961

Setting the Stage

Amid much enthusiasm and anticipation, John F. Kennedy was inaugurated as the nation's new president on January 20, but the euphoria in Washington was soon tempered by events elsewhere. First came the ill-fated Bay of Pigs operation in April, when Fidel Castro's forces crushed an invasion attempt by Cuban exiles armed and trained by the United States.

Then came more sobering reality. By the time (May 5) the U.S. finally put a man, Alan Shepard, in space, it had been three and a half weeks since Soviet cosmonaut Yuri Gagarin had become the first man in orbit around the Earth. In August, the Berlin Wall went up to halt the flow of refugees from East Berlin to West Berlin, and Nikita Khrushchev helped heat up the crisis by vowing to eventually rid Berlin of any U.S. presence. Later, in October, the Soviets made the world more uncomfortable by exploding a 50-megaton hydrogen bomb, the largest explosion in history.

In the meantime, the literary world lost one of its giants when Ernest Hemingway took his own life. On a more pleasant note, Hollywood couldn't sing loudly enough its praises for *West Side Story*, which was voted best picture and won a host of other Oscars. And Henry Mancini's "Moon River," from another top movie of the year, *Breakfast at Tiffany's*, won the Grammy.

Los Angeles and Washington, meanwhile, won expansion franchises in the new 10-team American League—Washington because the old Senators had fled for the Twin Cities to become the Minnesota Twins. In the expansion draft, the White Sox lost, among others, Dick Donovan and Ted Kluszewski. Yankee losses included Bobby Shantz, Bob Cerv, and Eli Grba. But there were other, more significant changes in Yankee personnel. Replacing Casey Stengel as manager was Ralph Houk, former Marine major, bullpen catcher, and, most recently, Yankee coach. Ex-Yankee pitcher Johnny Sain was Houk's new pitching coach, and Roy Hamey supplanted general manager George Weiss, who like Stengel had been forced to retire. One of the few new players was pitcher Roland Sheldon, 15-1 in Class D ball the year before. Missing from the scene, for the first time in 10 years, was Gil McDougald, who had announced his retirement at age 32.

At the White Sox camp in Sarasota, Florida, the 1960 cast was almost intact, with, besides those gone to the new clubs, one notable exception. Bill Veeck had traded Gene Freese to Cincinnati in a three-team deal also involving Milwaukee. To Chicago came two pitchers—35-year-old Calvin Coolidg Julius Caesar Tuskahoma McLish, a noted Yankee-killer (8-1 lifetime vs. New York), and 24-year-old lefty Juan Pizarro, who, by season's end, would develop into the staff's finest pitcher. Thus, Freese's stay in Chicago had lasted all of one season. Several years later, during his second stint as White Sox president, Veeck sat in the Bards Room at old Comiskey Park and recalled what had sparked the deal: "Al Lopez had told me that he simply wasn't going to play Freese, so I might as well get rid of the guy."

The new Chicago third baseman was to be rookie J.C. Martin, a .285 hitter at Triple-A San Diego in '60 and a converted first baseman. Soon he would be a converted third baseman: Found wanting with the bat, J.C. was made into a catcher, a career move that enabled him to stay in the big leagues through 1972. (As for Freese, he helped the Reds win the National League pennant with his 26 homers and 87 RBIs.)

Both the Yankees and White Sox started slowly. But whereas New York—on its way to a memorable year due in no small part to the assault on Babe Ruth's home-run record by Roger Maris and Mickey Mantle—quickly recovered, the White Sox didn't get straightened out until mid-June. By then, they were in last place, trailing even the ragtag expansion teams, and Veeck, suffering from what he feared was a brain tumor but what actually amounted to a chronic concussion, was being advised by doctors at the Mayo Clinic to get complete rest. So on June 10, he sold his 19-33 ballclub to a group headed by Chicago industrialist Arthur

Allyn and retired to an estate on Maryland's Eastern Shore. On that same day, the Sox—not the Yankees, remarkably—swung an eight-player deal with Kansas City, sending 1959 heroes Bob Shaw and Gerry Staley to the A's along with outfielders Wes Covington (purchased from Milwaukee only a month before) and Stan Johnson (then at San Diego). In return, Sox GM Hank Greenberg received Ray Herbert, a 14-game-winner in '60; reserve outfielder Al Pilarcik, and two longtime Yankees: Andy Carey, first actively sought by Chicago in 1956, and Don Larsen, 3-21 for Baltimore the year before he joined the Yankees and 1-10 for K.C. in the season after he left them—altogether, a nifty 4-31.

Carey stepped right in at third base, played terrific defense and began hitting well. Herbert took a spot in the starting rotation, Larsen pitched effectively in long relief and, suddenly, the Sox were red-hot, winning 19 of their next 20 games to climb back into the first division. But that was to be the dying gasp of what was becoming a dying ballclub. While the Yankees and Detroit battled it out into September—before the Yankee bombers blasted the Tigers three straight in New York to take command of the race (they then went on to beat the Reds in a five-game World Series)—the White Sox battled to stay above .500. The only bright spots were the development of Pizarro (14-7, 3.05 ERA despite not starting a game until mid-June); outfielder Floyd Robinson, a .310 hitter in his first full season; productive years from the aging veterans Al Smith (28 homers) and Roy Sievers (27); and a splendid all-around campaign by Jim Landis (22 homers, 85 RBIs, .283).

At season's end, the White Sox were in fourth place and 23 games behind the Yankees, to whom they had lost 12 of 18 meetings. Their pitchers had contributed 13 homers to Maris' record-smashing total of 61. The year had been a trifle embarrassing. The Chicago White Sox were ripe for rebuilding.

Rosters

Lists position players who appeared in 20 or more games, pitchers who appeared in 10 or more games, plus regulars who may have been traded/sold or acquired during the season.

1961 YANKEES

PITCHERS
Luis Arroyo, Tex Clevenger, Jim Coates, Bud Daley, Art Ditmar, Ryne Duren, Whitey Ford, Danny McDevitt, Hal Reniff, Roland Sheldon, Bill Stafford, Ralph Terry, Bob Turley

CATCHERS
John Blanchard, Elston Howard

INFIELDERS
Clete Boyer, Joe DeMaestri, Billy Gardner, Tony Kubek, Bobby Richardson, Bill Skowron, Earl Torgeson

OUTFIELDERS
Yogi Berra, Bob Cerv, Hector Lopez, Mickey Mantle, Roger Maris, Jack Reed

1961 WHITE SOX

PITCHERS
Frank Baumann, Warren Hacker, Ray Herbert, Russ Kemmerer, Don Larsen, Turk Lown, Cal McLish, Billy Pierce, Juan Pizarro, Bob Shaw, Gerry Staley, Early Wynn

CATCHERS
Camilo Carreon, Sherm Lollar, Bob Roselli

INFIELDERS
Luis Aparicio, Andy Carey, Sammy Esposito, Nellie Fox, Billy Goodman, J.C. Martin, Roy Sievers, Earl Torgeson

OUTFIELDERS
Wes Covington, Jim Landis, Minnie Minoso, Al Pilarcik, Floyd Robinson, Al Smith

1961

Most Devastating Defeat

Saturday, July 15

At Comiskey Park
Attendance: 37,730

A paid crowd of nearly 40,000 people for a Saturday afternoon game at Comiskey Park, even with the Yankees in town, was highly unusual. Friday nights, yes. Sunday doubleheaders, yes. But not Saturday afternoons.

The pennant race was not the reason for the turnout. The White Sox, trailing both New York and Detroit by 14 games, weren't in it. They were fifth, three games under .500. No, the reason was the home run. Roger Maris, with 34 homers, and Mickey Mantle, having hit No. 31 the night before off Juan Pizarro, both were well ahead of Babe Ruth's record pace of 1927. And the Yankees were well on their way to setting an all-time team record for home runs—240.

Before this afternoon was over, the fans would get their money's worth, and more.

It all started with a second-inning drive by Elston Howard off Ray Herbert that bounced on the roof—almost directly above the 375-foot sign—and across 34th Street and landed, supposedly, some 60 feet from the back wall of the ballpark. Sox mathematicians' estimate of the distance traveled: 490 feet. The fun had begun.

Next, Sherm Lollar evened things in the Chicago half of the second with a shot into the left-field seats off New York starter Ralph Terry. Then Maris clobbered one into the upper deck in right for his 35th homer and a 2-1 Yankee lead, but Herbert answered with a less-majestic home run in the bottom half of the third to tie the game. That Herbert got in on the action is not too great a surprise: With the Sox, he hit .226 with two homers in '61, .195 with two in '62, and .222 with one in '63—all good figures for a pitcher. But this homer was enough to convince Yankee manager Ralph Houk that this was not Terry's day. In came Jim Coates, and the tall, thin righthander got through the rest of the inning unscathed.

Such was not the case in the fourth. First, Minnie Minoso drilled a Coates' pitch into the left-field upper deck for his 11th home run of the year. Lollar walked and Andy Carey, eager to do well against his former teammates, lined one up the alley in right-center for an RBI triple and a 4-2 Chicago lead. Carey came home three batters later when the Yankees just missed doubling up Luis Aparicio on what they vociferously claimed was an inning-ending double play. Aparicio moved up when Nellie Fox walked, and both came home when Jim Landis, also getting into the long-ball mood, launched his 12th home run, this one into the upper seats in left.

So the Sox, after four innings, had hit four home runs and were up, 8-2. It was still 8-2 in the sixth when the Yankees began making things interesting again. Maris tripled to the wall in right-center to begin the assault on Herbert. Maris scored on Yogi Berra's sacrifice fly, two runs came across on a double by John Blanchard—getting an infrequent start—and when Hector Lopez delivered a pinch RBI single off reliever Turk Lown, it was an 8-6 ballgame.

After Lown zipped through the seventh and eighth, the Sox had an opportunity to add an insurance run in their eighth against Hal Reniff, the fourth New York pitcher. Aparicio walked, stole his 28th base, and took third on a wild pitch—all with none out. He couldn't score on Fox's shallow fly to Maris in right, but when Landis sent one a bit deeper in the same direction, Looie decided to give it a try. Maris, however, made a perfect throw to nail Aparicio at the plate, and the game moved to the ninth.

Bob Cerv, who had done this sort of thing before, batted for Reniff and sent Lown's first pitch of the ninth sailing into the top deck in left. Now it was 8-7. Bobby Richardson walked, and so did

Lown—to the clubhouse. In came lefty Frank Baumann; Tony Kubek bunted Richardson to second; and Maris, striking again, doubled down the right-field line, and the game was tied. The six-run lead was a memory.

Baumann walked Mantle intentionally, but when he walked Berra unintentionally, Al Lopez had seen enough. With the right-handed-hitting Howard coming up, Lopez called for 36-year-old Warren Hacker, who, years earlier as a Cub, had been known, quite unflatteringly, as "Home Run" Hacker. Out of the big leagues since 1958, he had been purchased by Bill Veeck on June 2 from Chattanooga of the Double-A Southern Association, where he had been 8-1 with a 1.57 earned-run average and 64 strikeouts and only 10 walks in 63 innings.

"At Chattanooga, it was like I was playing catch with the catcher," Hacker said from his home in Lenzburg, Illinois, about 30 miles southeast of St. Louis. "You could tell right there that baseball had really, you know, fallen off. Gosh, I know guys in that league went up to the big leagues, and they couldn't hit a fastball. I just threw it by 'em. And I wasn't an overpowering pitcher.

"Anyway, Bill Veeck told me he bought me out of *The Sporting News*. Saw my record in there, 8-1, and decided I could help."

And he had helped, but this was an entirely different set of circumstances: the mighty Yankees, bases loaded with one out, game tied, home runs flying out of the ballpark, and Elston Howard, who'd already hit one up on the roof, standing at the plate.

"I was scared to death," Hacker remembered. "I've heard relief pitchers say they couldn't wait to get in there. But I think myself, and the majority of them, are hoping the pitcher who's out there gets 'em out. I never did sit out there and say, 'Boy, I hope I get into this game.' I was the reverse. I was hoping I'd never get in.

"But a lot of times, you come into a game like that and you're kinda scared to death and, I don't know, it seems like you get a little extra energy. And you actually throw a little better then you're capable of."

Which, as it turned out, is what happened. After getting some guidance from his catcher, Hacker went to work on Howard.

"Sherm Lollar told me Howard likes the ball high and in—you know, a high-ball hitter. So Sherm said, 'You pitch him low and away, you can get him.' I threw four pitches. He swung at the first two and missed them. Next one, boom, right in the same spot. Umpire called it a ball. Came back right to the same spot again on the fourth pitch and struck him out."

Now there were two outs, but Hacker wasn't out of it yet. The batter was Blanchard, a left-handed pull hitter who was already 2 for 3 on the afternoon. "Blanchard then hit one—he hit it good, put it darn near out of the ballpark," Hacker remembered. Al Smith raced toward the wall in deep right-center, gloved the ball, had it pop loose, and then, just as the ball was dropping toward the ground, grabbed it again to end a most exciting half-inning.

But it all started up again in the Yankee 10th, after Luis Arroyo and his screwball had set down the White Sox in order in their ninth. Clete Boyer reached second with a double that Landis almost turned into an out with his diving attempt, and Arroyo's sacrifice bunt sent Boyer to third with one out. Hacker got Richardson to pop out, but Kubek solved him for a base hit to center for the tiebreaking run.

Thus, a game that had seen seven home runs, one of them a roof shot, in the end was decided on a single.

"Yeah, I got in trouble with Kubek," said Hacker. "The little guys, they were tough on me. See, the good strong hitters—well, like Howard—if they had a weakness, I had good control and I could hit that spot pretty good. But Tony Kubek—he's what I call one of those slap hitters. You don't know where to pitch 'em. I tried to overpower him, and he hit a little semi-line drive into center field for the base hit."

A little line drive...the little guys...the little things. The Yankees, even the '61 Yankees, won because of them, not just because of the big home runs. Two double plays. Maris throwing out Aparicio at the plate. Kubek and Arroyo getting their bunts down. Berra delivering his sacrifice fly and Kubek, finally, the game-winning single. Recalled Kubek: "We'd hit the home run, yes, but it was a team of players that played the game right and knew how to play it. Even with Mickey and Roger, the great home-run hitters that they were, we were always taught to play defense and if you get the chance to take the extra base, you do it. Most of us ran well, we were good baserunners. So we broke up double plays and we got to balls other teams didn't. That was more of a trademark than anything else."

But the trademark Warren Hacker will always remember were those big bats—and the guys who swung them.

"You look at that lineup, from top to bottom," he marveled. "And a guy like Blanchard sitting on the bench? God, you know they're tough."

1961

Most Glorious Victory

Tuesday Night, August 15

At Yankee Stadium
Attendance: 49,059

For a young man of 24, Juan Pizarro was quickly becoming accustomed to pitching against the New York Yankees in front of enormous crowds.

As a 20-year-old Milwaukee Braves' rookie, he had worked, briefly, in relief of Bob Buhl in Game 3 of the 1957 World Series before 45,804 at County Stadium. In the 1958 World Series, he had seen action in Game 5 before 65,279 in Yankee Stadium. Since his December 1960 acquisition by the White Sox, he had beaten the Yanks, 6-1, on July 14 at Comiskey Park as 43,450 looked on, and he had lasted less then three innings in a 12-0 loss July 25 at Yankee Stadium in front of 46,240.

Now, here he was again, back at Yankee Stadium, where almost 50,000 were settling in to cheer the first-place Yankees, Whitey Ford with his inconceivable 20-2 won-lost record and, most of all, Roger Maris and Mickey Mantle, both with 45 home runs and 15 games ahead of Babe Ruth's 1927 pace that produced a record 60 homers.

Pizarro was singular in purpose on this hot August night: His goal was a victory, revenge for that July 25 blowout. Stopping Maris and Mantle in their pursuit of "the Babe" was secondary.

"When you go out on that mound," Pizarro said during a 1994 visit to Chicago, "you don't think about records or nothing like that.

You try to get the guys out. See, if you think about the records these guys are trying to break, you make a lot of mistakes. But if you don't think about it, you don't make a mistake."

Besides, there were people other than Maris and Mantle in the Yankee lineup to worry about. "The guy who was real tough for me," Pizarro remembered, "was Bobby Richardson. He was tough to strike out; he didn't swing at no bad balls. He was tough. And the strongest swinging the bat was Moose Skowron. Now, for distance, it was Mantle. But Skowron, you pitch him low and away, he hit it nine miles to right field. Pitch him inside and low, he takes it to left field, with power."

This evening, however, Skowron went 0 for 4. Richardson went 0 for 4. Mantle went 0 for 4. There were singles by Tony Kubek and Clete Boyer, and Maris had a pop-fly double and a—well, what else? This, after all, was 1961.

"Roger Maris hit a home run that night off me—I remember that," said Pizarro. "I hung a curveball. But Mantle didn't do anything. Mantle, right-handed, you could throw him hard stuff and throw it by him. But don't throw him no slow stuff."

Pizarro, on this sweltering night, wasn't throwing too much slow stuff to anybody. His 96-M.P.H. fastball was crackling, helping him to strike out 10 Yankees, eight in the first six innings, as he clung to the lead provided him by his teammates in the second. In that inning, Roy Sievers had singled off Ford and Minnie Minoso doubled him to third, but they held their ground as Al Smith bounced to Boyer and Andy Carey, in an 0-for-20 nosedive, popped to shallow left. Now came rookie Camilo Carreon. With first base open, Ford could have pitched around him to get to Pizarro, but Carreon was just a rookie. So Whitey went ahead and pitched to him, and the young catcher, who had turned 24 only nine days earlier, lined a single to center to give his batterymate a 2-0 lead.

"Cammy Carreon," Pizarro said, brightening. "He was the guy who caught me a lot. Cammy Carreon. 'The Tequila Man.' He was Mexican-American. He loved those Margaritas.

"So did I."

The Margaritas could wait. There was a lead to protect. Maris, with one swing, cut it in half in the fourth with his 46th home run, a bullet well over the 344-foot sign in right. Carey, playing third that night, was an admiring witness.

"I'll never forget how hard he hit the ball that year," he said. "The ball would absolutely just jump out of the ballpark."

In the sixth, Maris crushed another one, this one into the third tier in right, but just inches foul. The giant crowd roared, then groaned. Pizarro sighed in relief, then struck Maris out. And then, he fanned Mantle, too, to end the inning with his eighth strikeout.

There were some more nervous moments to come. After the White Sox had squandered chances against Ford in the sixth and seventh and against Luis Arroyo the next inning, Maris, with one out in the home eighth, lifted a high pop fly to shallow center. Jim Landis, playing deep in center for reasons obvious, made a long run for the ball and dived for it—but came up empty. The Yankees had a runner at second base with one out, and the crowd came alive, sensing victory, with ample reason. For the White Sox were in fifth place, 18 games out and just two over .500 because they'd been losing these kinds of contests all year.

But Pizarro wasn't going to go down easily. Landis caught up with Mantle's flyball, and Carreon caught Elston Howard's popup in front of the Yankee dugout. After a scoreless Chicago ninth, Pizarro, still ahead 2-1, came out firing heat. He blew away Skowron, his 10th strikeout victim, on three pitches and got Hector Lopez on a roller back to the mound. Here, Boyer, No. 8 hitter in the lineup, grounded a single between Luis Aparicio and second base, and the Yankees were not through just yet.

Now the noise was thunderous, for, from the Yankee dugout, swinging a pair of bats, emerged Yogi Berra, hero of countless late-inning Yankee victories of seasons past. In Detroit, the second-place Tigers were beating Baltimore in a doubleheader. A Yankee loss would mean New York's league lead would shrink to two games. A long one by Berra, however, would pull this one out and keep the Yankees three games ahead.

Pizarro, from the stretch, fired and missed with ball one. He threw again and Berra lifted a towering popup near the mound. Carey, Sievers, Aparicio, and Nellie Fox all converged on it before Fox called everyone off and gloved it for the final out. Pizarro, who hadn't even made his first American League start until June 10, was now 8-5, had beaten Whitey Ford and the mighty Yankees, and silenced the Yankee Stadium throng. The transformation from a wild thrower to a solid pitcher was nearly complete.

"Pizarro, when he came to us," recalled the longtime Sox pitching coach, Ray Berres, "pitched with an arched back and a rushed delivery and consequently all he could throw was one fastball after another, and his best pitches—with the most velocity and the most movement—were up out of the strike zone. Well, you might as well throw it out the window. It took a long time to convince him to change his delivery just a little bit."

"Ray Berres, that was my man," Pizarro said, smiling. "He's the one who taught me how to throw strikes. I used to open up [on my delivery] too quick. So every time I opened up too soon, he'd whistle at me or holler at me and let me know. Then I'd concentrate: Don't open up too soon."

And then he'd close the door on the opposition—even the Yankees.

1962

Setting the Stage

The Berlin crisis continued to unnerve Europe—indeed, the world—with Chairman Khrushchev threatening to drive U.S. troops from West Berlin and President Kennedy responding by activating two divisions. On February 20, Col. John Glenn became the first American to orbit the Earth, and on May 31, Adolf Eichmann was executed in Israel.

In October, the world watched anxiously as Kennedy, revealing the Soviets were building missile bases in Cuba, demanded that Khrushchev have them dismantled and the weapons taken back to the USSR. Then, JFK ordered a naval blockade to keep out the next shipment of missiles. Millions feared imminent nuclear war, but Khrushchev backed down and the Soviet ships turned around and headed home. The world breathed a little easier.

Lawrence of Arabia won the Oscar for best picture and landed David Lean the Oscar for best director. The Grammy for best record went to Tony Bennett for "I Left My Heart in San Francisco," and while Shelley Fabares longed for "Johnny Angel," the Four Seasons yearned for "Sherry."

To their glittering world championship cast, meanwhile, the New York Yankees, training for the first time in Ft. Lauderdale, added a left-handed pitcher, Marshall Bridges, who would become the club's top reliever. They also added four impressive rookies: There was a trio from Amarillo in the Texas League—shortstop Phil Linz (a league-leading .349), center fielder-first baseman Joe Pepitone (21 homers, .316), and pitcher Jim Bouton (13-7, 2.97)—plus a shortstop from Central Michigan University, Tom Tresh, who had hit .315 in the International League the year before and was the son of Mike Tresh, the White Sox's No. 1 catcher through the '40s. Young Tresh and Linz were presented with an immediate job opening: Tony Kubek's Army reserve unit had been one of those called up to active duty because of the Berlin crisis, so Kubek would be lost to the Yankees until August at the earliest. Tresh beat out Linz and made the most of his opportunity.

As for the White Sox, they had spent the off-season undergoing an overdue face-lift. Not only were there new uniforms—the black-with-red-trim motif was replaced with a deep navy blue—but there were several new people wearing them. New GM Ed Short, with Al Lopez providing ample input, had begun rebuilding the club by dealing off two South Side legends, Billy Pierce and Minnie Minoso, plus the team's top home-run hitter of the last two seasons, Roy Sievers. Pierce, 35, was sent to San Francisco with Don Larsen, 32, for two players of some significance (pitchers Eddie Fisher, 25, and Dom Zanni, 30) and two of none (Bob Farley, a big young left-handed hitter who for some inexplicable reason reminded Sox broadcaster Bob Elson of Mickey Mantle, and pitcher Verle Tiefenthaler, who had the distinction of giving up a grand slam—to Detroit's Billy Bruton—in the first inning he pitched in the big leagues). Minoso, 39, was shipped to St. Louis for Joe Cunningham, 30, a fancy-fielding first baseman who could spray singles and doubles all over the ballpark. The man he was to replace, Sievers, 35, was banished to Philadelphia in a deal Short had hoped would include Johnny Callison but instead yielded a 25-year-old pitcher, John Buzhardt, and a 24-year-old third baseman, Charlie Smith.

Short and Lopez had decided the Sox had to get younger and faster and that the pitching staff must be reconstructed. That the whole operation was going to take a while became evident rather quickly, as the Sox struggled to stay above .500 for most of the season's first four months. A closing push helped them finish 85-77, which was good enough only for fifth place, one game out of third but 11 out of first.

The Yankees, meanwhile, even with Mickey Mantle sidelined from May 18 to June 22 and with Roger Maris' inevitably falling off to 33 homers and 100 RBIs, got 23 wins from Ralph Terry, 17 from Whitey Ford and 14 from Bill Stafford—not to mention 20 homers, 93 RBIs and a .286 average from the rookie Tresh—and fought off challenges from Cleveland and surprising Los Angeles in the first half and from Minnesota in the second to win their third pennant in a row and seventh in the last eight years. A thrilling seven-game World Series victory over the Giants—despite two fine outings by Pierce, one a three-hit triumph over Ford—was to follow.

Thus, it was, for the second consecutive year, a season without a pennant race on Chicago's South Side. But the White Sox had come up with two decent-looking rookies, pitcher Joe Horlen and outfielder Mike Hershberger; Ray Herbert won 20 games and was the winning pitcher in the All-Star Game at Wrigley Field; Floyd Robinson put together a second straight solid season (.312, 45 doubles, 109 RBIs); Cunningham hit .295 with 32 doubles and 70 RBIs, and Fisher and Buzhardt had their moments. At season's end, callups from the minors included outfielder Ken Berry, infielder Al Weis, and the towering, hard-throwing bonus baby Dave DeBusschere, the basketball star out of the University of Detroit. Also, a 21-year-old farmhand named Tommy McCraw had just won the American Association batting title at Indianapolis.

Yes, Norm Cash had blasted 39 homers at Detroit, John Romano hit 25 for Cleveland, Earl Battey batted .280 and won a Gold Glove at Minnesota, and Callison hit .300 with 23 homers and an incredible 24 outfield assists for the Phillies. And yes, Dick Donovan had won 20 games for Cleveland, Ken McBride was 11-5 for the Angels, and Bob Shaw 15-9 with a 2.80 ERA at Milwaukee. But the rebuilding program in Chicago was slowly but surely taking shape. The White Sox were one blockbuster deal away from shooting back into the 90-win class—and pennant contention.

Rosters

Lists position players who appeared in 20 or more games, pitchers who appeared in 10 or more games, plus regulars who may have been traded/sold or acquired during the season.

1962 YANKEES

PITCHERS
Luis Arroyo, Jim Bouton, Marshall Bridges, Tex Clevenger, Jim Coates, Bud Daley, Whitey Ford, Roland Sheldon, Bill Stafford, Ralph Terry, Bob Turley

CATCHERS
John Blanchard, Elston Howard

INFIELDERS
Clete Boyer, Tony Kubek, Phil Linz, Dale Long, Joe Pepitone, Bobby Richardson, Bill Skowron, Tom Tresh

OUTFIELDERS
John Blanchard, Hector Lopez, Mickey Mantle, Roger Maris, Jack Reed

1962 WHITE SOX

PITCHERS
Frank Baumann, Johnny Buzhardt, Dave DeBusschere, Eddie Fisher, Ray Herbert, Joe Horlen, Mike Joyce, Russ Kemmerer, Turk Lown, Juan Pizarro, Dean Stone, Early Wynn, Dom Zanni

CATCHERS
Camilo Carreon, Sherm Lollar, Bob Roselli

INFIELDERS
Luis Aparicio, Joe Cunningham, Sammy Esposito, Bob Farley, Nellie Fox, Bob Sadowski, Al Smith, Charlie Smith

OUTFIELDERS
Mike Hershberger, Jim Landis, Charlie Maxwell, Floyd Robinson

1962

Most Devastating Defeat

Wednesday Night, May 2

At Comiskey Park
Attendance: 25,547

The White Sox had entered the 1962 season with a number of new pitchers, among them Eddie Fisher, Johnny Buzhardt, Dom Zanni, and Joe Horlen. It was about time that one of their number be initiated into the ways of the Yankees. Tonight, it was to be Horlen's turn.

Horlen, a 24-year-old rookie from San Antonio, had gone 1-1 to date and had been fairly impressive during Chicago's 11-8 start. He was quick to win the approval of manager Al Lopez, who had looked with special admiration upon Horlen's 12-9 record and 2.51 earned-run average in the hitter-happy Pacific Coast League the season before. Now, he faced his first test against the defending world champions, who were one and a half games ahead of the White Sox. Against the champs, he would employ his usual repertoire of fastball, slider, and "cutter," the so-called "cut" fastball taught him by Warren Hacker, a Sox teammate the previous September during Horlen's brief look-see and, for a spell later, Horlen's minor-league pitching coach.

"You hold it like a slider," said Hacker, explaining the cutter, "just off center, only it doesn't break down. It's an ideal pitch for a righthander to use against a left-handed batter, because it runs right in on their hands. You know, a [righthander's] slider kinda breaks away from a right-handed hitter and sinks, but a cut fastball will just sail on you. Joe had a good motion for it, over the top, and gosh, he'd just give it that little twist, just off center, and he perfected it."

He had not perfected it quite yet. But, even so, Horlen pitched brilliant baseball on this cool spring evening, holding the Yankees to four singles and a double through the first eight innings, at which point he led, 3-2. He had simply thrown what veteran catcher Sherm Lollar called for, and he had attained excellent results. Only in the first inning—when, perhaps wisely, he walked both Roger Maris and Mickey Mantle with Bobby Richardson aboard to set up a New York run—and in the sixth—when Clete Boyer just did beat a relay to the plate on Maris' double—had Horlen encountered difficulty.

"Before the game started, I was wonderin' a little bit what's gonna happen," admitted Horlen, back home in San Antonio after serving another year as pitching coach for San Francisco's Triple-A club at Phoenix. "But once the game started, I'm just out there thinking about the batter. It was the catcher's game to call, not the pitcher's. Whatever the catcher puts down, I'm throwin'. He knows these guys better than a rookie pitcher knows 'em."

But he knew of them, of course, so when he struck out Mantle, with Maris at second base, to end the Yankee eighth and protect his one-run lead, he had to feel a special sense of accomplishment.

"Oddly enough," he revealed, "I never had too much trouble with Mantle. Richardson always got his bat on the ball. He was tough. Yogi Berra, Elston Howard, every one of 'em was capable of breaking a game open at any time."

By this time, the Sox were up by one, having scored all their runs off starter Ralph Terry, two of them driven home by Al Smith, who collected three hits on the night. The Sox might have had more than those three runs, but reliever Jim Coates had escaped a base-loaded jam in the seventh by getting Jim Landis to bounce to Boyer at third.

The first two hitters in the visitors' ninth were Berra and Howard. Horlen had closed the sixth by striking out both with Maris and Mantle on base. This time, the results would be different, as Horlen, more than 30 years later, recalled all too well. "I remember it, sure. I remember the losses more than the wins. Yogi Berra hit a double and Elston Howard hit a home run."

Minnie Minoso is greeted by Eddie Robinson (46) and Paul Lehner after his two-run homer on his first time up in a White Sox uniform, May 1, 1951. He hit it off the Yankees' Vic Raschi. Catcher is Yogi Berra. [UPI/Bettman]

Sox teammates Phil Masi (left), Eddie Robinson, and Nellie Fox (right) surround Saul Rogovin after the righthander beat the Yankees, 5-2, on June 21, 1951 in New York. Masi caught the game, Robinson homered, and Fox collected three hits. [AP/World Wide Photos]

Sox shortstop Chico Carrasquel gives fielding "tips" to the Yankees' Phil Rizzuto before the July 17, 1951 game at Comiskey Park. Chico was the All-Star starter one week earlier, Rizzuto the backup. [*Chicago Tribune* photo]

Manager Paul Richards welcomes Sam Mele (left) and his league-leading .429 batting average to the White Sox on May 4, 1952 at Yankee Stadium, one day after his acquisition from Washington. Sox then lost pair to the Yankees, scoring only one run all day. [AP/World Wide Photos]

Three Sox-killers talk things over at Comiskey Park before the game on June 18, 1954: from left, Whitey Ford, Allie Reynolds, and Eddie Lopat. [*Chicago Tribune* photo by Ed Feeney]

On the night of June 3, 1955, just 16 days after Bob Grim of the Yankees had beaned Minnie Minoso at Yankee Stadium, the two get together at Comiskey Park to show there are no hard feelings. Minnie suffered a hairline skull fracture as a result of the beaning, but he was back in the starting lineup June 5. [*Chicago Tribune* photo by Chester Gabrysiak]

Billy Pierce delivers to the plate against the Yankees on June 5, 1955 at Comiskey Park. The Yankees went on to win, 3-2, in 10 innings. [*Chicago Tribune* photo by Ed Feeney]

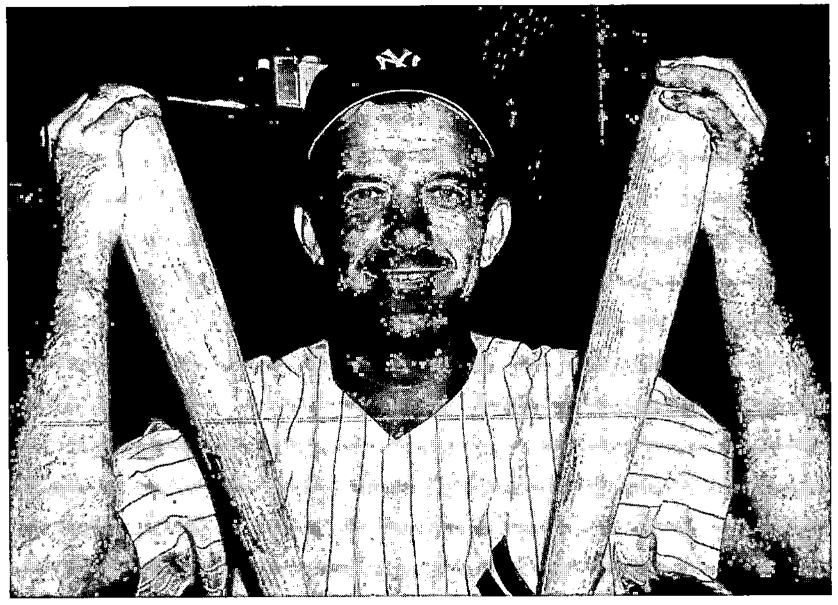

Joe Collins in Yankee clubhouse after his two home runs off Dick Donovan beat the White Sox, 5-4, on September 9, 1955. (See 1955, Most Devastating Defeat) [UPI/Bettman]

Mickey Mantle is flanked by Gil McDougald (left) and Andy Carey after the Yankees' 8-7 victory in 10 innings the night of May 18, 1956 at Comiskey Park. Mantle homered from both sides of the plate, and his two-out blast in the ninth tied the game. Carey singled in McDougald with the winning run in the 10th. [AP/Wide World Photos]

Sox VP Chuck Comiskey (center) beams as Dick Donovan (left) presents White Owl cigars to rookie Sammy Esposito, after Esposito's bases-loaded single defeated the Yankees, 5-4, in 12 innings the night of June 22, 1956, at Comiskey Park. Donovan had pitched no-hit ball into the eighth inning. (See 1956, Most Glorious Victory) [*Chicago Tribune* photo by Ed Feeney]

Sequence of duel between Dave Philley (6) of the Sox and Bob Grim of the Yankees, June 23, 1956, at Comiskey Park. Philley was ejected, Grim stayed in and lost, 2-0, in the second game of Chicago's four-game weekend sweep. (See The Fights) [*Chicago American* photos]

Walt Dropo and the Yankees' Enos Slaughter (17) square off as part of the half-hour-long free-for-all at Comiskey Park on June 13, 1957. Dropo got the best of this one. (See The Fights) [*Chicago Tribune* photo]

Slaughter, showing the effects of his bout with Dropo, leaves the field after the June 13, 1957 brawl. (See The Fights) [*Chicago Tribune* photo]

Roger Maris, chasing Babe Ruth's record, at the plate before the typically jammed Sox-Yankee night game crowd, September 12, 1961. [*Chicago Tribune* photo by Al Phillips]

Mickey Mantle takes his mighty swing but manages only a flyball to right field off the Sox's Juan Pizarro on August 15, 1961 at Yankee Stadium. Pizarro beat the Yankees, 2-1. (See 1961, Most Glorious Victory) [AP/ Wide World Photos]

Whitey Ford works against the White Sox on June 20, 1964, en route to a 1-0, 11-inning victory over Gary Peters. This was the seventh of 10 straight Sox losses to New York that year. [*Chicago Tribune* photo by Phil Mascione]

Johnny Buzhardt gets down a suicide-squeeze bunt that scored Ron Hansen from third base during the Sox's 5-0 victory on August 20, 1964—manager Al Lopez's 56th birthday. The victory completed the Sox's four-game sweep and moved them into first place by a half game. Yankee catcher is Elston Howard. (See 1964, Most Glorious Victory) [*Chicago Tribune* photo]

And suddenly, the Yankees, seemingly beaten, were ahead, 4-3. Berra's ball had split the gap between center fielder Landis and rookie right fielder Mike Hershberger, and Howard's drive, his fourth homer of the young season, had reached the seats in right-center.

"The ball Berra hit," said Horlen, chuckling in remembrance, "was a foot outside, probably a little over his head. And he jerked it into right-center. Then Elston Howard hit one to the opposite field. He had real good power the other way."

Howard's homer came, interestingly, on the pitch that eventually would help make Horlen the standout pitcher he was to become. "I threw him a cut fastball. It was supposed to break away from him. It forgot to cut. So there it was, right over the middle of the plate."

And Howard knew what to do with it. The White Sox, stunned, proceeded to go scoreless in the ninth against Coates, who got Lollar to rap into a game-ending Boyer-to-Richardson-to-Bill Skowron double play. Thus, a brand-new White Sox pitcher had fallen victim to the age-old Yankee treatment. Horlen, however, knew he had fought the good fight. In the next day's newspapers, he read the Yankees' glowing critiques of his performance. Yogi Berra's was typical:

"The kid pitched a good ballgame. We'll see a lot more of him."

Joe Horlen, decades later, repaid the compliment. "I think they had great teams, and they brought out the best in us, really."

But on this night, as usual, the White Sox's best had not been quite enough.

1962

Most Glorious Victory

Friday Night, September 21

At Comiskey Park
Attendance: 32,711

Only eight games remained on the schedule, the Yankees' magic number for clinching their third straight pennant was down to four and the White Sox (81-73) were in fourth place, 10 games out of first.

And yet, this game attracted nearly 33,000 paying customers, many of whom no doubt had purchased their tickets in the spring, hoping a September showdown between the Yankees and White Sox might prove to be one with title ramifications. In keeping with tradition, Whitey Ford was paired against Chicago's top lefty, in this case Juan Pizarro, and, also in keeping with tradition, rain was in the forecast.

The Yankees led, 3-1, in the sixth, when Pizarro walked Hector Lopez just before it began pouring. Out came the grounds crew with the tarpaulin, and the crowd settled back for a one-hour and three-minute delay. One out after play resumed, Bill Skowron hit his 22nd home run of the year—and the last one he would hit against the White Sox as a Yankee—and Ford led, 5-1.

Ford's arm stiffened in the bottom half of the sixth, and he was replaced by another lefthander, Bud Daley, who baffled Chicago batters through the eighth. When Tom Tresh, the splendid rookie who already had collected two hits, doubled in a run off Johnny Buzhardt in the ninth, Daley had a five-run lead with which to work as the White Sox came up for their last chance. A large percentage of the original crowd was still on hand, waiting—despite the discouraging display on the field—for the season's final fireworks display, advertised as the biggest of the year. Little did these fans anticipate the fireworks the Sox were about to produce.

It all began with a Nellie Fox base hit to left field. Camilo Carreon singled to left as well, and third-string catcher Bob Roselli was summoned from the center-field bullpen to bat for Buzhardt. Roselli had gotten into just 22 games the year before and would appear in but 35 this season, so he had to make the most of his limited opportunities. That he did here, driving a double to deep right-center to score Fox and send Carreon to third. Ralph Houk, slightly perturbed that Daley hadn't retired any of the lower third of the Chicago batting order, waved in another lefty, Marshall Bridges, his No. 1 reliever in '62. Bridges annoyed Houk even more by walking Luis Aparicio to fill the bases, still with nobody out. Now, the possibility of victory began crossing the minds of some people, including a 28-year-old September callup named Grover "Deacon" Jones, who was seated in the White Sox's dugout.

"It was incredible," remembered Jones, from his home in suburban Houston. "Guys just kept getting on—base hits, walks, somethin', one way or the other. Then, after a while, you start feelin' it, you know what I'm saying?"

That was especially so when Joe Cunningham brought the crowd to its feet by slicing a double down the left-field line, clearing the bases and leaving the White Sox only one run behind with, again, still nobody out. The Sox were "feelin' it," all right.

"It was exciting in that dugout, boy," Jones said. "And I've managed in the minor leagues. And I've had teams that had big leads and start losing it. And no matter what I do, I know, in the back of my mind, that nothing will stop this bleeding. I *know* that." By now, perhaps, Ralph Houk knew it, too, particularly after the lefty Bridges walked the left-handed-hitting Floyd Robinson. Houk trudged back out to the mound and called for righthander Jim Coates to face Al Smith. Smith failed twice in his attempt to bunt the runners over, then whacked a double past third base and into the corner. Cunningham came around with the tying run, but coach Tony Cuccinello held up Robinson at third—there were, remember, no outs.

Now the place was in an uproar. People could not believe what they were witnessing. The White Sox had rallied from five runs down in the ninth to tie the mighty Yankees, and the Yankees had yet to retire one Chicago batter.

Houk ordered Coates to walk Jim Landis on purpose to fill the bases, setting up a force play at homeplate. He also brought his infield and outfield in close. On the other side of the field, Al Lopez called back the due hitter, Mike Hershberger, even though the latter already had gone 2 for 4 this night and had beaten Coates with an extra-inning base hit just six weeks earlier. Instead, the batter was to be Jones, something of a minor-league vagabond who finally had made it to the majors—seven years and three months after Frank Lane signed him in the wake of a Comiskey Park workout.

He had made his debut 13 days before, as a pinch hitter against Washington. He'd worn that day a uniform style not used by the Sox since 1960. There was no name on the back—just a big No. 20. Now, here he was with J-O-N-E-S neatly sewn on his uniform, above a new number, 50. And, unlike that first appearance, when his knees were shaking as he stood in the box—before lining a base hit to right field on the first pitch thrown to him—this night he was far more relaxed. And more established, as well, having collected four hits in nine tries since his break-in.

"I'd gotten over my nervousness," he recalled. "I had my own uniform by then, too. First one didn't even have my name on the back. But I didn't care. I was just worried that it would be in my locker every time I got to the ballpark."

"The Deacon" took Coates' first pitch for a ball, then drilled the next one. "I remember I got a line drive into left-center, off a fastball," Jones said, "to knock in the winning run." By the time the ball had stopped rolling, it was at the wall and the White Sox had come up with an improbable 7-6 victory. In a normal situation, the hit would have been a bases-clearing double—or, perhaps, with Jones' speed, a triple. But this one went down simply as an RBI single. Which was just fine with him.

"That was awesome," he said. "Big crowd. The Yankees. Pinch-hitting with the bases loaded."

The winning hit triggered both an on-field celebration and an inquiry into just who was this Deacon Jones fellow and where had he come from. Unknown to most White Sox fans, he was hardly unknown to the organization. As a 17-year-old, he had been American Legion Player of the Year in 1951, hitting .408 in the national tournament for his team out of White Plains, New York. The Sox had signed him after graduation from Ithaca (NY) College in June 1955, and off he went on a tour of Sox farm clubs, where he always managed to hit up a storm: Waterloo (.318), Dubuque (.409, tops in organized baseball in 1956, with 26 home runs and 120 RBIs), Lincoln (.299), San Diego (.299), Charleston (.283), and, in '62, Savannah, where he'd hit .319 with 26 homers and 101 RBIs.

Unfortunately for him and the Sox, he couldn't play his normal position—second base—at all, and he couldn't play his adopted position—first base—up to major-league standards because of a 1956 spring-training injury suffered when he slid headfirst into third. On the play, Jones said, "all the weight came down on my right arm. I heard something pop, like when you crack your knuckles. Next morning, when I got out of bed, I couldn't move my shoulder."

He soon learned the extent of the damage. "I'd torn the long-headed biceps tendon in my right shoulder. It eventually healed, but scar tissue covered it and limited the range of motion. So when I started my arm up, the pain would be excruciating. I couldn't get my arm up, so I had to throw underhanded—little flip jobs."

There was no designated hitter back then; hence, his lengthy sojourn in the minors—which, eventually, led to a career as a major-league hitting instructor with Houston and San Diego.

"If they were as advanced medically in those days as they are now," said the Deacon, "I probably would've had a more successful career, in terms of staying longer in the big leagues."

His big-league stay as a player amounted to 49 at-bats, spread over parts of three seasons. Not very long, true, but long enough to include one memorable hit in one memorable game.

1963

Setting the Stage

No one who lived through it will forget the defining event of this year, an event that took place more than a month after the final pitch of the World Series had been thrown, more than a month after the Yankees had been humiliated, in four straight games, by the Los Angeles Dodgers. The date was Friday, November 22, the place was Dallas. A president was shot and killed. A disbelieving nation mourned. Two days later, the accused assassin was himself assassinated, as a still-disbelieving nation watched on television.

That weekend's horror climaxed a historic year: Martin Luther King stirred some 200,000 assembled for a civil rights rally in Washington with his "I have a dream" speech; the Washington-Moscow "hot line" was installed; a nuclear test-ban treaty was signed by the U.S., the Soviet Union, and Britain; and the number of U.S. advisors was up to 15,000 in South Vietnam, where President Ngo Dinh Diem, three weeks before President Kennedy's death, was murdered by officers of his own army.

Escape was provided by motion pictures like *Hud, Lilies of the Field, The V.I.P.s* and the Oscar-winning *Tom Jones.* The Grammy for best record went, for the second time in three years, to Henry Mancini, this time for "The Days of Wine and Roses."

The Yankees had prepared for their title defense by making only one change, but it involved a big name. With young Joe Pepitone deemed ready for full-time duty, the Yankees traded Bill Skowron to the Dodgers ("I tried hard to get him," said White Sox GM Ed Short, years later, "but when the Yankees did deal him, they made sure they dealt him out of the league"). For "the

Moose," New York got pitcher Stan Williams, who'd won 14, 15, and 14 games the previous three seasons.

Short and Al Lopez, in the meantime, were continuing the face-lift at Comiskey Park. Luis Aparicio, 29, who had spent 1962 squabbling with Lopez, slumping at the plate and slipping a bit in the field, was traded with Al Smith, 35, on January 14 to Baltimore. In return, Chicago received four players—the incomparable, 39-year-old relief pitcher, Hoyt Wilhelm; a shortstop replacement for Aparicio, Ron Hansen, Rookie of the Year in 1960 and still just 25; outfielder Dave Nicholson, five years removed from signing for a $110,000 bonus but just 23 and still possessed of great power potential ("Even in our park," gushed Short that spring, "he can hit 30 homers"); and finally, the key to the deal, a 23-year-old third-base prospect named Pete Ward, coming off a year in the International League in which he had batted .328 with 22 home runs. The Sox, who had also released Early Wynn, 43, had gotten younger and deeper, but the experts were hardly impressed: In *The Sporting News*' annual poll of baseball writers, the White Sox were picked to finish sixth.

It became apparent almost immediately that the White Sox would not finish sixth. With Ray Herbert firing shutout after shutout (he finished with seven of them) and with Juan Pizarro and John Buzhardt throwing superlatively, Chicago's pitching was remarkably stingy. And then it got better: When Pizarro came down with the flu one May night in Kansas City, Lopez gave lefty Gary Peters, a 26-year-old farm product expecting to be released on cutdown day, an opportunity to start. All Peters did was hit a home run and, with late relief help from the just-acquired noted author, Jim Brosnan, beat the A's, 5-1. Peters went on to put together an 11-game winning streak plus a final record of 19-8, a league-best 2.33 earned-run average and the Rookie of the Year Award.

With that kind of pitching, and with Ward, Floyd Robinson, and Joe Cunningham all hitting for average, Nicholson for power and Hansen in the clutch, the White Sox were in and out of first place through June, even taking three out of four from the Yankees in Chicago during that month's final week. Injuries, however, began taking their toll. First, Cunningham broke his collarbone, and Buzhardt (9-4, 2.42 at June's end) came up with a sore shoulder and was shelved for the season. After the Yankees beat Chicago three of four July 2-4 in New York, Hansen having missed the entire series with a sore neck, the Sox were four and a half games behind. By month's end, the deficit was eight games.

But the White Sox could not cry about injuries, because the Yankees' big guns, Mickey Mantle and Roger Maris, missed huge chunks of the season. Mantle missed two months with a broken foot and got into only 65 games. Maris, with ankle and back miseries, got into 90. And yet the Yankees still ended up winning 104 games and beating out the runner-up White Sox by 10½ games, biggest American League victory margin since the 1947 Yankees won by 12. With their big boppers sidelined, the Yankees, the mighty Yankees, won with pitching (Whitey Ford went 24-7, 2.74; Jim Bouton 21-7, 2.53; Ralph Terry 17-15, 3.22; and rookie Al Downing 13-5, 2.56) and with defense: Their infield of Clete Boyer, Tony Kubek, Bobby Richardson, and Pepitone was the league's finest. Also, Elston Howard was the league MVP, young Tom Tresh—with Kubek back at short—simply moved to left field and hit 25 home runs and Pepitone added 27 more.

The White Sox's return to the No. 2 spot in the standings could be traced to the blossoming of Peters (who allowed, remarkably, only nine homers in 243 innings) and the big trade with Baltimore. Ward led the club with his .295 average and 84 RBIs and hit 22 homers, a total matched by Nicholson, who, on the negative side, set a big-league record with his 175 strikeouts. Hansen was second to Aparicio (.9826 to .9825) among the league's shortstops in fielding, and Wilhelm's 21 saves were 15 more than Turk Lown's 1962 team-leading total. Additionally, three rookies—Tommy McCraw, Al Weis, and Dave DeBusschere—had shown promise. Al Lopez's team had been rebuilt almost overnight, and another batting champion from Indianapolis, Don Buford, was being readied for 1964 delivery. Lopez would spend the winter in Tampa playing golf and thinking pennant.

Rosters

Lists position players who appeared in 20 or more games, pitchers who appeared in 10 or more games, plus regulars who may have been traded/sold or acquired during the season.

1963 YANKEES

PITCHERS
Jim Bouton, Marshall Bridges, Al Downing, Whitey Ford, Steve Hamilton, Bill Kunkel, Hal Reniff, Bill Stafford, Ralph Terry, Stan Williams

CATCHERS
Yogi Berra, Elston Howard

INFIELDERS
Clete Boyer, Harry Bright, Tony Kubek, Phil Linz, Joe Pepitone, Bobby Richardson

OUTFIELDERS
John Blanchard, Hector Lopez, Mickey Mantle, Roger Maris, Jack Reed, Tom Tresh

1963 WHITE SOX

PITCHERS
Frank Baumann, Jim Brosnan, Johnny Buzhardt, Dave DeBusschere, Eddie Fisher, Ray Herbert, Joe Horlen, Gary Peters, Juan Pizarro, Hoyt Wilhelm, Dom Zanni

CATCHERS
Camilo Carreon, Sherm Lollar, J.C. Martin

INFIELDERS
Joe Cunningham, Nellie Fox, Ron Hansen, Jim Lemon, Tommy McCraw, Pete Ward, Al Weis

OUTFIELDERS
Mike Hershberger, Jim Landis, Charlie Maxwell, Dave Nicholson, Floyd Robinson

1963

Most Glorious Victory

Tuesday Night, June 25

At Comiskey Park
Attendance: 46,711

The evening before, the White Sox had won the opener of this four-game first-place showdown and now trailed the Yankees by one game. This night, the largest Sox home crowd since August 1960 gathered with hope that the home team could pull even with the New Yorkers, who were missing the big bat of Mickey Mantle, sidelined by a broken foot.

Juan Pizarro (8-3), off to the best start of his major-league career, went up against Ralph Terry, the Yankees' 23-game winner of 1962 but only 7-7 thus far in '63 despite some excellent performances. Thirty-two years to the date of this duel with Pizarro, Terry remembered his ill fortune.

"The first half of that season," he said from his home in Larned, Kansas, "I pitched nine ballgames where I went seven innings or more and gave up two runs or less. And I lost seven of 'em and got no-decisions in the other two. You know, that's the difference between an ordinary year and a real good year. But the team wasn't hittin', so what can you do? But that should've been a really big year for me, because I pitched my butt off that first half."

He did just that on this night against the White Sox, giving the big crowd nothing to cheer about for the first five innings. Terry had faced the minimum, 15 batters. Only a leadoff walk in the first to Mike Hershberger, who was subsequently thrown out by

Elston Howard on a steal attempt, separated Terry from perfection as the Chicago sixth began. The Yankees had gone ahead, 1-0, in the top half when Bobby Richardson singled, took second base on Tom Tresh's infield out, and came home on Roger Maris' line single to right.

Now came one of the night's pivotal plays. Ron Hansen, No. 7 man in the White Sox batting order, smacked a ball that bounded past the bag at third and into foul territory down the left-field line. The third-base umpire, Chicagoan John Rice, signaled fair ball, ruling the ball was still fair when it had crossed the bag, even though its first bounce after crossing the base had indeed been on the foul side of the chalk line. Hansen went into second base with a double, and Terry—far from joyous about losing his no-hitter on such a close call—joined third baseman Clete Boyer, catcher Howard and Yankee manager Ralph Houk in a rousing, though fruitless, argument with Rice. "He blew the call," Houk complained later. "Rice stood there like a stick. The ball was foul."

Said Hansen, grinning: "It was fair when I hit it."

Rice drew more of the Yankees' ire when, two outs later, Hershberger lined a single to center to drive home Hansen with the tying run. Now, Terry knew, it was a new game, three innings to go, he and Pizarro, and may the best man win, John Rice or no John Rice.

"We never had any real trouble with him, really," Terry said of Rice. "Although Rice is the only umpire I ever saw kick Elston Howard out of a game. And Ellie was a real gentleman, a real pro behind that plate. He just wasn't an argumentative guy. He was just a real champion. But they got into an argument once and Rice ran him.

"We'd give him a hard time once in a while. We used to say, 'What comes out of a Chinaman's ass?' And everybody'd holler, 'Rice!' But he was a good-natured guy. A good umpire."

The Yankees went out quickly in their seventh, and Terry retired the red-hot Sox rookie, Pete Ward (whose 18-game hitting streak came to a close this night) to open the Chicago half. Now the batter was Floyd Robinson, the Sox's leading hitter but, at the moment, in an 0-for-10 drought. Despite the mini-slump, Terry pitched respectfully. "He was a good hitter there for a few years," he said of Robinson. "Liked the ball out over the plate. And so he was a problem at Yankee Stadium. Because you had to be careful. You didn't want to come inside on him there, with the short right field, so that he could pull it. So he got a lot of good pitches to hit in Yankee Stadium, out over the plate."

But here, in Comiskey Park, where the home-run distance down the right-field line was 352 feet instead of Yankee Stadium's 296, Terry could afford to come inside on Robby. Or so he thought. With the count three balls and a strike, Terry tried to curve Robinson inside. But Robinson swung and belted the pitch high and deep toward the right-field corner. It had home-run distance, but the question was whether it would stay fair or curve foul. The ball landed in the first row of the upper deck, just a few feet to the left of the yellow foul screen, for Robinson's seventh homer of the year and a 2-1 White Sox lead. The 46,000-plus erupted, as did the exploding scoreboard in center field.

In the Yankee eighth, Pizarro, who had struck out 10 batters through the first seven innings, let his outfielders do the work, as Boyer, Richardson, and Tresh, in order, all flied out. In the Sox half, Terry, finishing off his own brilliant performance—a three-hitter, with just one walk—quickly disposed of Hansen, J.C. Martin, and Pizarro, and the game moved to the ninth. First up for New York was the perpetually menacing Maris, producer of 133 home runs over the previous three seasons. Maris was going to have to hit Pizarro's, not Maris', pitch in order to do any damage in this situation.

"See, I know that in Chicago, when you were pitching to those left-handed pull hitters, that ball to right field, it go like hell," Pizarro recalled, sitting in the lounge of an O'Hare-area hotel some 30 years later. "It'd carry really well. Right-center, the ball didn't carry good, but down the line, it carried good in Chicago. Maris was a pull hitter. If you pitched him away, he'd extend those arms, he's gonna pull the ball, because he was quick with his arms. The only way you pitch him was inside, way in, because then, if he pulls that, he's gonna pull it foul. And you gotta keep the ball down, because if you throw him from the knee up, he's gonna hurt you. Gotta pitch him below the knee, get him to chase a bad ball."

Which is what Pizarro tried to do, on four straight deliveries. Maris, however, did not bite, and trotted to first base, the recipient of Pizarro's second walk of the evening. The next batter, journeyman Harry Bright, fouled out, bringing up Howard, like Maris an eminently proficient home-run hitter. When Pizarro lost him on a 3-1 pitch, the go-ahead run was on base, and Hector Lopez, who routinely ripped Pizarro's pitching and already had a double and a single this game, was up. But here, Juan bore down and got Lopez to fly to Hershberger near the right-field line, Maris taking third after the catch.

Now the batter was Tony Kubek, whose popout—with two men on base—had ended the previous night's 5-2 Chicago victory. "Tony Kubek, he wasn't a problem," said Pizarro. "He didn't have no power." No, but all he needed was a single to tie the game. Pizarro, though, throwing nothing but fastballs, would not allow it. After Kubek fouled off four straight pitches, he swung at and missed a letter-high fastball. And that was it. Pizarro had his 11th strikeout, his ninth victory, and the American League strikeout lead—by six over Detroit's Jim Bunning.

And the White Sox were just .009 from first place.

1963

Most Devastating Defeat

Friday Night, August 16

At Comiskey Park
Attendance: 35,444

Juan Pizarro and the White Sox appeared to be on the brink of a brilliant victory as the ninth inning began, and hopes were being revived that the Sox might be able to present a late challenge to the Yankees in the American League race, after all.

The rain that had delayed the game's start by an hour and a half was long forgotten. Whitey Ford had departed the scene after seven innings, having given up the only two runs of the game, so he was through for the four-game weekend series. Mickey Mantle, available only for pinch-hitting duty because of various ailments, had batted for Ford in the eighth and grounded out, so he was out of the game as well. Also inactive—for the entire series—was Mantle's erstwhile slugging partner, Roger Maris, sidelined by a bad back.

So things were looking up on the South Side. Pizarro need only negotiate his way though the ninth, and the White Sox would cut the New York lead to seven and a half games. The amazing, almost unhittable rookie, Gary Peters, was to pitch Saturday's game, so the lead could be down to six and a half. And the shutout king, Ray Herbert (he had seven this season, two of them against the Yankees), would be going in Game 1 on Sunday, to be followed by Joe Horlen, who had pitched masterfully since his return from a two-and-a-half-week banishment to Triple-A Indianapolis in July. By weekend's completion, optimists were pointing out, the Sox could quite conceivably be just four and a half games from the top. Pizarro's pitching had much to do with the optimism. Entering the ninth, the hard-throwing lefty had allowed just four hits, had allowed no Yankee to reach third base, and had retired the last 13 batters to face him. He could have had a bigger lead, but his teammates—after an unearned run in the first inning and rookie Pete Ward's home run into the center-field bullpen in the second—had squandered scoring chances in the fourth, fifth and seventh. But Pizarro didn't mind that the score was still just 2-0 instead of 4-0 or 5-0.

"I believe you pitch better when you got a close game, because you try to make no mistakes," he said, many, many years later. "See, when you're 4-5 runs ahead, you just start messing around—you walk the No. 8 hitter, and the No. 9 hitter gets a base hit. And now you have the top of the lineup coming up. You just throw the ball—you don't think about what you're doing. But in a close game, you gotta think what you're gonna do: 'Don't make no mistakes. Don't walk this guy. You gotta get him out. 'Cause if you walk him, they gonna yank you out of the game.' By that, you push yourself and you pitch better. That's what I believe. That's what I used to do."

The first man to face him in the ninth was the switch-hitting Tom Tresh. Tresh, though only in his second year in the majors, already had begun to establish himself as something of a thorn in the side of the White Sox, much to the chagrin of older Sox fans who recalled with fondness the career of Tom's father, Mike, a competent catcher on the South Side from 1938 through '48. Mike Tresh had taught his son how to switch-hit by pitching to him hours before games at Comiskey Park, using the outfield wall as a backstop. As a rookie in 1962, the younger Tresh had beaten the Sox with a ninth-inning homer in Yankee Stadium. In the years ahead, he would enjoy a three-homer game against the Sox, steal home runs from them with great catches, and twice within a two-week period (in 1965) defeat bullpen ace Eddie Fisher with extra-inning home runs.

"I had some great ballgames against the White Sox," agreed Tresh, who among other duties at his alma mater, Central Michigan University, serves as assistant baseball coach. "And I had some good ones against Detroit, too. And I think I probably concentrated more on those teams because they meant more to me. Chicago had a definite warm spot in my heart, obviously, for a lot of years, so even though I was playing against them, I was more intense against them. And Detroit the same thing, because I grew up in Detroit."

So far this night, he had singled in three tries against Pizarro. He was batting right-handed, his natural side and the side from which he had always felt the most confident.

"Pizarro was a very fine pitcher," Tresh remembered, "but early in my career, I was a much superior hitter right-handed than left-handed. I was definitely a .320, .330, .340 hitter right-handed and maybe .240, .250 left-handed—although I had some power left-handed. I'd always relied on my right-handed hitting to be my superior side. At that time, I really didn't feel there was a left-handed pitcher in the world that I couldn't hit. I even hit a home run off Koufax in the World Series that year. He struck me out three times, so he won his share, too, but I really felt when I got the bat in my hands right-handed that I was capable of beating anybody out there."

Out there at the moment was Pizarro. Tresh swung at a 1-1 pitch and drove it into the seats in left-center for his 20th homer of the year. Now it was 2-1, and that old Yankee late-inning magic was starting to assert itself once again.

"We felt like we owned the seventh, eighth, and ninth innings," Tresh recalled, "and that if we could just stay in it, those were our innings. And momentum is such a huge thing. In that era, when the Yankees were winning so much and had such dominant players, you know, it's like we went into a ballgame feeling we were going to get the breaks to win it. And the other team felt like we were going to get the breaks to win it. It was like they were waiting for a mistake to happen, for us to pull it out. And we were waiting for that mistake, so we could pull it out. The power of positive energy was all on our side."

Elston Howard was next, and when Pizarro walked him, the tying run was aboard and, in the Sox bullpen, Hoyt Wilhelm and Jim Brosnan began loosening up in anticipation of a call that never came from manager Al Lopez. "The Senor" figured Pizarro was still throwing well, even after a veteran reserve named Harry

Bright sent Jim Landis into deep center for his long drive. Yet the Senor also had to have been aware of Pizarro's past difficulties with the next New York hitter, Hector Lopez, not to mention the Panamanian's career success at Chicago in general. But the Sox's Lopez never left the dugout. Pizarro went to work on the Yankees' Lopez, who from 1960 through '64 hit .295 in Comiskey Park and had entered this game with a lifetime .353 average (12 for 34) against his Puerto Rican "cousin."

"Oh yeah, I had very, very good luck against Pizarro," Lopez said while taking a break from his job as manager of the Yankees' Gulf Coast Rookie League club in Tampa. "I was from Panama, he was from Puerto Rico. I didn't meet him until he got to the big leagues. We were kinda friends; we'd always talk to each other, stuff like that. But he was a fastball pitcher who tried to keep the ball down, and I was a low-ball hitter. He was going with his best against my best."

And this time, Lopez's best was better. After taking ball one, he sent a fastball deep into the lower deck in left, and the Yankees were ahead, 3-2. Hector Lopez had done it again, coming through in the clutch against the White Sox.

"I was pretty lucky against the White Sox," he said. "I had a lot of base hits against them. And I got a lot of hits in Chicago, so I was always happy to get back there. It was a tough park for hitters, but I always did well there. I have no idea why. Some teams you hit better than others. They had a pretty good pitching staff those years, but I had good luck against all of them—Pizarro, Peters, and before that Billy Pierce. They were low-ball pitchers and I was a low-ball hitter. That's about the only reason I can think of."

Lopez's home run was not the end of the sudden New York barrage. With two out and the bases empty, Clete Boyer belted another Pizarro fastball over the center-field fence to make it 4-2. Understandably unnerved, Pizarro walked the next batter, relief pitcher Bill Kunkel—later an American League umpire—before retiring Phil Linz to end the inning. He then, according to some accounts, walked off the field and fired his glove against the back wall of the dugout. One writer called it the hardest pitch Pizarro had thrown all inning. Juan, years later, denied the reports.

"I remember the home runs," he said, "but I don't remember doing that. Because I never used to throw anything. Like when I struck out, I never threw the bat, because I remember a long time ago, 1957, my first year in the big leagues at Milwaukee, we almost got a fight between teammates, because Johnny Logan, he strike out and he flipped the helmet and it almost hit Wes Covington in the face. After that, I never, never, never throw no bat, no helmet. Never throw my glove."

Had he done so, he certainly had good cause, particularly when Charlie Maxwell, after a one-out pinch single by Floyd Robinson, bounded into a game-ending double play started by second baseman Bobby Richardson. The Sox, instead of being seven and a half games out and with Peters set to go on the morrow, were nine and a half back and all but finished for 1963. Pizarro, however, was not going to dwell on this disaster, which likely is one explanation for his success in his chosen profession.

"You can do nothing about it," he said. "Right after the game, you forget it. After the game was over, five minutes later, you gotta think, 'That game is gone.' Gotta think about what you did wrong, and don't do it again in the next one.

"Took me five minutes to forget it."

Even so, some 30 years later, that ninth inning was still rather clear in Juan Pizarro's memory.

1964

Setting the Stage

This was Lyndon Baines Johnson's year, the year in which he pushed through sweeping civil rights legislation, officially declared "War on Poverty" and unofficially declared war on North Vietnam. He did the latter when, despite being on somewhat shaky legal ground, he succeeded in getting Congress to pass the Gulf of Tonkin Resolution, which provided the president full authorization to prosecute the conflict in Southeast Asia by whatever means he deemed necessary. The resolution, passed in August, and the subsequent bombing, for the first time, of North Vietnam served to demonstrate to voters that LBJ was every bit as tough on communism as his Republican opponent, Barry Goldwater, had shown himself to be. And so, when Johnson was a landslide winner in the election in November, one month after Nikita Khrushchev was ousted in the Soviet Union and replaced by Leonid Brezhnev and Aleksei Kosigyn, not many people were astonished.

During 1964, too, civil war raged in the Congo, China exploded its first atomic bomb, three civil rights workers were murdered in Mississippi, and, despite significant evidence that seemed to indicate otherwise, the Warren Commission concluded that Lee Harvey Oswald had acted alone in the assassination of John F. Kennedy.

This was also the year *My Fair Lady* dominated the Oscar Awards, the year "The Girl from Ipanema" won the Grammy for best record, and the year of the "British Invasion," led by The Beatles, who were escorted across the Atlantic by The Dave Clark Five, Chad and Jeremy, Peter and Gordon, and all the rest.

Change, however, was not limited to world leaders and to

music. Although few realized it, the sun was beginning to set on the Yankee dynasty. Ralph Houk, an exceptional field manager, was promoted to the position of general manager, an assignment for which he was not well suited. Yogi Berra, after serving one year as a player-coach, was given Houk's old job, an assignment for which he was not well suited. Johnny Sain, after presiding over a pitching staff that had produced the league's second-best team ERA and at least one 20-game winner each of the previous three years, was cashiered and replaced by Whitey Ford, who would coach the pitchers in between his own starts. The only newcomer, of any significance, to the 25-man roster was rookie sinkerballer Pete Mikkelsen, whom Berra quickly made his late-inning stopper.

On the Chicago front, another hero had been given his walking papers. Nellie Fox, 15 days before his 36th birthday, was sent to Houston—and GM Paul Richards—for some cash and two minor-league pitchers, Jim Golden and Danny Murphy, a former Cub bonus baby. Nellie was dealt to clear a spot at second base for switch-hitting Don Buford, "the best prospect in the minors in '63," according to even some of the less-enthusiastic scouting reports. A former USC football star, Buford had hit .336 with 41 doubles and 42 stolen bases at Indianapolis, but he had spent the season playing 143 of his 152 games at third base, not second. Ed Short, Al Lopez & Co. had filled their hole at third base with Pete Ward. Why they did not have Buford spend 1963 preparing for his 1964 assignment at second base by actually playing there remains a mystery. As it happened, coach Tony Cuccinello was dispatched to Puerto Rico to give Buford a winter-league crash course on second-base play. That it was too little, too late, would quickly become sadly apparent.

Regardless, when the season swung into June, there were the White Sox, having been joined in spring training by veteran reliever Don Mossi and old (41) friend Minnie Minoso, leading the Orioles by a little and the Yankees by a lot. Even with Buford feeling his way and with only Tommy McCraw and Floyd Robinson hitting well, the Sox (31-15) had a one-and-a-half-game lead on Baltimore and a five-game bulge on New York when they arrived in Yankee Stadium June 12 to open a five-game weekend series. But when the five games were over, the Yankees, having won them all, were right back in it, tied with Chicago for second place, one game behind Baltimore.

More frustration followed for Chicago the next weekend in Comiskey Park. Ford beat Gary Peters, 1-0, in 11 innings, Jim Bouton beat Juan Pizarro 2-0 in Game 1 of a Sunday doubleheader and, though finally breaking through for a fifth-inning run in the nightcap (after 28 consecutive scoreless innings against Yankee pitching), the White Sox lost, 2-1, in 17 when Al Weis bobbled Bill Stafford's bases-loaded groundball. The next night, the Sox shocked Chicago by scoring five runs. Alas, the Yankees scored six, and the Sox were now 0-10 on the year against New York—and three and a half games behind the league-leading Yankees (Baltimore was second, a half-game back).

Quite obviously, the White Sox needed a bat. Short got one on July 13 when he landed Bill Skowron, the Chicago native and long-time Yankee, from Washington for Joe Cunningham and rookie lefty Frank Kreutzer. The Moose's presence provided an instant lift and gave overdue protection in the lineup for Ward, who'd been hitting just .254 at the All-Star break. Ward immediately started hitting like the Ward of '63, and the Sox began rolling, even against the Yankees. They split four games in New York August 11-13—while the Yankees were being sold to CBS—then swept them four straight August 17-20 in Chicago to take a half-game lead on Baltimore and four-and-a-half-game advantage on the Yanks. Back in New York, Houk, who already had decided that Berra would not be back, began looking toward 1965.

But then, things began to get interesting. In Chicago, where pennant fever had returned after a five-year absence, the Orioles cooled off the White Sox by winning three out of four. The Sox went to Baltimore the next weekend and won three of five. While the two leaders beat up on each other, the Yankees, with Roger Maris and Mickey Mantle clicking together as they had not done since 1961, crept back into the picture after falling as much as five and a half games behind. On September 4, Ward and Skowron hit back-to-back homers in the last of the 10th for a 6-5 White Sox victory over Cleveland. The next day, the Yankees, three games back, got journeyman pitcher Pedro Ramos from the Indians for $75,000 and two players to be named later (one turned out to be Ralph Terry, a resident of Houk's doghouse).

As Labor Day dawned, the White Sox (84-56) led the Orioles (82-55) by a half game, the Yankees (79-56) by two and a half. The Sox were in Washington for a pair with the ninth-place Senators, who had lost seven straight and had gone 2-11 against Chicago. The Sox promptly lost both games, 3-0 to Bennie Daniels (7-10) and 6-2 to Dave Stenhouse (2-7), not even scoring until the ninth inning of Game 2. They never regained the top spot, but they remained close. Indeed, when Chicago and not New York picked up veteran National League pinch hitter deluxe Smoky Burgess for the stretch drive, people continued to believe 1964 was not going to be a Yankee year. But the Yankees were not to be denied. Led by rookie Mel Stottlemyre (9-3 with a 2.06 ERA after his August 11 callup) and the suddenly overpowering Ramos (1.25 ERA, seven saves in 13 games for New York after going 7-10, 5.14 with Cleveland), the Yankees put together a five-game winning streak and then a pennant-clinching 11-gamer, during which Maris batted .381 with one big hit after another.

At one point, New York had won 26 of 33 while the White Sox and Orioles had been merely treading water. The end, for all intents and purposes, came September 23, when the Yankees swept a second successive doubleheader at Cleveland to go four games up on both Chicago and Baltimore. That was it, and though the White Sox won their final nine games to finish 98-64, they were still one victory short. If only they had kept Nellie Fox around for one more year, moaned those who had seen too many crucial errors at second base by the inexperienced Buford. If only they had beaten the Yankees once or twice in those first 10 meetings, lamented many, many others.

Even so, when it was all over, Sox fans—and fans around the American League—had reason to be of good cheer. Mantle, Maris, and Ford, though rallying late, were not getting any younger or healthier. The Sox and Orioles had more than held their own against the Yankees in head-to-head play the final two months and could only benefit from that experience. The Minnesota Twins, 91-game winners in both 1962 and '63 before falling back in '64, figured to rebound in 1965. The competition was getting stiffer for the Yankees, and, with the imminent implementation of the amateur free-agent draft, the competition would get stiffer still. The Yankee farm system, neglected since George Weiss' departure, was hardly brimming from top to bottom. As Bill Veeck had keenly noted, the Yankees no longer could trade minor-league averages for major-league players, for they no longer had those minor-league averages. Despite this latest pennant, the feeling was growing stronger and stronger that the Yankees were about to see their era of domination come to an end.

So it was that, on the eve of the World Series opener in St. Louis, one long-suffering White Sox fan stunned a friend of his by announcing that, for once, he was going to root for the Yankees in the Series. When his companion's face registered disbelief, he explained himself:

"I have a feeling it's going to be a long time before the Yankees get into a World Series again. I'd like to see them go out as winners."

He had no idea he would be so right.

Rosters

Lists position players who appeared in 20 or more games, pitchers who appeared in 10 or more games, plus regulars who may have been traded/sold or acquired during the season.

1964 YANKEES

PITCHERS
Jim Bouton, Bud Daley, Al Downing, Whitey Ford, Steve Hamilton, Pete Mikkelsen, Pedro Ramos, Hal Reniff, Roland Sheldon, Bill Stafford, Mel Stottlemyre, Ralph Terry, Stan Williams

CATCHERS
John Blanchard, Elston Howard

INFIELDERS
Clete Boyer, Pedro Gonzalez, Tony Kubek, Phil Linz, Joe Pepitone, Bobby Richardson

OUTFIELDERS
Hector Lopez, Mickey Mantle, Roger Maris, Archie Moore, Tom Tresh

1964 WHITE SOX

PITCHERS
Frank Baumann, Johnny Buzhardt, Eddie Fisher, Ray Herbert, Joe Horlen, Frank Kreutzer, Don Mossi, Gary Peters, Juan Pizarro, Fred Talbot, Hoyt Wilhelm

CATCHERS
Camilo Carreon, J.C. Martin, Jerry McNertney

INFIELDERS
Don Buford, Joe Cunningham, Ron Hansen, Jeoff Long, Tommy McCraw, Bill Skowron, Pete Ward, Al Weis

OUTFIELDERS
Mike Hershberger, Jim Landis, Minnie Minoso, Dave Nicholson, Floyd Robinson, Gene Stephens

1964

Most Devastating Defeat

Sunday, June 21

At Comiskey Park
Attendance: 39,316

The remarkable hex the Yankees had held over the 1964 White Sox was about to become even more remarkable. The day before, New York had recorded its seventh victory over Chicago in as many tries, a 1-0, 11-inning decision by Whitey Ford over Gary Peters. Now, on this bright, sunny afternoon, the city's biggest crowd of the season to date turned out to see if the White Sox, their hitless heroes, could finally beat the Yankees or, failing that, at least score a run against them, something the Sox had been unable to do in two home games with the Yankees thus far in '64.

Juan Pizarro, off to another 8-3 start, opposed the Yankees' Jim Bouton in the opener, and the Puerto Rican lefty was his usual outstanding self: He went eight innings, struck out five, didn't walk anybody, and allowed only four hits. Unfortunately for him, two of the hits were home runs—a liner into the lower deck in left by Elston Howard in the second and an upper-deck shot to left in the seventh by Mickey Mantle. Bouton was even better. He took a 2-0 lead and a two-hitter into the eighth, when he gave way to reliever Pete Mikkelsen after a two-out single by J.C. Martin. Mikkelsen, a rookie whose sinkerballer had made a believer of his rookie manager, Yogi Berra, encountered some difficulty in the ninth when he hit Al Weis with a pitch and allowed a single by Floyd Robinson. But the Yankees did not have to worry: Pete

Ward and Joe Cunningham were easily retired, and the Sox's 1964 frustration string against Yankee pitching in Comiskey Park had now reached 29 innings.

"It seemed like we were in that same situation with other teams, too, besides the Yankees," remembered Weis, who started both games that day at second base. "It seemed like every game we played was either 1-0 or 2-1 or 3-1 or 3-2. The game was always on the line. We could've won games that we lost, and we could've lost games that we won. We were always in the game, because of our pitching and defense." Meanwhile, first-place Baltimore had lost at Boston, so the Yankees, five games behind the then-first-place White Sox just nine days earlier, were now but a half game from the league lead. Also, word had arrived from New York that the Phillies' Jim Bunning had just pitched a perfect game against the Mets. It was not exactly the thing struggling White Sox batters had to hear about, particularly with fireballing Yankee lefty Al Downing going against them in Game 2.

But the scoreless string came to an end, at last, in the home fifth, after four more runless innings. With the Sox and Joe Horlen trailing, 1-0, Ron Hansen opened the Chicago fifth with a single, moved up on a Downing wild pitch and came home, to some derisive cheering, on Tommy McCraw's line single to right-center. That was in the fifth. Three relievers—and several blown opportunities—for both sides later, it was going on 9 P.M. and the game was in the 17th inning, still tied, 1-1. The Sox had used 19 players, the Yankees 17. Don Mossi, the lefthander who had made a name for himself with Cleveland under Al Lopez a decade earlier, had been entrusted by Lopez with the pitching duties to start the 17th.

With one out, Hector Lopez drilled his fourth hit of the game, a double, just inside the bag at third. Mossi walked Howard intentionally to get to the light-hitting Phil Linz, which made sense, but then he walked Linz unintentionally, which did not. Bill Stafford, the fourth Yankee pitcher, was allowed to bat for himself and, with the bases filled, the infield moved in close for a play at the plate. By now, Weis, a skilled gloveman best known today for his unlikely offensive heroics as a New York Met in the 1969 World Series upset of Baltimore, had moved over to shortstop. He was ready. "I used to have the feeling, 'I want the ball hit to me,' " he remembered. "I believe a good fielder wants the ball hit to him.

That's the way I always felt. I wanted the ball hit to me, because basically, that's what I was paid for—my defense."

Weis was granted his wish. Stafford hit a groundball right to him, but he bobbled it. By the time he recovered, Hector Lopez had slid across the plate and Howard was starting his slide into third. There was no way to get Linz at second and Stafford was going to be safe at first on the error.

"He overcharged the ball," was the postgame complaint of Al Lopez, who, some writers observed, was more dejected than usual on this particular evening. "If he had stayed back, he would've had a nice, high hop, and it would've been easy."

But he hadn't, and it wasn't, so it was 2-1 New York, and even though Mossi managed to retire both Clete Boyer and Bobby Richardson without further damage, the score might as well have been 10-1, because everyone knew the Sox were not going to score again. They went down in order: Weis wrapped up an 0-for-7 game and an 0-for-10 afternoon; Robinson also failed; and Stafford finished it by striking out Jim Landis at 8:59 P.M. The Yankees had moved into first place by .008 and the Sox, now 0-9 vs. New York on the season, were two and a half games behind.

"You're bringing up some bad memories," Weis said, chuckling. "But I can remember, talking about errors, the first game I played for the Mets, in 1968, was that 24-inning game at Houston. I made an error in the 24th inning with the bases loaded to lose the game. And I was playing shortstop that game, too, because Buddy Harrelson was hurt. Then we go back to New York the following day, and I'm in the starting lineup. We're playing the Giants. And it's the home opener, you know, where they introduce the starting lineups and you go out to line up along the foul lines. Well, I didn't hear too many cheers that day."

Yet making the key error in a game between bottom-of-the-heap clubs like those '68 Mets and Astros was hardly as devastating as making it in a pressure-laden game against the Yankees, particularly for Weis, whose youth had been spent on Long Island during the 1950s.

"I think I was in awe of them somewhat," he said. "Like myself, growing up in New York, the name Mantle—it sticks out in anybody's mind. And the first time I go into Yankee Stadium, I'm playing against him. It's really hard to fathom that you're on the same playing field as a person of his stature.

"And all the players on that team, it seemed, were All-Stars. You go right down the line: Kubek, Clete Boyer, Bobby Richardson, Mantle, Maris, Yogi Berra, Elston Howard. But I think when you play against the best people in the game, you play better yourself."

Well, some of the time, perhaps.

1964

Most Glorious Victory

Thursday, August 20

At Comiskey Park
Attendance: 36,677

Something had to give this afternoon as the White Sox went for a four-game series sweep of the suddenly stumbling American League champions, who had fallen four lengths behind first-place Baltimore.

The White Sox, just a half game out after thrilling 2-1, 4-3, and 4-2 victories over New York, were sending righthander Johnny Buzhardt against Whitey Ford. Buzhardt had yet to lose to the Yankees in his three years in the AL, while Ford hadn't lost to Chicago since May 3, 1962—when he was outdueled, interestingly enough, by Buzhardt, 1-0—and hadn't even been scored on by the Sox since the previous August 16. So it was a Yankee-killer versus a Sox-killer. The Yankee-killer, however, was just 4-0 lifetime against the Yankees, whereas the Sox-killer was 33-19 against the Sox. And one of Buzhardt's victories over the Yankees had come in relief. Also, in his last start against New York, a no-decision on June 22, he had been knocked out in the fifth inning of a game the Sox eventually lost, 6-5.

Ford had a string of 43 consecutive scoreless innings going against Chicago, but by this point in this particular season, he wasn't at 100 percent health-wise. Bothered by a sore right hip—he later discovered the pain was caused by a calcium deposit—Whitey hadn't pitched in 12 days. Indeed, it was testimony to how badly manager Yogi Berra wanted this game that he turned to Ford to start it.

Buzhardt, too, was something of an emergency starter. Joe Horlen, originally scheduled to go, complained of stiffness in his right shoulder and was rescheduled to work Game 2 of the upcoming weekend series with Baltimore. So manager Al Lopez, on this his 56th birthday, turned instead to Buzhardt, who had not pitched since the previous Friday in Boston. Pitching on five, six days' rest served, at times, to annoy Buzhardt, but he held his tongue and watched as Horlen, Gary Peters, Juan Pizarro, and Ray Herbert worked on regular rest while he and rookie Fred Talbot worked as spot starters.

"Sure I wanted to pitch, but you didn't complain to the Senor," remembered Buzhardt, retired after 29 years with Carolina Eastman (a Kodak subsidiary) in his native Prosperity, South Carolina. "You communicated with the Senor through his coaches. Although one year we did sit down and talk about it. And he called me in his office later and told me, 'John, you're gonna start the rest of the year.' And I did. I didn't miss a turn the rest of that season. It was the year I won 13 games [1965]."

Recalled Lopez: "The toughest part of being a manager is keeping everybody satisfied, because every pitcher wants to start and everybody on the bench wants to play. And I don't blame them, because that's how you're gonna make the money. But for some reason or another, John thought I didn't like him, because I wasn't using him in rotation. But I had other pitchers I thought should pitch in rotation; otherwise, if I didn't, it was gonna hurt the whole ballclub. And John was always the No. 5 pitcher, in spots, so he thought I didn't like him personally. But I didn't have anything against him. He had a good sinker. He had a pretty good fastball. His problem was, every once in a while, his control hurt him."

This day was not to be one of those times, however. From the start, he had his control and he was in control. He did allow first-inning singles—harmless, as it turned out—to Tony Kubek and Roger Maris, but thereafter it was smooth sailing. Maris reached him for one more hit and Kubek two ("Kubek and Bobby Richardson, those boys gave me as much trouble as the free swingers," Buzhardt said), but the rest of the lineup—which for the fourth straight day did not include the ailing Mickey Mantle—was completely stymied.

In the meantime, the White Sox, perhaps inspired by the "4" that the eighth-place Red Sox had put up on the scoreboard in the second inning of their game with Baltimore at Fenway Park, finally broke through against Ford. With one out in the second, Mike Hershberger, Ron Hansen, and Camilo Carreon singled in succession, accounting for one run and leaving Sox runners at first and third. With two strikes on Buzhardt, Lopez flashed the squeeze sign, and Buzhardt got the bunt down, about halfway between the plate and the pitcher's mound. Ford scrambled in and flipped an underhand toss to catcher Elston Howard, who had to reach up for the ball while Hansen slid in underneath him. It was 2-0 Chicago, and the old South Side joint was jumping.

More excitement developed in the following inning. Floyd Robinson and Bill Skowron—0 for 12 against his former teammates in the series up until now—opened with singles, and Hershberger's second hit drove in Robinson to make it 3-0. In the fourth, Buzhardt and Jim Landis singled to start things, and out came Berra and out went Ford. Whitey had gone three-plus innings and allowed nine hits. And when Skowron, facing reliever Roland Sheldon, singled in Buzhardt and Pete Ward's sacrifice fly plated Landis, Ford was responsible for five Chicago runs—usually about a season's worth for the White Sox against the little lefty.

Thereafter, the game sped along, Buzhardt dominating Yankee hitters, the Sox mustering no additional offense against either Bill Stafford or Steve Hamilton. The scoreboard declared that Boston had beaten the Orioles, 4-3. Suddenly it was the ninth inning. First place and a four-game sweep of the Yankees were just three outs away. Kubek delivered his third single, and after Richardson and Maris were retired, Howard delivered his first. Tom Tresh dragged a bunt down the first-base line. Buzhardt got over quickly, scooped up the ball, and tagged Tresh, who had gone into a head-first slide, before he could reach first base. Photographers recorded the moment: Buzhardt, all-conquering, tagging out the fallen Yankee, with the former Yankee, first baseman Skowron, standing over Tresh and wearing a huge smile.

"Yeah, I remember that game," Buzhardt said, three decades later, of the 5-0 triumph. "I remember that well, sure do. That was one of my more memorable games. And that win made me 5-0 against the Yankees, right? Well, I wound up 7-0 against them in my career. And even in spring training, I remember I pitched a game against them in Sarasota, and they were expecting rain any second. And they had a real good turnout, and they didn't want to have to give up that gate. I just went out there and threw strikes and gave 'em only two hits in seven innings or so in a spring-training game."

Why the amazing success against baseball's most feared offensive machine? After his shutout this day, Buzhardt told Brent Musburger, then a young sportswriter with the *Chicago American*: "They've got a lot of strong hitters on that team who don't take too many pitches. My most effective pitch is the sinker, and if I'm hitting my spots, they'll hit a lot of balls into the ground rather than over the fence."

Thirty years later, Johnny's explanation hadn't changed much. "They were the type of ballclub that they wanted to hit the long ball, the kind of guys I always called free swingers. And I had a fastball that would sink, and occasionally I could get the curveball over the plate, and they were probably just a little bit anxious. That's the only thing I can think of, 'cause I wasn't what you could call overpowering. But I did pitch some real good games against them.

"But it wasn't all success. It wasn't easy. Yeah, I beat 'em seven times, but our team beat 'em seven times while I was pitching. Gracious, it wasn't easy. Every game was a battle."

After this particular one, two memory-making events took place. First came the victory/birthday celebration in the Sox clubhouse, with players crowding around Lopez in an attempt to (a) secure a piece of birthday cake and (b) assure themselves a spot in one of the many pictures the newspaper photographers were taking.

"That," recalled Lopez, "was one of the nicest birthday presents I ever had. Four wins against the Yankees was quite a present."

Added Buzhardt: "I've still got a picture of us around that birthday cake. It's in my scrapbook."

And rest assured that Phil Linz still has a scrapbook filled with clippings describing an incident that took place on the Yankees' team bus as it made the long journey—in rush-hour traffic—from 35th and the Dan Ryan Expressway on the South Side to O'Hare International Airport on the Far Northwest Side. Jerry Coleman, the longtime Yankee infielder who was just beginning a new career in radio, will never forget it.

"I was sitting in the front of the bus—that was my first year in broadcasting," he remembered. "There's almost complete silence. All of a sudden, you hear the harmonica."

Linz had just purchased one. Now he had decided to get in some practice. For his opening number, he chose a little ditty familiar to all preschoolers. Said Coleman: "I'm thinking, 'Mary Had A Little Lamb??? What the hell is that? We just got swept. We just lost the pennant.'

"[Coach] Frankie Crosetti says to Berra, 'Ya hear the guy? Ya hear the guy?' Berra's out of his seat and down that aisle, just like that."

Berra screamed at Linz to cease and desist, and Linz screamed back at Berra and flipped the harmonica toward him. Yogi slapped the harmonica out of the air and it ricocheted off the knee of Joe Pepitone, who feigned injury and hollered for a medic, thereby taking some of the edge off the moment. Berra told Linz he'd deal with him later and trudged back to his seat.

"That was the only time all year I saw Yogi provoked," Coleman said. "And hell, it turned us around. We won something like 24 of the next 31 and won the pennant." Coleman's memory is almost perfect. Actually, the Yankees won 26 of their next 33—including an 11-game winning streak—while the White Sox were going 14-17 and the Orioles, after taking the opening three games of their showdown series in Chicago, lost 17 of their next 30. So when the Sox began their season-closing nine-game winning streak, they were already four and a half games back and the race was all but over.

"It wasn't that we didn't play well, because we did play well down the stretch," remembered Buzhardt. "They just played better. But that series in August, that was like a turning point, where we thought now maybe we might have a good chance to win the pennant. Baltimore was right there with us, but the feeling I had, and most of the team had, was we weren't too worried about Baltimore. The Yankees, we knew, was the team we had to beat.

"And even after we swept 'em that series, we were still lookin' over our shoulders at 'em."

But not for long. On September 17, the Yankees vaulted past the Sox and Orioles into first place—to stay.

The Fights

By 1956, the White Sox had been futilely battling the Yankees for the American League lead for half a decade. It was probably inevitable that, at some point, the emotions that had been simmering for five years would, finally, boil over into full-fledged fisticuffs on the playing field.

There had been brief skirmishes, to be sure, generally caused by the leveling and/or spiking of smallish Chicago middle infielders such as Chico Carrasquel and Nellie Fox by large Yankees such as Hank Bauer, Johnny Lindell, and Bob Cerv. But it was not until a Saturday afternoon in 1956—June 23, in Chicago—that people actually started swinging at each other. The main combatants were the White Sox's Dave Philley and Yankee pitcher Bob Grim, already on Chicago's blacklist because he had beaned Minnie Minoso a year earlier in New York—and also because he had a 7-0 lifetime record against the Sox.

The game was scoreless when Philley, rescued from Baltimore and the second division one month before, came up to lead off the home sixth. Grim, almost four decades later, recalled what happened next.

"Philley was pretty aggressive. What I remember was he had stepped on Joe Collins' foot at first base earlier in that game, and our players didn't particularly like that gesture. So I threw one in close—I'll have to admit that. It kinda glanced off his shoulder and hit him in the helmet—knocked his helmet off. Next thing I know, he's chargin' like a raging bull."

Philley, though 10 years older than the 26-year-old Grim, was ready for action. He simply had had enough. "I'd been thrown at quite a bit, and I was sick and tired of it," remembered the retired cattle rancher and former Paris, Texas, city councilman. "You always hear, 'Well, if they throw at you, they got respect for you.' But I found out later that Stengel just didn't like me at all, 'cause

I'd go in there hard at second base to break up double plays. That's the way I played. So he had 'em throwin' at me."

Philley advanced toward Grim. Both benches cleared. From center field came the two clubs' bullpen corps. "I was ready to run," Grim remembered, "because he still had his bat in his hand. He finally dropped the bat, so I just kinda stood my ground. And I swung a good one at him, and I'm glad I missed him 'cause I had a good shot at him. I still have the pictures in my scrapbook, and the pictures make it look like I really cold-cocked him. But it was one of those typical baseball fights. He didn't hit me and I didn't hit him."

Instead, apparently, they merely swung and missed a few times, despite what the photographs and game accounts indicate. Peacemakers managed to separate the pair before too many punches could be thrown. Said Philley: "I mighta hurt that boy if they hadn't stopped us. I'd boxed quite a bit before that. In high school, we had a boxing club, and we used to put on exhibitions every now and then. We wore out those gloves pretty good."

Surprisingly, none of Grim's or Philley's teammates squared off. There was only the usual pushing and shoving until order was restored. And, when it was, Philley was ejected—indeed, he was later fined $250, a hefty sum at 1956 prices—for his role in the altercation. Before leaving the field, however, he barked at Grim's batterymate, Yogi Berra. "I remember I told Yogi, 'One of these days I'm gonna get the pitcher, Stengel and you, all at the same time.' He comes back with somethin' like, 'Well, I didn't have anything to do with it.' But I'll tell ya, Grim never threw at me after that."

Speaking of Grim, he was allowed to remain in the game, but, perhaps shaken by the preceding events, he was tagged in that same inning for two runs. They were the only runs in a 2-0 Sox victory, the second of four straight on what would become a memorable weekend.

★ ★ ★

Almost exactly a year after the Philley-Grim bout, the two teams were at it again, and again the scene was Comiskey Park. It was Thursday afternoon, June 13, and the first-place White Sox, leading the Yankees by five games, had split the first two matches of a three-game series. Tempers had flared the night before, so perhaps the free-for-all that would erupt this day could have been expected.

The previous evening, during the Sox's 7-6 victory, Yankee reliever Al Cicotte had thrown dangerously close to Minnie Minoso's head. Minoso had hit the dirt, then pulled himself up and screamed various epithets at Cicotte. Shouted Cicotte, a rookie who had served a long minor-league apprenticeship: "Anytime you want to start something, I'll be around to finish it!" To which Sherm Lollar, the on-deck hitter, responded: "By that time, you'll be back in the minors." On the next pitch, Minnie swung and missed but let go of the bat, which went sailing out toward Cicotte, who just did manage to get his head out of the way as Minoso's bat went flying by. Everyone was even now, and cooler heads prevailed thereafter.

But this was a new day. Art Ditmar was pitching for the Yankees, and the Sox had runners at first and second with two out in the first inning and Larry Doby at the plate. Ditmar fired one high and tight—extremely high and tight. Doby ducked out of the way, catcher Elston Howard was unable to flag down the pitch, and the Sox runners—Nellie Fox and Minoso—moved up a base. Ditmar, seeing Fox round third, raced in to cover homeplate. Doby was waiting for him, and that's when all the excitement really began. Nearly 40 years later, several of the key participants recalled the ensuing events.

"I remember it like it was yesterday," said ex-Sox first baseman Walt Dropo, who was in the on-deck circle. "What happened was they had two strikes on Larry, and Ditmar threw the next pitch behind his head. As you know, Larry took offense to it. There were some obscenities said. And there were racial slurs thrown around there."

Ditmar disputed both the claim that he was throwing at Doby and that there were racially charged comments made. "When I threw the pitch to Doby, it wasn't even close to him. It was about a foot and a half to two feet over his head. But Doby used to hit me pretty good when he played for Cleveland, so I used to brush him back. And so a lot of times players think you're throwing at them because they're black or white or whatever, and not because they're good hitters. I never brushed back a bad hitter."

"It'd been going on for a couple years," Doby said of Ditmar's high-and-tight pattern. "It didn't just happen that one day in '57. It happened before that. It had started when I was with Cleveland. Normally, if that's the first time you have a ball thrown behind you, there's no reaction. But if it happens a number of times, if the same person keeps doing that, then certainly you're gonna have some kind of reaction."

Doby's reaction, besides the preliminary trading of angry words, was a left hook that, according to photographs, most witnesses, and newspaper accounts, sent Ditmar to the Comiskey Park turf. Again, Ditmar's version varied somewhat. "I think Doby said somewhere that he broke my jaw. But he actually just knocked my cap off when he swung at me. But he never hit me. I fell down after he swung at me, but the thing that probably forced me down was the umpire, Larry Napp, jumped between us and I lost my balance."

"He fell down because of what?" Doby said when told of Ditmar's explanation. "Oh yeah? OK. If he wants to believe that, fine."

Regardless, there were Doby and Ditmar going at it, with Napp, the plate ump, trying to separate the pugilists. Onto the scene came Dropo and Bill Skowron—both aptly nicknamed "Moose"—and, finally, the always-combative Billy Martin. "I told Skowron, 'Let's get these guys cooled down,' " said Dropo. "We were the peacemakers, see? Martin was there, too. He was chirpin' away. But then everything seemed to be settled down, and Martin started to spout off again. So we were in the middle of the diamond, with nobody around but Doby, myself, Ditmar, Martin and Skowron and the umpires. And all of a sudden both benches start flyin' out. We didn't know who was coming at who."

Skowron's story is slightly different. "Doby dropped the bat and went after Ditmar," recalled the former Purdue football star. "And I happened to dive and I caught Doby—I made a good tackle—and I got him down. Then Billy Martin started hitting him, and then Walt Dropo thought I was hitting Doby, so he pulled me off him—almost pulled my pants off. And Enos Slaughter thought Dropo was hitting me, so then he got into it. And Dropo just beat the heck out of Slaughter."

Said Dropo: "Like I mentioned, we didn't know who was coming at who. So the first guy out was Slaughter, so I said this is the end of the peacemaking, and I took a shot at him. I had no more intentions of settling any disputes. That's when the free-for-all broke out, see? And you saw the picture. Slaughter left there kinda disheveled. I think it made *Look* magazine. It was a famous picture. I have it on my wall here at home. But I had nothing against Slaughter. I just figured the first guy comin' out there is gonna get it, and he came barreling out there. He was the first one out.

"Well, the thing became a fiasco. I tore his shirt off, gave him a couple good shots. But those things are impulsive things. I had no hostility toward Slaughter. I didn't even know the guy."

Chicago broadcaster Jack Brickhouse did, however, and it was no surprise to him that ol' Enos, then 41, had decided to take on a man who was eight years younger, seven and a half inches taller, and 40 pounds heavier than he was. Declared Brickhouse: "There's never ever been any questioning Slaughter's courage. After all, there's a guy who's been married five times."

Slaughter's teammates, most notably Whitey Ford, tried to separate him from Dropo, but their efforts proved fruitless. Meanwhile, other Sox and Yankees were pushing and shoving, and the bullpen brigades from both teams had by that time arrived to join the fray. The lone Johnny-come-lately was Sox pitcher Bob Keegan. When the hostilities broke out, Keegan, a Yankee farmhand until his break-in as a White Sox rookie at age 30, leaped onto the bullpen fence and began to vault over. "I want Ford!" he shouted. "Whitey Ford is mine!" But somehow his spikes caught, and down he came, landing on his posterior—and in one of the many puddles left over from the previous night's heavy rains. This dampened not only his uniform, but his fighting spirit as well.

Another non-combatant was Yankee right fielder Hank Bauer, just a couple weeks removed from being served a summons for his part in the famed Copacabana brawl that allegedly had involved himself, Martin, and a drunken patron or two in that noted New York night spot. "We didn't have to post bond," Bauer recalled. "The D.A. said he knew where I was gonna be. And I didn't dare get in the goddamn fight in Chicago. We were goin' in front of the grand jury, you know. So I just stayed out in right field. I was cheerin' 'em on."

But by now, the umpires had managed to bring a semblance of calm to the situation. Players were milling around, collecting their equipment—and their composure. Just then, Martin's temper boiled over once again. "After it was all quieted down," recalled Ditmar, "Martin asked me, 'What did Doby say to you?' And I told him what he'd said, and he took off after Doby, and so he got thrown out, too."

Neither Ditmar nor Doby disclosed what was said, but a number of others have claimed that it was along the lines of: "If you ever do that again, I'm gonna stick a knife in your back." Whatever was said, it was enough to set off Martin, who was rather easily set off, anyway. But before Martin and Doby could resume hostilities, the four umpires and several players got in between them and order was restored. Altogether, the donnybrook had used up 30 minutes. Said Brickhouse: "Best baseball fight I ever saw." Added Slaughter, who'd been in the majors since 1938: "It's the best one I've ever been in." Wrote the *Chicago Tribune*'s Irv Vaughan, who'd been covering baseball since the early '20s: "The best fight I have ever seen on a ballfield." But now came the ejections: Besides Martin, the umps gave Doby, Dropo, and Slaughter the heave-ho. Ditmar, the man who had fired the pitch that had touched off the fireworks, was allowed to stay, which, as could be expected, angered the Chicagoans. "There's always been that question in my mind," said Doby. "If the guy that creates the initial problem, if he stays in, and the guy who responds has to leave—I've never been able to understand that."

Responded Ditmar: "I remember Lopez was the manager, and he complained about me staying in the game and pitching, so Napp told him what Doby had said to me, and he didn't complain about it after that. Doby was the one who instigated it, although he probably figures I was the one because I threw at him. But I did get fined for it by the American League, $100, 'for instigating the brawl,' they said."

The ejections robbed the White Sox of their Nos. 5-6 hitters, while the Yankees lost a bench player (Slaughter) and their third baseman (Martin, who was replaced, with no dropoff, by Andy Carey), and were able to keep their starting pitcher. That lopsided result prompted speculation about the Yankees' motives, speculation still fresh in Dropo's mind when he discussed the matter more than three and a half decades later. "I really believe this," he began. "We didn't have the depth the Yankees had. The only power hitters we had were Minoso, myself, and Doby. Now, all of a sudden they got me and Larry out of the game. I think some of it might've been their intent to try and get Doby out of the game. They didn't think I was gonna get into a fight. Nobody realized there was gonna be a melee. But they probably wanted to get Doby out of the game or somehow intimidate him. That's my honest, gut reaction as to what precipitated that one."

Could the Yankees, who had been struggling on their western trip and were in danger of falling six games behind the Sox if they would lose again this day, have been guilty of provoking an on-field incident that might prove beneficial to their cause? Admitted Skowron: "If we were in a slump, Casey used to tell Billy Martin, 'If a guy slides into you hard, start a fight. Or if you get knocked down, start a fight.' Just to get the guys motivated again, you know. That's the way we got our motivation, was to start somethin'. Because we were probably kinda lackadaisical, you know, from winnin' every year."

If indeed the Yankees had planned this particular incident, it worked supremely well. They won this game, 4-3, defeating Billy Pierce, and embarked on a 10-game winning streak that enabled them to overtake the White Sox by the following weekend.

★ ★ ★

The Yankees were in town Wednesday, September 7, 1960 for a night game against the third-place White Sox. Both teams were trailing Baltimore, the surprising league-leaders—New York by one and a half games, Chicago by four and a half. Each team needed a victory badly, but the Sox were at a distinct disadvantage: Their star second baseman, Nellie Fox, was home in bed with a virus, his streak of 798 consecutive games having been forced to an abrupt ending. In his place was the utility man for all seasons, Sammy Esposito, who would never forget this night.

The White Sox and Early Wynn led, 4-1, when things began coming undone in the visitors' eighth inning. With one out, Roger

Maris singled and Mickey Mantle walked. Up stepped Skowron, who sent a double-play ball right to Esposito. Alas, Sammy booted the ball, couldn't make a play anywhere, and all hands were safe. Yogi Berra batted for Elston Howard and singled to center for two runs, making it 4-3 and sending Wynn to the clubhouse. Al Lopez sent for Gerry Staley, and another pinch hitter, John Blanchard, sent a drive to left-center that was misplayed by Al Smith, bringing in two more runs. The Yankees were en route to a 6-4 victory. Esposito could only stare at the ground. Luis Aparicio came over and offered an encouraging word. "I'm standing out at second talking to Looie," Esposito recalled, "and all of a sudden this guy comes out of the stands toward me. And he said he'd bet a lot of money on us and I'd just blown the game. And some punches were thrown. It was a very embarrassing situation for me."

But at least Sammy got in a couple good shots against his opponent, Willie Harris, a fan from the South Side who had jumped over the box-seat railing along the right-field line. Harris' pal, Jesse James, likewise of the South Side, also dashed onto the field, but members of the park police detail collared him before he could reach the fight scene. Meanwhile, Aparicio, with help from police and ushers, had separated Esposito and Harris, and the latter was led away by security people. Under the stands, Harris managed to get in one final blow, a punch to the Burns Detective Agency's Jack Moran, who lost a couple of teeth because of it. Finally, Harris was taken to the nearby Deering district police station and booked for disorderly conduct. The story was not quite over, however.

"I was sued by this guy afterwards," Esposito said. "Some lawyer got with him and they brought this lawsuit. Of course, it was thrown out of court. They sued the White Sox, too. They figured they could get some money out of it. But he had come out onto the field, so he was in the wrong, right from the start. But that was a most embarrassing time for me. What made it more embarrassing was losing the game. I had a tough time getting over that. It was a tough night for me."

It was a tough night, too, for Jim Landis, who had watched the whole episode, in disbelief, from center field. "Sammy and I were pretty good friends," he said. "It was something I'll never forget,

The Chicago Side:

The White Sox Remember the Yankees and New York

(Note: Years with Sox during rivalry indicated in parentheses)

BILLY PIERCE, pitcher (1951-61):

"When I was young and when I first started playing ball, the fall of the year it was the World Series and Yankee Stadium and Mel Allen. If you beat the Yankees, every ballplayer felt more elated than if you'd beaten one of the other clubs. You always wanted to win, of course, no matter who you were playing. But they were the tops. It's like a team beats Notre Dame in football; it makes their season. It's the same thing in all sports. You play a team that's kind of a perennial power and they're rated higher than anyone else and you beat them—that's it. It means a little more.

"We had good success against Cleveland. Even when they had that great team in '54, we broke even with them. We were the only team in the league to do that. But the Yankees would always beat us. We'd beat 'em some games, but they would always win more than we did. Of course, they always had a little more depth than we did. And that made all the difference in the world. We tried to save pitchers for them and we'd lose other games because of it, because we didn't have the hitting to make up for it. The Yankees could overwhelm Philadelphia—later Kansas City—and some other clubs, but we couldn't overwhelm anybody with our hitting, so we couldn't spot our pitching. They had Johnny Kucks and Tom Sturdivant, who they could spot against certain clubs, and they could save Whitey Ford for the White Sox and Cleveland. Stengel could do it, but our managers couldn't. We didn't have the depth. We always had to keep low runs because we didn't score 10-12 runs a game.

"The Yankees would go into Kansas City after beating us 2-1

and 3-2 and they'd beat Kansas City, 8-6. We were the other way around. We'd get done playing those real tough games with the Yankees and because we didn't have the depth in pitching or the good hitting, we'd go to Kansas City and lose 5-4 or 4-3, all the time. That's what hurt us. We didn't have the depth."

On pitching to the Yankees: "You had Mantle and Berra. Bauer was tough on left-handed pitching. Now, you get past them, and psychologically maybe you tend to relax a little bit, and Skowron would kill you. Bill was a good hitter. He gave the White Sox a lot of trouble. Mantle and Berra were the 3-4 men in the lineup, and they probably beat us more games, but probably batting average-wise, Skowron did as well against us as anybody.

"Mantle was almost an 80-point better hitter right-handed than he was left-handed, because he knew the strike zone. Left-handed, he'd swing and miss the ball up above the letters and also the ball in the dirt. Right-handed, he wouldn't swing at those pitches. I wish he would have. But Mickey right-handed was probably as good a hitter as there was."

On the White Sox's approach: "There was a lot of pride in the ballclub. There were a lot of guys who had to work hard to accomplish something. They couldn't play halfway and still do well. They had to go with everything they had. No, we were a good ballclub. Nobody ever said they beat us easy. They knew they were in a fight. Even the Yankees."

MINNIE MINOSO, outfielder (1951-57, '60-61, '64):

On homering off Vic Raschi of the Yankees his first time up with the Sox (May 1, 1951): "That was one of the greatest days of my life. That day, I never forget. It helped that I finally know I have regular position. With Cleveland, I was on the bench, play maybe two-three times a week. Some guy get hurt, I go in and play. But when I come over here, to Chicago, left field or third base or whatever, I know I'm in the lineup every day. The people that day, the fans, made me feel at home, completely. So after that, I figured I had a home here for a hundred years. It's true. The people gave me good welcome."

(So did the press that afternoon, as Paul Richards recalled: "After the game, the sportswriters stormed him for an interview.

He couldn't speak hardly any English at all then, and Luis Aloma, the Cuban relief pitcher, was his interpreter. They asked a lot of questions, and Aloma relayed them to Minnie. Finally, one of the guys asked: 'Don't you think it's gonna be hard to play major-league baseball if you can't speak any English?' So Aloma relayed the question and Minnie answered in English: 'Ball, bat, glove—she no speak English.' ")

On being hit in the head—causing a hairline skull fracture—by Yankee pitcher Bob Grim in May 1955: "In this case, I always said before and I say it now: Things like this happen in baseball. But I don't think Bob Grim threw baseball intentional to hit me. Probably, you know, he gonna pitch me close, and the pitch was a little wild. But I never had it on my mind that he do it on purpose—even though it almost killed me."

CHICO CARRASQUEL, shortstop (1951-55):

"One series in New York, we had a meeting before the first game, and Paul Richards say, 'Bed check tonight. It's $500 if you're not in your room at midnight.' Five hundred, at that time, is a lot of money. So after that, [coach] Luman Harris come and say, 'Richards want to see you.' So I'm thinking he gonna talk to me about baseball, right? I go in and Richards say, 'For you, it's a thousand.' See, he knew I had this girlfriend in New York, a Cuban girl. I didn't see her that trip."

On toughest Yankees: "Allie Reynolds was their toughest pitcher, for me. Ooh, he threw hard. They played tough. Gene Woodling, Bob Cerv, Hank Bauer. I was one of the first shortstops to come across and throw from down here [across the body] to make that runner [coming into second base to break up the double play] get down. And Hank Bauer's the reason. One day, he spike me on that play. I needed 20 stitches later. This was in second inning. I no tell the trainer. I tell Nellie [Fox], 'Don't tell anybody. If trainer find out, they'll take me out of the game. I'm gonna get Bauer. I'm gonna throw at his head.' So later in the game, Hank Bauer is on first base, there's a groundball to Nellie, he gives me the ball and I let it go—missed Bauer's head by this much [Chico held his fingers about an inch apart]. Hank Bauer, he say, 'Hey, Chico, why you do that?' He knew why."

SAUL ROGOVIN, pitcher (1951-53):

"The Yankees never made a mistake. It was incredible. Their defense was unbelievable. And you know the pitchers they had: Ford, Reynolds, Raschi, Eddie Lopat, Johnny Sain. And they had that great infield, with Rizzuto, McDougald, Collins, and later Richardson. And those great outfielders. Where are you gonna hit the ball? Wherever you hit the ball, they're gonna get it. So they'd beat you 1-0 and they'd beat you 14-2.

"DiMaggio hit a few shots off me. Woodling was a tough man to pitch to—hit to all fields, had good power to all fields. Yogi beat us so many times that Richards told us at one time, 'The next son of a bitch that allows him to beat us with a home run in the seventh, eighth, or ninth inning on a fastball, I'm gonna fine him $500.' Yogi, it seemed, used to sleep the first five, six innings. He'd be sort of lackadaisical, kinda nonchalant. But all of a sudden, you try to waste a pitch on him, in the seventh, eighth, or ninth inning, and he'd put one in the stands on you. He beat us so many times with a home run in the late innings, it's not even funny.

"Now Yogi, he could pull Bob Feller in his prime. Anybody who walked out there, he could pull. And nobody ever seemed to try a change-of-pace on him. They kept throwing this guy fastballs. I couldn't understand it. I threw him a fastball one day, at Chicago. I had two strikes and no balls, and I was gonna waste a pitch on him, throw one up under his chin, move him away from the plate, you know? I threw this pitch. To me, the ball was a little bit over his head—wasn't eye-high, it was over his head. I threw it as hard as I could throw it, and inside. And the first thing you know, he chopped down on that ball, and the wind was blowing a gale in from right field, and he hit that ball into the teeth of that gale, and he hit a line shot into the right-field stands. I couldn't believe it. So I said, 'That's the last fastball this guy is ever gonna see from me, unless I bounce it up there.' So what I wound up doing was throwing him change-of-paces and slow curveballs, and wasting a fastball way outside. And I got him out very well that way.

"Mize was another tough hitter. He'd hit a line drive over shortstop for a single, or he'd pull the ball to right field for a home run. And he was one of those hitters—Ted Williams the same way—if he didn't swing, it was a ball. Great, great eye."

JIM RIVERA, outfielder (1952-61):

"I'll tell you somethin'. We were up against *some* team. And you've got to give them credit. They were the best team I ever saw in baseball. And Whitey Ford was the best pitcher I ever faced. I don't care what they tell you about the Cincinnati Big Red Machine and all that. Those guys couldn't even play with the Yankees. They were tough. Super ballplayers. They had pitching, defense, running, everything."

On the four-game sweep of the Yankees in June 1956: "I'd tell everybody, if we beat the Yankees one out of four, we'd celebrate. If we beat 'em two straight, it's a hell of a thing. But four straight? That never happened. It's like beating Mayor Daley—which is impossible, right?"

He was stationed in right field during the late innings of Game 2 of that Sunday sweep, when hundreds of fans came out onto the field to celebrate: "One gal, she climbed down from the seats in right field. She ran right past me and went to Nellie. I don't know, I guess she was a Nellie fan. Hell, so was I. We all were."

SAM MELE, outfielder (1952-53):

"Vic Raschi was terrific. You give him a one-run lead in the seventh inning and forget it. Reynolds was tough. I used to hit Lopat pretty good. Then he came up with a screwball, and that made him tough for me, too.

"We knew the Yankees were tough. And I'll tell you, they knew that we played tough against them, too. They knew that. As you look back, you can tell by the scores, there were an awful lot of tough ballgames. We had some good pitchers—not the greatest staff. But they knew how to pitch those Yankee hitters pretty damned good."

FERRIS FAIN, first baseman (1953-54):

"Admire the Yankees? I don't know how you can admire someone who's kickin' your ass all the time, no. You gotta realize we played 154 ballgames a year, every day against another team, and there wasn't any of this hero-worship. It didn't exist, at least not from my point of view. I wasn't awed. I might've admired a player or two, like Joe DiMaggio. He was without a doubt the best all-around ballplayer I ever saw. But falling over in a faint because we were playing the Yankees, no, it didn't make any difference to me. All in a day's work.

"What I'm telling you is, I didn't give a shit about the Yankees, frankly. As far as I was concerned, they were just another ballclub we had to play. I wasn't 'thrilled' that I was playing against 'em. We were just as good as they were. And we were gonna beat their ass if we could, just like they were gonna try to do to us. I just wish I could've contributed more when I was there in Chicago. As it was, it didn't turn out that way. I was out of the lineup more than I was in it. I didn't have a complete season either year. In '54, my second year, I was having a hell of a year, and so was the ballclub. And we'd gotten George Kell, and he was helping. Well, then we both got hurt. But I enjoyed every minute that I played and I didn't give a goddamn who we were playin'."

On the toughest pitchers he had to face: "It was a different situation back then than now. When you went into Cleveland in those days, you had Early Wynn, Feller, Lemon, Garcia. You're not lookin' at one soft touch at all. The Yankees were the same way. Looking back, they had Ford and Lopat, Reynolds and Raschi. The top clubs had real good pitchers. You didn't get a breather. Lopat—there might be a day when I'd get a couple hits off him, and then the next time he'd get me out with that slow-slower-slowest stuff, and then stand out on the mound and laugh at you when he did get you out. But they were all tough. In other words, I can't tell you a *bad* pitcher on that club. It was no picnic htting against any of them. You're always looking at it from your standpoint. So I'm thinking, 'Hey, I'm looking for this mediocre pitcher. Where is he?' In those days, you were looking at tough pitching every day. In the major leagues now, I couldn't name you, on the 28 goddamn teams they got goin' now, more than 10 pitchers who were qualified to be starters on the ballclubs in the years I was playing. There's a hell of a difference."

JACK HARSHMAN, pitcher (1954-57):

"I never really ever sensed any real animosity between us and the Yankees. It's just that they were so tough to beat, that you had that extra incentive going in—that you knew you had to bust your ass, and that you really would love to kick their butts, because they really were the cream of the league."

On the aftermath of the May 18, 1955 incident at Yankee Stadium, when Hank Bauer blatantly leveled Nellie Fox in the baseline, breaking up a potential inning-ending double play and setting the stage for Mickey Mantle's game-winning grand slam: "See, the sportswriters all jumped on that play in New York, how mean old Hank Bauer took unfair advantage of our second baseman. And of course, that's what Bauer's supposed to do. Anyway, [Sox VP] Chuck Comiskey comes to me before that first game against the Yankees back in Chicago [June 3] and, in kind of a quiet way, said to me, 'Jack, if you take care of Bauer tonight, there may be a little white envelope in your locker for you.' And I was a little leery about how I was gonna go about this and still protect my position on the club—this was just my second year. If the situation had come up where I could've knocked Bauer on his butt without doing any damage, I would have. But it just never came up. I never got the chance. I was in trouble most of the way, men on base all the time. So the ballgame's over and I've beaten them, 3-2, and I felt pretty good about that. But Chuck never even said, 'Nice game.' And certainly there was no white envelope waiting for me."

DICK DONOVAN, pitcher (1955-60):

"I remember pitching against the Yankees one night in Chicago. And Bob Cerv was on first base. He was about 6-1 or 6-2, 215 or so. Legs and arms like Alley Oop. Just a real big guy. There's a ball hit to Aparicio in the hole, over to Fox for the force—and Cerv knocked Nellie out into short left field. Nelson was pained, sore—my God, it took him about four or five minutes to get back to his position. Cerv came up next time with a guy on first. Nellie called time and came to the mound: 'Tricky, do me a favor.' I said, 'Nelson, anything. You name it.' 'How 'bout putting one up under that S.O.B.'s chin?' I said, 'Nelson, consider it done.' Next pitch, I put one high and tight. Cerv went down, the bat went up in the air, the ball hit the bat, and it bounced back out to me for an easy 1-4-3 double play. Nellie came over to me in the dugout and told me, 'Tricky, you're my friend for life.' "

On his 2-1, 11-inning loss on August 29, 1957, when he allowed a leadoff homer to Hank Bauer and a game-winning homer to Enos Slaughter, giving the Yankees a sweep of the three-game series and putting New York ahead by six and a half games instead of four and a half: "The plate umpire that day was Bill Summers, a guy who'd been around a long time [in the AL since 1933, in organized ball since 1921]. Wasn't the best umpire, wasn't the worst umpire. But he took a lot of crap that day, from the fans, from our bench. After the game, in our clubhouse, guys were throwing things around, really upset. Which was unusual, because we were an older club. And after a while, I walked out of our clubhouse and over to the umpires' dressing room, which was next to our clubhouse. There were three police or Andy Frains outside the door, and they wouldn't let me in. I said, 'I want to see Summers. He called a hell of a game, and I wanna tell him he called a hell of a game.' Finally [umpire] Nestor Chylak comes out to see what's going on. He says, 'Come on, let him in.' There's Summers, sitting on a stool by his locker, in his underwear, his head down, a can of Budweiser in his hand. I sat down on the stool next to him. He looks over, sees my spikes, the socks, the uniform pants of this guy sitting next to him. I tell him, 'I just wanted to tell you I thought you called a hell of a game.' He looks up at me finally and says, 'You know, I've been umpiring for 40 years, and I have never seen a pitching performance like that one—just two bad pitches in 11 innings.'

"Kind of a boring story, I suppose. But when you talk about the White Sox and the Yankees, that's a memorable game. Because it was such a big game. But I thought I really pitched well that day. And to have the plate umpire tell you something like that—I kinda feel self-conscious telling you about it. But it made me feel good."

MARTY MARION, coach (1954), manager (1955-56):

"The greatest series that was ever played in Marty Marion's life was when we beat the Yankees four straight at Comiskey Park [June 22-24, 1956]. Everybody thought I was the greatest manager in the world.

"The ballclub was very exuberant, very excited. We didn't pour champagne down anybody's neck, but we had a few Cokes—or something. The feeling was great. The Yankees—everybody appreciated how great they were. You had to do something to beat them four straight. People thought the sweep was the greatest thing that ever happened. All the newspapermen, they'd never seen anything like it before.

"Everybody in Chicago went wild. To me, it was a great thing, but not the greatest. After all, you're paid to win a pennant, not to beat the Yankees four straight games.

"We had our 'differences' with the Yankees, but there was no bad blood between the two teams. It was just part of competition. We had bad blood against anybody we played. We didn't like anybody. We wasn't your buddy, you know. I never liked that 'buddy-buddy' stuff.

"I'll never forget Casey, the first year I was with the White Sox as a coach for Paul Richards. The All-Star Game was in Cleveland, and Casey called me up and says, 'Marty, you know more about the National League than anybody else. Why don't you be my coach?' Fine. So I'm in the clubhouse, everybody's gettin' dressed. Casey comes in and says, 'Marty, here's the scorecard. You take over, and I'll see ya all later.' And he went out. So, I start goin' over the hitters. Whitey Ford was gonna start. I said, 'Whitey, now, Granny Hamner'—the old Phillies' shortstop, who was gonna be leadin' off—'he's a hell of a high-ball hitter. Don't you get the ball up on him, or he'll hurt ya.' So Whitey's on the mound, and I'm sittin' on the edge of the dugout. Whitey throws the first pitch—a high fastball. Hamner swings at it and misses. Whitey looks over at me: 'I'm trying to get it down, I'm trying to get it down.' He struck him out on three high fastballs.

"Casey'd come up to homeplate for the meeting—with the umpires, you know, before the game—and he'd always tell a joke. He never talked about baseball. He always wanted to tell you a joke. Then we'd exchange lineups, and then he'd beat the hell out of us."

On the reception he got from a crowd of 50,990 when he pulled Billy Pierce with two out, the bases filled, and the Sox leading the Yankees, 3-2, in the seventh inning of Game 2 of the August 28, 1955 doubleheader showdown: "Billy was the fair-haired boy in Chicago then. And I recall John Carmichael [*Chicago Daily News* columnist] telling me later, 'Boy, you've sure got a lot of guts taking him out in a situation like that.' I never got booed so loud in my life as when I took Billy Pierce out of that ballgame. But Hank Bauer, he was just murder on left-handed pitchers, and Billy was struggling. So Dixie Howell pitched to Bauer, and Bauer hit a shot—I mean a shot—right at Minoso in left. Right at him. Almost pinned him to the wall, he hit it so hard. But that was the third out. And that saved my life." (The Sox held on to win.)

WALT DROPO, first baseman (1955-58):

"Yankee Stadium, for a right-handed hitter like me, that's another Comiskey Park, only worse. Whitey Ford and Eddie Lopat used to let me hit long flies that would be caught out by the monuments, and they'd laugh at me as I'd go back to the dugout. Easy outs, 450 feet away. Don't forget, too, they had some real hard throwers, like Raschi and Reynolds, so you had a difficult time trying to pull them right down the line. And the power alley was Death Valley.

"But we were right there with them for several years. Their reserves were deeper than ours. Plus relief pitchers. We had Gerry Staley have a couple great years for us, but they always had two or three of those kinds of guys. They had Sain for a while, Bobby Shantz, Jim Konstanty. They all came from different clubs. Our starting lineups were not that much different in talent. The White Sox had George Kell, Aparicio, Fox, Torgeson, and myself. We had Minoso, Doby and Rivera—that's a good outfield. And Lollar catching. You always heard about Berra, but Sherm was an outstanding catcher, in my book. Good handler of pitchers, a good hitter.

"When we played the Yankees, every pitch seemed to be a crucial pitch. We knew when we played New York, it was gonna be a tight ballgame. 'Cause we had good pitching, they had good pitching. We knew it wasn't gonna be a blowout, 'cause those ballparks were too big for anybody, including Mantle. Those games were clinics. Every game was a World Series game. And I believe that. That's why I enjoyed my stay in Chicago so much."

LARRY DOBY, outfielder (1956-57, '59):

"I enjoyed playing in Yankee Stadium, because I was comin' home. I lived in Paterson, New Jersey, in those years, so it was great to be home. And I think you have to motivate yourself in baseball. Three or four coaches in those days, plus a manager, they can't motivate 25 players. So you have to motivate yourself most of the time. And I think playing against really good players like the DiMaggios, the Henrichs, and the Mantles motivated me. I always used to say, 'I'm gonna play a better center field and have a better day than DiMaggio'—or, later, Mantle.

"I was pretty fortunate against the Yankees. My first few years, the guy who was really tough on me was Allie Reynolds. But outside of Reynolds those first couple years, I hit the Yankee pitchers all right. Lopat, I had fairly good luck against. Raschi, Ford, the same thing."

On his huge day at the plate on June 24, 1956, when his pair of three-run homers, one in each game, led the Sox to a sweep of the afternoon's doubleheader—completing a sweep of the series: "One of my greatest days in baseball, and my greatest day with the White Sox, without a doubt. It was a great moment for us, it was a great moment for the fans. Because without the fans, we're nothing—let's face it. So when they're involved to that degree, it gives you that really happy feeling, that tingling feeling, inside.

"After you beat the Yankees, it's a happy time. You go out to eat and you feel good about it. You go to sleep and you feel good about it."

FRED HATFIELD, third baseman (1956-57):

"Everybody shot the works against the Yankees, and when they left town, you might've won one of three or split with them, or even won a series from them. But you were depleted. And the next club would come into town, even a last-place club, and they'd beat you three straight times. So the Yankees not only wounded you when they played you, they left you for bait for the next club. They either beat you to death or you had to wear yourself out to beat them."

JIM LANDIS, outfielder (1957-64):

"For me, it wasn't really a rivalry with the Yankees, because I was always—I don't want to use the word 'awe'—but I got to be close with a lot of those guys. I used to go into their clubhouse, and with that atmosphere and everything else—I don't know why—but in more cases than not, I was much closer to the Yankee ballplayers than to a lot of other teams' players. I think a few of us, like Roger Maris and Johnny Blanchard, we all came up together, and so all of a sudden, it's 'Hey, Jim, this is Elston,' and so on. And it got to be more of a nice friendship of great guys. Maybe it sounds weird, but I never really looked at it as a rivalry.

"But all my games with the Yankees, it was a sense of, what a great ballclub they were. I keep wanting to come out with the word 'awe,' but it wasn't awe. I was just so fascinated with that ballclub.

And when you got close to them, I'll be honest with you—Elston Howard, God bless him, I'd call him 'the Black Hercules,' and he'd laugh like hell. Tony Kubek, I'd call him 'the White Ghost,' 'cause he never did have a tan in his life. It was just that type of situation. That's how the camaraderie was. It was quite fun for me to play against them and also to see a great ballclub in action.

"I went into that clubhouse a fair amount of times, and I'd just stand there and say, 'No wonder you want to be a Yankee.' I remember this, too. I went into their training room one day, and there's Mickey Mantle getting a stretch wrap put on his leg, getting wrapped all the way from his ankle to his thigh. And Johnny Blanchard said, 'Hey, Jim, he goes through that every day.' Well, you see that, and you admire a guy like that even more.

"You'll think I'm crazy, but I remember Mickey Mantle hitting a 385-foot homer to right-center at Comiskey Park, and I heard his bat crack, from out in center field. He got jammed, and I could hear the bat crack, and the ball still went 385 feet. That astounded me, too. I said, 'My, what a man.' He was amazing. I've always appreciated watching greatness, and not many get to watch it. And I got to see how many games every year, watching Mantle. I really admired him."

On whether the White Sox choked against the Yankees (Landis was told of Nellie Fox's response many years earlier, that good clubs don't choke, they get beat by a better club, like the Yankees' losing to the Milwaukee Braves in the 1957 World Series: "I agree with that. No way in the world [we choked]. There's too much talent all the way through. I think if you look at it closely, you'll find that we played a lot of hard ballgames against the Yankees. There weren't many blowouts. The series were always close. So it was a real good rivalry that way. I think we proved we were a little bit better than we thought we were ourselves."

On Whitey Ford: "I honestly had fairly good luck against him. It was just one of those things, where another lefthander who didn't have as good stuff as he had might get me out easily. But for a certain reason, I bore down more and I didn't do too badly against him. He tried to keep the ball in on me, and after so long you learn a little bit and you start going with him. But I'm not trying to say how great it was to hit against him, because he was tough. I just battled him a lot harder than some other guys.

"I kidded him about his spitter once. He threw me a wet one, and he walked me. And, as I'm going to first, I said to him, 'You're gonna have to improve on that thing.' And he started laughing. He was just fiddling with it, and he was having trouble controlling it."

On Ryne Duren, who threw 100-M.P.H. heat and invariably ended up nailing Landis with pitched balls more than any player in the league: "Nellie told me later, 'Hey, Jim, I finally talked to Duren. Told him you better stop throwing at Landis.' And Ryne told Nellie, 'Believe me, I am honestly not trying to throw at him. It's just one of those things.' Well, I had to believe it too because, see, when I was in winter ball, before I got to the big leagues, Ryne and I and Sandy Koufax were on the same team in Puerto Rico. And we'd go fishing together and do a lot of stuff together. There was never any conflict. But boy, I'd go up there and stand in the farthest corner of the batter's box, and he'd still get me."

AL LOPEZ, manager (1957-64):

On Casey Stengel, his longtime rival: "His best trait, to me, was that he loved to play young guys. He wanted to help young guys. He wanted to develop young kids and get credit for developing them. The Yankees, actually, were lucky to get Stengel when they did because their club had started to deteriorate at that time, and they were lucky enough to come up with Mantle, Whitey Ford, McDougald, Billy Martin, and Hank Bauer—a bunch of guys. And they were all young when Casey got there. And I think Casey, by playing those young guys, they developed quicker, and they became a damn good ballclub again.

"And Casey was fortunate that he had that farm system. The Yankees had a great farm system back then. They had both Kansas City and Newark at the Triple-A level, and both had tremendous, good-looking young ballplayers. Kansas City and Newark used to win the American Association and International League practically every year. Then, down the line, they had Birmingham in the Southern Association and Beaumont in the Texas League. A great farm system, no question about it."

On pitching to Mantle: "In my experience with him, I used to tell my pitchers, 'Don't ever throw him a changeup, 'cause he'll hit it out of town.' He wasn't a pull hitter, really. He hit straightaway.

And you're not gonna fool a straightaway hitter with a changeup. The pull hitter, you'll fool, because he's gonna be way out in front."

GARY PETERS, pitcher (1959-64):

"I got to talking to Whitey [Ford] the last year he played, '67. And I'd never beaten him. And he beat me five times, and four of them were by one run—either 1-0, 2-1, or 3-2. Almost all during those two years, '63 and '64. I was trying to get him to go one more year so I could get another shot at him. But he retired."

PETE WARD, third base-outfield (1963-64):

"It was a heck of a thrill, playing the Yankees, 'cause they were loaded. And the thing that I remember most was that guys like Hector Lopez used to beat us. You look at their whole lineup, and not that those other guys didn't beat you, but it seemed like Elston Howard and Hector Lopez did the most damage.

"Some people were asking me the other day, how it seems like when teams go up against the 49ers, it seems like they don't think they can win. And I mentioned to them that we used to go up against the Yankees, but we thought we could win, even though we thought they were great. I remember in '64, the 'harmonica deal,' they came into Chicago and for once we beat them, four straight. For once, we nailed them. Usually in a showdown series, they'd come in, win it, and that was the end of it. I'm sure people would say that, man for man, they had a better ballclub than we did, but we whipped them, and I felt like we had a good ballclub, too. When we swept them, I would say nobody took it for granted that we had knocked them out of the race, but we thought we hurt 'em real bad." But not badly enough, as it turned out. "No, but I went to the World Series that year, anyway. Nick Kladis [Ward's pal and the owner of One Stop Food & Liquors in Chicago] and I went to the games in St. Louis. And we didn't have a room. We wound up renting one of the johns in one of the downtown hotels. They brought in rollaway beds. Here you've got this big successful businessman from Chicago and a ballplayer sleeping in the john."

On Yankee pitching: "We always had great pitching—I thought probably the best in the league. But the Yankees had guys who could shut you out, too. They weren't easy. Ford was the toughest for me. I just think he was a pitcher's pitcher. He had control of everything, he knew how to pitch, he didn't want to waste pitches. I remember one time, I'd fouled off a number of pitches and then I flied out or something, and after the game, I'm on this radio show with him. And I talked about that one particular time at bat, and he came out and said he felt he wasted a lot of pitches there. In other words, he was saying he should've gotten me out quicker. And I thought that was pretty interesting. People said he didn't throw hard. But he could throw as hard as he wanted to—not like Sandy Koufax or Nolan Ryan, but he could throw hard, too, and he had everything else to go with it.

"They always had a good bullpen, too. They had that damn Steve Hamilton. He'd come in and get lefthanders out. That's how he made his living. He would come in and throw you 800 sliders and then throw you one fastball. So then you'd look for the fastball and then he'd get you out with the slider.

"I really think that we always felt, even probably after they weren't good, we always thought they were. And I think probably the single area where they stood out more than anybody else was defense. That infield—Pepitone, Richardson, Kubek, and Boyer—it was just real hard to get one through. I really think that's the last thing people point out when they talk about the Yankees."

AL WEIS, infielder (1962-64):

"I grew up in Farmingdale, New York, on Long Island. I was probably more partial to the Giants as a kid. I liked them a little better than the Dodgers or the Yankees. But we had a great rivalry with the Yankees in Chicago. It was just a great feeling to go out there and play against people like Whitey Ford, Mickey Mantle, Maris, Elston Howard, Tresh. I think playing against people like that makes you play better too. Like when I play with someone who plays a good game of golf, I think I play a better game of golf, too. Whereas if you play someone who's a 20-handicapper and you're maybe a 10-handicapper, somehow you just don't play as well. You look at him play and it seems to rub off on you. But gosh, the Yankees. When I got released by the Mets in 1971, the Yankees were one of the teams I gave a call to. But at that time, their roster was completely filled. But I would've loved to put on the old pinstripes and played a few games for them.

"We didn't have the home-run hitters. We had to scratch, you

The New York Side:

The Yankees Remember the White Sox and Chicago

(Note: Years with Yankees during rivalry indicated in parentheses)

JERRY COLEMAN, infielder (1951-57):

"We liked good competition. Fox, Aparicio, Minoso, Rivera, Lollar—you had a good ballclub. Good pitching. Billy Pierce. Saul Rogovin earlier. In any event, it was an exciting ballclub. Paul Richards came in and turned a Jack Onslow snail club into the Go-Go Sox. And I'd known Frank Lane. He was a commander in the Navy. He used to run us off the volleyball court so he and his wife could play. Then, later, he became my general manager at Kansas City in 1946."

Bad blood between the two clubs? "There were some guys who didn't like each other. But we never really went into a town and said, 'We're gonna get these guys.' We knew we could win, and we went in and won. The game was the thing."

On the underrated Yankee defense: "What we did was—and people don't realize this—we brought our gloves to the park. We made the plays. The only guy I ever remember them finding a position for was Bill Skowron. He couldn't play anywhere, but they said, 'The way this guy can hit, we gotta find a place for him.' So they found first base for him. But if you didn't bring your glove to the park, hell, you didn't play."

On their many come-from-behind victories over the White Sox: "We were never behind in a game. The game just wasn't finished yet. That's what happens when you're used to winning. I never knew how many double plays I'd made, how many sacrifice bunts I'd made. We didn't care. The bottom line was winning. And there was a lot of peer pressure. The older guys would let you know it if you weren't doing the job. I remember many times one of our pitchers would read Mantle the riot act for not hustling out on the field—or anybody else. I was more concerned with what Tommy Henrich would say to me than Stengel. That peer pressure was very evident then.

"I've said this many times: Being a Yankee wasn't my job—it was my religion. And that attitude permeated the clubhouse."

HANK BAUER, outfielder (1951-59):

"I'll tell ya what: When Paul Richards was there, we didn't take 'em that seriously. But when Lopez got over there, we did. He always had damn good pitching, wherever he went. I'm not saying we didn't take 'em seriously before that, but I think they was a better ballclub later. I'll tell ya what: They didn't have that much offense in those days. Looie'd get on first—somehow—and steal second. Nellie'd bunt him to third, and they'd score a run and now you had to fight like hell. They'd beat ya 1-0.

"The guy who gave me the most problem—I know he gave 'em to me, and I think he gave 'em to most of us—was Billy Pierce. The guy I used to hit—I don't know how well I hit him—was Dick Donovan. Those hanging sliders. Wynn? Well, Early, you'd go 0 for 4 against him, but it was a comfortable 0 for 4. He'd always pitch the ball up, and you'd pop it up or you'd do somethin' with it. He was all right, as long as you didn't hit the ball through the middle. You'd hit the ball back up the middle, the next time you was gonna get thrown at."

"We were playin' in New York [May 18, 1955]. And I was on first, and Andy Carey hit a squib to Nellie Fox. And I let him field the ball, and then I knocked him on his ass. And then Mickey came up and hit a home run and we win the game. And the White Sox all told me if I wanted to play football to go get a helmet and some shoulder pads. Now we go into Chicago [June 3], and I'm leadin' off the game, and now here comes one of them great big steel marbles, from the upper deck. Hit right on homeplate. Then, out in right field, one guy threw a deck of Bicycle playing cards at me. And then I look around and another guy threw a whole can of Schlitz at me. This was before pop-top cans. And I saw who it was, and I picked it up and gave it back to him and I said, 'You son of a bitch—the least you could've done was open it up.' And they all laughed, and it was over with.

"I used to like to come into Chicago and get interviewed by Jack Brickhouse. Jack'd give me a hell of a nice radio. That was a big deal in them days. There weren't many perks. Hell, no. The only place we got a perk was in Chicago."

CHARLIE SILVERA, catcher (1951-56):

As Yogi Berra's backup, spent much of the time in the bullpen out in center field at old Comiskey Park: "Those fans out there could be pretty rough. We used to have to hide out back there underneath the stands, where the grounds crew kept their stuff. Once somebody threw a beer cup with human excrement in it down at us. Oh yeah, it could get bad out there.

"Ol' Richards, he could cuss more in 30 seconds than some guys could in a lifetime. Once he left the dugout and came out to argue, he was gone. He knew it, everybody knew it. But Richards was a hell of a manager. He was just always one man short on that bench when he played us."

On the Chicago cabbie who, after the Yankees beat the Sox 18-2 one June afternoon in 1953, threatened to crash his cab with Silvera, Yogi Berra, and Joe Collins still in it: "Oh, the cabbie picked us up and took us back to where we were staying, at the old Del Prado Hotel. The book [*Dynasty*—by Peter Golenbock] said 'when he found out who we were.' Hell, he knew who we were. But yeah, he started driving like a kamikaze pilot.

"In that 18-2 game [in which he started and went 3 for 6 with three RBIs], I'd even played some third base, and Ralph Houk came in to catch. Casey got all the reserves in. Next day, Richards was still steamed. He came out with the lineup card and handed it to the umps with his back turned to 'em, so he wouldn't have to look at Casey."

Were the Yankees more fearful of the Sox once they got the fiery Ferris Fain from the A's for Eddie Robinson? "No, because he didn't have the power Eddie Robinson had. He was a singles and doubles hitter. Eddie hit the long ball."

TOMMY BYRNE, pitcher (1951, '54-57):

"Don't you ever think that when the Yankees played anybody

we didn't take 'em seriously, because we always knew we were gonna be hitting against everybody's best pitching. Donovan, that guy, he'd thrown down at the knees pretty good. He threw a heavy ball. He was tough. He'd get a lot of groundballs, a lot of double plays. Pierce was sneaky fast, a good breaking ball. He was tough. For several years there he was right up there on a par with Ford."

ANDY CAREY, third baseman (1952-60):

"We always had respect for the White Sox. They were always contenders, always finished second or third. They were our nemesis. They and Cleveland. They reminded people of the old Cardinals, running the bases, stealing. Doing anything they could to beat you."

On the May 1956 rumors that he was about to be traded to the White Sox: "Sure, we heard the rumors. And I loved Chicago. Still do. My wife loved Chicago. I'd tell my wife, 'Yeah, you love Chicago—State Street and Michigan Avenue.' But at that time, there was no finer ballclub to play for than the Yankees. And no finer city than New York City. You can have it now.

"I remember this: When we used to come to Chicago, the groundskeepers, down the third-base line from homeplate to the bag, they would make it so that any balls bunted down there would stay fair. And they'd always wet the field in front of homeplate to slow down groundballs."

Most admired players: "Ol' Minoso, I made a hero out of him. That sucker in left field, it seemed like every time I'd hit a ball down the left-field line, he would be right there to catch it. I went to an old-timers' game and I did the same damn thing, and I told him, 'You son of a bitch, you're still over there.'

"I didn't like Nellie. There was always something about him that irritated me—until I went over to the White Sox in 1961 and played with him, and found out that he was such a nice man. Same thing with Early Wynn. I don't know what it was. Just Nellie's aggressiveness, I think. I'd always had like a challenge with Nellie, 'cause he'd like to try and bunt down the third-base line, and I'd come way in and play 15 feet in front of the bag at third and just kinda dare him to hit it down to me. 'Cause he was such a great bunter, so I just tried to take that away from him. I mean, I just came in like I was playing patty-cake with him, 'cause I knew he couldn't hurt me if he hit it my way. So I just tried to make him think a little."

Toughest pitchers: "Virgil Trucks pitched high and inside—rising fastballs. He pitched very much like Early Wynn. They were both tough."

BOB CERV, outfielder (1951-56, '60, '61-62):

"I always remember the games when Pierce and Ford would lock up. Those were great ballgames—2-1, 3-2. Usually, if they'd get beat, Mantle would hit a home run. I can remember the day [June 5, 1955] Mantle hit one on the roof off Pierce and we won by a run. I'd play in those games, being a right-handed hitter. I used to say I always had to play against those tough lefthanders, like Pierce, Parnell, Shantz, Hoeft, Herb Score. You never saw any easy lefthanders back then in the big leagues, and I'd always chuckle: 'Sure, that's when I get to play—against these guys.'

"I'll always remember that grand slam I hit off Early Wynn [May 28, 1961]. He had a 6-2 lead. It was a 3-2 pitch, and I hit a grand slam. But I'd always hit Early fairly well. And I know that was one of the longest home runs I ever hit in Yankee Stadium. It was over the third exit in the bleachers in left-center."

On his recent hip-replacement surgery, after being asked if it was caused by running into Nellie Fox too many times at second base while breaking up double plays: "Yeah, I used to take him out once in a while. I couldn't do that anymore. They'd throw me out of the game now. But hell, I used to tell him, 'Turn the double play the right way, and you won't get hurt.' "

BOB GRIM, pitcher (1954-58):

On beaning Minnie Minoso, May 18, 1955 in New York: "He was always right on the plate, you know. And he just froze. It scared me to death—scared me to death. [Laughing] What scared me even more was he got up. But then they eventually found a hairline fracture. But, oh God, what a terrible feeling. But he was very gracious, 'cause he knew I wasn't throwing at him. He'd always lead the league in getting hit by pitches. And that time he just froze. But all he had to do was move his head four to five inches, and he's clear.

"He was well liked, even by the opposition, 'cause he was

always chattering. He was just a very happy-go-lucky-guy. I'm sure he's still the same way."

"I had good luck against the White Sox. I don't know for what reason, but I always pitched well against them. And they had some good ballclubs—fast, aggressive—and some good hitters. But everybody has a team that they pick on, and then there's always some teams that knock your jock off, too."

BILL SKOWRON, first baseman (1954-62):

"That was the team we had to beat—the White Sox. And Detroit and Cleveland. But we were more worried about the Sox, because they had great pitching, and we were always up for them games.

"When I was in high school at Weber, I only competed in football and basketball because the Catholic schools at that time didn't have baseball. I played a lot of softball midweek—Windy City softball—and on Sundays I played hardball, sandlot ball. Then I went to Purdue on a football scholarship, and the Cubs and Sox both thought I'd finish my college education, so they never offered me anything. And the Sox scout, Doug Minor, he didn't like my dad for some reason, so he blackballed me, said 'Moose'll never make it.' So I hit good against the Sox in my career because I wanted to prove to them that their scouts had made a mistake not offering me a contract. As it turned out, though, I could never complain, because I got into seven World Series with the Yankees. I get traded to the Dodgers, we win the pennant, we win the World Series. So I was in eight World Series out of my 14 years in the big leagues."

BOB TURLEY, pitcher (1955-62):

"The White Sox always had a pretty good team, but they didn't have enough depth in their ballclub to be able to hold on in September. But we took 'em seriously. They always had a good pitching staff. They didn't have the home-run hitting that would give them the big inning, so they had to scratch out one or two runs. But they always had the good pitching—those guys like Billy Pierce, Connie Johnson, Jack Harshman—and they always had the good defense—Busby in center, Minnie Minoso in the outfield. Most of the games we'd win off them seemed to come in the late innings. I remember Early Wynn, in the years he pitched for them, he'd have us beat by a run or two runs coming into the late innings, and they didn't have the great reliever to come in, and we'd get a home run or two off him and we'd win the ballgame.

"I guess one of my closest friends was Nellie Fox. Nellie and I were always good friends. I lived near Baltimore, in Lutherville, Maryland, and he lived in Pennsylvania. We both owned bowling alleys. He had one in Chambersburg and I had one in Bel Air, Maryland. We used to bowl against each other. And I admired him. He was the toughest hitter for me to get out. If he hit two homers a year, he hit 'em both off me. He could do about anything with the bat he wanted to. He was a good, winning ballplayer."

On stealing signs and relaying them, by whistling, to Mickey Mantle: "Some of the signs I would steal from the pitcher, then I would let Mickey know, and sometimes Mickey could read 'em himself, so he wouldn't have to worry about me callin' 'em. But I had three pitchers on the White Sox I could get the signs from pretty well. You'll get a shock when I tell you now. Connie Johnson was one. He had that great screwball. And Mickey loved to hit the screwball off of him. Connie Johnson, during his windup, would move his right foot all the way over to the left side of the rubber before he would throw the screwball. We were in a ballgame, and Mickey was at the plate, and Marty Marion's coming out to take Connie Johnson out. And I'm saying, 'Please leave him in. Please leave him in.' And Mickey's looking at me like, 'Oh God, don't take him out.' And so he left him in there, and the very first pitch, I watched his foot, and he moved it over to the left-hand side of the rubber. He threw a screwball, and Mickey darn near hit it over the roof, and we beat ya the ballgame.

"Another guy was Early Wynn. He was another guy we didn't have to call 'em on. We just had to get somebody on base. We would use his nose as the focal point. In the stretch, when he went above his nose with his glove, it was a fastball. If he went below his nose, it was a curveball. If he only went to his belly with the glove, it was a knuckleball.

"And then Billy Pierce was the other one. Billy had a habit when he pitched. He'd put his hand way inside his glove. And, when he was wearing long sleeves, you could see his wrist. When you could see his bare wrist, he was throwing fastball. When you could see no wrist, he was throwing curveball, 'cause he went further into his glove.

"So I'd see these things, and I'd whistle. We started off assuming everything was a curveball. And then if I whistled one time, that would change it from a curveball to a fastball. If I didn't whistle again, it was another fastball. But if I whistled again, it was a curveball. So we kept switching off, so nobody could ever catch on to what we were doing. And then Mickey and I had a sign if he got screwed up, which he did a lot. He'd hit the top of his head, and then we'd start all over again."

BOBBY RICHARDSON, second baseman (1955, '56, '57-64):

"The thing I remember about Chicago was the fact they usually weren't high-scoring games. It was kinda hard to hit home runs there. And I remember the fans there, especially for a doubleheader in the afternoon, they'd drink a lot, they were kinda rowdy, but they loved their White Sox."

Most admired Sox player: "Naturally, it was Nellie Fox. I liked the way he got a piece of the ball all the time. He could work you for a walk and he could hit the ball anywhere he wanted to. I found myself on occasion thinking, 'Boy, he really helps that ballclub. I wish I could help our club like that.' And I don't remember how many times I made the All-Star team behind him. It was three, to four times at least that he was the second baseman and I was his reserve. But between him and Aparicio, I just felt that they were the key to that ballclub.

"[In the '57 fight], I went out and I grabbed Nellie Fox. You know, no one stays in the dugout when the teams go out. And for some reason, the little second basemen always go after each other. But I remember that day very well. And Larry Doby and I have since become great friends. He's from South Carolina, from Camden, and he was voted into the state Hall of Fame a few years ago, and he helps head up marketing for Major League Baseball. I respected him and admired him as a ballplayer."

On the oft-married Enos Slaughter, a combatant in that Sox-Yankee brawl and, much later, the baseball coach at Duke when Richardson coached at South Carolina: "I roomed with Slaughter one year when he had come over from Kansas City. And I called my wife and said, 'Honey, I'm rooming with a guy from North Carolina; he's a farmer, he gets up early. You can really appreciate that.' Next day, she called me up, said she'd talked to somebody who had told her he'd been married five times—and she wanted to know if I could get a new roommate.

"I remember one year, I didn't have a real good ballclub at South Carolina, and we went up to Duke and he beat me a doubleheader. Boy, I mean he just poured it on. He didn't hold the score down at all.

"I looked forward to coming to Chicago, I really did. You know, two of my kids later graduated from Wheaton College. But I enjoyed going into Chicago because Lee Pfund, the basketball coach at Wheaton, was a friend of mine and he's the one who first arranged for me to speak at Christian Service Brigade [a youth ministry then based in Wheaton]. His background was in baseball, and he just called me up one day, came up to the room, and visited with me, asked if I could come out and speak the next time we were in Chicago. And we just became good friends. So when my kids got to be high school age, I rented a motor home and we took my two boys and two girls and visited Wheaton and Taylor University [in Upland, Indiana], and it ended up two went to each school.

"I had another friend who ran a delicatessan in Chicago. His name was Oscar Friedman. And he'd always make me three corned beef sandwiches and bring 'em down to the ballpark, and I'd leave tickets for him. And Elston Howard and Kubek would just love those sandwiches.

"I remember when Early Wynn was going after his 300th win [September 1962]. Well, I laid a bunt down, and of course, he didn't like that a bit. He didn't even wait 'til I got up to bat the next time. He threw at me at first base."

RALPH TERRY, pitcher (1956-57, '59-64):

"The White Sox were always tough. I remember the harmonica game, when they swept us four straight [August 1964]. No, they were always tough. Lopez was a good manager, and he always had a terrific coaching staff, and they had Aparicio, Fox, Landis, Sherm Lollar catching—strength up the middle. They had a really fine team, a good defensive team, and they'd play for that one run. They were real good at playing for that one run. Wonderful ballclub. It was always 3-2, 2-1. Lopez always insisted on pitching low—keep that ball low.

"One night [June 26, 1959], we had a game at Comiskey the same night Ingemar Johansson knocked out Floyd Patterson [for the heavyweight title]. I remember that night. I was in the bullpen. It was a big upset. And a white guy beat a black guy. That night, the cops were draggin' 'em down to the bullpen and loadin' 'em on the paddy wagon. It was a Friday night, everybody had their paychecks. I mean, there were fights all over that place that night.

"I remember one night, we came out for batting practice at Comiskey. It was a nice, calm night, wind not blowin' much at all. Mantle was feeling good. He said, 'I'll betcha I can take five swings in batting practice and put three balls up on the roof.' Whenever he wanted to put on a show for distance, he'd bat right-handed. He'd even have Ford pitch to him, or John Blanchard. And Blanchard had a nice motion, for a catcher, nothing herky-jerky or anything. And he laid it in there, and Mantle took five swings and he put three of 'em up on that roof. Now, that's impressive."

TONY KUBEK, shortstop-outfielder (1957-64):

"We always had real good crowds here [in Chicago] 'cause you usually had pretty good teams. Aparicio at short, Fox at second, Landis in center, Smith in the outfield. They always had pretty good teams. There was always a lot of excitement coming here—especially for me, 'cause my folks would always come down from Milwaukee to see me play. So that made it more meaningful to me.

"Jim Coates used to come in high and tight on people, start fights. And after a while, we got tired of defending him. One day he hit Early Wynn, and they glared at each other for a while, and I came in to the mound, and I look at their dugout and see Earl Torgeson and Jim Rivera already on their way out. And I look around and realize Moose is still at first base, Clete and Bobby are still at their positons, and I'm out here alone with Coates, and Rivera and Torgeson are comin'. I say to myself, 'I don't want any part of this.' Just then, Wynn holds up his hand to those guys, as if to tell 'em, 'Hey, I'll take care of this.' And he did. He went to first base, took forever to put his jacket on, and then, next inning, he took care of us. Richardson, Kubek, Mantle—he went right down the line. Didn't hit any of us. But we all went down.

"I signed in '54, right here in Chicago. I'd worked out with the Braves, oh yeah—I did that to get free tickets. But a Yankee scout, the late Freddie Hasselman, he'd scouted me. He brought me down here to work out. In fact, Jerry Coleman and Frankie Crosetti came out early at old Comiskey Park, and Stengel was there, and some of the other coaches. And I hit, threw and ran, and I ended up signing right there.

"You knew if you were going against the White Sox, sure, you were gonna face good pitching. But the reason we felt we were gonna beat teams with good pitching like the White Sox was because we caught the ball and ran the bases well. Frankie Crosetti, one of the first things he ever told us was, 'You don't beat good pitching 10-9, you beat 'em 2-1 and 3-2. You hold 'em close until something happens.' I remember Hank Bauer, one of the first years I was up, sitting on the bench saying, 'Hold 'em right there—we'll get to him.' To hold 'em right there and then make something happen, you have to hold the other team with your pitching and your defense."

BOBBY SHANTZ, pitcher (1957-60):

"The White Sox were always tough, especially in 1959. Our club always respected them. And I guess the guy I admired the most was my old roommate, Nellie Fox. We roomed together at Lincoln, Nebraska, in 1948. He made himself into a fine ballplayer, with the help of Paul Richards. I really think Nellie Fox should be in the Hall of Fame."

TOM TRESH, shortstop-outfielder (1961-64):

"Hoyt Wilhelm, no question, was the toughest White Sox pitcher for me. Anytime I got a hit off him, it was lucky. For me, there wasn't any way to hit him. I tried, in the beginning, to swing real slow and just punch the ball, and heck, I couldn't hit it. Later on, I had a little bit more success when I did start to swing harder, because I finally came to the conclusion, the way his knuckleball broke a couple different ways, my best chance at hitting him was to swing as quick as I could and try to get it where I thought it was going with the first turn, before it had a chance to turn again. And so I made more contact—I never did hit him that well, but I think I became more of a challenge for him.

"Eddie Fisher had a good knuckleball, but it wasn't Hoyt Wilhelm's knuckleball. Hoyt threw his really slow, and it just really floated up there. It was just different than the other ones, like Wilbur Wood's. But again, Eddie and Wilbur threw the other pitches, too, and so you had a chance to hit some of the other stuff. You didn't have to hit the knuckleball all the time. With Hoyt, you had to hit the knuckleball."

Both Sides Now

Not may ballplayers wore the uniform of both the White Sox and Yankees in the '50s and early '60s, for which there was an excellent explanation: The two clubs did not trade with each other. The White Sox were not about to do anything that might make the Yankees even stronger, and the Yankees were not about to help out another American League contender. Besides, whenever the Yankees needed help, they would simply trade four or five players they no longer needed to their farm club, the Philadelphia/Kansas City Athletics, and in return receive the player required to keep them on top.

Even Frank Lane, for all of his wheeling and dealing as Sox general manager, never made a deal of any substance with New York. "The Yankees," he once sneered, "always wanted to steal something." The only trade Lane, as Chicago GM, ever made with the Yankees came in December 1948, a month after he took over the White Sox, when he traded a young outfielder, Jim Delsing, to New York for Steve Souchock, a big (6' 2½," 203 pounds) first baseman-outfielder who'd always put up big numbers in the Yankee farm system but was, essentially, a big zero in the major leagues.

Also, there was Lane's conditional purchase, in January 1949, of Floyd "Bill" Bevens, the Yankee pitcher who had lost a no-hitter, and the game, with two outs in the ninth inning during the 1947 World Series. Bevens, his arm and shoulder aching, was shipped back to the Yankees even before spring training had run its course.

Oh, Lane tried once to swing something meaningful with New York, in the early '50s, when Whitey Ford was in military service. Recalled Lane in Chicago in 1978: "Dan Daniel, one of their writers, came in here and said, 'We need a lefthander. We need Billy Pierce. You don't need him down here.' I said, 'Screw the Yankees. You want him, you'll pay for him.' That's when I went after them."

Lane was amenable to giving up Pierce and another player—

quite possibly outfielder Al Zarilla—for Hank Bauer, Jerry Coleman, and Joe Collins. "George Weiss [Yankee GM] called me up," Lane remembered, "and said, 'Well, I'm gonna make you a deal.' I said, 'Who?' He mentioned a guy who was playing first base for their club at Binghamton. I said, 'That doesn't sound like Joe Collins to me.' He mentioned a guy named Frank Verdi who was playing second base at Birmingham. 'Well, that doesn't sound like Jerry Coleman.' Then he mentioned the name of a guy who was playing left field at Binghamton. And I said, 'That doesn't sound like Hank Bauer.' He said, 'That's the closest you'll ever come to making a deal with me.' Which it was."

When Lane departed for the St. Louis Cardinals, however, his successors, Chuck Comiskey and John Rigney, tried again. In May 1956, they were close to a deal that would have sent Dick Donovan to the Yankees for Andy Carey, Johnny Kucks, and a third player. But the teams couldn't agree on the third player.

So Carey remained in New York. Eventually, however, he and a few others made their way to Chicago. Among the handful of men who played for both teams during 1951-64 were Willie Miranda, Virgil Trucks, Tommy Byrne, Harry Byrd, Gerry Staley, Earl Torgeson, Harry Simpson, Don Larsen, and three players who were key members of both clubs—Carey, Bill Skowron, and Eddie Robinson.

Carey, whose stay in Chicago was hampered by back problems that cut short a budding batting binge, spoke almost reverently of Al Lopez in comparison to his longtime manager in New York, Casey Stengel.

"I learned more from Al Lopez about hitting in one year than I did from anybody else in all my previous years. In fact, if I'd have been with Lopez earlier, he'd have helped me tremendously. He helped me with my stance and my preparation before the pitch—the actual presentation, the shoulder turn. He said he'd always thought that, if he'd gotten hold of me earlier, I'd have been a hell of a lot better hitter. He'd watched me for a long time and they'd been trying to get me for a long time. And so I tried out what he taught, and it really worked."

Carey, who had come from Kansas City with a .244 average on June 10, 1961, caught on rather quickly. In his first six games in a

Chicago uniform, he went 2 for 20 as he tried to put Lopez's teachings into practice. Then, everything clicked. He began hitting line drives everywhere. Over the next 15 games, he went 23 for 52, a .442 clip, to bring his average up to .282. That's when he reinjured his back.

"It had been kind of a chronic condition all during my career," he said. "In fact, there were three-four times when I thought I'd never play again. It was in the lower lumbar section. If I didn't keep myself in good shape or if I tried to lift things or tried to do certain things, it would go out on me. Most of the time, it wouldn't happen during the season. That's what was unusual with the White Sox. I hurt my back stepping off a curb in Los Angeles, when we came out to play at old Wrigley Field."

The Sox were in L.A. to play the expansion Angels on June 30. Carey tried to play with the pain, but he only lasted one inning. He missed the next two weeks. "I tried to protect it and not let anybody know what was going on. And I think it got Lopez pissed off at me because he thought I was just jakin' around. He just got mad at me. But I was just trying to hide the fact that I had a bad back."

And yet, his respect for Lopez remains high, mostly for the aid he provided Carey's approach to hitting. The same cannot be said of his feelings toward Stengel, for whom he played six full seasons and parts of three others.

"Stengel always liked Billy Martin, and George Weiss liked me, and I know Stengel resented me in many ways—because I played third base only. And most of the guys on the team played two or three positions. Like Gil McDougald played third, short, and second; Billy played third, short, and second. And the Old Man wanted me to be a shortstop. And I told him, 'You can have shortstop. I don't want any part of it. I'd rather be a good third baseman than a mediocre shortstop.' "

Stengel also would become perturbed with Carey's refusal, at first, to be anything but a pull hitter. "Stengel used to tell me, after I'd hit a 420-foot flyball to left-center and they'd catch it, 'Well, nice goin', Carey. How'd that feel?' He'd just completely lash you all over the place after you hit the shit out of the ball, right in front of everybody else."

So Carey finally gave in and started to go to the opposite field. And his average went from .302 in 1954 to .257 in '55 and .237 in

'56. "I finally said, 'Screw it,' went back to being a pull hitter and hit .286 in '58." Which got Ol' Case more annoyed with his strong-minded third baseman.

"And," said Carey, "he used to always get on my ass because he knew if he got me mad I would play better. He continually made me mad. Stengel would play Martin at third base, Tony Kubek played over there, Jerry Lumpe played over there. Whatever Stengel could do to irritate me, he did."

Furthermore, Carey insisted, "I don't think Stengel was revered as much as a lot of people think. They put up with him because he was successful and you were in the World Series every year. I mean, how are you gonna argue with that?"

On the other hand, Skowron, nine years a Yankee, enjoyed playing for Stengel. "Casey used a lot of psychology on ballplayers, as far as giving them heck in the newspapers. And you'd read your name in the paper, and it'd motivate you to get out there the next day and prove him wrong.

"Casey was harder to play for when we won than when we lost. We'd win eight-nine games in a row, and he'd be on our ass all the time. But if we were losin', he'd go the other way—a little sympathy for the guys."

The Yankees didn't lose too often, though, because they played the game the right way, running the bases well and always, but always, moving the runners along by hitting behind them. "They all teach you that—man on second, nobody out, get him over," Skowron said. "You get two shots to shoot it out that way, toward right field. Then you're on your own. But Casey was always pushing us, 'Get that guy over.' And, bases loaded, score tied, try to get hit by a pitched ball. Casey'd give you $50 if you got hit in that situation. That check would be on your chair in the clubhouse after the ballgame. That's the way he operated. He wanted to win."

So did Lopez, Skowron's manager in Chicago for the first year and a half of the Moose's three-season stint with the White Sox. "Lopez hated to lose. A tough game, and we'd get beat by our own mistake, that's when he would get angry. A guy not taggin' up, a collision between the second baseman and right fielder, nobody callin' for it—that's when he'd get hot.

"Al's pet peeve was if a guy hit a flyball and didn't run. That's when he would get out of his seat and be on the dugout steps waiting for you. Like Floyd Robinson. Boy, Floyd would hit a flyball and he wouldn't run and the guy would drop the ball—and Floyd would still be at first base. Lopez would fine him $400, $500, on the spot. That was Lopez. As long as you gave 100 percent, you did your job. But if you loafed, he was on top of you."

Eddie Robinson was on top of the world both with the White Sox (1950-52) and with the Yankees (1954-56). In successive years with the Sox, he hit 21, 29, and 22 homers, drove in 86, 117, and 104 runs and hit .295, .282, and .296. After another big power year with the Philadelphia A's in 1953 (22 homers, 102 RBIs), he was traded, at age 34, to the Yankees and became Stengel's No. 1 pinch hitter. In '54, Casey sent him up 49 times, tops in the American League, and he responded with 15 pinch hits, also best in the league, for a .306 average, terrific for a pinch hitter. The next year, in just 173 total at-bats, he had 16 home runs among his 36 hits and drove in 42 runs. By the following June, however, Eddie, at 36, had been exiled to Kansas City.

"Really, my career started sliding when I left the White Sox. I loved the White Sox. I loved playing for the White Sox, and I loved playing for Paul Richards. When they traded me [to the A's for Ferris Fain], that was a stunning blow for me. I really didn't want to be traded, especially to a second-division team. I just loved playing for Richards, and it had nothing to do with us both being Texans. It's just that I respected him as a manager and I played well for him and felt he appreciated it."

"Robby" ended his playing career in 1957 with Baltimore, then managed by Richards. The two were together, also, in the building of the Houston organization and, later, in Atlanta.

"I always felt and I still feel that I know a lot of baseball that other people may not know simply because I had the privilege of being associated with him. He was a 'teaching' manager, and he wanted you to play the game right. The difference between him and Stengel was Stengel never taught you anything. He just ran you out there and expected you to play. Richards, of course, inherited a team that he had to make better. He had to get the most out of mediocre players, so he had to get them to do everything they could do to the best of their ability in order to win some games."

With the Yankees, Stengel never had such a problem. "They had good players, good talent," said Robinson. "As a Yankee, it didn't matter who we were gonna play. We felt like we were gonna win, whether it was the White Sox, the Red Sox, whoever. They had such a good feeling on that club. They really wanted to win, and they went out there and won. You never thought about losing when you were with the Yankees."

And you never thought about losing when you were with the White Sox, either, except when you were playing the Yankees.

Epilogue

Much has changed about the Yankees and White Sox since the events described in this book. The Yankees play in a completely remodeled Yankee Stadium and are talking about leaving the Bronx. The White Sox play in a totally new Comiskey Park across the street from their former home, which is now a parking lot. Casey Stengel, Al Lopez, and the rest have departed from the scene. Mickey Mantle, like Nellie Fox and Sherm Lollar before him, has lost his battle with cancer. The rivalry between these two clubs is gone, like so many of the participants.

And so much about baseball has changed, guaranteeing that this rivalry could never again exist. Baseball has 28 alleged major-league clubs, with two more set to join before the turn of the century. Where there were eight clubs in the American League in 1951 when our story began and 10 in 1964 when it ended, there are now 14. During the 1950s, there were 22 games each season between the Yankees and White Sox, 18 during the 1960s. Today, there are 12, and that number is likely to shrink when interleague play becomes a reality. It is difficult to maintain a rivalry in baseball when teams play each other only 12 times a year.

Expansion, too, has brought with it divisional play, and the Yankees and White Sox have been in different divisions since 1969. It is difficult to maintain a rivalry in baseball when the two would-be rivals are in different divisions, pursuing separate championships.

Finally, there is the matter of free agency. Seldom now do players spend lengthy periods of their career with one club. Players move from one club to another with such frequency that even fans who consider themselves avid have difficulty keeping track of who is with whom. Even in the days of Frantic Frank Lane, there was some semblance of continuity.

Here's an example: In 1954, you could have gone out to Comiskey Park or Yankee Stadium and seen Billy Pierce pitch against Whitey Ford. In the Yankee lineup would have been Mickey Mantle, Yogi Berra, Bill Skowron, and Gil McDougald. The Sox lineup would have had Nellie Fox, Sherm Lollar, Minnie Minoso, and Jim Rivera. If you had returned, say, six years later, you would have seen the same players in the same uniforms—and, quite possibly, another Pierce-Ford matchup. In '52, Mantle and Berra were in the Yankee lineup, Fox and Lollar in the Sox lineup. They were all still there in '62. Pierce was challenging Yankee hitters in '51 as well as '61; Ford was fooling Chicago batsmen in '53 and still doing so in '63.

Such things simply do not occur today. If the '50s could somehow be transported to the '90s, there would not be a Yankee dynasty, nor a pesky White Sox team to duel with it. Can't you just picture it? Mantle, with his business interests in Dallas and roots in northeastern Oklahoma beckoning, might sign a long-term deal with the Texas Rangers or Kansas City Royals when his chance at free agency arrived. Berra, a St. Louis native, quite likely would want to become a St. Louis Cardinal. McDougald, from the Bay Area, would leave New York to accept a big-bucks contract with the Oakland A's or San Francisco Giants. Hank Bauer, an East St. Louis, Illinois, native who has long lived in the Kansas City area, might yearn to be a Royal or a Cardinal.

On the White Sox side, Pierce, a Tiger fan as a youth in Detroit, would return to the Motor City to play for the team that originally signed him. Fox's former home in Chambersburg, Pennsylvania, was not far from either Pittsburgh or Baltimore. Imagine Nellie in an Oriole uniform at Camden Yards. And rest assured that Minoso, still a hero to Cuban Americans, would be playing left field in Miami for the Florida Marlins once he became a free agent.

One can continue on and on, but the point is clear. The White Sox-Yankee rivalry is dead and gone, as is the chance of its ever returning as it once was. Too much—baseball, the country, the world—has changed. It can never be the same.

And yet, with all the change, there is one thing that remains reassuringly unchanging. In the '50s and '60s, whenever the Yankees came to Chicago for big showdowns with the White Sox, the constant—in addition to big, noisy crowds and late-inning Yankee home runs—was rain. As this is being written, the White Sox are preparing to play host to the Yankees for a three-game series.

Sure enough, rain is in the forecast.

Appendix A
White Sox vs. Yankees
1951-1964

Year-by-Year, Game-by-Game

1951 Season

THE DATE: Tuesday, May 1
THE PLACE: Comiskey Park
THE CROWD: 14,776
THE STARTERS: Vic Raschi (NY), Bob Cain (Chi)
THE FINAL: Yankees 8, White Sox 3
THE WINNER: Raschi
THE LOSER: Ken Holcombe
THE KEYS: First black Chicago major-leaguer, Minnie Minoso, acquired one day earlier in three-way trade with Indians and A's, homers in first at-bat in Sox uniform; rookie Mickey Mantle, 19, hits first big-league homer, off Randy Gumpert; Yogi Berra hits his first '51 homer. Raschi now 12-2 lifetime vs. Sox.

THE DATE: Wednesday, May 2
THE PLACE: Comiskey Park
THE CROWD: 8,802
THE STARTERS: Frank Shea (NY), Dick Littlefield (Chi)
THE FINAL: Yankees 6, White Sox 4
THE WINNER: Joe Ostrowski
THE LOSER: Harry Dorish
THE KEYS: Sox blow 4-0 first-inning lead; Joe Collins' triple off wall in right-center breaks tie in ninth.

THE DATE: Friday, May 18
THE PLACE: Yankee Stadium
THE CROWD: 7,353
THE STARTERS: Billy Pierce (Chi), Frank Shea (NY)
THE FINAL: White Sox 7, Yankees 4
THE WINNER: Pierce
THE LOSER: Shea
THE KEYS: Former Yankee Eddie Stewart's grand slam in the eighth snaps 3-3 tie in first game of 11-game road trip, on which Sox go 11-0 to sweep into first place.

THE DATE: Friday night, June 8
THE PLACE: Comiskey Park
THE CROWD: 53,940
THE STARTERS: Vic Raschi (NY), Ken Holcombe (Chi)

THE FINAL: Yankees 4, White Sox 2
THE WINNER: Raschi
THE LOSER: Holcombe
THE KEYS: Eddie Robinson's 11th homer gives Sox quick 2-0 lead before record all-time Comiskey Park night-game crowd, but Yankees break 2-2 tie in fifth on RBI singles by Gene Woodling and Bobby Brown and cool off Chicagoans, who had entered 32-11 with 4 1/2-game lead.

THE DATE: Saturday, June 9
THE PLACE: Comiskey Park
THE CROWD: 24,726
THE STARTERS: Frank Shea (NY), Billy Pierce (Chi)
THE FINAL: Yankees 10, White Sox 5
THE WINNER: Tommy Byrne
THE LOSER: Pierce
THE KEYS: Jerry Coleman and rookie Gil McDougald each drive in two runs and Phil Rizzuto collects three hits as Pierce (7-3) is stopped in his bid for sixth straight victory.

THE DATE: Sunday, June 10
THE PLACE: Comiskey Park
THE CROWD: 52,054
THE STARTERS (1st): Eddie Lopat (NY), Saul Rogovin (Chi)
THE STARTERS (2nd): Allie Reynolds (NY), Joe Dobson (Chi)
THE FINALS: Yankees 2, White Sox 1; White Sox 11, Yankees 7
THE WINNER (1st): Lopat
THE LOSER (1st): Rogovin
THE WINNER (2nd): Randy Gumpert
THE LOSER (2nd): Joe Ostrowski
THE KEYS: Gene Woodling's eighth-inning sacrifice fly is the difference as Lopat improves to 9-1; Eddie Robinson, with score 7-7 in the seventh of Game 2, singles for go-ahead run, and Don Lenhardt follows with RBI double and rookie Jim Busby a two-run single.

THE DATE: Tuesday, June 19
THE PLACE: Yankee Stadium
THE CROWD: 60,441
THE STARTERS (1st): Marv Rotblatt (Chi), Stubby Overmire (NY)
THE STARTERS (2nd): Joe Dobson (Chi), Vic Raschi (NY)
THE FINALS: Yankees 11, White Sox 9; White Sox 5, Yankees 4
THE WINNER (1st): Joe Ostrowski
THE LOSER (1st): Lou Kretlow
THE WINNER (2nd): Randy Gumpert
THE LOSER (2nd): Raschi
THE KEYS: Joe DiMaggio misses entire series to attend mother's funeral in San Francisco; Mickey Mantle goes 3 for 4 with three-run homer in opener of afternoon twin bill, but Bob Dillinger's pinch double off Allie Reynolds in ninth of Game 2 scores Jim Busby with tie-breaking run to enable Sox to maintain 3 1/2-game lead.

THE DATE: Wednesday, June 20
THE PLACE: Yankee Stadium
THE CROWD: 21,020
THE STARTERS: Billy Pierce (Chi), Eddie Lopat (NY)

Appendix A

THE FINAL: Yankees 2, White Sox 1
THE WINNER: Lopat
THE LOSER: Pierce
THE KEYS: Hank Bauer singles home Mickey Mantle to break 1-1 eighth-inning tie as Lopat cools off red-hot Sox hitters like Minnie Minoso (AL-leading .370) and Nellie Fox (third at .344).

THE DATE: Thursday, June 21
THE PLACE: Yankee Stadium
THE CROWD: 30,670
THE STARTERS: Saul Rogovin (Chi), Frank Shea (NY)
THE FINAL: White Sox 5, Yankees 2
THE WINNER: Rogovin
THE LOSER: Shea
THE KEYS: With Gen. Douglas MacArthur and his wife on hand, Rogovin allows two home runs to Johnny Mize but only two other hits to record one of his 17 complete games this season. Eddie Robinson hits No. 13 for Chicago off Bob Kuzava, former Sox lefty.

THE DATE: Tuesday night, July 17
THE PLACE: Comiskey Park
THE CROWD: 45,580
THE STARTERS: Allie Reynolds (NY), Saul Rogovin (Chi)
THE FINAL: White Sox 4, Yankees 3 (10 innings)
THE WINNER: Rogovin
THE LOSER: Stubby Overmire
THE KEYS: See "Most Glorious Victory"

THE DATE: Wednesday, July 18
THE PLACE: Comiskey Park
THE CROWD: 36,713
THE STARTERS: Vic Raschi (NY), Billy Pierce (Chi)
THE FINAL: Yankees 5, White Sox 1
THE WINNER: Raschi
THE LOSER: Pierce
THE KEYS: Raschi singles in go-ahead run in the seventh, and Johnny Mize adds two-run homer in the eighth off Marv Rotblatt before largest weekday crowd, to date, in Comiskey Park history. Sox's Chico Carrasquel has his AL shortstop record string of 297 consecutive errorless chances snapped when he boots Gene Woodling's first-inning grounder. Sox get 11 hits, one a homer by Minnie Minoso.

THE DATE: Thursday, July 19
THE PLACE: Comiskey Park
THE CROWD: 34,297
THE STARTERS: Eddie Lopat (NY), Howie Judson (Chi)
THE FINAL: White Sox 2, Yankees 1
THE WINNER: Judson
THE LOSER: Lopat
THE KEYS: Bob Dillinger (sacrifice fly) and Nellie Fox (bloop double) drive in the Chicago runs and Billy Pierce, who had worked seven innings the day before, enters in the ninth and saves the win for Judson (4-2). Sox now .003 behind AL-leading Boston, the Yankees and Indians 1½ games out.

THE DATE: Friday night, July 27
THE PLACE: Yankee Stadium
THE CROWD: 50,125
THE STARTERS: Billy Pierce (Chi), Tom Morgan (NY)
THE FINAL: Yankees 3, White Sox 1
THE WINNER: Morgan
THE LOSER: Pierce
THE KEYS: See "Most Devastating Defeat"

THE DATE: Sunday, July 29
THE PLACE: Yankee Stadium
THE CROWD: 70,972
THE STARTERS (1st): Lou Kretlow (Chi), Vic Raschi (NY)
THE STARTERS (2nd): Saul Rogovin (Chi), Bob Kuzava (NY)
THE FINALS: Yankees 8, White Sox 3; Yankees 2, White Sox 0
THE WINNER (1st): Raschi
THE LOSER (1st): Kretlow
THE WINNER (2nd): Kuzava
THE LOSER (2nd): Rogovin
THE KEYS: Joe DiMaggio hits game-tying two-run homer in first inning of Game 1 and adds a three-run blast five innings later to help boost Raschi's record to 15-6. Kuzava throws five-hitter in Game 2 and strikes out nine as Chicago falls 61/2 games behind first-place Yankees.

THE DATE: Sunday, August 26
THE PLACE: Comiskey Park
THE CROWD: 43,593
THE STARTERS (1st): Tom Morgan (NY), Saul Rogovin (Chi)
THE STARTERS (2nd): Art Schallock (NY), Billy Pierce (Chi)
THE FINALS: White Sox 3, Yankees 2; Yankees 8, White Sox 6
THE WINNER (1st): Rogovin
THE LOSER (1st): Kuzava
THE WINNER (2nd): Schallock
THE LOSER (2nd): Pierce
THE KEYS: Joe DiMaggio's final home run in Chicago has New York ahead 2-1 in the eighth inning before Eddie Robinson's 22nd homer of the year ties it and, in the ninth, Nellie Fox's two-out double wins it. In Game 2, six unearned runs enable Yankees to build 8-1 lead after 61/2 before two-run pinch home run by Bert Haas and two-run homer by Don Lenhardt help make things close. Allie Reynolds escapes two-on, one-out jam in ninth to earn a save.

THE DATE: Tuesday night, September 18
THE PLACE: Yankee Stadium
THE CROWD: 44,214
THE STARTERS: Billy Pierce (Chi), Vic Raschi (NY)
THE FINAL: White Sox 7, Yankees 1
THE WINNER: Pierce
THE LOSER: Raschi
THE KEYS: Eddie Stewart's fifth homer of the year, fourth at Yankee Stadium, third off Raschi, is Sox's lone run until the eighth, when Chicago scores six runs to bust 1-1 tie. Highlights: bases-loaded, two-run singles by Stewart and Nellie Fox. Loss leaves Yankees in first-place tie with Cleveland.

THE DATE: Wednesday, September 19

THE PLACE: Yankee Stadium
THE CROWD: 12,127
THE STARTERS: Lou Kretlow (Chi), Tom Morgan (NY)
THE FINAL: Yankees 5, White Sox 3
THE WINNER: Bob Kuzava
THE LOSER: Kretlow
THE KEYS: With score tied 2-2 and two out in the fourth, Kretlow walks Phil Rizzuto and Kuzava, a lifetime .086 hitter, before giving up a three-run homer to Mickey Mantle. Chicago's final run comes on catcher Gus Niarhos' one and only career homer (691 career at-bats).

THE DATE: Thursday, September 20
THE PLACE: Yankee Stadium
THE CROWD: 13,712
THE STARTERS: Saul Rogovin (Chi), Johnny Sain (NY)
THE FINAL: Yankees 5, White Sox 4
THE WINNER: Bob Hogue
THE LOSER: Rogovin
THE KEYS: Joe Collins (14 for 29 vs. Chicago pitching in '51) hits three-run homer in the eighth over the 344-foot sign in right to win game for Yankees, who entered with .003 lead over Cleveland with 10 games left.

1952 Season

THE DATE: Sunday, May 4
THE PLACE: Yankee Stadium
THE CROWD: 44,628
THE STARTERS (1st): Marv Grissom (Chi), Tom Morgan (NY)
THE STARTERS (2nd): Billy Pierce (Chi), Bill Miller (NY)
THE FINALS: Yankees 8, White Sox 0; Yankees 3, White Sox 1
THE WINNER (1st): Morgan
THE LOSER (1st): Grissom
THE WINNER (2nd): Miller
THE LOSER (2nd): Pierce
THE KEYS: Nine men bat in New York's four-run first in the opener (Joe Collins' two-run, two-out triple is the big blow) and Morgan goes on to post Yankees' first shutout of '52. In Game 2, newcomer Sam Mele, acquired from Washington for Jim Busby the evening before (Yankees get Irv Noren from Senators the same day for Jackie Jensen), scores Chicago's only run of the afternoon, while Sam Dente grounds into a double play in the seventh inning. It's Miller's first big-league victory and complete game. The Sox fall to 7-10 and sixth place.

THE DATE: Tuesday night, May 20
THE PLACE: Comiskey Park
THE CROWD: 33,294
THE STARTERS: Johnny Sain (NY), Ken Holcombe (Chi)
THE FINAL: Yankees 4, White Sox 3
THE WINNER: Sain
THE LOSER: Holcombe
THE KEYS: Mickey Mantle goes 4 for 5 with an RBI and Sain helps his own cause with an RBI single.

THE DATE: Wednesday, May 21
THE PLACE: Comiskey Park

THE CROWD: 7,841
THE STARTERS: Allie Reynolds (NY), Billy Pierce (Chi)
THE FINAL: Yankees 5, White Sox 1
THE WINNER: Reynolds
THE LOSER: Pierce
THE KEYS: With Chicago up 1-0 after six on Sam Mele's homer, Yankees score four in seventh on Reynolds' RBI triple (Mele's shoestring try comes up short), Phil Rizzuto's two-out infield hit and Yogi Berra's two-run single—his third hit off Pierce this day.

THE DATE: Tuesday night, June 3
THE PLACE: Yankee Stadium
THE CROWD: 32,125
THE STARTERS: Billy Pierce (Chi), Vic Raschi (NY)
THE FINAL: Yankees 4, White Sox 3 (13 innings)
THE WINNER: Bob Hogue
THE LOSER: Pierce
THE KEYS: Pierce goes route, allowing one hit from the fourth through the 12th, before Yankees load bases with two out in the 13th and the game tied at 3-3. Johnny Sain pinch-hits for Joe Collins and when Minnie Minoso slips and falls to the turf in pursuit of Sain's drive to left, the ball drops for the game-winning hit.

THE DATE: Wednesday, June 4
THE PLACE: Yankee Stadium
THE CROWD: 10,488
THE STARTERS: Joe Dobson (Chi), Eddie Lopat (NY)
THE FINAL: Yankees 6, White Sox 3
THE WINNER: Lopat
THE LOSER: Dobson
THE KEYS: Nellie Fox's own batting-practice foul tip hits him above the left eye, forcing him to miss rest of series and Willie Miranda into the lineup in his place. Back-to-back home runs by Sherm Lollar and Ray Coleman put Sox ahead 2-0 in the second, but Yankees go ahead in third 4-2 on Yogi Berra's two-run homer and add two more runs in the sixth. Dobson is chased in that inning, as is manager Paul Richards and fellow umpire-baiter Saul Rogovin (for questioning plate ump Bill McKinley's calls). Minnie Minoso's 0 for 4 drops him to .239.

THE DATE: Thursday, June 5
THE PLACE: Yankee Stadium
THE CROWD: 8,699
THE STARTERS: Saul Rogovin (Chi), Johnny Sain (NY)
THE FINAL: Yankees 6, White Sox 4
THE WINNER: Sain
THE LOSER: Rogovin
THE KEYS: Chico Carrasquel's first 1952 homer gives Chicago 4-3 lead in the fourth, but Sain's two-run single puts New York on top in the fifth. Yanks now 1 1/2 games out of first, sixth-place Sox (22-24) 1 1/2 out of seventh.

THE DATE: Friday night, June 20
THE PLACE: Comiskey Park
THE CROWD: 39,444
THE STARTERS: Vic Raschi (NY), Saul Rogovin (Chi)
THE FINAL: White Sox 8, Yankees 5 (11 innings)

THE WINNER: Harry Dorish
THE LOSER: Bob Hogue
THE KEYS: See "Most Glorious Victory"

THE DATE: Saturday, June 21
THE PLACE: Comiskey Park
THE CROWD: 17,019
THE STARTERS: Eddie Lopat (NY), Chuck Stobbs (Chi)
THE FINAL: White Sox 5, Yankees 1
THE WINNER: Stobbs
THE LOSER: Lopat
THE KEYS: Third baseman Leo Thomas, acquired in June 15 deal with St. Louis Browns, delivers bases-loaded, two-run single in fourth, and when Mickey Mantle overruns the ball in center, Sherm Lollar scores all the way from first for 3-0 White Sox lead. Eddie Stewart follows with squeeze bunt to score Thomas, who collects only three more hits in a Sox uniform and, after '52, never plays in the major leagues.

THE DATE: Sunday, June 22
THE PLACE: Comiskey Park
THE CROWD: 47,970
THE STARTERS (1st): Bob Kuzava (NY), Billy Pierce (Chi)
THE STARTERS (2nd): Marv Grissom (Chi), Bill Miller (NY)
THE FINALS: Yankees 3, White Sox 0; White Sox 2, Yankees 1
THE WINNER (1st): Kuzava
THE LOSER (1st): Pierce
THE WINNER (2nd): Grissom
THE LOSER (2nd): Miller
THE KEYS: Yogi Berra's two-run homer snaps 0-0 tie in seventh of Game 1, in which Kuzava allows just two Chicago hits; in Game 2, Sherm Lollar's RBI double in eighth puts Sox ahead 2-1, and Grissom, a 34-year-old righthander plucked from Pacific Coast League over the winter, hangs on to lead by retiring pinch-hitter Johnny Mize on a hot smash to first baseman Eddie Robinson with runners at first and third to end the game. Grissom's fifth straight win leaves Sox two games behind first-place Yanks.

THE DATE: Friday, July 18
THE PLACE: Yankee Stadium
THE CROWD: 7,618
THE STARTERS: Chuck Stobbs (Chi),Tom Gorman (NY)
THE FINAL: Yankees 6, White Sox 3
THE WINNER: Gorman
THE LOSER: Stobbs
THE KEYS: Hank Bauer hits three-run homer in third inning, Gene Woodling a two-run shot in fourth as White Sox drop fifth in a row.

THE DATE: Saturday, July 19
THE PLACE: Yankee Stadium
THE CROWD: 20,854 (15,397 paid)
THE STARTERS: Billy Pierce (Chi), Tom Morgan (NY)
THE FINAL: Yankees 4, White Sox 2
THE WINNER: Morgan
THE LOSER: Pierce
THE KEYS: Misplays in left field by Ray Coleman (Minnie Minoso is in center

as Sox continue searching for replacement for traded Jim Busby) help Yankees to a pair of gift runs; seldom-used Charlie Silvera chips in sacrifice fly and RBI single. Nine days later, Coleman is banished to the Browns.

THE DATE: Sunday, July 20
THE PLACE: Yankee Stadium
THE CROWD: 26,051
THE STARTERS: Saul Rogovin (Chi), Bob Kuzava (NY)
THE FINAL: White Sox 5, Yankees 4
THE WINNER: Rogovin
THE LOSER: Kuzava
THE KEYS: Before the game, Rogovin, a native New Yorker, is honored by his neighbors with several gifts, including a new car, presented to him by New York Mayor Vincent Impellitteri. Sox then present Rogovin with a solo homer (No.16) by Eddie Robinson and a two-run blast by Sherm Lollar to forge 5-1 lead after 7 1/2. Harry Dorish rescues Sox in eighth, escaping two-on, one-out jam, then retires Yankees in order in ninth.

THE DATE: Tuesday night, July 29
THE PLACE: Comiskey Park
THE CROWD: 38,967
THE STARTERS: Jim McDonald (NY), Billy Pierce (Chi)
THE FINAL: Yankees 10, White Sox 7
THE WINNER: Joe Ostrowski
THE LOSER: Chuck Stobbs
THE KEYS: See "Most Devastating Defeat"

THE DATE: Wednesday, July 30
THE PLACE: Comiskey Park
THE CROWD: 15,103
THE STARTERS: Bob Kuzava (NY), Lou Kretlow (Chi)
THE FINAL: White Sox 7, Yankees 0
THE WINNER: Kretlow
THE LOSER: Kuzava
THE KEYS: Kretlow wrecks Casey Stengel's 61st birthday by firing two-hitter, striking out six and walking four; Jim Rivera, acquired from Browns two days before, hits two-run homer and swipes first of 146 bases he will steal in a Sox uniform.

THE DATE: Thursday night, July 31
THE PLACE: Comiskey Park
THE CROWD: 34,548
THE STARTERS: Vic Raschi (NY), Saul Rogovin (Chi)
THE FINAL: Yankees 6, White Sox 2
THE WINNER: Raschi
THE LOSER: Rogovin
THE KEYS: Raschi (12-2) blanks Sox after third inning on one hit—a ninth-inning double by Hector Rodriguez—while Yankees get three hits and three RBIs from Gene Woodling and three hits from Gil McDougald.

THE DATE: Tuesday night, August 19
THE PLACE: Yankee Stadium
THE CROWD: 34,166
THE STARTERS: Marv Grissom (Chi), Johnny Schmitz (NY)

THE FINAL: White Sox 3, Yankees 1
THE WINNER: Grissom
THE LOSER: Schmitz
THE KEYS: Former Cub lefty Schmitz, picked up on waivers from Brooklyn Aug. 1, is KOd in three-run Chicago first featuring RBI singles by Minnie Minoso and Eddie Robinson and Sam Mele's sacrifice fly. Grissom goes the distance, annoyed only by Yogi Berra's 25th homer. Chico Carrasquel back in lineup after missing eight weeks (broken finger).

THE DATE: Wednesday, Aug. 20
THE PLACE: Yankee Stadium
THE CROWD: 14,456
THE STARTERS: Saul Rogovin (Chi), Johnny Sain (NY)
THE FINAL: White Sox 12, Yankees 3
THE WINNER: Rogovin
THE LOSER: Sain
THE KEYS: Six-run Chicago third, in which Hector Rodriguez singles twice and Rogovin helps own cause with RBI single, is biggest against New York all season. Rogovin's five-hitter cuts Yanks' lead over Cleveland to one game.

THE DATE: Thursday, August 21
THE PLACE: Yankee Stadium
THE CROWD: 11,238
THE STARTERS: Billy Pierce (Chi), Tom Gorman (NY)
THE FINAL: White Sox 6, Yankees 1
THE WINNER: Pierce
THE LOSER: Gorman
THE KEYS: Pierce, who enters 12-3 vs. rest of league but 0-5 vs. New York, throws five-hitter as Sox complete series sweep. Gorman's bad throw to third on Minnie Minoso's sacrifice bunt attempt enables two runs to score in three-run Chicago first.

THE DATE: Friday night, September 12
THE PLACE: Comiskey Park
THE CROWD: 40,137
THE STARTERS: Tom Gorman (NY), Hector "Skinny" Brown (Chi)
THE FINAL: Yankees 6, White Sox 4
THE WINNER: Ray Scarborough
THE LOSER: Bill Kennedy
THE KEYS: Billy Martin's two-run homer in the fourth breaks 3-3 tie, and sidearmer Ewell Blackwell blanks the White Sox over the final three innings as Yankees remain a half-game ahead of Cleveland.

THE DATE: Saturday, September 13
THE PLACE: Comiskey Park
THE CROWD: 25,542
THE STARTERS: Vic Raschi (NY), Marv Grissom (Chi)
THE FINAL: Yankees 6, White Sox 5
THE WINNER: Raschi
THE LOSER: Grissom
THE KEYS: Sam Mele's 16th homer of '52, a two-run shot, ties game 3-3 before Irv Noren's RBI double in fifth puts Yankees up for good. Grissom fans 13 but allows 13 hits in eight innings. Sox rally for runs in eighth and ninth before Allie Reynolds enters to save Raschi's 16th victory against five losses.

1953 Season

THE DATE: Thursday, April 30
THE PLACE: Comiskey Park
THE CROWD: 7,656
THE STARTERS: Whitey Ford (NY), Gene Bearden (Chi)
THE FINAL: Yankees 6, White Sox 1
THE WINNER: Ford
THE LOSER: Bearden
THE KEYS: Solo homers off Bearden by Mickey Mantle and rookie Bill Renna plus a three-run ninth against Harry Dorish (bases-loaded, two-run single by Phil Rizzuto puts things out of reach) make it easy for young lefty Ford, fresh out of the Army.

THE DATE: Friday night, May 1
THE PLACE: Comiskey Park
THE CROWD: 23,901
THE STARTERS: Johnny Sain (NY), Billy Pierce (Chi)
THE FINAL: White Sox 6, Yankees 5
THE WINNER: Pierce
THE LOSER: Sain
THE KEYS: Nellie Fox gets a triple and double, Sherm Lollar homers and Jim Rivera steals two bases and scores twice as Sox build 5-1 for Pierce after six. But the real hero on this rainy night is Saul Rogovin, who relieves with the bases loaded and one out in the ninth and strikes out Yogi Berra and retires Billy Martin on a flyball to Sam Mele in right.

THE DATE: Saturday, May 2
THE PLACE: Comiskey Park
THE CROWD: 11,907
THE STARTERS: Eddie Lopat (NY), Tommy Byrne (Chi)
THE FINAL: White Sox 8, Yankees 7
THE WINNER: Earl Harrist
THE LOSER: Ray Scarborough
THE KEYS: Ex-Yankee Byrne is KOd in a four-run second and Sox trail 6-1 after 61/2 before their comeback begins. Down 7-4 in the ninth, Sox tie it on Ferris Fain's three-run homer off lefty Johnny Schmitz, then win it when, after walks to Minnie Minoso and Sam Mele, Billy Martin throws double-play relay into first-base dugout, allowing Minnie to score from second. Yankees are now 11-5, Chicago 10-6.

THE DATE: Thursday, May 14
THE PLACE: Yankee Stadium
THE CROWD: 8,516
THE STARTERS: Tommy Byrne (Chi), Johnny Sain (NY)
THE FINAL: White Sox 7, Yankees 5
THE WINNER: Harry Dorish
THE LOSER: Tom Gorman
THE KEYS: Down 4-1 in the seventh, White Sox get RBI single from Vern Stephens and 420-foot, three-run homer from Sherm Lollar off Sain to go up 5-4 before Don Bollweg's pinch homer ties game in eighth. But Sam Mele and Nellie Fox single a run home apiece in the visitors' ninth.

THE DATE: Saturday, May 16

THE PLACE: Yankee Stadium
THE CROWD: 24,966
THE STARTERS: Billy Pierce (Chi), Vic Raschi (NY)
THE FINAL: White Sox 5, Yankees 3
THE WINNER: Luis Aloma
THE LOSER: Raschi
THE KEYS: See "Most Glorious Victory"

THE DATE: Tuesday night, June 2
THE PLACE: Comiskey Park
THE CROWD: 46,428
THE STARTERS: Eddie Lopat (NY), Mike Fornieles (Chi)
THE FINAL: Yankees 4, White Sox 3
THE WINNER: Lopat
THE LOSER: Harry Dorish
THE KEYS: Sam Mele's RBI double scores Minnie Minoso with the tying run in the eighth, but Joe Collins' second homer of the night breaks up the ballgame in the ninth.

THE DATE: Wednesday, June 3
THE PLACE: Comiskey Park
THE CROWD: 14,032
THE STARTERS: Whitey Ford (NY), Bob Keegan (Chi)
THE FINAL: Yankees 18, White Sox 2
THE WINNER: Ford
THE LOSER: Keegan
THE KEYS: Ford improves to 5-0 on the year as Yankees total 19 hits off 30-year-old rookie Keegan, Joe Dobson, newcomer Sandy Consuegra, and Lou Kretlow. Joe Collins gets four hits, Mickey Mantle four RBIs and Irv Noren the game's lone homer as Yanks continue on winning streak that eventually will reach 18.

THE DATE: Thursday, June 4
THE PLACE: Comiskey Park
THE CROWD: 10,011
THE STARTERS: Vic Raschi (NY), Billy Pierce (Chi)
THE FINAL: Yankees 9, White Sox 5 (10 innings)
THE WINNER: Allie Reynolds
THE LOSER: Gene Bearden
THE KEYS: Mickey Mantle's three-run homer into the centerfield bullpen helps stake New York to 5-3 lead before Sox gain 5-5 tie in eighth, tying run scoring on Bearden's pinch single off Reynolds. Gil McDougald's two-run upper-deck homer off Bearden highlights four-run Yankee 10th. New York leads third-place White Sox by 7 1/2 games.

THE DATE: Tuesday night, June 23
THE PLACE: Yankee Stadium
THE CROWD: 46,756
THE STARTERS: Virgil Trucks (Chi), Allie Reynolds (NY)
THE FINAL: White Sox 11, Yankees 3
THE WINNER: Trucks
THE LOSER: Reynolds
THE KEYS: Nellie Fox triples in two teammates in a six-run fifth and does so again during a three-run sixth and Eddie Stewart collects three straight hits as

Trucks, acquired 10 days earlier from the St. Louis Browns, coasts to the first of 47 wins he'll amass in a Chicago uniform from '53 through '55.

THE DATE: Wednesday, June 24
THE PLACE: Yankee Stadium
THE CROWD: 14,621
THE STARTERS: Saul Rogovin (Chi), Jim McDonald (NY)
THE FINAL: White Sox 8, Yankees 4
THE WINNER: Rogovin
THE LOSER: McDonald
THE KEYS: Sam Mele, pinch-hitting for lefty-hitting cleanup man Eddie Stewart in first inning after McDonald walks first three hitters, singles for a run off lefty reliever Bob Kuzava before recent addition Bob Elliott, 36, triples to 457-foot sign in left-center to clear the bases. Red Wilson then singles to cap five-run first. Minnie Minoso's two-run homer extends his hitting streak to 16 games.

THE DATE: Thursday, June 25
THE PLACE: Yankee Stadium
THE CROWD: 12,670
THE STARTERS: Billy Pierce (Chi), Johnny Sain (NY)
THE FINAL: White Sox 4, Yankees 2
THE WINNER: Pierce
THE LOSER: Sain
THE KEYS: Pierce improves to 9-3 and even plays first base (so Harry Dorish can pitch to two righthanded hitters, Hank Bauer and Gil McDougald, to start the ninth) before returning to the mound to close out the victory by retiring Johnny Mize and striking out pinch-hitter Bill Renna. Pierce is one of a record five first basemen used by manager Paul Richards this day. The others: Ferris Fain (ejected), Sherm Lollar, Freddie Marsh, and Sam Mele. Sox sweep series—and win ninth straight at Yankee Stadium—but still trail Yankees by 91/2.

THE DATE: Sunday, July 19
THE PLACE: Comiskey Park
THE CROWD: 54,215
THE STARTERS (1st): Eddie Lopat (NY), Mike Fornieles (Chi)
THE STARTERS (2nd): Vic Raschi (NY), Billy Pierce (Chi)
THE FINALS: Yankees 6, White Sox 2; Yankees 3, White Sox 0
THE WINNER (1st): Lopat
THE LOSER (1st): Fornieles
THE WINNER (2nd): Raschi
THE LOSER (2nd): Pierce
THE KEYS: Yankees, before record Comiskey Park crowd, cool off Sox, who had won 25 of 31, including their last eight in a row, and had crept to within four games of the lead. New York breaks 2-2 tie in ninth inning of opener on Mickey Mantle's two-out, two-run double; in Game 2, Raschi allows only two hits and stops Sam Mele's hitting streak at 22 games to beat Pierce, who allows Hank Bauer's solo homer in the second and nothing more until two unearned runs in the eighth.

THE DATE: Friday, August 7
THE PLACE: Yankee Stadium
THE CROWD: 27,063
THE STARTERS: Connie Johnson (Chi), Eddie Lopat (NY)
THE FINAL: Yankees 6, White Sox 1

THE WINNER: Lopat
THE LOSER: Johnson
THE KEYS: Sox, 11-2 on road trip and five games out, fall behind 4-1 in the third on Mickey Mantle's three-run, inside-the-park homer and Yogi Berra's solo shot, both off Johnson, a 1-0 winner six days before at Washington. Billy Martin later adds two-run homer off Mike Fornieles.

THE DATE: Saturday, August 8
THE PLACE: Yankee Stadium
THE CROWD: 68,529
THE STARTERS (1st): Sandy Consuegra (Chi), Whitey Ford (NY)
THE STARTERS (2nd): Virgil Trucks (Chi), Bob Kuzava (NY)
THE FINALS: Yankees 1, White Sox 0; Yankees 3, White Sox 0
THE WINNER (1st): Ford
THE LOSER (1st): Consuegra
THE WINNER (2nd): Kuzava
THE LOSER (2nd): Trucks
THE KEYS: See "Most Devastating Defeat"

THE DATE: Sunday, August 9
THE PLACE: Yankee Stadium
THE CROWD: 42,504
THE STARTERS: Billy Pierce (Chi), Vic Raschi (NY)
THE FINAL: White Sox 5, Yankees 0
THE WINNER: Pierce
THE LOSER: Raschi
THE KEYS: Bob Boyd (7 for 13 in series) leads off game with line drive into left-field seats for his first major-league homer and later singles in a run; Pierce(15-7) throws three-hitter, strikes out eight, gets his fifth shutout of '53 and lowers ERA to 2.39. Sox trail by 7 games.

THE DATE: Sunday, August 30
THE PLACE: Comiskey Park
THE CROWD: 35,097
THE STARTERS (1st): Vic Raschi (NY), Sandy Consuegra (Chi)
THE STARTERS (2nd): Jim McDonald (NY), Billy Pierce (Chi)
THE FINALS: Yankees 10, White Sox 6; White Sox 1, Yankees 0
THE WINNER (1st): Raschi
THE LOSER (1st): Fornieles
THE WINNER (2nd): Pierce
THE LOSER (2nd): McDonald
THE KEYS: In 98-degree heat, Sox split to stay 8 1/2 behind New York (86-43); Consuegra (back spasms) departs after one batter and Yankees pound lumps on Gene Bearden, Mike Fornieles and, in particular, Luis Aloma, who allows home runs to Gil McDougald, Joe Collins, and Yogi Berra in the third. In Game 2, Pierce scores his seventh shutout, a four-hitter, and takes the big-league strikeout lead over the Phillies' Robin Roberts, 161-160. Billy gets Mickey Mantle to pop to Chico Carrasquel with two on to end it.

THE DATE: Tuesday night, September 1
THE PLACE: Comiskey Park
THE CROWD: 45,003
THE STARTERS: Whitey Ford (NY), Virgil Trucks (Chi)
THE FINAL: Yankees 3, White Sox 2

THE WINNER: Ford
THE LOSER: Trucks
THE KEYS: Mickey Mantle homers in seventh to extend Ford's lead to 3-1, and Sox manage only one run from a bases-loaded, no-out opportunity in their half. Ford, with relief help from Johnny Sain, improves to 16-5, 4-0 vs. Sox. Trucks falls to 18-7, 13-3 with Chicago.

THE DATE: Wednesday night, September 9
THE PLACE: Yankee Stadium
THE CROWD: 34,691
THE STARTERS: Billy Pierce (Chi), Whitey Ford (NY)
THE FINAL: Yankees 9, White Sox 3
THE WINNER: Ford
THE LOSER: Pierce
THE KEYS: Pierce extends scoreless-innings streak vs. New York to $23\frac{1}{3}$ before Yanks get seven runs in the fifth, highlighted by Hank Bauer's bases-loaded double and Mickey Mantle's two-run homer. Paul Richards is ejected for seventh time in '53, fifth in games with NY.

THE DATE: Thursday, September 10
THE PLACE: Yankee Stadium
THE CROWD: 14,656
THE STARTERS: Sandy Consuegra (Chi), Eddie Lopat (NY)
THE FINAL: Yankees 1, White Sox 0
THE WINNER: Lopat
THE LOSER: Consuegra
THE KEYS: In Yankees' second, Gene Woodling slices a home run to left field, just inside the foul pole at the 301 sign, and Lopat ups his record to 15-3. Consuegra, finishing with six-hitter, loses 1-0 for the second straight time at Yankee Stadium.

1954 Season

THE DATE: Tuesday, April 27
THE PLACE: Yankee Stadium
THE CROWD: 4,461
THE STARTERS: Don Johnson (Chi), Whitey Ford (NY)
THE FINAL: White Sox 4, Yankees 3
THE WINNER: Johnson
THE LOSER: Ford
THE KEYS: Two-run single by Johnny Groth in the fourth and Minnie Minoso's two-run homer in the fifth lift ex-Yankee Johnson to the victory on a cold, drizzly day. Harry Dorish gets Bob Cerv to ground out to Ferris Fain with two runners on to end game and hand Ford his first career loss to the White Sox after seven wins.

THE DATE: Thursday, April 29
THE PLACE: Yankee Stadium
THE CROWD: 9,943
THE STARTERS: Billy Pierce (Chi), Eddie Lopat (NY)
THE FINAL: Yankees 5, White Sox 4
THE WINNER: Lopat
THE LOSER: Pierce
THE KEYS: Johnny Groth's two-run homer to right gives Sox a 4-3 lead in the

fourth, but pinch RBI singles by ex-Cardinal star Enos Slaughter and former Sox first baseman Eddie Robinson account for the tying and go-ahead runs in the Yankee sixth. Allie Reynolds allows no hits and one walk over final three innings for the save.

THE DATE: Tuesday night, May 18
THE PLACE: Comiskey Park
THE CROWD: 37,158
THE STARTERS: Tom Morgan (NY), Virgil Trucks (Chi)
THE FINAL: Yankees 4, White Sox 3
THE WINNER: Johnny Sain
THE LOSER: Don Johnson
THE KEYS: Ferris Fain's homer and RBI single have Sox ahead 3-1 before Gene Woodling ties game with two-run homer off Trucks in eighth and Yogi Berra wins it with two-out RBI single off Johnson in ninth.

THE DATE: Wednesday, May 19
THE PLACE: Comiskey Park
THE CROWD: 18,942
THE STARTERS: Eddie Lopat (NY), Billy Pierce (Chi)
THE FINAL: Yankees 3, White Sox 2
THE WINNER: Lopat
THE LOSER: Pierce
THE KEYS: Pierce's four-hit shutout and 2-0 lead evaporate in the eighth when Yankees tie with RBI singles by Phil Rizzuto and Yogi Berra; Yanks then win in ninth when, with one out, Enos Slaughter beats Nellie Fox's double-play relay, scoring Gil McDougald from third.

THE DATE: Friday night, June 11
THE PLACE: Yankee Stadium
THE CROWD: 44,445
THE STARTERS: Don Johnson (Chi), Allie Reynolds (NY)
THE FINAL: Yankees 3, White Sox 2
THE WINNER: Reynolds
THE LOSER: Mike Fornieles
THE KEYS: Sox, having won seven in a row, enter action $1\frac{1}{2}$ games up on Cleveland and four on New York, but Irv Noren's RBI single, only hit off Fornieles in $3\frac{2}{3}$ innings of relief, scores Phil Rizzuto with the game-winner in the eighth. Johnny Sain gets Ferris Fain to fly out to end game with Nellie Fox and Minnie Minoso on base.

THE DATE: Saturday, June 12
THE PLACE: Yankee Stadium
THE CROWD: 31,569 (24,870 paid)
THE STARTERS: Jack Harshman (Chi), Whitey Ford (NY)
THE FINAL: Yankees 2, White Sox 0
THE WINNER: Ford
THE LOSER: Harshman
THE KEYS: Ford, now 8-1 lifetime vs. Chicago, throws two-hitter to beat rookie lefty Harshman, who surrenders RBI single to Gil McDougald and suicide-squeeze bunt by Phil Rizzuto in the fifth. Cleveland, meanwhile, wins to grab first place for good. George Kell, new Sox third baseman, hit on right hand by pitch and misses rest of series.

THE DATE: Sunday, June 13

THE PLACE: Yankee Stadium
THE CROWD: 60,070
THE STARTERS (1st): Sandy Consuegra (Chi), Eddie Lopat (NY)
THE STARTERS (2nd): Virgil Trucks (Chi), Harry Byrd (NY)
THE FINALS: Yankees 4, White Sox 2; White Sox 8, Yankees 0
THE WINNER (1st): Lopat
THE LOSER (1st): Consuegra
THE WINNER (2nd): Trucks
THE LOSER (2nd): Byrd
THE KEYS: Gene Woodling's three-run homer, his first since the previous Sept. 10—also off Consuegra and also a slicing flyball just inside the left-field foul pole—wipes out 2-1 Sox lead in sixth in opener; Byrd is KOd during four-run first in Game 2, and Nellie Fox adds a home run in the second inning for one of his three hits. Trucks (9-3) now 24-9 in his first calendar year (acquired previous June 13) with Chicago.

THE DATE: Friday night, June 18
THE PLACE: Comiskey Park
THE CROWD: 45,216
THE STARTERS: Harry Byrd (NY), Virgil Trucks (Chi)
THE FINAL: Yankees 7, White Sox 6
THE WINNER: Bob Grim
THE LOSER: Morrie Martin
THE KEYS: Rookie Grim victimizes lefty reliever Martin, acquired from A's one week earlier, with two-run single and two-run homer to let Yankees take 7-4 lead into ninth. Ex-Cub great Phil Cavarretta socks pinch homer off Grim in bottom half to make it interesting before Johnny Sain relieves and—after allowing Nellie Fox's fourth hit of night, RBI fielder's-choice grounder by Minnie Minoso and single to Ferris Fain—gets George Kell to ground to third to end it.

THE DATE: Saturday, June 19
THE PLACE: Comiskey Park
THE CROWD: 27,595
THE STARTERS: Eddie Lopat (NY), Sandy Consuegra (Chi)
THE FINAL: White Sox 3, Yankees 0
THE WINNER: Consuegra
THE LOSER: Lopat
THE KEYS: Consuegra, on his way to club-record 16-3 season, throws six-hitter to improve to 8-2 on the year; George Kell's RBI single in fourth and Jim Rivera's bases-loaded, two-run single in sixth hand Lopat his first loss to Chicago since Saturday, June 21, 1952.

THE DATE: Sunday, June 20
THE PLACE: Comiskey Park
THE CROWD: 37,075
THE STARTERS (1st): Allie Reynolds (NY), Billy Pierce (Chi)
THE STARTERS (2nd): Whitey Ford (NY), Bob Keegan (Chi)
THE FINALS: Yankees 16, White Sox 6; White Sox 7, Yankees 3
THE WINNER (1st): Bob Grim
THE LOSER (1st): Mike Fornieles
THE WINNER (2nd): Keegan
THE LOSER (2nd): Tom Morgan
THE KEYS: In Game 1, two-run homers by Minnie Minoso and Carl Sawatski contribute to Sox's six-run third, but Yankees rally on homers by Gil McDougald

and Mickey Mantle for 9-6 lead, then break game open with six-run ninth off rookie Vito Valentinetti. Keegan improves to 10-2 in nightcap, helped by George Kell's solo homer off Ford and Sherm Lollar's two-run blast off Bob Kuzava.

THE DATE: Tuesday night, July 20
THE PLACE: Yankee Stadium
THE CROWD: 38,072
THE STARTERS: Bob Keegan (Chi), Whitey Ford (NY)
THE FINAL: Yankees 4, White Sox 1
THE WINNER: Ford
THE LOSER: Keegan
THE KEYS: Minus injured All-Stars Ferris Fain (out for year) and George Kell (one month), Sox fall to Ford for ninth time in 10 career decisions. Mickey Mantle and Irv Noren each drive in two runs.

THE DATE: Wednesday, July 21
THE PLACE: Yankee Stadium
THE CROWD: 18,597
THE STARTERS: Virgil Trucks (Chi), Bob Wiesler (NY)
THE FINAL: White Sox 15, Yankees 3
THE WINNER: Trucks
THE LOSER: Wiesler
THE KEYS: Johnny Groth goes 4 for 5 with four RBIs, Minnie Minoso 4 for 6 with three doubles and two RBIs and Phil Cavarretta 3 for 5 with three RBIs as Trucks coasts to his 13th victory.

THE DATE: Thursday, July 22
THE PLACE: Yankee Stadium
THE CROWD: 36,722
THE STARTERS (1st): Sandy Consuegra (Chi), Bob Grim (NY)
THE STARTERS (2nd): Billy Pierce (Chi), Harry Byrd (NY)
THE FINALS: Yankees 4, White Sox 3 (10 inn.); Yankees 11, White Sox 1
THE WINNER (1st): Johnny Sain
THE LOSER (1st): Don Johnson
THE WINNER (2nd): Byrd
THE LOSER (2nd): Pierce
THE KEYS: In opener, Eddie Robinson's pinch homer off Consuegra and Mickey Mantle's two-out RBI single off Jack Harshman tie game 3-3 in the eighth, and Mantle's opposite-field homer off Johnson with two out in 10th is the game-winner. Rookie Bill Skowron collects RBI single in three-run third and two-run homer in six-run fifth against Pierce, who goes the route, though allowing all 11 runs, five of them unearned. Yanks stay a half-game behind Cleveland while the Sox fall 61/2 back.

THE DATE: Tuesday night, July 27
THE PLACE: Comiskey Park
THE CROWD: 53,067
THE STARTERS: Harry Byrd (NY), Virgil Trucks (Chi)
THE FINAL: White Sox 4, Yankees 0
THE WINNER: Trucks
THE LOSER: Byrd
THE KEYS: See "Most Glorious Victory"

THE DATE: Wednesday, July 28

THE PLACE: Comiskey Park
THE CROWD: 38,056
THE STARTERS: Eddie Lopat (NY), Billy Pierce (Chi)
THE FINAL: Yankees 7, White Sox 5
THE WINNER: Bob Grim
THE LOSER: Jack Harshman
THE KEYS: See "Most Devastating Defeat"

THE DATE: Thursday, July 29
THE PLACE: Comiskey Park
THE CROWD: 22,995
THE STARTERS: Whitey Ford (NY), Jack Harshman (Chi)
THE FINAL: Yankees 10, White Sox 0
THE WINNER: Ford
THE LOSER: Harshman
THE KEYS: Harshman, who had faced four batters in the fateful ninth inning the day before, lasts only into the second, when Ford greets reliever Don Johnson with a two-run double. Assault continues against Harry Dorish and rookie Dick Strahs. Ford finishes with four-hitter and is now 10-1 lifetime vs. Chicago.

THE DATE: Sunday, August 29
THE PLACE: Yankee Stadium
THE CROWD: 41,783
THE STARTERS: Virgil Trucks (Chi), Whitey Ford (NY)
THE FINAL: Yankees 4, White Sox 1
THE WINNER: Ford
THE LOSER: Trucks
THE KEYS: Yankees enter 3½ back, Sox eight behind Cleveland (despite 85-46 record). Yogi Berra's two-run double in first and Joe Collins' homer in seventh prevent Trucks from notching his 19th win.

THE DATE: Friday night, September 10
THE PLACE: Comiskey Park
THE CROWD: 22,352
THE STARTERS: Bob Grim (NY), Virgil Trucks (Chi)
THE FINAL: Yankees 6, White Sox 3
THE WINNER: Grim
THE LOSER: Trucks
THE KEYS: Andy Carey's two-run homer off upper-deck facade in left and Irv Noren's bases-loaded single help eliminate Sox from pennant race. Trucks, once 18-5, falls to 18-9; he'll finish 19-12. Paul Richards verbally agrees to new deal as GM/manager of Orioles.

THE DATE: Saturday, September 11
THE PLACE: Comiskey Park
THE CROWD: 15,334
THE STARTERS: Eddie Lopat (NY), Jack Harshman (Chi)
THE FINAL: White Sox 6, Yankees 5 (10 innings)
THE WINNER: Morrie Martin
THE LOSER: Jim Konstanty
THE KEYS: Sox tie game in ninth on Minnie Minoso's RBI double and George Kell's RBI single—both with two out—then win it when Chico Carrasquel singles home pinch-runner Bob Cain with two out in 10th. Yankees fall 6½ behind Cleveland with two weeks to go.

Appendix A

1955 Season

THE DATE: Tuesday, April 26
THE PLACE: Comiskey Park
THE CROWD: 21,847 (12,297 paid)
THE STARTERS: Bob Turley (NY), Mike Fornieles (Chi)
THE FINAL: Yankees 5, White Sox 0
THE WINNER: Turley
THE LOSER: Fornieles
THE KEYS: Sox are shut out a second straight time since exploding for 29-6 rout of A's April 23 in Kansas City. Ex-Oriole Turley allows one hit, Sherm Lollar's single in the second, walks nine and fans 10.

THE DATE: Wednesday, April 27
THE PLACE: Comiskey Park
THE CROWD: 10,043
THE STARTERS: Whitey Ford (NY), Virgil Trucks (Chi)
THE FINAL: White Sox 13, Yankees 4
THE WINNER: Billy Pierce
THE LOSER: Ford
THE KEYS: Ford's afternoon, as well as his streak of 21 scoreless innings, ends in first when Sox score five times. Inning is capped by Sherm Lollar's two-run homer off Johnny Sain. Walt Dropo homers twice, and Pierce, in relief of Trucks, goes 6 2/3 innings, striking out seven.

THE DATE: Tuesday night, May 17
THE PLACE: Yankee Stadium
THE CROWD: 21,206
THE STARTERS: Billy Pierce (Chi), Whitey Ford (NY)
THE FINAL: Yankees 1, White Sox 0
THE WINNER: Ford
THE LOSER: Pierce
THE KEYS: Pierce allows three hits—but four walks—in his seven innings, Ford just seven singles in his nine innings. Yankees score in sixth as Mickey Mantle comes across when Eddie Robinson hits into a force play. This is one of four 1-0 defeats Pierce will suffer in '55.

THE DATE: Wednesday, May 18
THE PLACE: Yankee Stadium
THE CROWD: 10,600
THE STARTERS: Virgil Trucks (Chi), Bob Grim (NY)
THE FINAL: Yankees 11, White Sox 6
THE WINNER: Grim
THE LOSER: Trucks
THE KEYS: Grim beans Minnie Minoso, causing hairline skull fracture and sidelining Minnie for nearly three weeks. Down 5-1 after three, Sox close to 7-6 by seventh on two homers by recent waiver pickup Vern Stephens and one each by Clint Courtney and Jim Rivera. With bases loaded and one out in seventh, Hank Bauer, runner at first, knocks over Nellie Fox to prevent double play. Sox holler for interference and completion of inning-ending double play, but umpire Ed Hurley calls only Bauer out and returns runners to third and second and awards batter, Andy Carey, first base. Mickey Mantle follows with grand slam off Mike Fornieles.

THE DATE: Friday night, June 3
THE PLACE: Comiskey Park
THE CROWD: 40,020
THE STARTERS: Bob Turley (NY), Jack Harshman (Chi)
THE FINAL: White Sox 3, Yankees 2
THE WINNER: Harshman
THE LOSER: Turley
THE KEYS: Hank Bauer is greeted with verbal abuse—and some garbage—by fans in right field who remembered his block on Nellie Fox in New York. Harshman allows solo homers by Bill Skowron and Mickey Mantle but not much else, and he drives in two runs with a single and a sacrifice fly to beat the Yankees for the first time in his career.

THE DATE: Saturday, June 4
THE PLACE: Comiskey Park
THE CROWD: 19,899
THE STARTERS: Eddie Lopat (NY), Bob Keegan (Chi)
THE FINAL: Yankees 4, White Sox 3
THE WINNER: Lopat
THE LOSER: Keegan
THE KEYS: Bill Skowron's RBI single in fourth, ninth hit off Keegan, puts Yankees ahead 3-2, and Irv Noren singles in fourth run in sixth. Minnie Minoso appears as pinch-hitter, his first action since his beaning. Yanks increase lead over second-place Sox to 4 1/2 games.

THE DATE: Sunday, June 5
THE PLACE: Comiskey Park
THE CROWD: 37,561
THE STARTERS (1st): Tommy Byrne (NY), Dick Donovan (Chi)
THE STARTERS (2nd): Whitey Ford (NY), Billy Pierce (Chi)
THE FINALS: White Sox 5, Yankees 3; Yankees 3, White Sox 2 (10 innings)
THE WINNER (1st): Donovan
THE LOSER (1st): Byrne
THE WINNER (2nd): Tom Morgan
THE LOSER (2nd): Pierce
THE KEYS: Jim Rivera hits two-out grand slam in first inning of opener and Sherm Lollar follows with solo blast to put rookie Donovan (6-2) in command. In Game 2, Andy Carey homers and Mickey Mantle blasts one over the roof in left-center for 2-0 lead, but Sox tie on Chico Carrasquel's homer in fifth and Johnny Groth's two-out RBI single in seventh. In top of 10th, career .219 hitter Billy Hunter's drive off wall in left-center goes for game-winning, inside-the-park homer.

THE DATE: Friday night, June 17
THE PLACE: Yankee Stadium
THE CROWD: 33,744
THE STARTERS: Dick Donovan (Chi), Whitey Ford (NY)
THE FINAL: White Sox 2, Yankees 1
THE WINNER: Donovan
THE LOSER: Ford
THE KEYS: Walt Dropo's first home run since May 6 is countered by Mickey Mantle's two-out third-tier blast in the eighth for a 1-1 tie, but George Kell's RBI single in ninth provides the winning run. Sandy Consuegra gets the save as Chicago moves to within a game of the first-place New Yorkers.

Appendix A

THE DATE: Saturday, June 18
THE PLACE: Yankee Stadium
THE CROWD: 24,947 (21,586 paid)
THE STARTERS: Harry Byrd (Chi), Bob Turley (NY)
THE FINAL: White Sox 6, Yankees 3
THE WINNER: Byrd
THE LOSER: Turley
THE KEYS: Byrd, purchased from last-place Baltimore on June 15, makes White Sox debut and shuts out his former teammates on three hits for six innings before Yankees finally score on him in seventh. By then, Sox are up 4-0, thanks in part to Bob Nieman's two-run pinch double in the top of the seventh. Sandy Consuegra again gets save as Sox move into AL lead by percentage points.

THE DATE: Sunday, June 19
THE PLACE: Yankee Stadium
THE CROWD: 44,060
THE STARTERS (1st): Billy Pierce (Chi), Eddie Lopat (NY)
THE STARTERS (2nd): Jack Harshman (Chi), Johnny Kucks (NY)
THE FINALS: Yankees 7, White Sox 1; Yankees 5, White Sox 2
THE WINNER (1st): Lopat
THE LOSER (1st): Pierce
THE WINNER (2nd): Jim Konstanty
THE LOSER (2nd): Harshman
THE KEYS: Pierce is tagged for six hits—including rookie Elston Howard's two-run homer—and departs after three innings behind 4-0. Lopat goes distance to even record at 4-4. In Game 2, Gil McDougald homers off Harshman to break 2-2 tie in seventh and Mickey Mantle adds two-run homer in same inning off Sandy Consuegra. New York is back in first by two games over Sox and four games over Cleveland.

THE DATE: Tuesday night, July 19
THE PLACE: Comiskey Park
THE CROWD: 46,711
THE STARTERS: Tommy Byrne (NY), Connie Johnson (Chi)
THE FINAL: Yankees 4, White Sox 3
THE WINNER: Byrne
THE LOSER: Harry Byrd
THE KEYS: Walt Dropo's two-run homer forges 2-2 tie in sixth, and George Kell singles home new center-fielder Jim Busby (acquired from Washington for three players on June 7) with two out in seventh for 3-2 Chicago lead. But reliever Byrd, between strikeouts of Irv Noren and Mickey Mantle, walks Yogi Berra and then gives up game-deciding homer to Elston Howard in eighth.

THE DATE: Wednesday night, July 20
THE PLACE: Comiskey Park
THE CROWD: 36,869
THE STARTERS: Bob Turley (NY), Dick Donovan (Chi)
THE FINAL: White Sox 8, Yankees 6
THE WINNER: Donovan
THE LOSER: Turley
THE KEYS: With slumping Minnie Minoso moved into leadoff spot, Sox get four in first and four more in third (Walt Dropo doubles twice, Donovan delivers two-run single), then hold off Yankees, who KO Donovan with five-run seventh. In ninth, Sandy Consuegra is bailed out by Billy Pierce, who retires Mickey Mantle

on grounder to short to save victory for Donovan (13-2). Sox now two games back.

THE DATE: Thursday, July 21
THE PLACE: Comiskey Park
THE CROWD: 30,962
THE STARTERS: Whitey Ford (NY), Virgil Trucks (Chi)
THE FINAL: White Sox 9, Yankees 6
THE WINNER: Dixie Howell
THE LOSER: Eddie Lopat
THE KEYS: Two-run double by Bob Kennedy off Lopat breaks 6-6 tie in seventh, and Dixie Howell, 35-year-old righthander purchased from Memphis on June 8, blanks Yanks over final six innings, striking out Mickey Mantle twice, to get the win that closes gap to one game.

THE DATE: Tuesday night, July 26
THE PLACE: Yankee Stadium
THE CROWD: 37,369
THE STARTERS: Dick Donovan (Chi), Tommy Byrne (NY)
THE FINAL: Yankees 1, White Sox 0
THE WINNER: Byrne
THE LOSER: Donovan
THE KEYS: Yankees, who enter with one-game lead over Chicago, two ahead of Cleveland and four in front of Boston, win on Yogi Berra's homer in sixth. Byrne (9-2) goes route with four-hitter, though walking five and hitting two batters. Donovan drops to 13-4.

THE DATE: Wednesday, July 27
THE PLACE: Yankee Stadium
THE CROWD: 18,252
THE STARTERS: Harry Byrd (Chi), Eddie Lopat (NY)
THE FINAL: White Sox 7, Yankees 4
THE WINNER: Byrd
THE LOSER: Lopat
THE KEYS: Walt Dropo drives in three runs, giving him 17 RBIs in his last 16 games, as Sox KO Lopat in his final appearance in a Yankee uniform (he was sold to Baltimore three days later). Byrd takes 6-1 lead into eighth before wilting a bit in 95-degree heat.

THE DATE: Thursday, July 28
THE PLACE: Yankee Stadium
THE CROWD: 14,062
THE STARTERS: Connie Johnson (Chi), Bob Turley (NY)
THE FINAL: White Sox 3, Yankees 2
THE WINNER: Johnson
THE LOSER: Turley
THE KEYS: George Kell, hitting .418 over his last 27 games, is sidelined by back spasms and replaced at third base by Bobby Adams, just bought from Cincinnati. Johnson, thanks to Jim Rivera's RBI single and Walt Dropo's two-run homer, takes 3-0 lead into ninth before Mickey Mantle belts two-run homer to make it 3-2. Two misplays by Adams help load bases with two out, when Billy Pierce relieves and strikes out Jerry Coleman to end game and move Sox into AL lead by .002.

THE DATE: Sunday, August 28
THE PLACE: Comiskey Park
THE CROWD: 50,990
THE STARTERS (1st): Whitey Ford (NY), Connie Johnson (Chi)
THE STARTERS (2nd): Bob Turley (NY), Billy Pierce (Chi)
THE FINALS: Yankees 6, White Sox 1; White Sox 3, Yankees 2
THE WINNER (1st): Ford
THE LOSER (1st): Johnson
THE WINNER (2nd): Pierce
THE LOSER (2nd): Turley
THE KEYS: Mickey Mantle's 34th homer, a three-run shot in the fourth inning of the opener, provides a 4-0 cushion for Ford (15-6), who fans nine and allows five hits, among them Walt Dropo's 18th homer. Bob Kennedy's three-run homer in the first inning is the difference in the nightcap. Dixie Howell works the final 2 1/3 innings to save the win for Pierce, escaping a bases-loaded, two-out jam in the seventh. At day's end, Yankees lead Sox by a half-game, Cleveland by one, Boston by 3 1/2.

THE DATE: Friday, September 9
THE PLACE: Yankee Stadium
THE CROWD: 18,158
THE STARTERS: Dick Donovan (Chi), Don Larsen (NY)
THE FINAL: Yankees 5, White Sox 4
THE WINNER: Larsen
THE LOSER: Donovan
THE KEYS: See "Most Devastating Defeat"

THE DATE: Saturday, September 10
THE PLACE: Yankee Stadium
THE CROWD: 31,486
THE STARTERS: Billy Pierce (Chi), Rip Coleman (NY)
THE FINAL: White Sox 9, Yankees 8 (10 innings)
THE WINNER: Dixie Howell
THE LOSER: Johnny Kucks
THE KEYS: See "Most Glorious Victory"

1956 Season

THE DATE: Sunday, May 6
THE PLACE: Yankee Stadium
THE CROWD: 49,016
THE STARTERS (1st): Jack Harshman (Chi), Whitey Ford (NY)
THE STARTERS (2nd): Harry Byrd (Chi), Rip Coleman (NY)
THE FINALS: Yankees 4, White Sox 0; Yankees 4, White Sox 0
THE WINNER (1st:) Ford
THE LOSER (1st): Harshman
THE WINNER (2nd): Coleman
THE LOSER: (2nd): Byrd
THE KEYS: Yogi Berra's two-run homer and Hank Bauer's blast with the bases empty help Ford coast to eight-hit shutout in opener; Gil McDougald triples in a run and Elston Howard singles him home in the second inning of Game 2, and Bauer robs Walt Dropo of a grand slam with a sensational two-out catch in the sixth. Yankees improve to 13-5; Sox slip to 6-6.

THE DATE: Thursday, May 17
THE PLACE: Comiskey Park
THE CROWD: 18,082 (10,335 paid)
THE STARTERS: Whitey Ford (NY), Jack Harshman (Chi)
THE FINAL: Yankees 10, White Sox 3
THE WINNER: Ford
THE LOSER: Harshman
THE KEYS: Ford raises record to 6-0 and lowers ERA to 0.83 (errors by shortstop Phil Rizzuto, 37, lead to all Chicago runs) as Yankees snap Sox's six-game winning streak and increase lead over South Siders to 2½ games. Yogi Berra hits 11th homer (Sox season total is 10).

THE DATE: Friday night, May 18
THE PLACE: Comiskey Park
THE CROWD: 36,192
THE STARTERS: Rip Coleman (NY), Billy Pierce (Chi)
THE FINAL: Yankees 8, White Sox 7 (10 innings)
THE WINNER: Tom Sturdivant
THE LOSER: Dixie Howell
THE KEYS: RBI singles by Jim Rivera and Nellie Fox off Tommy Byrne send Sox ahead 7-6 in eighth, but Mickey Mantle's second homer of the night—this one lefthanded, off Howell—ties game with two out in ninth. In 10th, Andy Carey—a key figure in Sox-Yankee trade talks—singles past a diving George Kell at third for decisive run.

THE DATE: Saturday, May 19
THE PLACE: Comiskey Park
THE CROWD: 17,294
THE STARTERS: Bob Turley (NY), Howie Pollet (Chi)
THE FINAL: Yankees 6, White Sox 4
THE WINNER: Turley
THE LOSER: Pollet
THE KEYS: Pollet, 35-year-old ex-Cardinal star and old teammate of Sox manager Marty Marion, lasts 2⅓ innings in his first AL start and is charged with five runs. The Sox drop two to Boston the next day, then, a day later, trade George Kell, Bob Nieman, Mike Fornieles, and Connie Johnson to Baltimore for pitcher Jim Wilson and outfielder-1B Dave Philley.

THE DATE: Tuesday night, June 12
THE PLACE: Yankee Stadium
THE CROWD: 34,662
THE STARTERS: Dick Donovan (Chi), Whitey Ford (NY)
THE FINAL: Yankees 4, White Sox 2
THE WINNER: Ford
THE LOSER: Donovan
THE KEYS: Two-run homer by Andy Carey, still with Yankees, helps beat Donovan, still with Chicago despite all the trade rumors. Nellie Fox breaks up Ford's no-hit bid in seventh. Ford now 8-3. Sox do stop Mickey Mantle (0 for 3), who is hitting .388 with 21 homers and 52 RBIs.

THE DATE: Wednesday, June 13
THE PLACE: Yankee Stadium
THE CROWD: 11,822
THE STARTERS: Bob Keegan (Chi), Bob Turley (NY)

THE FINAL: White Sox 7, Yankees 5
THE WINNER: Howie Pollet
THE LOSER: Rip Coleman
THE KEYS: Ron Northey hits three-run pinch homer for 4-3 Sox lead in fourth, Larry Doby's first homer of season snaps 4-4 tie in fifth and rookie shortstop Luis Aparicio drives in three runs with a pair of singles as Sox beat Yankees for first time in '56.

THE DATE: Thursday, June 14
THE PLACE: Yankee Stadium
THE CROWD: 9,315
THE STARTERS: Jim Wilson (Chi), Bob Grim (NY)
THE FINAL: Yankees 5, White Sox 1
THE WINNER: Grim
THE LOSER: Wilson
THE KEYS: Minnie Minoso drops Gil McDougald's two-out liner in third for an error, and Yankees jump on the opportunity for three runs, getting RBI doubles by Joe Collins and Mickey Mantle and RBI single from Bill Skowron. Mantle later hits 22nd homer. Dave Philley homers for lone run off Grim, who finishes with four-hitter and is now 7-0 lifetime vs. Sox. Yankees lead second-place Sox by five games.

THE DATE: Friday night, June 22
THE PLACE: Comiskey Park
THE CROWD: 48,346
THE STARTERS: Tom Sturdivant (NY), Dick Donovan (Chi)
THE FINAL: White Sox 5, Yankees 4 (12 innings)
THE WINNER: Sandy Consuegra
THE LOSER: Rip Coleman
THE KEYS: See "Most Glorious Victory"

THE DATE: Saturday, June 23
THE PLACE: Comiskey Park
THE CROWD: 29,832
THE STARTERS: Bob Grim (NY), Jim Wilson (Chi)
THE FINAL: White Sox 2, Yankees 0
THE WINNER: Wilson
THE LOSER: Grim
THE KEYS: In a game highlighted by an unscheduled bout between Grim and Dave Philley (see "The Fights"), Sherm Lollar doubles for one sixth-inning run and Luis Aparicio singles for another as Wilson (10-3 overall, 6-1 with Sox) throws four-hit shutout. Sox three games out.

THE DATE: Sunday, June 24
THE PLACE: Comiskey Park
THE CROWD: 47,255
THE STARTERS (1st): Whitey Ford (NY), Billy Pierce (Chi)
THE STARTERS (2nd): Mickey McDermott (NY), Gerry Staley (Chi)
THE FINALS: White Sox 14, Yankees 2; White Sox 6, Yankees 3
THE WINNER (1st): Pierce
THE LOSER (1st): Ford
THE WINNER (2nd): Staley
THE LOSER (2nd): McDermott
THE KEYS: Larry Doby slugs a three-run homer in the first inning of each game

to provide the spark for the completion of Chicago's most glorious baseball weekend of the decade. Pierce improves to 10-2 as Sox collect 18 hits in Game 1, four apiece by Doby and Dave Philley. Fans by the hundreds storm onto the field after Luis Aparicio throws out Hank Bauer to end Game 2 victory, which leaves Sox one game out of AL lead.

THE DATE: Sunday, July 15
THE PLACE: Yankee Stadium
THE CROWD: 61,351
THE STARTERS (1st): Billy Pierce (Chi), Whitey Ford (NY)
THE STARTERS (2nd): Dick Donovan (Chi), Rip Coleman (NY)
THE FINALS: Yankees 2, White Sox 1; Yankees 6, White Sox 5 (10 innings)
THE WINNER (1st) Ford:
THE LOSER (1st): Pierce
THE WINNER (2nd): Johnny Kucks
THE LOSER (2nd): Jim Wilson
THE KEYS: See "Most Devastating Defeat"

THE DATE: Tuesday night, July 24
THE PLACE: Comiskey Park
THE CROWD: 33,316
THE STARTERS: Tom Sturdivant (NY), Billy Pierce (Chi)
THE FINAL: White Sox 11, Yankees 5
THE WINNER: Pierce
THE LOSER: Sturdivant
THE KEYS: Larry Doby leads way with two-run homer (3 for 4 on night with four RBIs) and hard slide at second base that breaks up double play and knocks second baseman Billy Martin out of the game. Doby's slide is in retaliation for Bob Cerv's similar block on Nellie Fox. Minnie Minoso also homers—as do Yankees Cerv, Gil McDougald, and Bill Skowron—and Pierce improves record to 15-4.

THE DATE: Wednesday night, July 25
THE PLACE: Comiskey Park
THE CROWD: 34,745
THE STARTERS: Whitey Ford (NY), Dick Donovan (Chi)
THE FINAL: Yankees 10, White Sox 1
THE WINNER: Ford
THE LOSER: Donovan
THE KEYS: Yankees, now 13 1/2 games ahead of fourth-place Chicago, KO Donovan in sixth, then add three runs in seventh off lefty Paul LaPalme and three more in ninth off 42-year-old Ellis Kinder. Ford fires four-hitter to improve to 13-4 on season and 18-4 lifetime vs. Sox.

THE DATE: Thursday, July 26
THE PLACE: Comiskey Park
THE CROWD: 26,741
THE STARTERS: Tommy Byrne (NY), Jack Harshman (Chi)
THE FINAL: Yankees 8, White Sox 5
THE WINNER: Don Larsen
THE LOSER: Harshman
THE KEYS: Sox take 3-1 lead in second on Les Moss' homer and Jim Rivera's two-run triple before Yankees KO Harshman during five-run third. Larsen works final six innings, allowing five hits and one run. Harshman drops to 1-8 lifetime vs. New York.

Appendix A

THE DATE: Thursday, August 23
THE PLACE: Yankee Stadium
THE CROWD: 22,971
THE STARTERS (1st): Bob Keegan (Chi), Rip Coleman (NY)
THE STARTERS (2nd): Dixie Howell (Chi), Bob Turley (NY)
THE FINALS: White Sox 8, Yankees 3; White Sox 6, Yankees 4
THE WINNER (1st): Keegan
THE LOSER (1st): Coleman
THE WINNER (2nd): Howell
THE LOSER (2nd): Turley
THE KEYS: In opener, Nellie Fox goes 5 for 5 with four RBIs and Keegan goes route to beat Yankees for first time since June 20, 1954. Fox adds two more hits in first two times up in Game 2 (raising his average to .318) and Larry Doby rips two-run triple in first inning in support of Howell, who lasts 5 2/3 innings in rare start. Mickey Mantle, against Paul LaPalme, hits 43rd homer, a 480-foot shot that puts him five games ahead of Babe Ruth's 60-homer pace in 1927.

THE DATE: Friday, August 24
THE PLACE: Yankee Stadium
THE CROWD: 14,189
THE STARTERS: Jack Harshman (Chi), Johnny Kucks (NY)
THE FINAL: Yankees 2, White Sox 0
THE WINNER: Kucks
THE LOSER: Harshman
THE KEYS: Kucks, 22, pitches four-hitter to outduel Harshman, who allows solo homer by Gil McDougald in sixth. Mickey Mantle doubles home insurance run in eighth off Ellis Kinder.

THE DATE: Saturday. August 25
THE PLACE: Yankee Stadium
THE CROWD: 54,449
THE STARTERS: Dick Donovan (Chi), Whitey Ford (NY)
THE FINAL: White Sox 4, Yankees 2
THE WINNER: Donovan
THE LOSER: Ford
THE KEYS: On Old-Timers Day, Sox make it 18 out of their last 24 as Donovan, though allowing two-run homer in fourth to Mickey Mantle (No. 44), finishes with six-hitter to win his fourth straight decision after starting 4-7. RBI single by rookie Luis Aparicio (.324 hitter vs. Yanks on the year) is the decisive hit. Sox still 10 1/2 games behind Yanks, who reacquire Enos Slaughter from A's and release Phil Rizzuto.

THE DATE: Tuesday night, September 18
THE PLACE: Comiskey Park
THE CROWD: 31,694
THE STARTERS: Whitey Ford (NY), Billy Pierce (Chi)
THE FINAL: Yankees 3, White Sox 2 (11 innings)
THE WINNER: Ford
THE LOSER: Pierce
THE KEYS: Walt Dropo's eighth-inning homer puts Pierce ahead 2-1, but Yogi Berra's bloop single to short left-center scores Billy Martin (leadoff triple) to tie game in ninth. With two out in 11th, Mickey Mantle, whom Pierce had

fanned with Martin at third in ninth, belts his 50th home run, into the upper deck in left-center. Bob Grim rescues Ford from two-on, no-out jam in bottom half, and Yanks clinch another pennant. Ford now 19-5, Pierce 20-8.

1957 Season

THE DATE: Saturday, May 4
THE PLACE: Comiskey Park
THE CROWD: 19,216 (14,796 paid)
THE STARTERS: Whitey Ford (NY), Jim Wilson (Chi)
THE FINAL: Yankees 3, White Sox 2
THE WINNER: Art Ditmar
THE LOSER: Wilson
THE KEYS: Ditmar relieves ailing Ford in second and blanks Sox till ninth. Andy Carey's two-run homer in fifth and botched double-play ball by third baseman Bubba Phillips in ninth give Yankees 3-0 lead before Minnie Minoso's two-run single KOs Ditmar. Tommy Byrne enters to fan Larry Doby to end it, cutting Sox's AL lead over New York to 1 1/2 games.

THE DATE: Sunday, May 5
THE PLACE: Comiskey Park
THE CROWD: 41,304
THE STARTERS (1st): Bobby Shantz (NY), Billy Pierce (Chi)
THE STARTERS (2nd): Johnny Kucks (NY), Jack Harshman (Chi)
THE FINALS: Yankees 4, White Sox 2; Yankees 3, White Sox 0
THE WINNER (1st): Shantz
THE LOSER (1st): Pierce
THE WINNER (2nd): Kucks
THE LOSER (2nd): Harshman
THE KEYS: Mickey Mantle's two-run upper-deck homer to left and Billy Martin's RBI single highlight three-run fourth inning in Game 1. Shantz goes distance, allowing seven hits. In Game 2, Kucks retires 17 straight in one stretch and finishes with three-hitter. Elston Howard's two-run triple in fourth the key blow. Yankees are back in first place.

THE DATE: Tuesday night, May 21
THE PLACE: Yankee Stadium
THE CROWD: 28,059
THE STARTERS: Billy Pierce (Chi), Whitey Ford (NY)
THE FINAL: White Sox 3, Yankees 1
THE WINNER: Pierce
THE LOSER: Ford
THE KEYS: Sox score all their runs in sixth, on RBI singles by Jim Rivera and Pierce and a suicide-squeeze bunt by Bubba Phillips. Pierce improves to 6-2, retiring the last 16 Yankees in order. He strikes out eight and allows four hits as Sox increase AL lead to three games.

THE DATE: Wednesday, May 22
THE PLACE: Yankee Stadium
THE CROWD: 11,756
THE STARTERS: Jim Wilson (Chi), Johnny Kucks (NY)
THE FINAL: White Sox 8, Yankees 4
THE WINNER: Wilson
THE LOSER: Kucks

THE KEYS: Sox snap Kucks' scoreless-innings streak against them at 20 and go on to win their ninth straight game. Three-base error by Mickey Mantle and Minnie Minoso's RBI double are key plays in four-run sixth. Nellie Fox's homer off Tommy Byrne in eighth caps victory.

THE DATE: Tuesday night, June 11
THE PLACE: Comiskey Park
THE CROWD: 49,114
THE STARTERS: Bobby Shantz (NY), Jim Wilson (Chi)
THE FINAL: Yankees 3, White Sox 2
THE WINNER: Shantz
THE LOSER: Wilson
THE KEYS: Sox enter with five-game lead on second-place Yankees, Mickey Mantle with 15 homers and .360 average, Nellie Fox with .362 average (second to Ted Williams' .380). Mantle homers into right-field upper deck and Hank Bauer adds RBI single in first inning. Bob Grim relieves Shantz in eighth and retires last four Sox batters.

THE DATE: Wednesday night, June 12
THE PLACE: Comiskey Park
THE CROWD: 40,033
THE STARTERS: Johnny Kucks (NY), Jack Harshman (Chi)
THE FINAL: White Sox 7, Yankees 6
THE WINNER: Harshman
THE LOSER: Kucks
THE KEYS: Rain holds down crowd and holds up game's start by 21 minutes. Game is soon interrupted by rain delay of 1 hour 9 minutes. Bases-empty homers by Mickey Mantle, Bill Skowron, and Hank Bauer are countered by Walt Dropo's two-run homer and solo shot by Jim Rivera, and Sox lead 7-4 in ninth before Mantle homers off Bob Keegan (giving Mick one from each side of the plate) with Gil McDougald aboard to cut lead to 7-6. Dixie Howell finally strikes out Bauer to end game.

THE DATE: Thursday, June 13
THE PLACE: Comiskey Park
THE CROWD: 23,401
THE STARTERS: Art Ditmar (NY), Billy Pierce (Chi)
THE FINAL: Yankees 4, White Sox 3
THE WINNER: Ditmar
THE LOSER: Pierce
THE KEYS: After the day's main event (see "The Fights"), Jim Rivera gives Sox 2-0 lead with two-run homer off foul pole in right. But Yankees rip Pierce (10-3) for 11 hits in 4 1/3 innings and take lead in fifth on Bill Skowron's RBI single. Sherm Lollar's homer cuts New York lead to 4-3 in eighth, but Bob Grim shuts Sox down in ninth, and Yankees now trail Chicago by four games.

THE DATE: Friday night, June 21
THE PLACE: Yankee Stadium
THE CROWD: 51,947
THE STARTERS: Jim Wilson (Chi), Johnny Kucks (NY)
THE FINAL: Yankees 4, White Sox 2
THE WINNER: Kucks
THE LOSER: Wilson
THE KEYS: Sox, minus Sherm Lollar (broken wrist) and Larry Doby and Jim

Landis (leg injuries), strand three runners at third base and have their lead sliced to a half-game. Bob Grim works final three innings, striking out Jim Rivera to end the eighth and Earl Battey and pinch-hitters Ron Northey and Dixie Howell in the ninth.

THE DATE: Saturday, June 22
THE PLACE: Yankee Stadium
THE CROWD: 33,136
THE STARTERS: Jack Harshman (Chi), Art Ditmar (NY)
THE FINAL: Yankees 6, White Sox 5 (13 innings)
THE WINNER: Tommy Byrne
THE LOSER: Paul LaPalme
THE KEYS: Sox lead 5-2 after three innings, but Bill Skowron's two-run homer in sixth and Harry Simpson's two-out single in seventh tie the score. Byrne blanks Sox over final nine innings, allowing one hit (but seven walks), and Yogi Berra leads off bottom of 13th with homer off LaPalme to send Yankees into AL lead for first time since May 8.

THE DATE: Sunday, June 23
THE PLACE: Yankee Stadium
THE CROWD: 63,787
THE STARTERS (1st): Billy Pierce (Chi), Bobby Shantz (NY)
THE STARTERS (2nd): Dick Donovan (Chi), Al Cicotte (NY)
THE FINALS: Yankees 9, White Sox 2; White Sox 4, Yankees 3
THE WINNER (1st): Shantz
THE LOSER (1st): Pierce
THE WINNER (2nd): Donovan
THE LOSER (2nd): Cicotte
THE KEYS: Before season's biggest crowd (including Japanese Prime Minister Nobuske Kishi, who throws out ceremonial first ball), Yankees pound Pierce for seven runs and 11 hits (among them a homer by Hank Bauer and RBI doubles by Elston Howard, Mickey Mantle, and Andy Carey) in five-plus innings of opener as New York's winning streak reaches 10. In Game 2, Donovan leads 4-0 entering ninth (thanks in part to solo home run by Nellie Fox off Don Larsen) before Mantle crushes three-run homer to right that almost clears the Stadium roof. Reliever Paul LaPalme then escapes two-on, none-out jam to keep Sox a half-game back.

THE DATE: Sunday, July 14
THE PLACE: Comiskey Park
THE CROWD: 48,244
THE STARTERS (1st): Bobby Shantz (NY), Billy Pierce (Chi)
THE STARTERS (2nd): Whitey Ford (NY), Dick Donovan (Chi)
THE FINALS: White Sox 3, Yankees 1; Yankees 6, White Sox 4
THE WINNER (1st): Pierce
THE LOSER (1st): Shantz
THE WINNER (2nd): Tommy Byrne
THE LOSER (2nd): Jim Wilson
THE KEYS: See "Most Glorious Victory" and "Most Devastating Defeat"

THE DATE: Tuesday night, July 23
THE PLACE: Yankee Stadium
THE CROWD: 42,522
THE STARTERS: Bob Keegan (Chi), Don Larsen (NY)

THE FINAL: Yankees 10, White Sox 6
THE WINNER: Art Ditmar
THE LOSER: Jack Harshman
THE KEYS: Yankees, down 6-4 entering seventh, go ahead when Harshman walks Gil McDougald with bases filled to force in a run and then gives up bases-clearing triple to Mickey Mantle, who earlier had homered, singled, and doubled. Yankees lead second-place Chicago by $5\frac{1}{2}$ games.

THE DATE: Wednesday, July 24
THE PLACE: Yankee Stadium
THE CROWD: 24,594
THE STARTERS: Billy Pierce (Chi), Whitey Ford (NY)
THE FINAL: White Sox 7, Yankees 2
THE WINNER: Pierce
THE LOSER: Ford
THE KEYS: Even without Minnie Minoso (groin pull), Sox—especially Luis Aparicio (4 for 5, two runs scored and RBI)—get to Ford, scoring three times in first inning. Pierce, notching 14th win, shackles Mickey Mantle, who enters with AL-best .367 average but fails to get ball out of infield in four tries.

THE DATE: Thursday, July 25
THE PLACE: Yankee Stadium
THE CROWD: 17,971
THE STARTERS: Dick Donovan (Chi), Bobby Shantz (NY)
THE FINAL: White Sox 6, Yankees 2
THE WINNER: Donovan
THE LOSER: Shantz
THE KEYS: Donovan (10-3) throws four-hitter and helps his own cause with a home run as Sox cut Yanks' AL lead to $3\frac{1}{2}$ games. Chicago even scores twice in ninth off Sox-killer Art Ditmar. Shantz drops to 9-4.

THE DATE: Tuesday night, August 27
THE PLACE: Comiskey Park
THE CROWD: 46,830
THE STARTERS: Art Ditmar (NY), Jim Wilson (Chi)
THE FINAL: Yankees 12, White Sox 6
THE WINNER: Bob Grim
THE LOSER: Bill Fischer
THE KEYS: Sox, down 5-0 after $1\frac{1}{2}$, KO Ditmar in third and tie score at 6-6 in seventh on RBI single by Minnie Minoso. But after one-out singles by Enos Slaughter and Mickey Mantle in eighth off rookie Fischer, Al Lopez calls on lefty Paul LaPalme to face Yogi Berra, and Berra hits LaPalme's first pitch into the upper deck in right for a 9-6 lead. Berra adds single in ninth for the sixth RBI of his 4-for-5 night. Sox, who had won six straight, fall $4\frac{1}{2}$ games behind New York, which uses Whitey Ford and Bob Turley (next night's scheduled starter) in relief to nail down this victory. New York's lead is $4\frac{1}{2}$ games.

THE DATE: Wednesday night, August 28
THE PLACE: Comiskey Park
THE CROWD: 36,917
THE STARTERS: Don Larsen (NY), Billy Pierce (Chi)
THE FINAL: Yankees 5, White Sox 4
THE WINNER: Larsen
THE LOSER: Pierce

THE KEYS: After 1-hour-15-minute rain delay and having their first 10 batters retired by Pierce, Yankees take 5-2 lead entering last of seventh, fifth run scoring in top half on Hank Bauer's homer. Earl Torgeson's two-run homer off Bob Turley makes it 5-4, and singles by Minnie Minoso and Larry Doby (four hits on the night) and a walk to Sherm Lollar load bases. But Jim Rivera pops out and pinch-hitter Fred Hatfield strikes out to end threat, and Turley fans Sammy Esposito with runners at second and third in ninth to end the game.

THE DATE: Thursday, August 29
THE PLACE: Comiskey Park
THE CROWD: 39,357
THE STARTERS: Tom Sturdivant (NY), Dick Donovan (Chi)
THE FINAL: Yankees 2, White Sox 1 (11 innings)
THE WINNER: Whitey Ford
THE LOSER: Donovan
THE KEYS: Before largest weekday crowd, to date, in Comiskey Park history, Sox match Hank Bauer's solo homer with Earl Torgeson's sacrifice fly and teams battle into 11th with score tied 1-1. Enos Slaughter then leads off Yankee half with upper-deck homer to hand Donovan just his fourth loss in 19 decisions and to end, for all practical purposes, the AL pennant race.

THE DATE: Friday, September 13
THE PLACE: Yankee Stadium
THE CROWD: 13,374
THE STARTERS: Billy Pierce (Chi), Whitey Ford (NY)
THE FINAL: Yankees 7, White Sox 1
THE WINNER: Ford
THE LOSER: Pierce
THE KEYS: Mickey Mantle, back in lineup after missing 10 games with shin splints, doubles in two runs in first and triples and scores in third as Yankees KO Pierce (19-11). Walt Dropo collects three hits but commits three errors. Sox six games out with 15 left.

THE DATE: Saturday, September 14
THE PLACE: Yankee Stadium
THE CROWD: 29,275
THE STARTERS: Dick Donovan (Chi), Tom Sturdivant (NY)
THE FINAL: White Sox 5, Yankees 2
THE WINNER: Donovan
THE LOSER: Bob Grim
THE KEYS: With score tied 2-2 in eighth, Minnie Minoso leads off with single against reliever Grim and Jim Rivera follows with homer into third tier in right field to give Donovan his 16th win (against five losses). Donovan ends up 3-1 vs. Yanks in '57, allowing 33 hits and 12 runs in 45 innings.

1958 Season

THE DATE: Tuesday night, May 20
THE PLACE: Comiskey Park
THE CROWD: 36,167
THE STARTERS: Johnny Kucks (NY), Dick Donovan (Chi)
THE FINAL: Yankees 5, White Sox 1
THE WINNER: Kucks

THE LOSER: Donovan
THE KEYS: See "Most Devastating Defeat"

THE DATE: Wednesday, May 21
THE PLACE: Comiskey Park
THE CROWD: 9,002
THE STARTERS: Whitey Ford (NY), Billy Pierce (Chi)
THE FINAL: Yankees 5, White Sox 2
THE WINNER: Ford
THE LOSER: Pierce
THE KEYS: Homers by Jim Landis and Al Smith put Pierce ahead 2-0 before Elston Howard's two-run shot into bullpen creates 2-2 tie in fifth. Gil McDougald unties it with three-run homer into upper deck in left in sixth. Yankees 21-5, last-place Sox 11-18. Pierce is 1-4.

THE DATE: Monday night, June 2
THE PLACE: Yankee Stadium
THE CROWD: 12,641
THE STARTERS: Jim Wilson (Chi), Whitey Ford (NY)
THE FINAL: Yankees 3, White Sox 0
THE WINNER: Ford
THE LOSER: Wilson
THE KEYS: In makeup of earlier rainout, Wilson allows six hits, but three are homers—two by Hank Bauer, one by Mickey Mantle. Ford, 23-7 lifetime vs. Chicago, throws seven-hit shutout and strikes out nine.

THE DATE: Tuesday night, June 3
THE PLACE: Yankee Stadium
THE CROWD: 30,970
THE STARTERS: Dick Donovan (Chi), Johnny Kucks (NY)
THE FINAL: Yankees 13, White Sox 0
THE WINNER: Kucks
THE LOSER: Donovan
THE KEYS: Kucks allows only two hits—singles by Billy Goodman—and Yankees KO Donovan in first when Mickey Mantle's three-run homer is followed by Bill Skowron's solo shot. Donovan falls to 2-6.

THE DATE: Wednesday, June 4
THE PLACE: Yankee Stadium
THE CROWD: 8,582
THE STARTERS: Billy Pierce (Chi), Tom Sturdivant (NY)
THE FINAL: White Sox 7, Yankees 2
THE WINNER: Pierce
THE LOSER: Sturdivant
THE KEYS: Two-run pinch single by Don Mueller breaks 2-2 tie in seventh and KOs Sturdivant, and Jim Rivera adds two-run homer in eighth off Bob Grim to enable Pierce to even record at 4-4.

THE DATE: Thursday, June 5
THE PLACE: Yankee Stadium
THE CROWD: 14,402
THE STARTERS (1st): Early Wynn (Chi), Don Larsen (NY)
THE STARTERS (2nd): Ray Moore (Chi), Bobby Shantz (NY)
THE FINALS: Yankees 12, White Sox 5; White Sox 3, Yankees 2

THE WINNER (1st): Larsen
THE LOSER (1st): Wynn
THE WINNER (2nd): Moore
THE LOSER (2nd): Shantz
THE KEYS: Wynn allows seven hits and seven runs—including inside-the-park homer by Mickey Mantle—in 4 2/3 innings of opener. In Game 2, Sherm Lollar hits two-run, first-inning homer and Moore shuts out Yankees on four hits through eight before New York breaks through in ninth for two runs, one unearned because of Earl Torgeson's error. Nellie Fox (6 for 9 on day) raises average to .350.

THE DATE: Monday night, June 23
THE PLACE: Comiskey Park
THE CROWD: 30,388
THE STARTERS: Whitey Ford (NY), Ray Moore (Chi)
THE FINAL: White Sox 2, Yankees 0
THE WINNER: Moore
THE LOSER: Ford
THE KEYS: Sherm Lollar hits two-run homer in first inning and Moore goes the route, allowing just three hits, in a snappy 2:05. He strikes out five and walks only two. Sox, still 9 1/2 games out, get reliever Turk Lown on waivers from Cincinnati, sell Walt Dropo to same club.

THE DATE: Tuesday night, June 24
THE PLACE: Comiskey Park
THE CROWD: 27,845
THE STARTERS: Bob Turley (NY), Early Wynn (Chi)
THE FINAL: Yankees 6, White Sox 2
THE WINNER: Turley
THE LOSER: Wynn
THE KEYS: Crowd held down by rain and by WGN-TV's first home night telecast of a Sox game since 1948 sees Wynn get bombed for three homers in the fourth: a solo shot by Mickey Mantle, Jerry Lumpe's three-run blast (his first homer in the major leagues) and another bases-empty homer by Norm Siebern. Turley improves to 11-3.

THE DATE: Thursday, June 26
THE PLACE: Comiskey Park
THE CROWD: 31,535 (18,214 paid)
THE STARTERS: Johnny Kucks (NY), Dick Donovan (Chi)
THE FINAL: Yankees 4, White Sox 3
THE WINNER: Kucks
THE LOSER: Donovan
THE KEYS: After rainout, Sox fall three games under .500 and 11 1/2 behind New York as Yankees break 1-1 tie on Bill Skowron's two-run single in the sixth and make it 4-1 on Norm Siebern's homer in the seventh. Jim Rivera's two-run homer in seventh makes it close.

THE DATE: Sunday, July 13
THE PLACE: Yankee Stadium
THE CROWD: 39,854
THE STARTERS (1st): Billy Pierce (Chi), Don Larsen (NY)
THE STARTERS (2nd): Ray Moore (Chi), Bobby Shantz (NY)
THE FINALS: White Sox 7, Yankees 4; Yankees 5, White Sox 4 (10 innings)

THE WINNER (1st): Pierce
THE LOSER (1st): Larsen
THE WINNER (2nd): Ryne Duren
THE LOSER (2nd): Bob Keegan
THE KEYS: Turk Lown nails down Game 1 victory with three scoreless innings, allowing one hit and striking out five after Billy Goodman helps stake Pierce to lead with triple and two-run single. Jim Landis' two-run homer ties Game 2 at 4-4 in fifth, but Jerry Lumpe's bases-loaded single in 10th off Keegan is the game-winner.

THE DATE: Monday, July 14
THE PLACE: Yankee Stadium
THE CROWD: 15,311
THE STARTERS: Early Wynn (Chi), Whitey Ford (NY)
THE FINAL: Yankees 5, White Sox 0
THE WINNER: Ford
THE LOSER: Wynn
THE KEYS: Hank Bauer opens Yankee first with home run and Mickey Mantle later homers—his 23rd of the year and seventh off Chicago pitching—to help Ford (three-hitter) improve to 11-4 on the season and 24-8 lifetime vs. Sox. Chicago is fifth, 15 1/2 games out.

THE DATE: Friday night, August 1
THE PLACE: Comiskey Park
THE CROWD: 38,832
THE STARTERS: Bob Turley (NY), Billy Pierce (Chi)
THE FINAL: Yankees 7, White Sox 0
THE WINNER: Turley
THE LOSER: Pierce
THE KEYS: Bill Skowron homers, singles twice and drives in four runs and Turley throws five-hitter to go to 16-4 on the season.

THE DATE: Saturday, August 2
THE PLACE: Comiskey Park
THE CROWD: 18,611
THE STARTERS: Art Ditmar (NY), Early Wynn (Chi)
THE FINAL: Yankees 6, White Sox 1
THE WINNER: Ditmar
THE LOSER: Wynn
THE KEYS: Yogi Berra singles in a run in the first, hits three-run homer in sixth and doubles home Yanks' final two runs in eighth; Ditmar goes distance, scattering eight hits.

THE DATE: Sunday, August 3
THE PLACE: Comiskey Park
THE CROWD: 35,695
THE STARTERS (1st): Whitey Ford (NY), Dick Donovan (Chi)
THE STARTERS (2nd): Johnny Kucks (NY), Ray Moore (Chi)
THE FINALS: White Sox 3, Yankees 1; White Sox 4, Yankees 0
THE WINNER (1st) Donovan
THE LOSER (1st): Ford
THE WINNER (2nd): Moore
THE LOSER (2nd): Kucks
THE KEYS: See "Most Glorious Victory"

THE DATE: Thursday night, August 21
THE PLACE: Yankee Stadium
THE CROWD: 26,829
THE STARTERS: Ray Moore (Chi), Bob Turley (NY)
THE FINAL: Yankees 6, White Sox 3
THE WINNER: Turley
THE LOSER: Moore
THE KEYS: Yankees expand 3-2 lead with three runs in seventh with sacrifice flies by Bill Skowron and Elston Howard and Tony Kubek's squeeze bunt—all against birthday boy Gerry Staley (38)—and Turley improves to 18-6 while halting Sox's seven-game winning streak. Moore now 9-4 overall, 3-1 vs. New York.

THE DATE: Friday, August 22
THE PLACE: Yankee Stadium
THE CROWD: 12,257
THE STARTERS: Early Wynn (Chi), Johnny Kucks (NY)
THE FINAL: Yankees 8, White Sox 5
THE WINNER: Duke Maas
THE LOSER: Wynn
THE KEYS: Billy Goodman (.323) goes 4 for 4 and Sherm Lollar's 17th homer puts Sox up 4-3 after 6½, but Yankees get four in seventh, Enos Slaughter singling in the tying run and Tony Kubek the tie-breaker.

THE DATE: Saturday, August 23
THE PLACE: Yankee Stadium
THE CROWD: 23,183
THE STARTERS: Billy Pierce (Chi), Whitey Ford (NY)
THE FINAL: White Sox 7, Yankees 1
THE WINNER: Pierce
THE LOSER: Ford
THE KEYS: Ray Boone highlights four-run seventh with three-run double, and Pierce (14-8) lowers ERA to 2.58, second in AL to Ford's 2.11.

THE DATE: Friday night, September 12
THE PLACE: Comiskey Park
THE CROWD: 24,892
THE STARTERS: Bob Turley (NY), Ray Moore (Chi)
THE FINAL: Yankees 5, White Sox 0
THE WINNER: Turley
THE LOSER: Moore
THE KEYS: Turley becomes Yanks' first 21-game winner since Vic Raschi and Eddie Lopat in '51 by allowing only four hits—one a double by 19-year-old rookie Johnny Callison. Moore drops fourth straight.

THE DATE: Saturday, September 13
THE PLACE: Comiskey Park
THE CROWD: 13,962
THE STARTERS: Bobby Shantz (NY), Early Wynn (Chi)
THE FINAL: Yankees 5, White Sox 4
THE WINNER: Murry Dickson
THE LOSER: Wynn
THE KEYS: Gil McDougald drives three-run homer into left-field upper deck off Wynn with two out in eighth to wipe out 4-2 Sox lead, and Ryne Duren fans

Ray Boone with two on in ninth to enable Yankees to clinch tie for pennant. Wynn finishes 0-6 vs. New York in '58.

1959 Season

THE DATE: Wednesday, April 29
THE PLACE: Comiskey Park
THE CROWD: 9,952
THE STARTERS: Bob Turley (NY), Ray Moore (Chi)
THE FINAL: Yankees 5, White Sox 2
THE WINNER: Turley
THE LOSER: Moore
THE KEYS: Mickey Mantle, Hank Bauer and Bill Skowron hit home runs as Yankees climb to .500 (7-7). Sherm Lollar fails to advance any of the seven baserunners aboard for him. Nellie Fox collects four hits.

THE DATE: Thursday night, April 30
THE PLACE: Comiskey Park
THE CROWD: 26,944
THE STARTERS: Whitey Ford (NY), Billy Pierce (Chi)
THE FINAL: White Sox 4, Yankees 3 (11 innings)
THE WINNER: Pierce
THE LOSER: Ryne Duren
THE KEYS: Jim Rivera's diving catch in top of 11th saves a run (and costs Rivera a cracked rib), and Al Smith's two-out bases-loaded single in bottom half wins it for Pierce (nine hits allowed in 11 innings).

THE DATE: Friday night, May 15
THE PLACE: Yankee Stadium
THE CROWD: 27,863
THE STARTERS: Billy Pierce (Chi), Whitey Ford (NY)
THE FINAL: White Sox 6, Yankees 0
THE WINNER: Pierce
THE LOSER: Ford
THE KEYS: Pierce fans seven, allows six hits, gets his 33rd career shutout, improves record to 5-2 and lowers ERA to 2.90 while becoming first lefty to blank the Yankees since Cleveland's Herb Score did so on Aug. 21, 1956. Sox's winning streak reaches seven.

THE DATE: Saturday, May 16
THE PLACE: Yankee Stadium
THE CROWD: 20,980
THE STARTERS: Ray Moore (Chi), Bob Turley (NY)
THE FINAL: White Sox 4, Yankees 3 (11 innings)
THE WINNER: Turk Lown
THE LOSER: Art Ditmar
THE KEYS: With Sox down 3-2 in ninth, Mickey Mantle loses Nellie Fox's drive in the sun (he's charged with three-base error) and Sherm Lollar follows with game-tying single; newcomer Del Ennis singles home Fox with game-winner in 11th, Turk Lown strikes out Mantle to end it, and Chicago's winning streak is at eight.

THE DATE: Tuesday night, June 16
THE PLACE: Yankee Stadium

THE CROWD: 30,097
THE STARTERS: Billy Pierce (Chi), Art Ditmar (NY)
THE FINAL: Yankees 5, White Sox 1
THE WINNER: Ditmar
THE LOSER: Pierce
THE KEYS: After Bill Veeck's trade-deadline offer for Washington's Roy Sievers is rejected, Sox lose when Yankees' new acquisition, Hector Lopez, doubles in tie-breaking run in the sixth. Ditmar finishes with four-hitter; Chicago is one game behind first-place Cleveland.

THE DATE: Wednesday, June 17
THE PLACE: Yankee Stadium
THE CROWD: 10,078
THE STARTERS: Ray Moore (Chi), Bob Turley (NY)
THE FINAL: Yankees 7, White Sox 3
THE WINNER: Turley
THE LOSER: Moore
THE KEYS: Moore lasts only 1 2/3 innings and slumps to 1-5 as Mickey Mantle caps five-run second with three-run homer off the facade above the third tier in right. Yanks move to 29-29; Sox are 33-27.

THE DATE: Thursday, June 18
THE PLACE: Yankee Stadium
THE CROWD: 12,217
THE STARTERS: Bob Shaw (Chi), Jim Bronstad (NY)
THE FINAL: Yankees 5, White Sox 4 (10 innings)
THE WINNER: Bobby Shantz
THE LOSER: Gerry Staley
THE KEYS: See "Most Devastating Defeat"

THE DATE: Friday night, June 26
THE PLACE: Comiskey Park
THE CROWD: 37,909
THE STARTERS: Art Ditmar (NY), Billy Pierce (Chi)
THE FINAL: Yankees 8, White Sox 4
THE WINNER: Ditmar
THE LOSER: Pierce
THE KEYS: Hector Lopez's two-run homer into centerfield bullpen puts Yanks ahead to stay in fifth, and Ryne Duren, pitching the final three innings, closes in overpowering fashion, striking out eight and allowing only one hit—and one hit batsman (Jim Landis)—in his 14th straight scoreless outing.

THE DATE: Saturday, June 27
THE PLACE: Comiskey Park
THE CROWD: 21,624
THE STARTERS: Bob Turley (NY), Bob Shaw (Chi)
THE FINAL: White Sox 5, Yankees 4
THE WINNER: Shaw
THE LOSER: Turley
THE KEYS: In perhaps most pivotal game of these teams' seasons (both entered with 36-32 records, two games behind first-place Cleveland), Turley takes 2-1 lead into the eighth, thanks to two homers by Hector Lopez. With two out, Nellie Fox walks, Earl Torgeson singles and Sherm Lollar walks to fill the bases. Even with lefty Bobby Shantz ready in bullpen, Casey Stengel elects to stay with

Turley against lefty-swinging Harry "Suitcase" Simpson, the ex-Yankee acquired from Kansas City in early May. Simpson responds with grand slam against upper-deck railing in right for 5-2 Sox lead. After solo homers by Norm Siebern and Bill Skowron off Rodolfo Arias, Gerry Staley fans Tony Kubek with runners at first and third to end game.

THE DATE: Sunday, June 28
THE PLACE: Comiskey Park
THE CROWD: 42,121
THE STARTERS (1st): Whitey Ford (NY), Early Wynn (Chi)
THE STARTERS (2nd): Don Larsen (NY), Dick Donovan (Chi)
THE FINALS: White Sox 9, Yankees 2; White Sox 4, Yankees 2
THE WINNER (1st): Wynn
THE LOSER (1st): Ford
THE WINNER (2nd): Donovan
THE LOSER (2nd): Larsen
THE KEYS: Two-run homers by Sherm Lollar and Earl Battey in sixth inning of opener wipe out 2-1 New York lead and KO Ford; Wynn notches 11th win of year and 260th of career. Lollar's three-run homer in first inning is decisive blow of Game 2. Sox one game out of first.

THE DATE: Friday night, July 17
THE PLACE: Yankee Stadium
THE CROWD: 42,020
THE STARTERS: Early Wynn (Chi), Ralph Terry (NY)
THE FINAL: White Sox 2, Yankees 0
THE WINNER: Wynn
THE LOSER: Terry
THE KEYS: See "Most Glorious Victory"

THE DATE: Saturday, July 18
THE PLACE: Yankee Stadium
THE CROWD: 27,959
THE STARTERS: Bob Shaw (Chi), Don Larsen (NY)
THE FINAL: White Sox 2, Yankees 1
THE WINNER: Shaw
THE LOSER: Larsen
THE KEYS: With runners at first and third and one out in ninth, Gerry Staley relieves Shaw—who had driven in go-ahead run with single in fourth—and throws one pitch to Hector Lopez, who raps into game-ending 4-6-3 double play. Sox's winning streak hits seven; they lead league by one game.

THE DATE: Sunday, July 19
THE PLACE: Yankee Stadium
THE CROWD: 57,057
THE STARTERS (1st): Barry Latman (Chi), Whitey Ford (NY)
THE STARTERS (2nd): Billy Pierce (Chi), Eli Grba (NY)
THE FINALS: Yankees 6, White Sox 2; Yankees 6, White Sox 4
THE WINNER (1st): Ford
THE LOSER (1st): Latman
THE WINNER (2nd): Grba
THE LOSER (2nd): Pierce
THE KEYS: Enos Slaughter hits the final two home runs of his glorious career, and Ryne Duren strikes out five in the final two innings to help Ford improve

to 10-6; Grba, rookie from Chicago's Southeast Side, gets first big-league win in Game 2, behind Mickey Mantle's 20th homer and relief help from Duren. Sox .001 out of first, Yankees 5 1/2 back.

THE DATE: Tuesday night, July 28
THE PLACE: Comiskey Park
THE CROWD: 43,829
THE STARTERS: Ralph Terry (NY), Billy Pierce (Chi)
THE FINAL: White Sox 4, Yankees 3
THE WINNER: Pierce
THE LOSER: Terry
THE KEYS: Nellie Fox's single scores Pierce with tie-breaking run in fifth and Al Smith hits two-run homer in eighth to provide cushion for Pierce in ninth, when Yankees score twice before Tony Kubek is called out on strikes (Pierce's 10th strikeout) to end game and send Sox into first place to stay.

THE DATE: Wednesday night, July 29
THE PLACE: Comiskey Park
THE CROWD: 43,599
THE STARTERS: Whitey Ford (NY), Bob Shaw (Chi)
THE FINAL: White Sox 4, Yankees 4 (tie)
THE KEYS: Ford departs because of elbow pain in second, and Sox break 2-2 tie in fifth against Duke Maas when Luis Aparicio triples in rookie Jim McAnany and scores on an infield out. But Yogi Berra's two-run homer in sixth ties game and, after Sox go 1-2-3 in their half, deluge hits.

THE DATE: Thursday, July 30
THE PLACE: Comiskey Park
THE CROWD: 30,858
THE STARTERS: Eli Grba (NY), Early Wynn (Chi)
THE FINAL: White Sox 3, Yankees 1
THE WINNER: Wynn
THE LOSER: Grba
THE KEYS: Billy Goodman's single scores Sherm Lollar to break 1-1 tie in seventh, and Al Smith's RBI single in eighth adds insurance for Wynn (14-6), who strikes out nine, walks one, and allows six hits.

THE DATE: Sunday, August 23
THE PLACE: Comiskey Park
THE CROWD: 44,520
THE STARTERS (1st): Art Ditmar (NY), Early Wynn (Chi)
THE STARTERS (2nd): Ralph Terry (NY), Bob Shaw (Chi)
THE FINALS: Yankees 7, White Sox 1; White Sox 5, Yankees 0
THE WINNER (1st): Ditmar
THE LOSER (1st): Wynn
THE WINNER (2nd): Shaw
THE LOSER (2nd): Terry
THE KEYS: Enos Slaughter's two-run pinch single breaks 1-1 tie in seventh inning of opener and Ditmar finishes with three-hitter; in nightcap, Sherm Lollar's 19th homer, a solo shot, snaps scoreless tie in seventh and ignites rally that produces four more runs and sends Shaw to his 13th win. Sox are 1 1/2 games ahead of second-place Indians.

THE DATE: Monday, August 24
THE PLACE: Comiskey Park
THE CROWD: 21,923
THE STARTERS: Don Larsen (NY), Ray Moore (Chi)
THE FINAL: White Sox 4, Yankees 2
THE WINNER: Moore
THE LOSER: Larsen
THE KEYS: In makeup of July 29 rainout, Jim Landis singles in two runs, rookie Norm Cash singles in one, Sherm Lollar contributes RBI double and Luis Aparicio steals his 41st and 42nd bases. Turk Lown relieves Moore in sixth and strikes out four in his 3 1/3 innings, twice getting Mickey Mantle, who had already been fanned twice by Moore. Sox clinch season series vs. Yanks for first time since 1925.

THE DATE: Tuesday, September 15
THE PLACE: Yankee Stadium
THE CROWD: 8,714
THE STARTERS: Billy Pierce (Chi), Ralph Terry (NY)
THE FINAL: White Sox 4, Yankees 3
THE WINNER: Pierce
THE LOSER: Whitey Ford
THE KEYS: Terry leads 2-1 but forced to depart after seven innings with strained back, and Sox greet Ford with single by Nellie Fox, walk to newcomer Ted Kluszewski and RBI hit by Sherm Lollar. Bob Turley relieves and hits Al Smith with pitch, and Jim Rivera and Norm Cash follow with sacrifice flies. Mickey Mantle's two homers go for naught as Sox reduce magic number to 5.

THE DATE: Wednesday, September 16
THE PLACE: Yankee Stadium
THE CROWD: 7,550
THE STARTERS: Early Wynn (Chi), Jim Coates (NY)
THE FINAL: Yankees 3, White Sox 1
THE WINNER: Coates
THE LOSER: Wynn
THE KEYS: RBI singles in the sixth by Yogi Berra, Hector Lopez and Hank Bauer provide all the runs off Wynn, beaten in his quest for his 21st victory by rookie Coates, who goes the route.

1960 Season

THE DATE: Sunday, May 8
THE PLACE: Yankee Stadium
THE CROWD: 19,053
THE STARTERS: Billy Pierce (Chi), Art Ditmar (NY)
THE FINAL: White Sox 8, Yankees 3 (10 innings)
THE WINNER: Gerry Staley
THE LOSER: Fred Kipp
THE KEYS: After Yankees rally for two runs to tie game at 3-3 in ninth, Minnie Minoso and Ted Kluszewski open Sox 10th with singles off lefty Kipp. Sherm Lollar and Al Smith follow with RBI singles off Jim Coates, and Jim Landis drills a three-run homer to right to clinch the victory for first-place Chicago, which leads New York by one game.

THE DATE: Friday night, May 20

THE PLACE: Comiskey Park
THE CROWD: 40,970
THE STARTERS: Whitey Ford (NY), Early Wynn (Chi)
THE FINAL: White Sox 5, Yankees 3
THE WINNER: Wynn
THE LOSER: Ford
THE KEYS: Ted Kluszewski hits two-out, two-run homer off Ford in fourth and then singles home two runs off Ryne Duren in eighth to help Wynn to 5-1 lead. Yankees cut deficit in half on Mickey Mantle's two-run homer in ninth before Turk Lown, with two on, strikes out Bill Skowron to end Sox's ninth victory in nine home games.

THE DATE: Saturday, May 21
THE PLACE: Comiskey Park
THE CROWD: 24,631 (14,385 paid)
THE STARTERS: Art Ditmar (NY), Dick Donovan (Chi)
THE FINAL: White Sox 9, Yankees 8
THE WINNER: Gerry Staley
THE LOSER: Bobby Shantz
THE KEYS: In game delayed three times by rain and hampered by 30 M.P.H. winds, Yankees get homers from Roger Maris, Gil McDougald and Bob Cerv to build 4-3 lead after 2 1/2 before Sox rally for 8-4 advantage in the fifth. Tony Kubek's two-run double in sixth and Roger Maris' two-run homer in seventh forge 8-8 tie, which Sox break in their half on Minnie Minoso's RBI single. Gerry Staley strikes out Yogi Berra for final out with tying run at third. Sox lead Indians by 1 1/2 games, Orioles by two and Yankees by 3 1/2.

THE DATE: Monday night, June 6
THE PLACE: Yankee Stadium
THE CROWD: 24,018
THE STARTERS: Billy Pierce (Chi), Whitey Ford (NY))
THE FINAL: White Sox 3, Yankees 2
THE WINNER: Gerry Staley
THE LOSER: Ford
THE KEYS: Minnie Minoso's two-run single sends Chicago ahead 2-1 in eighth, but Staley surrenders Roger Maris' 15th homer in home half before Luis Aparicio's bases-loaded infield hit sends winning run home in ninth. Dick Donovan picks up the save.

THE DATE: Tuesday, June 7
THE PLACE: Yankee Stadium
THE CROWD: 12,810
THE STARTERS: Early Wynn (Chi), Jim Coates (NY)
THE FINAL: Yankees 5, White Sox 2
THE WINNER: Coates
THE LOSER: Wynn
THE KEYS: Casey Stengel, hospitalized for two weeks, returns to Yankee dugout after absence of 13 games. Says Case: "They examined all my organs. Some are quite remarkable and others are not so good. A lot of museums are bidding for them." Coates fires four-hitter and benefits from Tony Kubek's two-run double in third off Wynn and Bill Skowron's two-run double in eighth off Dick Donovan.

THE DATE: Wednesday night, June 8

Appendix A

THE PLACE: Yankee Stadium
THE CROWD: 30,420
THE STARTERS: Bob Shaw (Chi), Bob Turley (NY)
THE FINAL: Yankees 6, White Sox 0
THE WINNER: Turley
THE LOSER: Shaw
THE KEYS: Turley throws three-hit shutout and Shaw allows two-run homer to Hector Lopez and solo blast by Mickey Mantle. Yanks clinch decision in eighth against Ray Moore with back-to-back homers by Mantle and Roger Maris.

THE DATE: Thursday, June 9
THE PLACE: Yankee Stadium
THE CROWD: 12,588
THE STARTERS: Frank Baumann (Chi), Ralph Terry (NY)
THE FINAL: Yankees 5, White Sox 2
THE WINNER: Johnny James
THE LOSER: Baumann
THE KEYS: Baumann, coming off successive shutouts, is tagged for three runs, including Mickey Mantle's two-run homer, and lasts only into the fourth. Bobby Shantz gets save with three innings of one-hit, shutout relief. Yankees move past Sox into third, 3 1/2 games behind Indians.

THE DATE: Friday night, June 17
THE PLACE: Comiskey Park
THE CROWD: 43,320
THE STARTERS: Art Ditmar (NY), Billy Pierce (Chi)
THE FINAL: Yankees 4, White Sox 2
THE WINNER: Ditmar
THE LOSER: Pierce
THE KEYS: Ditmar works seven-hit complete game and Yankees, spoofing Bill Veeck's new exploding scoreboard, light sparklers after home runs by Clete Boyer and Mickey Mantle. Yankees win 10th in last 12 games.

THE DATE: Saturday, June 18
THE PLACE: Comiskey Park
THE CROWD: 34,640 (20,981 paid)
THE STARTERS: Bob Turley (NY), Early Wynn (Chi)
THE FINAL: Yankees 12, White Sox 5
THE WINNER: Eli Grba
THE LOSER: Wynn
THE KEYS: Mickey Mantle and Roger Maris homer off ex-Cub Bob Rush and Bill Skowron victimizes Frank Baumann to highlight 19-hit attack, and Eli Grba, working over final six innings, allows only two-run homer by Roy Sievers. It's Sievers' sixth homer; he'll finish with 28.

THE DATE: Sunday, June 19
THE PLACE: Comiskey Park
THE CROWD: 48,139
THE STARTERS (1st): Jim Coates (NY), Bob Shaw (Chi)
THE STARTERS (2nd): John Gabler (NY), Russ Kemmerer (Chi)
THE FINALS: Yankees 7, White Sox 5; Yankees 5, White Sox 3
THE WINNER (1st): Coates
THE LOSER (1st): Shaw
THE WINNER (2nd): Johnny James

THE LOSER (2nd): Kemmerer
THE KEYS: Two-run singles by Bobby Richardson and Coates chase Shaw in the fifth inning of Game 1, and Mickey Mantle's two-out RBI triple followed by Roger Maris' single—both in sixth—are key blows in Game 2. Bob Turley saves both games for New York. Minnie Minoso homers twice for Sox, who fall to 30-29 and fifth place. Yankees take AL lead by .003 over Orioles.

THE DATE: Friday night, July 22
THE PLACE: Yankee Stadium
THE CROWD: 48,603
THE STARTERS: Early Wynn (Chi), Bob Turley (NY)
THE FINAL: White Sox 11, Yankees 5
THE WINNER: Frank Baumann
THE LOSER: Turley
THE KEYS: Sox collect 18 hits, giving them 70 hits and 47 runs in their last five games, and win their sixth straight to close to within .003 of the first-place Yankees.

THE DATE: Saturday, July 23
THE PLACE: Yankee Stadium
THE CROWD: 38,402 (28,402 paid)
THE STARTERS: Bob Shaw (Chi), Whitey Ford (NY)
THE FINAL: White Sox 5, Yankees 3
THE WINNER: Shaw
THE LOSER: Ford
THE KEYS: See "Most Glorious Victory"

THE DATE: Sunday, July 24
THE PLACE: Yankee Stadium
THE CROWD: 60,002
THE STARTERS (1st): Billy Pierce (Chi), Jim Coates (NY)
THE STARTERS (2nd): Herb Score (Chi), Eli Grba (NY)
THE FINALS: White Sox 6, Yankees 3; Yankees 8, White Sox 2
THE WINNER (1st): Pierce
THE LOSER (1st): Coates
THE WINNER (1st): Grba
THE LOSER (1st): Score
THE KEYS: Pierce pitches Sox to eighth straight win in opener as Nellie Fox gets 2,000th career hit, Roy Sievers hits No. 16—a two-run shot—and Gene Freese adds a two-run triple. In Game 2, Grba goes route, Roger Maris' two-out RBI single breaks 2-2 tie in fourth and Mickey Mantle belts 24th homer an inning later. Sox lead by one game.

THE DATE: Monday night, August 8
THE PLACE: Comiskey Park
THE CROWD: 48,323
THE STARTERS: Whitey Ford (NY), Billy Pierce (Chi)
THE FINAL: White Sox 9, Yankees 1
THE WINNER: Pierce
THE LOSER: Ford
THE KEYS: Roy Sievers breaks 1-1 tie in third with RBI double, and Minnie Minoso later adds bases-loaded two-run single and Sox—minus the injured Sherm Lollar for this series—go on to defeat Ford a fourth straight time. Pierce finishes with four-hitter and Sox close to within half-game of AL-leading Yankees.

Appendix A

THE DATE: Tuesday night, August 9
THE PLACE: Comiskey Park
THE CROWD: 48,408
THE STARTERS: Bob Turley (NY), Early Wynn (Chi)
THE FINAL: Yankees 7, White Sox 4
THE WINNER: Luis Arroyo
THE LOSER: Frank Baumann
THE KEYS: Gene Freese's three-run homer gives Sox 4-2 lead in fifth before Yankees tie with RBI singles by Tony Kubek and Hector Lopez. After Yankees load bases with none out in eighth, two misplays by Nellie Fox and one by Roy Sievers give Yankees 7-4 lead. With two out in home eighth and monsoon-like downpour just blocks away, Jim Landis chases Arroyo screwball for strike three, and the rains arrive seconds later, washing out game. Had Landis waited a few moments, the score might have reverted to the seventh inning, forcing a complete replay. Instead, Sox trail by 1 1/2 games.

THE DATE: Wednesday, August 10
THE PLACE: Comiskey Park
THE CROWD: 51,344 (48,109 paid)
THE STARTERS: Art Ditmar (NY), Herb Score (Chi)
THE FINAL: Yankees 6, White Sox 0
THE WINNER: Ditmar
THE LOSER: Score
THE KEYS: Before largest weekday crowd in Comiskey Park history, Score allows no walks and just one hit—Bill Skowron's 21st homer—through seven innings. But Bobby Shantz strikes out Joe Ginsberg with bases loaded and two out in Sox's seventh, and Yanks get two in eighth off Score (on Tony Kubek's two-run single) and three more in ninth off Turk Lown. Yankees now lead Orioles by one game, Sox by 2 1/2.

THE DATE: Tuesday night, August 23
THE PLACE: Yankee Stadium
THE CROWD: 43,275
THE STARTERS: Early Wynn (Chi), Eli Grba (NY)
THE FINAL: White Sox 5, Yankees 1
THE WINNER: Wynn
THE LOSER: Grba
THE KEYS: Wynn replaces Billy Pierce just before game's start because of Pierce's sore hip, and the 40-year-old righthander goes on to pitch four-hitter, New York's lone run coming on Grba's homer just inside left-field foul pole. Sox again just half-game out of first.

THE DATE: Wednesday, August 24
THE PLACE: Yankee Stadium
THE CROWD: 32,116
THE STARTERS: Herb Score (Chi), Art Ditmar (NY)
THE FINAL: Yankees 3, White Sox 2
THE WINNER: Ditmar
THE LOSER: Score
THE KEYS: See "Most Devastating Defeat"

THE DATE: Wednesday night, September 7
THE PLACE: Comiskey Park
THE CROWD: 36,372

THE STARTERS: Whitey Ford (NY), Early Wynn (Chi)
THE FINAL: Yankees 6, White Sox 4
THE WINNER: Luis Arroyo
THE LOSER: Wynn
THE KEYS: With Sox ahead 4-1 in the eighth and Yankee runners at first and second and one out, Bill Skowron raps double-play ball at second baseman Sammy Esposito (Nellie Fox is sidelined by a virus after 798 consecutive games), but Esposito bobbles ball, loading the bases. Yogi Berra follows with two-run single, John Blanchard with a pinch double, and the Yankees are ahead 5-4. Then come some fisticuffs between Esposito and an angry fan (see "The Fights"). Tony Kubek homers in ninth and Arroyo retires final seven Sox hitters. Yankees are 1 1/2 games behind first-place Orioles, while Sox are 4 1/2 back.

THE DATE: Thursday night, September 8
THE PLACE: Comiskey Park
THE CROWD: 32,152
THE STARTERS: Art Ditmar (NY), Billy Pierce (Chi)
THE FINAL: White Sox 5, Yankees 4
THE WINNER: Russ Kemmerer
THE LOSER: Luis Arroyo
THE KEYS: With Sox trailing 4-1 in seventh, Gene Freese homers off Ditmar, Al Smith rips two-out RBI single off Arroyo and Ted Kluszewski—making first start since July 4—greets Bobby Shantz with two-run double to left for 5-4 lead. Mike Garcia, 36, activated on Sept. 1 after serving as batting-practice pitcher, zips through eighth on five pitches, then fans Mickey Mantle and Bill Skowron in scoreless ninth to gain the save and keep Chicago's pennant hopes alive.

1961 Season

THE DATE: Sunday, May 28
THE PLACE: Yankee Stadium
THE CROWD: 44,435
THE STARTERS (1st): Early Wynn (Chi), Bob Turley (NY)
THE STARTERS (2nd): Cal McLish (Chi), Art Ditmar (NY)
THE FINALS: White Sox 14, Yankees 9; Yankees 5, White Sox 3
THE WINNER (1st): Turk Lown
THE LOSER (1st): Luis Arroyo
THE WINNER (2nd): Jim Coates
THE LOSER (2nd): McLish
THE KEYS: Grand slam into third tier by recent acquisition Wes Covington helps stake Wynn to 6-0 Game 1 lead before Yankees rally and tie on pinch grand slam by Bob Cerv in sixth. Yanks lead 9-6 after homers in seventh by Yogi Berra and Bill Skowron, but Sox get four in eighth and clinch in ninth on Floyd Robinson's three-run homer. In Game 2, homers by Covington and Roy Sievers provide McLish (8-1 lifetime vs. Yanks before this date) with 3-1 lead, but New York KOs him in fourth. Coates allows last-place Sox two hits over final six innings.

THE DATE: Friday night, June 2
THE PLACE: Comiskey Park
THE CROWD: 38,410
THE STARTERS: Whitey Ford (NY), Cal McLish (Chi)
THE FINAL: Yankees 6, White Sox 2
THE WINNER: Ford
THE LOSER: McLish

THE KEYS: Yogi Berra homers twice and Roger Maris once; Ford, though allowing two-run homer in first inning to Al Smith, settles down and coasts to seventh victory—his first over the White Sox since July 19, 1959.

THE DATE: Saturday, June 3
THE PLACE: Comiskey Park
THE CROWD: 16,480
THE STARTERS: Ralph Terry (NY), Bob Shaw (Chi)
THE FINAL: White Sox 6, Yankees 5 (10 innings)
THE WINNER: Warren Hacker
THE LOSER: Art Ditmar
THE KEYS: Roger Maris' three-run homer off Shaw in eighth unlocks 2-2 tie, but Sox get two-run pinch homer by Floyd Robinson and Minnie Minoso's sacrifice fly in home eighth, so game moves to extra innings tied 5-5. Hacker, ex-Cub who'd made AL debut the night before, works perfect 11th, 12th, and 13th, and Roy Sievers leads off Sox 13th with home run—his 11th—to beat Ditmar, on Ditmar's last pitch thrown against Sox in a New York uniform. (He was dealt to A's on June 14.)

THE DATE: Sunday, June 4
THE PLACE: Comiskey Park
THE CROWD: 28,362
THE STARTERS: Bill Stafford (NY), Billy Pierce (Chi)
THE FINAL: Yankees 10, White Sox 1
THE WINNER: Stafford
THE LOSER: Pierce
THE KEYS: Four-run first, keyed by Elston Howard's three-run double past the graceless Wes Covington in right, does in Pierce, who falls to 1-5, and Sox, who fall to 10th place again. Covington homers for lone Sox run, a week before he goes to A's in eight-player deal.

THE DATE: Thursday night, July 13
THE PLACE: Comiskey Park
THE CROWD: 43,960
THE STARTERS: Bill Stafford (NY), Early Wynn (Chi)
THE FINAL: Yankees 6, White Sox 2
THE WINNER: Stafford
THE LOSER: Wynn
THE KEYS: Roger Maris hits two-run shot (No. 34) and Mickey Mantle follows with his 30th to highlight four-run Yankee first inning. Sox get homers from Sherm Lollar and reliever Frank Baumann in 11th loss in last 15 games. Yanks take AL lead by percentage points over Detroit.

THE DATE: Friday night, July 14
THE PLACE: Comiskey Park
THE CROWD: 43,450
THE STARTERS: Roland Sheldon (NY), Juan Pizarro (Chi)
THE FINAL: White Sox 6, Yankees 1
THE WINNER: Pizarro
THE LOSER: Sheldon
THE KEYS: Pizarro, 24, improves to 5-3 by throwing seven-hitter, striking out eight, hitting two doubles and driving in a pair of runs. Ex-Yankee Andy Carey, acquired June 10, singles twice and scores once.

THE DATE: Saturday, July 15

THE PLACE: Comiskey Park
THE CROWD: 37,730
THE STARTERS: Ralph Terry (NY), Ray Herbert (Chi)
THE FINAL: Yankees 9, White Sox 8 (10 innings)
THE WINNER: Luis Arroyo
THE LOSER: Warren Hacker
THE KEYS: See "Most Devastating Defeat"

THE DATE: Tuesday night, July 25
THE PLACE: Yankee Stadium
THE CROWD: 46,240
THE STARTERS (1st): Frank Baumann (Chi), Whitey Ford (NY)
THE STARTERS (2nd): Juan Pizarro (Chi), Bill Stafford (NY)
THE FINALS: Yankees 5, White Sox 1; Yankees 12, White Sox 0
THE WINNER (1st): Ford
THE LOSER (1st): Baumann
THE WINNER (2nd): Stafford
THE LOSER (2nd): Pizarro
THE KEYS: Roger Maris cracks two homers in each game to reach the 40 mark and go 24 games ahead of Babe Ruth's '27 pace. Mickey Mantle hits No. 38 in Game 1, helping Ford improve to 18-2 on the season. Clete Boyer homers twice and Elston Howard once in Game 2 as Yanks take half-game lead on second-place Detroit.

THE DATE: Wednesday, July 26
THE PLACE: Yankee Stadium
THE CROWD: 22,366
THE STARTERS: Ray Herbert (Chi), Roland Sheldon (NY)
THE FINAL: Yankees 5, White Sox 2
THE WINNER: Sheldon
THE LOSER: Herbert
THE KEYS: Mickey Mantle belts No. 39, Clete Boyer also homers and John Blanchard hits two out—giving him a streak of four home runs in four at-bats over a three-game span (he had hit a pair of pinch homers three days earlier in Boston). Sheldon finishes with four-hitter.

THE DATE: Thursday night, July 27
THE PLACE: Yankee Stadium
THE CROWD: 20,529
THE STARTERS: Billy Pierce (Chi), Ralph Terry (NY)
THE FINAL: Yankees 4, White Sox 3
THE WINNER: Terry
THE LOSER: Pierce
THE KEYS: Mickey Mantle drives in a pair to help Terry to 4-0 lead after three, but Sox rally with three in ninth (rookie catcher Camilo Carreon singles off Luis Arroyo for two runs) to make it exciting before Sherm Lollar grounds into a game-ending double play.

THE DATE: Tuesday night, August 15
THE PLACE: Yankee Stadium
THE CROWD: 49,059
THE STARTERS: Juan Pizarro (Chi), Whitey Ford (NY)
THE FINAL: White Sox 2, Yankees 1
THE WINNER: Pizarro

THE LOSER: Ford
THE KEYS: See "Most Glorious Victory"

THE DATE: Wednesday, August 16
THE PLACE: Yankee Stadium
THE CROWD: 29,728
THE STARTERS: Billy Pierce (Chi), Roland Sheldon (NY)
THE FINAL: Yankees 5, White Sox 4
THE WINNER: Ralph Terry
THE LOSER: Turk Lown
THE KEYS: Roger Maris' 47th and 48th home runs, both off Pierce, are countered by Nos. 17 and 18 by Jim Landis, and game goes to ninth tied 4-4. Lown allows singles to Bill Skowron and Yogi Berra and intentional walk to John Blanchard before Warren Hacker enters and hits pinch-hitter Bob Cerv with a pitch to force in game-winning run.

THE DATE: Thursday, August 17
THE PLACE: Yankee Stadium
THE CROWD: 25,532
THE STARTERS: Frank Baumann (Chi), Bill Stafford (NY)
THE FINAL: Yankees 5, White Sox 3
THE WINNER: Stafford
THE LOSER: Baumann
THE KEYS: Stafford (10-6) takes 5-0 lead into ninth, when Sox score three times, closing to 5-3 on Floyd Robinson's two-out RBI single off Luis Arroyo. But pinch-hitter Bob Roselli flies to Mickey Mantle to end game and keep Yankees on top by two over Detroit.

THE DATE: Tuesday night, September 12
THE PLACE: Comiskey Park
THE CROWD: 36,166
THE STARTERS: Ralph Terry (NY), Billy Pierce (Chi)
THE FINAL: Yankees 4, White Sox 3 (6 innings)
THE WINNER: Terry
THE LOSER: Pierce
THE KEYS: Elston Howard triples in two runs in New York's three-run first and singles home another in the fifth, but Luis Aparicio homers in Chicago fifth to cut deficit to 4-3. With tying run at third and two out in Sox sixth, rains arrive, play is halted and game is called after wait of 1 hour 5 minutes, extending Yankees' winning streak to 13 and cutting their magic number to 7. Yanks now 100-45, Sox 78-68.

THE DATE: Thursday, September 14
THE PLACE: Comiskey Park
THE CROWD: 18,120
THE STARTERS (1st): Roland Sheldon (NY), Ray Herbert (Chi)
THE STARTERS (2nd): Jim Coates (NY), Juan Pizarro (Chi)
THE FINALS: White Sox 8, Yankees 3; White Sox 4, Yankees 3
THE WINNER (1st): Herbert
THE LOSER (1st): Sheldon
THE WINNER (2nd): Russ Kemmerer
THE LOSER (2nd): Luis Arroyo
THE KEYS: Sox not only sweep but hold Roger Maris at 56 homers and Mickey Mantle at 53—Mantle, in fact, goes hitless on the day. Sox put opener away in first inning when Floyd Robinson hits two-run homer and Jim Landis rips No.

20, a three-run blast. In Game 2, Sox trail 3-1 in ninth but Minnie Minoso, J.C. Martin, and Sherm Lollar deliver successive two-out RBI singles off Arroyo for the victory.

1962 Season

THE DATE: Tuesday, April 24
THE PLACE: Yankee Stadium
THE CROWD: 21,769
THE STARTERS: Johnny Buzhardt (Chi), Ralph Terry (NY)
THE FINAL: White Sox 3, Yankees 1
THE WINNER: Buzhardt
THE LOSER: Terry
THE KEYS: Trailing 1-0 with two out in eighth, Sox get RBI single from Joe Cunningham and two-run homer by Floyd Robinson (AL-leading 21 RBIs in 13 games) to take lead, and Frank Baumann and Turk Lown protect it.

THE DATE: Wednesday, April 25
THE PLACE: Yankee Stadium
THE CROWD: 22,497
THE STARTERS: Juan Pizarro (Chi), Whitey Ford (NY)
THE FINAL: Yankees 7, White Sox 6
THE WINNER: Roland Sheldon
THE LOSER: Eddie Fisher
THE KEYS: Jim Landis (fifth homer, plus triple and double), Al Smith (four hits) and rookie Mike Hershberger (three hits) stake Pizarro to 6-3 lead entering ninth. Yanks load bases with one out, and John Blanchard singles off Fisher for one run; Turk Lown walks Bill Skowron for another and Hector Lopez singles off Lown—on an 0-2 pitch—for the tying and winning runs.

THE DATE: Tuesday night, May 1
THE PLACE: Comiskey Park
THE CROWD: 16,942
THE STARTERS: Bill Stafford (NY), Juan Pizarro (Chi)
THE FINAL: Yankees 6, White Sox 1
THE WINNER: Stafford
THE LOSER: Pizarro
THE KEYS: Errors by Al Smith at third and Luis Aparicio at short lead to three unearned runs for New York, which blanks Chicago on zero hits until ninth. Roland Sheldon, in relief of Stafford (who departs in sixth due to strained hip), allows leadoff single to Nellie Fox and, later, RBI double to Floyd Robinson before lefty Marshall Bridges enters to nail down the victory in 40-degree temperatures. Elston Howard belts 425-foot, two-run homer off Herb Score in Yankee ninth.

THE DATE: Wednesday night, May 2
THE PLACE: Comiskey Park
THE CROWD: 25,547
THE STARTERS: Ralph Terry (NY), Joe Horlen (Chi)
THE FINAL: Yankees 4, White Sox 3
THE WINNER: Jim Coates
THE LOSER: Horlen
THE KEYS: See "Most Devastating Defeat"

Appendix A

THE DATE: Thursday night, May 3
THE PLACE: Comiskey Park
THE CROWD: 30,481
THE STARTERS: Whitey Ford (NY), Johnny Buzhardt (Chi)
THE FINAL: White Sox 1, Yankees 0
THE WINNER: Buzhardt
THE LOSER: Ford
THE KEYS: Jim Landis homers to lead off fourth and Buzhardt (4-1) allows only five hits and one walk as Sox snap Yankee winning streak at seven. Rookie rightfielder Mike Hershberger helps by hauling down deep drives by Mickey Mantle and Yogi Berra in ninth.

THE DATE: Friday night, July 27
THE PLACE: Yankee Stadium
THE CROWD: 28,395
THE STARTERS: Frank Baumann (Chi), Bill Stafford (NY)
THE FINAL: Yankees 4, White Sox 3 (12 innings)
THE WINNER: Bud Daley
THE LOSER: Turk Lown
THE KEYS: Nellie Fox singles home tying run in eighth, but veteran first baseman Dale Long, playing only because Bill Skowron is back home in Chicago for his father's funeral, hits two-out homer off Lown in 12th for Yankees' 13th win in last 16 games. Lown had retired eight straight hitters before the Long shot.

THE DATE: Saturday, July 28
THE PLACE: Yankee Stadium
THE CROWD: 52,038
THE STARTERS: Eddie Fisher (Chi), Whitey Ford (NY)
THE FINAL: Yankees 4, White Sox 3
THE WINNER: Jim Coates
THE LOSER: Fisher
THE KEYS: Down 3-0 in seventh, Yankees rally on Mickey Mantle's 21st homer and three-run pinch home run just out of Mike Hershberger's reach at the 296-foot sign by John Blanchard, whose only previous pinch hit all season had been a single off Fisher back on April 25. Sixth-place Sox fall to 51-52 and 11 1/2 games back of New York.

THE DATE: Sunday, July 29
THE PLACE: Yankee Stadium
THE CROWD: 41,883
THE STARTERS (1st): Juan Pizarro (Chi), Ralph Terry (NY)
THE STARTERS (2nd): Mike Joyce (Chi), Roland Sheldon (NY)
THE FINALS: Yankees 7, White Sox 4; White Sox 6, Yankees 2
THE WINNER (1st): Terry
THE LOSER (1st): Pizarro
THE WINNER (2nd): Pizarro
THE LOSER (2nd): Sheldon
THE KEYS: Pizarro, KOd in five-run first inning of opener (big blow is Bill Skowron's three-run homer), gets the win in Game 2 with 4 1/3 innings of one-hit, shutout relief. Charlie Maxwell, acquired in late June from Detroit, hits two homers in Game 2 after crashing three-run homer in opener. Rookie infielder Bob Sadowski hits three-run homer off Sheldon in nightcap.

THE DATE: Friday, August 3
THE PLACE: Comiskey Park
THE CROWD: 23,465
THE STARTERS: Ralph Terry (NY), Juan Pizarro (Chi)
THE FINAL: Yankees 10, White Sox 2
THE WINNER: Terry
THE LOSER: Pizarro
THE KEYS: In game played in afternoon to avoid conflict with that night's College All-Star football game at Soldier Field, Yankees get homers from rookie Tom Tresh, Elston Howard, and Bobby Richardson, four hits from Hector Lopez and a complete-game effort (win No. 15) from Terry. Seventh-place Sox drop 15 games behind AL-leading Yankees.

THE DATE: Saturday, August 4
THE PLACE: Comiskey Park
THE CROWD: 36,468
THE STARTERS: Bill Stafford (NY), Frank Baumann (Chi)
THE FINAL: White Sox 2, Yankees 1
THE WINNER: Baumann
THE LOSER: Stafford
THE KEYS: With score 1-1 in ninth, Stafford allows single to Charlie Maxwell, ground-rule double to Floyd Robinson and intentional walk to Joe Cunningham to fill bases with none out. Stafford then hits Al Smith in left shoulder with 1-0 pitch, forcing in winning run. Baumann goes the distance, finishing with five-hitter.

THE DATE: Sunday, August 5
THE PLACE: Comiskey Park
THE CROWD: 44,444
THE STARTERS: Whitey Ford (NY), Eddie Fisher (Chi)
THE FINAL: White Sox 3, Yankees 2 (13 innings)
THE WINNER: Juan Pizarro
THE LOSER: Jim Coates
THE KEYS: Shutout relief by New York's Bud Daley and Marshall Bridges and Chicago's Dean Stone, Turk Lown, and Pizarro set stage for dramatic finish. With two out in home 13th, Pizarro bats for himself and singles to center and, when ball bounces away from Jack Reed (replacement for injured Mickey Mantle), Pizarro takes second base. Mike Hershberger then lines a Coates fastball into right-center for game-winning run.

THE DATE: Friday night, September 21
THE PLACE: Comiskey Park
THE CROWD: 32,711
THE STARTERS: Whitey Ford (NY), Juan Pizarro (Chi)
THE FINAL: White Sox 7, Yankees 6
THE WINNER: Johnny Buzhardt
THE LOSER: Marshall Bridges
THE KEYS: See "Most Glorious Victory"

THE DATE: Saturday, September 22
THE PLACE: Comiskey Park
THE CROWD: 17,454
THE STARTERS: Ralph Terry (NY), Ray Herbert (Chi)

THE FINAL: White Sox 6, Yankees 2
THE WINNER: Herbert
THE LOSER: Terry
THE KEYS: Nellie Fox's RBI single snaps 2-2 tie during three-run Sox seventh, and Chicago adds three runs in eighth to deny Terry his 23rd victory. Herbert goes seven and improves to 18-9.

THE DATE: Sunday, September 23
THE PLACE: Comiskey Park
THE CROWD: 30,032
THE STARTERS: Bill Stafford (NY), Early Wynn (Chi)
THE FINAL: Yankees 5, White Sox 1 (10 innings)
THE WINNER: Stafford
THE LOSER: Wynn
THE KEYS: In Sox's home finale and Wynn's second bid for his 300th win, Sox tie game 1-1 in ninth on Floyd Robinson's RBI double. But Hector Lopez singles in tie-breaker in 10th and Elston Howard follows with three-run homer into upper deck in left, enabling Yankees to clinch tie for third straight pennant.

THE DATE: Friday night, September 28
THE PLACE: Yankee Stadium
THE CROWD: 11,444
THE STARTERS: Early Wynn (Chi), Jim Bouton (NY)
THE FINAL: Yankees 7, White Sox 3
THE WINNER: Tex Clevenger
THE LOSER: Wynn
THE KEYS: Wynn, in final appearance with Sox and still in quest of No. 300, leads 3-1 in seventh before rookie Joe Pepitone hits two-run pinch homer to tie game. Then, in eighth, Tony Kubek's single breaks tie and Dale Long adds three-run homer. Wynn, after release by Sox, signs with Cleveland and gets 300th the following June.

THE DATE: Saturday, September 29
THE PLACE: Yankee Stadium
THE CROWD: 10,461
THE STARTERS: Juan Pizarro (Chi), Whitey Ford (NY)
THE FINAL: Yankees 8, White Sox 6
THE WINNER: Bob Turley
THE LOSER: Frank Baumann
THE KEYS: Sox lead 6-3 entering ninth, but Yankees get close on John Blanchard's home run off Johnny Buzhardt and win it on rookie Tom Tresh's three-run, one-out blast off Baumann.

THE DATE: Sunday, September 30
THE PLACE: Yankee Stadium
THE CROWD: 14,685
THE STARTERS: Ray Herbert (Chi), Bill Stafford (NY)
THE FINAL: White Sox 8, Yankees 4
THE WINNER: Herbert
THE LOSER: Stafford
THE KEYS: In season finale, Herbert gains 20th win thanks to Eddie Fisher (four scoreless innings in relief) and September callup Brian McCall, 19, who had spent the '62 season in the Class B Northwest League. The lefthanded-hitting outfielder homers off Stafford in third inning and off Ralph Terry in seventh,

making him 3 for 8 in the big leagues. He never again gets a major-league hit.

1963 Season

THE DATE: Wednesday, April 24
THE PLACE: Yankee Stadium
THE CROWD: 4,206
THE STARTERS: Juan Pizarro (Chi), Stan Williams (NY)
THE FINAL: White Sox 6, Yankees 4 (12 innings)
THE WINNER: Hoyt Wilhelm
THE LOSER: Luis Arroyo
THE KEYS: Down 4-2 with two out in ninth, Yankees tie on Jack Reed's RBI triple and passed ball charged to J.C. Martin when a Wilhelm knuckler eludes him. But Wilhelm opens top of 12th with bloop single and eventually scores, along with Nellie Fox, on Mike Hershberger's two-out single off Bill Kunkel, Yankees' seventh pitcher of day.

THE DATE: Thursday night, May 9
THE PLACE: Comiskey Park
THE CROWD: 32,405
THE STARTERS: Ralph Terry (NY), Ray Herbert (Chi)
THE FINAL: White Sox 2, Yankees 0
THE WINNER: Herbert
THE LOSER: Terry
THE KEYS: In makeup of April 29 rainout, Herbert fires his third straight shutout, allowing two hits and lowering his ERA to 2.19. Ron Hansen's double in second inning drives in only runs of a game that lasts just 1:51. Sox lead second-place Yankees by two games.

THE DATE: Monday night, June 24
THE PLACE: Comiskey Park
THE CROWD: 42,748
THE STARTERS: Al Downing (NY), Johnny Buzhardt (Chi)
THE FINAL: White Sox 5, Yankees 2
THE WINNER: Buzhardt
THE LOSER: Downing
THE KEYS: Sox break 1-1 tie in fourth when rookie Downing walks rookie Tommy McCraw with bases filled and two out and Camilo Carreon follows with bases-clearing double to the fence in right-center. Hoyt Wilhelm saves Buzhardt's ninth win with scoreless eighth and ninth innings as Chicago closes to within one game of Yankees, who will be without Mickey Mantle (broken foot) until August.

THE DATE: Tuesday night, June 25
THE PLACE: Comiskey Park
THE CROWD: 46,177
THE STARTERS: Ralph Terry (NY), Juan Pizarro (Chi)
THE FINAL: White Sox 2, Yankees 1
THE WINNER: Pizarro
THE LOSER: Terry
THE KEYS: See "Most Glorious Victory"

THE DATE: Wednesday night, June 26
THE PLACE: Comiskey Park

THE CROWD: 44,305
THE STARTERS: Whitey Ford (NY), Gary Peters (Chi)
THE FINAL: Yankees 3, White Sox 2
THE WINNER: Ford
THE LOSER: Peters
THE KEYS: Tom Tresh's 12th homer and Elston Howard's RBI single have Ford ahead 2-1 before Roger Maris hits 16th homer to make it 3-1 in sixth. Camilo Carreon's RBI single in seventh KOs Ford, but Hal Reniff shuts down Sox thereafter as Yankees retake AL lead.

THE DATE: Thursday, June 27
THE PLACE: Comiskey Park
THE CROWD: 48,554 (30,040 paid)
THE STARTERS: Jim Bouton (NY), Ray Herbert (Chi)
THE FINAL: White Sox 6, Yankees 0
THE WINNER: Herbert
THE LOSER: Bouton
THE KEYS: Herbert pitches Sox back into first-place tie with his sixth shutout of '63, a five-hitter, beating New York in just 1:55 and handing Bouton only his third loss in 13 decisions. Floyd Robinson's two-run single with bases filled in first inning gets Sox rolling.

THE DATE: Tuesday night, July 2
THE PLACE: Yankee Stadium
THE CROWD: 20,998
THE STARTERS: Ray Herbert (Chi), Al Downing (NY)
THE FINAL: Yankees 3, White Sox 0
THE WINNER: Downing
THE LOSER: Herbert
THE KEYS: Downing strikes out 10 and allows just one hit, Camilo Carreon's two-out single in seventh, to lift Yankees 3 1/2 games ahead of second-place Chicago. After blanking Yankees for 20 innings in the season, Herbert is finally solved on Tony Kubek's bloop RBI single in the third. Hector Lopez adds two-run homer to right in fifth.

THE DATE: Wednesday, July 3
THE PLACE: Yankee Stadium
THE CROWD: 15,198
THE STARTERS: Johnny Buzhardt (Chi), Ralph Terry (NY)
THE FINAL: Yankees 5, White Sox 4
THE WINNER: Hal Reniff
THE LOSER: Jim Brosnan
THE KEYS: Sox tie game when Jim Landis draws bases-loaded walk from Reniff in ninth, but Hector Lopez catches Tommy McCraw's flyball in short left and guns down Al Weis at plate for inning-ending double play. Yankees then win in their half on Tony Kubek's RBI double, after Brosnan had walked his counterpart, Reniff.

THE DATE: Thursday, July 4
THE PLACE: Yankee Stadium
THE CROWD: 38,130
THE STARTERS (1st): Gary Peters (Chi), Whitey Ford (NY)
THE STARTERS (2nd): Juan Pizarro (Chi), Bill Stafford (NY)
THE FINALS: Yankees 9, White Sox 1; White Sox 4, Yankees 2

THE WINNER (1st): Ford
THE LOSER (1st): Peters
THE WINNER (2nd): Pizarro
THE LOSER (2nd): Stafford
THE KEYS: Elston Howard hits No, 16 with none on (off Peters) and Roger Maris hits No. 18 with two on (off Frank Baumann) to aid Ford (13-3), who works six-hitter and fans 12 in Game 1. Then, Floyd Robinson drives in two runs and Nellie Fox lines homer over 296-foot sign with one on as Pizarro improves to 10-4. Yankees lead by 4 1/2 games.

THE DATE: Friday night, August 16
THE PLACE: Comiskey Park
THE CROWD: 35,444
THE STARTERS: Whitey Ford (NY), Juan Pizarro (Chi)
THE FINAL: Yankees 4, White Sox 2
THE WINNER: Bill Kunkel
THE LOSER: Pizarro
THE KEYS: See "Most Devastating Defeat"

THE DATE: Saturday, August 17
THE PLACE: Comiskey Park
THE CROWD: 29,719
THE STARTERS: Al Downing (NY), Gary Peters (Chi)
THE FINAL: White Sox 2, Yankees 0
THE WINNER: Peters
THE LOSER: Downing
THE KEYS: Pete Ward collects three hits, a sacrifice fly and two RBIs to help fellow rookie Peters win his eighth straight game and 13th of the year. Peters allows just four hits and lowers ERA to 1.88, best in majors among starting pitchers.

THE DATE: Sunday, August 18
THE PLACE: Comiskey Park
THE CROWD: 44,659
THE STARTERS (1st): Ralph Terry (NY), Ray Herbert (Chi)
THE STARTERS (2nd): Jim Bouton (NY), Joe Horlen (Chi)
THE FINALS: Yankees 8, White Sox 2; Yankees 8, White Sox 4
THE WINNER (1st): Terry
THE LOSER (1st): Herbert
THE WINNER (2nd): Bouton
THE LOSER (2nd): Horlen
THE KEYS: Hector Lopez homers in opener and Elston Howard does so in Game 2 (in which he goes 4 for 4) to help Terry improve to 14-12 and Bouton to 16-6. Yanks, even without Roger Maris and Mickey Mantle, collect 23 hits as they stretch their lead over Chicago to 10 1/2 games.

THE DATE: Friday night, August 23
THE PLACE: Yankee Stadium
THE CROWD: 30,014
THE STARTERS: Hoyt Wilhelm (Chi), Jim Bouton (NY)
THE FINAL: Yankees 7, White Sox 2
THE WINNER: Bouton
THE LOSER: Wilhelm
THE KEYS: Wilhelm, in second of three 1963 starts, departs with 3-2 deficit after six innings, and Yanks add four in seventh off Jim Brosnan and Bouton

coasts to 17th win. Pete Ward collects three hits to raise average vs. New York to .328.

THE DATE: Saturday, August 24
THE PLACE: Yankee Stadium
THE CROWD: 20,140
THE STARTERS: Ray Herbert (Chi), Whitey Ford (NY)
THE FINAL: Yankees 3, White Sox 0
THE WINNER: Ford
THE LOSER: Herbert
THE KEYS: Ford needs just 21 pitches to get through first three innings and finishes with six-hitter and 29th shutout of his career. Tony Kubek doubles in a run in fifth and then scores on Bobby Richardson's single, and John Blanchard adds "short porch" home run in eighth. Sox now trail New York by 12 games.

THE DATE: Sunday, August 25
THE PLACE: Yankee Stadium
THE CROWD: 41,646
THE STARTERS (1st): Juan Pizarro (Chi), Al Downing (NY)
THE STARTERS (2nd): Gary Peters (Chi), Stan Williams (NY)
THE FINALS: Yankees 4, White Sox 0; White Sox 2, Yankees 1 (12 innings)
THE WINNER (1st): Downing
THE LOSER (1st): Pizarro
THE WINNER (2nd): Peters
THE LOSER (2nd): Williams
THE KEYS: In opener, Downing (10-4) fans 14 and allows just two hits, the first being Ron Hansen's leadoff single in eighth. Elston Howard hits Nos. 25 and 26, one off Pizarro and one off Jim Brosnan. In Game 2, Floyd Robinson's sacrifice fly in 12th breaks tie and Peters, going the route and allowing only six hits, wins his 10th in a row and improves to 15-5 on the year.

1964 Season

THE DATE: Wednesday night, April 23
THE PLACE: Comiskey Park
THE CROWD: 29,703
THE STARTERS: Whitey Ford (NY), Gary Peters (Chi)
THE FINAL: Yankees 3, White Sox 0
THE WINNER: Ford
THE LOSER: Peters
THE KEYS: Ford posts 200th career victory and 35th career shutout and lifts lifetime record vs. Chicago to 31-19. Yankee outfield records just two putouts. Clete Boyer homers in fifth for first Yankee run.

THE DATE: Friday, June 12
THE PLACE: Yankee Stadium
THE CROWD: 38,135
THE STARTERS (1st): John Buzhardt (Chi), Steve Hamilton (NY)
THE STARTERS (2nd): Joe Horlen (Chi), Whitey Ford (NY)
THE FINALS: Yankees 6, White Sox 1; Yankees 3, White Sox 0
THE WINNER (1st): Hamilton
THE LOSER (1st): Frank Baumann
THE WINNER (2nd): Ford
THE LOSER (2nd): Horlen

THE KEYS: Joe Pepitone's two-run homer and Roger Maris' two-run single highlight five-run Yankee sixth in opener, and Tony Kubek's two-run homer in sixth inning of nightcap snaps scoreless tie as Ford records 39th career shutout and ups '64 record to 8-1. Sox had entered with 1 1/2-game lead on Orioles and 5-game lead on New York.

THE DATE: Saturday, June 13
THE PLACE: Yankee Stadium
THE CROWD: 20,532 (15,531 paid)
THE STARTERS: Frank Kreutzer (Chi), Al Downing (NY)
THE FINAL: Yankees 6, White Sox 3
THE WINNER: Bill Stafford
THE LOSER: Hoyt Wilhelm
THE KEYS: Mickey Mantle hits 430th career homer in fourth (off rookie lefty Kreutzer), Tom Tresh delivers tie-breaking single in fifth and Stafford contributes 4 1/3 innings of one-hit, shutout relief.

THE DATE: Sunday, June 14
THE PLACE: Yankee Stadium
THE CROWD: 37,148
THE STARTERS (1st): Juan Pizarro (Chi), Bud Daley (NY)
THE STARTERS (2nd): Gary Peters (Chi), Roland Sheldon (NY)
THE FINALS: Yankees 8, White Sox 3; Yankees 4, White Sox 3 (10 innings)
THE WINNER (1st): Daley
THE LOSER (1st): Pizarro
THE WINNER (2nd): Hal Reniff
THE LOSER (2nd): Hoyt Wilhelm
THE KEYS: Pizarro and Peters both enter with 7-2 records to Daley's 1-2 and Sheldon's 0-0, but Yankees pay no heed: Elston Howard and Phil Linz hit two-run homers in opener and Reniff saves win for Daley with three perfect innings of relief; in Game 2, after Dave Nicholson's three-run, 450-foot homer into bleachers in left-center gives Peters 3-0 lead in sixth, Yanks get run in seventh and then tie game in ninth on Bobby Richardson's sacrifice fly. In 10th, Joe Pepitone, with two out, singles off lefty Don Mossi to drive in game-winning run. Yankees and Sox now tied for second, one game behind Orioles.

THE DATE: Saturday, June 20
THE PLACE: Comiskey Park
THE CROWD: 27,366 (22,453 paid)
THE STARTERS: Whitey Ford (NY), Gary Peters (Chi)
THE FINAL: Yankees 1, White Sox 0 (11 innings)
THE WINNER: Ford
THE LOSER: Peters
THE KEYS: After rightfielder Mike Hershberger throws out Roger Maris at the plate for second out of 11th, Elston Howard bloops single to center to drive in game's lone run. Ford then finishes off yet another shutout to improve to 10-1; Peters falls to 7-4 as Sox drop seventh straight to New York.

THE DATE: Sunday, June 21
THE PLACE: Comiskey Park
THE CROWD: 39,316
THE STARTERS (1st): Jim Bouton (NY), Juan Pizarro (Chi)
THE STARTERS (2nd): Al Downing (NY), Joe Horlen (Chi)
THE FINALS: Yankees 2, White Sox 0; Yankees 2, White Sox 1 (17 innings)

THE WINNER (1st): Bouton
THE LOSER (1st): Pizarro
THE WINNER (2nd): Bill Stafford
THE LOSER (2nd): Don Mossi
THE KEYS: See "Most Devastating Defeat"

THE DATE: Monday night, June 22
THE PLACE: Comiskey Park
THE CROWD: 26,026
THE STARTERS: Steve Hamilton (NY), Johnny Buzhardt (Chi)
THE FINAL: Yankees 6, White Sox 5
THE WINNER: Hamilton
THE LOSER: Frank Baumann
THE KEYS: In makeup of previous Friday night's rainout, Yankees make it 10 straight over Sox, even with Mickey Mantle, Elston Howard, and Tony Kubek all given the evening off. RBI singles off Baumann by Joe Pepitone and Hamilton in fifth help erase 2-1 Sox lead and put Yanks ahead 5-2. Down 6-2 in ninth, Chicago rallies but comeback falls short when Joe Cunningham grounds to pitcher to end game with tying run at third. Yankees grab AL lead by half-game over Baltimore; Sox are 31/2 out.

THE DATE: Tuesday, August 11
THE PLACE: Yankee Stadium
THE CROWD: 14,576
THE STARTERS: Joe Horlen (Chi), Ralph Terry (NY)
THE FINAL: White Sox 6, Yankees 4
THE WINNER: Don Mossi
THE LOSER: Terry
THE KEYS: In afternoon half of day-night double-header, Pete Ward's 17th homer, a two-out, two-run shot over the 407-foot marker in right-center in the seventh, puts Sox ahead 4-3, and Hoyt Wilhelm protects lead over final three innings to give Chicago its first victory over Yankees in 1964.

THE DATE: Tuesday night, August 11
THE PLACE: Yankee Stadium
THE CROWD: 25,203
THE STARTERS: Juan Pizarro (Chi), Jim Bouton (NY)
THE FINAL: White Sox 8, Yankees 2
THE WINNER: Pizarro
THE LOSER: Bouton
THE KEYS: Leading 2-1 in sixth, Sox break it open on RBI singles by ex-Yankee star Bill Skowron (5 for 7 on the day) and J.C. Martin and 420-foot homer to right-center by Pizarro, who goes on to become AL's first 15-game winner. Sox now trail first-place Baltimore by one game; Yankees drop 31/2 games back.

THE DATE: Wednesday, August 12
THE PLACE: Yankee Stadium
THE CROWD: 16,945
THE STARTERS: Ray Herbert (Chi), Mel Stottlemyre (NY)
THE FINAL: Yankees 7, White Sox 3
THE WINNER: Stottlemyre
THE LOSER: Herbert
THE KEYS: Mickey Mantle homers lefthanded (off Herbert) over the 461-foot marker in dead center (blast is measured at 502 feet) to tie game in fourth, then

homers righthanded (off Frank Baumann) in eighth—the 10th and final time "the Mick" homers from both sides of plate in same game. Beneficiary is Stottlemyre, just called up from Triple-A Richmond and making big-league debut. He goes distance, allowing seven hits, for first of 167 career victories.

THE DATE: Thursday night, August 13
THE PLACE: Yankee Stadium
THE CROWD: 24,711
THE STARTERS: Gary Peters (Chi), Al Downing (NY)
THE FINAL: Yankees 5, White Sox 2
THE WINNER: Downing
THE LOSER: Peters
THE KEYS: With game tied 2-2 in eighth and Roger Maris and Tom Tresh both aboard with walks, Elston Howard crushes two-out, 400-foot blast into visitors' bullpen in left to drop Sox three games behind Orioles. Yanks trail by 3 1/2.

THE DATE: Monday night, August 17
THE PLACE: Comiskey Park
THE CROWD: 38,885
THE STARTERS: Ralph Terry (NY), Juan Pizarro (Chi)
THE FINAL: White Sox 2, Yankees 1
THE WINNER: Pizarro
THE LOSER: Terry
THE KEYS: Yankees, with Mickey Mantle (jammed knee) limited to pinch-hitting duty for series, fall behind 1-0 in sixth on J.C. Martin's sacrifice fly and 2-0 in seventh on Pete Ward's RBI single off Whitey Ford, making cameo relief appearance. Bobby Richardson singles in run in eighth before Hoyt Wilhelm enters and retires Roger Maris and Elston Howard to end eighth and then sets down side in order in ninth. Sox are 1 1/2 games behind AL-leading Orioles.

THE DATE: Tuesday night, August 18
THE PLACE: Comiskey Park
THE CROWD: 35,403
THE STARTERS: Al Downing (NY), Gary Peters (Chi)
THE FINAL: White Sox 4, Yankees 3 (10 innings)
THE WINNER: Eddie Fisher
THE LOSER: Downing
THE KEYS: Floyd Robinson's three-run homer in eighth forges 3-3 tie, and with runners at first and third and two out in 10th, Mike Hershberger—0 for his last 16 and, vs. New York, just 2 for 40 on the season—lines 2-2 fastball to right-center for game-winning single.

THE DATE: Wednesday night, August 19
THE PLACE: Comiskey Park
THE CROWD: 37,354
THE STARTERS: Jim Bouton (NY), Ray Herbert (Chi)
THE FINAL: White Sox 4, Yankees 2
THE WINNER: Herbert
THE LOSER: Bouton
THE KEYS: With Yanks up 1-0 and bases loaded with two out in Sox third, Joe Pepitone fields Pete Ward's two-hopper and flips to Bouton covering, but umpire Lou DiMuro rules Bouton missed bag, enabling tying run to score. Bouton, enraged, fires ball into ground, and Jim Landis keeps coming from second to score go-ahead run. Bases-loaded walk to Landis and Don Buford's sacrifice

fly in seventh makes it 4-2, and Sox's victory, coupled with Baltimore's loss in Boston, leaves Chicago a half-game from AL lead.

THE DATE: Thursday, August 20
THE PLACE: Comiskey Park
THE CROWD: 36,677
THE STARTERS: Whitey Ford (NY), Johnny Buzhardt (Chi)
THE FINAL: White Sox 5, Yankees 0
THE WINNER: Buzhardt
THE LOSER: Ford
THE KEYS: See "Most Glorious Victory"

Appendix B
Year-by-Year Comparisons
1951-1964

White Sox and Yankees

*Note: *= led league **= with Sox ***= with Yankees #= All-time record*

1951 (8-team league)	**NEW YORK**	**CHICAGO**
Won-lost	98-56	81-73
Finish	1st	4th
Games behind	....	17
Home attendance	1,950,107	1,328,234
Team batting avg.	.269 (2nd)	.270 (1st)
Team slugging pct.	.408 (1st)	.385 (5th)
Team ERA	3.56 (3rd)	3.50 (2nd)
Team fielding pct.	.975 (4th-T)	.975 (4th-T)
Total DP	190 (2nd)	176 (5th)
Total strikeouts	644 (1st)	572 (5th)
Total shutouts	24 (1st)	11 (2nd)
Total runs scored	798 (2nd)	714 (4th)
Total HR	140 (1st-T)	86 (6th-T)
Total SB	78 (2nd)	99 (1st)
Batting leader	McDougald .306	Minoso .326
HR leader	Berra 27	E. Robinson 29
RBI leader	Berra 88	E. Robinson 117
Pitching (W)	Raschi, Lopat 21	Pierce 15
Pitching (ERA)	Lopat 2.91	Rogovin 2.78*
Left field (Player, HR, RBI, AVG.)	Woodling 15, 71, .281	Minoso (RF) 10, 76, .326
	Jensen 8, 25, .298	Stewart 6, 40, .276
Center field	DiMaggio 12, 71, .263	Busby 5, 68, .283
Right field	Bauer 10, 54, .296	Zarilla 10, 60, .257
	Mantle 13, 65, .267	Lenhardt (LF) 10, 45, .266**
Third base	McDougald 14, 63, .306	Dillinger 0, 20, .301
	Brown 6, 51, .268	
Shortstop	Rizzuto 2, 43, .274	Carrasquel 2, 58, .264
Second base	Coleman 3, 43, .249	Fox 4, 55, .313
First base	Collins 9, 48, .286	Robinson 29, 117, .282
Catcher	Berra 27, 88, .294	Masi 4, 28, .271
		Niarhos 1, 10, .256
Starters	Raschi 21-10	Pierce 15-14
	Lopat 21-9	Rogovin 12-8
	Reynolds 17-8	Holcombe 11-12
	Morgan 9-3	Gumpert 9-8
		Dobson 7-6

Relievers	Kuzava 2.40 Ostrowski 3.49 Shea 4.33	Dorish 3.54 Aloma 1.82 Rotblatt 3.40 Judson 3.77

1952	**NEW YORK**	**CHICAGO**
Won-lost	95-59	81-73
Finish	1st	3rd
Games behind	...	14
Home attendance	1,629,665	1,231,675
Team batting avg.	.267 (1st)	.252 (5th)
Team slugging pct.	.403 (2nd)	.348 (7th)
Team ERA	3.14 (1st)	3.25 (2nd)
Team fielding pct.	.979 (2nd)	.980 (1st)
Total DP	199 (1st)	158 (4th)
Total strikeouts	666 (4th)	774 (1st)
Total shutouts	17 (1st)	13 (2nd)
Total runs scored	727 (2nd)	610 (5th)
Total HR	129 (2nd)	80 (7th)
Total SB	52 (3rd-T)	61 (1st)
Batting leader	Mantle .311	Fox, E. Robinson .296
HR leader	Berra 30	E. Robinson 22
RBI leader	Berra 98	E. Robinson 104
Pitching (W)	Reynolds 20	Pierce 15
Pitching (ERA)	Reynolds 2.06*	Dobson 2.51
Left field	Woodling 12, 63, .309	Minoso 13, 61, .281
Center field	Mantle 23, 87, .311	Rivera 7, 48, .253
Right field	Bauer 17, 74, .293	Mele 16, 69, .259
Third base	McDougald 11, 78, .263	Rodriguez 1, 40, .265
Shortstop	Rizzuto 2, 43, .254	Carrasquel 1, 42, .248
Second base	Martin 3, 33, .267	Fox 0, 39, .296
First base	Collins 18, 59, .280	Robinson 22, 104, .296
Catcher	Berra 30, 98, .273	Lollar 13, 50, .240
Starters	Raschi 16-6 Lopat 10-5 Reynolds 20-6 Sain 11-6	Pierce 15-12 Rogovin 14-9 Dobson 14-10 Grissom 12-10 Stobbs 7-12
Relievers	Kuzava 3.45 Morgan 3.07 Hogue 5.32 Miller 3.48	Dorish 2.47 Aloma 4.28 Kennedy 2.80

1953	**NEW YORK**	**CHICAGO**
Won-lost	99-52	89-65
Finish	1st	3rd
Games behind	....	11 1/2
Home attendance	1,537,811	1,141,353
Team batting avg.	.273 (1st)	.258 (6th)
Team slugging pct.	.417 (1st)	.364 (7th)
Team ERA	3.20 (1st)	3.41 (2nd)
Team fielding pct.	.979 (2nd-T)	.980 (1st)
Total DP	182 (2nd)	144 (8th)
Total strikeouts	604 (6th)	714 (1st)
Total shutouts	16 (1st-T)	16 (1st-T)

Total runs scored	801 (1st)	716 (3rd)
Total HR	139 (2nd)	74 (7th)
Total SB	34 (4th)	73 (1st)
Batting leader	Bauer .304	Minoso .313
HR leader	Berra 27	Minoso 15
RBI leader	Berra 108	Minoso 104
Pitching (W)	Ford 18	Trucks 20
Pitching (ERA)	Lopat 2.42*	Pierce 2.72
Left field	Woodling 10, 58, .306	Minoso 15, 104, .313
Center field	Mantle 21, 92, .295	Rivera 11, 78, .259
Right field	Bauer 10, 57, .304	Mele 12, 82, .274
Third base	McDougald 10, 83, .285	Elliott 9, 61, .255
Shortstop	Rizzuto 2, 54, .271	Carrasquel 2, 47, .279
Second base	Martin 15, 75, .257	Fox 3, 72, .285
First base	Collins 17, 44, .269	Fain 6, 52, .256
Catcher	Berra 27, 108, .296	Lollar 8, 54, .287
Starters	Ford 18-6	Trucks 20-10
	Lopat 16-4*	Pierce 18-12
	Raschi 13-6	Fornieles 8-7
	Sain 14-7	Dobson 5-5
	McDonald 9-7	Rogovin 7-12
Relievers	Kuzava 3.31	Dorish 3.40
	Gorman 3.39	Keegan 2.74
	Reynolds 3.41	Consuegra 2.54

1954	**NEW YORK**	**CHICAGO**
Won-lost	103-51	94-60
Finish	2nd	3rd
Games behind	8	17
Home attendance	1,475,171	1,231,629
Team batting avg.	.268 (1st)	.267 (2nd)
Team slugging pct.	.408 (1st)	.379 (4th)
Team ERA	3.26 (3rd)	3.05 (2nd)
Team fielding pct.	.979 (2nd-T)	.982 (1st)
Total DP	198 (1st)	149 (6th)
Total strikeouts	655 (5th)	701 (2nd)
Total shutouts	12 (4th)	21 (1st)
Total runs scored	805 (1st)	711 (3rd)
Total HR	133 (2nd)	94 (4th-T)
Total SB	34 (6th)	98 (1st)
Batting leader	Noren .319	Minoso .320
HR leader	Mantle 27	Minoso 19
RBI leader	Berra 125	Minoso 116
Pitching (W)	Grim 20	Trucks 19
Pitching (ERA)	Ford 2.82	Consuegra 2.69
Left field	Noren 12, 66, .319	Minoso 19, 116, .320
Center field	Mantle 27, 102, .300	Groth 7, 60, .275
Right field	Bauer 12, 54, .294	Rivera 13, 61, .286
Third base	Carey 8, 65, .302	Kell 5, 58, .276
		Michaels 7, 44, .262
Shortstop	Rizzuto 2, 15, .195	Carrasquel 12, 62, .255
Second base	McDougald 12, 48, .259	Fox 2, 47, .319
First base	Collins 12, 46, .271	Fain 5, 51 .302
	Skowron 7, 41, .340	Cavarretta 3, 24, .316

Catcher	Berra 22, 125, .307	Lollar 7, 34, .244
Starters	Grim 20-6	Trucks 19-12
	Ford 16-8	Pierce 9-10
	Lopat 12-4	Keegan 16-9
	Byrd 9-7	Harshman 14-8
	Reynolds 13-4	Consuegra 16-3*
Relievers	Sain 3.16	Dorish 2.72
	Morgan 3.34	M. Martin 3.52
		D. Johnson 3.13

1955	**NEW YORK**	**CHICAGO**
Won-lost	96-58	91-63
Finish	1st	3rd
Games behind	....	5
Home attendance	1,490,138	1,175,684
Team batting avg.	.260 (5th)	.268 (1st)
Team slugging pct.	.418 (1st)	.388 (5th)
Team ERA	3.23 (1st)	3.37 (2nd)
Team fielding pct.	.978 (3rd)	.981 (1st-T)
Total DP	180 (1st)	147 (7th)
Total strikeouts	731 (2nd)	720 (3rd)
Total shutouts	18 (1st)	17 (2nd)
Total runs scored	762 (2nd)	725 (4th)
Total HR	175 (1st)	116 (6th)
Total SB	55 (2nd)	69 (1st)
Batting leader	Mantle .306	Kell .312
HR leader	Mantle 37*	Dropo 19
RBI leader	Berra 108	Kell 81
Pitching (W)	Ford 18*	Pierce 15
		Donovan 15
Pitching (ERA)	Ford 2.63	Pierce 1.97*
Left field	Noren 8, 59, .253	Minoso 10, 70, .288
	Howard 10, 43, .290	
Center field	Mantle 37, 99, .306	Busby 7, 41, .239
Right field	Bauer 20, 53, .278	Rivera 10, 52, .264
		Nieman 11, 53, .283
Third base	Carey 7, 47, .257	Kell 8, 81, .312
		Kennedy 9, 43, .304**
Shortstop	Hunter 3, 20, .227	Carrasquel 11, 52, .256
Second base	McDougald 13, 53, .285	Fox 6, 59, .311
First base	Collins 13, 45, .234	Dropo 19, 79, .280
	Skowron 12, 61, .319	
Catcher	Berra 27, 108, .272	Lollar 16, 61, .261
Starters	Ford 18-7	Pierce 15-10
	Turley 17-13	Donovan 15-9
	Byrne 16-5*	Trucks 13-8
	Larsen 9-2	Harshman 11-7
	Kucks 8-7	C. Johnson 7-4
Relievers	Grim 4.19	Howell 2.93
	Morgan 3.25	M. Martin 3.63
	Konstanty 2.32	Consuegra 2.64
		Byrd 4.65

1956	NEW YORK	CHICAGO
Won-lost	97-57	85-69
Finish	1st	3rd
Games behind	....	12
Home attendance	1,491,784	1,000,090
Team batting avg	.270 (3rd)	.267 (4th)
Team slugging pct.	.434 (1st)	.397 (4th)
Team ERA	3.63 (2nd)	3.73 (3rd)
Team fielding pct.	.977 (4th-T)	.979 (1st)
Total DP	214 (1st)	160 (5th)
Total strikeouts	732 (3rd)	722 (4th)
Total shutouts	9 (5th)	11 (2nd)
Total runs scored	857 (1st)	776 (4th)
Total HR	190 (1st)	128 (5th)
Total SB	51 (2nd)	70 (1st)
Batting leader	Mantle .353*	Minoso .316
HR leader	Mantle 52*	Doby 24
RBI leader	Mantle 130*	Doby 102
Pitching (W)	Ford 19	Pierce 20
Pitching (ERA)	Ford 2.47*	Harshman 3.10
Left field	Howard 5, 34, .262	Minoso 21, 88, .316
	Siebern 4, 21, .204	
Center field	Mantle 52, 130, .353	Doby 24, 102, .268
Right field	Bauer 26, 84, .241	Rivera 12, 66, .255
Third base	Carey 7, 50, .237	Hatfield 7, 33, .262
		Esposito 3, 25, .228
Shortstop	McDougald 13, 56, .311	Aparicio 3, 56, .266
Second base	Martin 9, 49, .264	Fox 4, 52, .296
First base	Skowron 23, 80, .308	Dropo 8, 52, .266
		Philley 5, 64, .247
Catcher	Berra 30, 105, .298	Lollar 11, 75, .293
Starters	Ford 19-6*	Pierce 20-9
	Kucks 18-9	Donovan 12-10
	Sturdivant 16-8	Harshman 15-11
	Larsen 11-5	Wilson 13-14
	Turley 8-4	
Relievers	Grim 2.72	Howell 4.62
	Morgan 4.16	Staley 3.26
	Byrne 3.36	LaPalme 2.35
	R. Coleman 3.67	Kinder 2.70

1957	NEW YORK	CHICAGO
Won-lost	98-56	90-64
Finish	1st	2nd
Games behind	....	8
Home attendance	1,497,134	1,135,668
Team batting avg.	.268 (1st)	.260 (3rd)
Team slugging pct.	.409 (1st)	.375 (6th)
Team ERA	3.00 (1st)	3.35 (2nd)
Team fielding pct.	.980 (3rd-T)	.982 (1st)
Total DP	183 (1st)	169 (3rd)
Total strikeouts	810 (1st)	665 (7th)
Total shutouts	13 (2nd-T)	16 (1st)
Total runs scored	723 (1st)	707 (3rd)
Total HR	145 (3rd)	106 (7th)

Total SB	49 (3rd)	109 (1st)
Batting leader	Mantle .365	Fox .317
HR leader	Mantle 34	Doby 14
		Rivera 14
RBI leader	Mantle 94	Minoso 103
Pitching (W)	Sturdivant 16	Pierce 20*
Pitching (ERA)	Shantz 2.45	Donovan 2.77
Left field	Kubek 3, 39, .297	Minoso 12, 103, .310
	Slaughter 5, 34, .254	
Center field	Mantle 34, 94, .365	Doby 14, 79, .288
Right field	Bauer 18, 65, .259	Rivera 14, 52, .256
		Landis 2, 16, .212
Third base	Carey 6, 33, .255	Phillips 7, 42, .270
	Lumpe 0, 11, .340	
Shortstop	McDougald 13, 62, .289	Aparicio 3, 41, .257
Second base	Richardson 0, 19, .256	Fox 6, 61, .317
First base	Skowron 17, 88, .304	Dropo 13, 49, .256
	Simpson 13, 63, .270	Torgeson 8, 51, .286
Catcher	Berra 24, 82, .251	Lollar 11, 70, .256
	Howard 8, 44, .253	
Starters	Sturdivant 16-6*	Pierce 20-12
	Ford 11-5	Donovan 16-6*
	Shantz 11-5	Wilson 15-8
	Kucks 8-10	Keegan 10-6
	Larsen 10-4	Harshman 8-8
	Turley 13-6	
Relievers	Grim 2.63	Staley 2.06
	Ditmar 3.25	LaPalme 3.35
	Byrne 4.36	Howell 3.29
		Fischer 3.48

1958	**NEW YORK**	**CHICAGO**
Won-lost	92-62	82-72
Finish	1st	2nd
Games behind	....	10
Home attendance	1,428,428	797,451
Team batting avg.	.268 (1st)	.257 (4th)
Team slugging pct.	.416 (1st)	.367 (6th)
Team ERA	3.22 (1st)	3.61 (4th)
Team fielding pct.	.978 (6th)	.981 (2nd)
Total DP	182 (1st)	160 (6th)
Total strikeouts	796 (2nd)	751 (5th)
Total shutouts	21 (1st)	15 (2nd)
Total runs scored	759 (1st)	634 (6th)
Total HR	164 (1st)	101 (8th)
Total SB	48 (3rd-T)	101 (1st)
Batting leader	Mantle .304	Fox .300
HR leader	Mantle 42*	Lollar 20
RBI leader	Mantle 97	Lollar 84
Pitching (W)	Turley 21*	Pierce 17
Pitching ERA)	Ford 2.01*	Pierce 2.68
Left field	Siebern 14, 55, .300	Smith 12, 58, .252
	Howard 11, 66, .314	
Center field	Mantle 42, 97, .304	Landis 15, 64, .277
Right field	Bauer 12, 50, .268	Rivera 9, 35, .225
Third base	Carey 12, 45, .286	Goodman 0, 40, .299

Shortstop	Kubek 2, 48, .265	Aparicio 2, 40, .266
Second base	McDougald 14, 65, .250	Fox 0, 49, .300
First base	Skowron 14, 73, .273	Boone 13, 61, .242
		Torgeson 10, 30, .266
Catcher	Berra 22, 90, .266	Lollar 20, 84, .273
Starters	Turley 21-7*	Pierce 17-11
	Ford 14-7	Donovan 15-14
	Ditmar 9-8	Wynn 14-16
	Shantz 7-6	Moore 9-7
	Kucks 8-8	Wilson 9-9
Relievers	Duren 2.02	Staley 3.16
	Larsen 3.07	Lown 3.98
	Maas 3.82	

1959	**NEW YORK**	**CHICAGO**
Won-lost	79-75	94-60
Finish	3rd	1st
Games behind	15	....
Home attendance	1,552,030	1,423,144
Team batting avg.	.260 (2nd)	.250 (6th)
Team slugging pct.	.402 (2nd)	.364 (7th)
Team ERA	3.60 (3rd)	3.29 (1st)
Team fielding pct.	.978 (2nd-T)	.979 (1st)
Total DP	160 (3rd)	141 (5th)
Total strikeouts	836 (1st)	761 (3rd)
Total shutouts	15 (1st-T)	13 (3rd)
Total runs scored	687 (4th)	669 (6th)
Total HR	153 (4th)	97 (8th)
Total SB	45 (4th)	113 (1st)
Batting leader	Richardson .301	Fox .306
HR leader	Mantle 31	Lollar 22
RBI leader	Mantle 75	Lollar 84
Pitching (W)	Ford 16	Wynn 22*
Pitching l(ERA)	Ditmar 2.90	Shaw 2.69
Left field	Siebern 11, 53, .271	Smith 17, 55, .237
Center field	Mantle 31, 75, .285	Landis 5, 64, .272
Right field	Bauer 9, 39, .238	Rivera 4, 19, .220
		McAnany 0, 27, .276
Third base	Lopez 22, 93, .283	Phillips 5, 40, .264
Shortstop	Kubek 6, 51, .279	Aparicio 6, 51, .257
	McDougald 4, 34, .251	
Second base	Richardson 2,33, .301	Fox 2, 70, .306
First base	Skowron 15, 59, .298	Torgeson 9, 45, .220
	Howard 18, 73, .273	Cash 4, 16, .240
Catcher	Berra 19, 69, .284	Lollar 22, 84, .265
Starters	Ford 16-10	Wynn 22-10
	Maas 14-8	Shaw 18-6*
	Ditmar 13-9	Pierce 14-15
	Turley 8-11	Donovan 9-10
	Terry 5-11	Latman 8-5
Relievers	Duren 1.88	Staley 2.25
	Shantz 2.38	Lown 2.90
	Coates 2.87	

Appendix B

1960	NEW YORK	CHICAGO
Won-lost	97-57	87-67
Finish	1st	3rd
Games behind	....	10
Home attendance	1,627,349	1,644,460
Team batting avg.	.260 (4th)	.270 (1st)
Team slugging pct.	.426 (1st)	.396 (2nd)
Team ERA	3.52 (1st-T)	3.60 (3rd)
Team fielding pct.	.979 (3rd-T)	.982 (1st-T)
Total DP	162 (4th)	175 (1st)
Total strikeouts	712 (6th)	695 (7th)
Total shutouts	16 (1st)	11 (2nd-T)
Total runs scored	746 (1st)	741 (2nd)
Total HR	193 (1st)	112 (7th)
Total SB	37 (5th-T)	122 (1st)
Batting leader	Skowron .309	Smith .315
HR leader	Mantle 40*	Sievers 28
RBI leader	Maris 112*	Minoso 105
Pitching (W)	Ditmar 15	Pierce 14
Pitching (ERA)	Ditmar 3.06	Baumann 2.67*
Left field	Lopez 9, 42, .284	Minoso 20, 105, .311
Center field	Mantle 40, 94, .275	Landis 10, 49, .253
Right field	Maris 39, 112, .283	Smith 12, 72, .315
Third base	Boyer 14, 46, .242	Freese 17, 79, .273
	McDougald 8, 34, .258	
Shortstop	Kubek 14, 62, .273	Aparicio 2, 61, .277
Second base	Richardson 1,26, .252	Fox 2, 59, .289
First base	Skowron 26, 91, .309	Sievers 28, 93, .295
Catcher	Berra (LF) 15, 62, .267	Lollar 7, 46, .252
	Howard 6, 39, .245	
Starters	Ford 12-9	Wynn 13-12
	Ditmar 15-9	Shaw 13-13
	Turley 9-3	Pierce 14-7
	Coates 13-3	Baumann 13-6
	Terry 10-8	Score 5-10
Relievers	Duren 4.96	Staley 2.42
	Shantz 2.79	Lown 3.88
	Arroyo 2.88	Kemmerer 3.59
	Maas 4.09	Donovan 5.38

1961 **NEW YORK** **CHICAGO**

(First year of 10-team league, 162-game schedule)

1961	NEW YORK	CHICAGO
Won-lost	109-53	86-76
Finish	1st	4th
Games behind	....	23
Home attendance	1,747,736	1,146,019
Team batting avg.	.263 (4th)	.265 (3rd)
Team slugging pct.	.442 (1st)	.395 (6th)
Team ERA	3.46 (2nd)	4.06 (4th)
Team fielding pct.	.980 (1st-T)	.980 (1st-T)
Total DP	180 (4th)	138 (10th)
Total strikeouts	866 (4th)	814 (7th)
Total shutouts	14 (2nd-T)	3 (10th)
Total runs scored	827 (2nd)	765 (3rd)
Total HR	240# (1st)	138 (7th)

Total SB	28 (10th)	100 (1st)
Batting leader	Mantle .317	F. Robinson .310
HR leader	Maris 61#	Smith 28
RBI leader	Maris 142*	Smith 93
Pitching (W)	Ford 25*	Pizarro 14
Pitching (ERA)	Stafford 2.68	Pizarro 3.05
Left field	Berra 22, 61, .271	Minoso 14, 82, .280
Center field	Mantle 54, 128, .317	Landis 22, 85, .283
Right field	Maris 61, 142, .269	F. Robinson 11, 59, .310
Third base	Boyer 11, 55, .224	Smith 28, 93, .278
Shortstop	Kubek 8, 46, .276	Aparicio 6, 45, .272
Second base	Richardson 3,49, .261	Fox 2, 51, .251
First base	Skowron 28, 89, .267	Sievers 27, 92, .295
Catcher	Howard 21, 77, .348	Lollar 7, 41, .282
		Carreon 4, 27, .271
Starters	Ford 25-4*	Pizarro 14-7
	Stafford 14-9	Herbert 12-12
	Terry 16-3	Pierce 10-9
	Daley 12-17	McLish 10-13
	Sheldon 11-5	Wynn 8-2
Relievers	Arroyo 2.19	Lown 2.76
	Coates 3.44	Hacker 3.77
		Kemmerer 4.38
		Larsen 4.12
		Baumann 5.61

1962	**NEW YORK**	**CHICAGO**
Won-lost	96-66	85-77
Finish	1st	5th
Games behind	....	11
Home attendance	1,493,574	1,131,562
Team batting avg.	.267 (1st)	.257 (5th)
Team slugging pct.	.426 (1st)	.372 (10th)
Team ERA	3.70 (2nd)	3.73 (4th)
Team fielding pct.	.979 (3rd-T)	.982 (1st)
Total DP	151 (8th)	153 (4th-T)
Total strikeouts	838 (6th)	821 (8th)
Total shutouts	10 (6th-T)	13 (2nd)
Total runs scored	817 (1st)	707 (6th-T)
Total HR	199 (2nd)	92 (10th)
Total SB	42 (7th)	76 (2nd-T)
Batting leader	Richardson .302	F. Robinson .312
HR leader	Maris 33	Smith 16
RBI leader	Maris 100	F. Robinson 109
Pitching (W)	Terry 23*	Herbert 20
Pitching ERA)	Ford 2.90	Fisher 3.10
Left field	Lopez 6, 48, .275	F. Robinson 11, 109, .312
	Blanchard 13, 39, .232	
Center field	Mantle 30, 89, .321	Landis 15, 61, .228
Right field	Maris 33, 100, .256	Hershberger 4, 46, .262
Third base	Boyer 18, 68, .272	Smith 16, 82, .292
Shortstop	Tresh 20, 93, .286	Aparicio 7, 40, .241
Second base	Richardson 8,59, .302	Fox 2, 54, .267
First base	Skowron 23, 80, .270	Cunningham 8, 70, .295
Catcher	Howard 21, 91, .279	Carreon 4, 37, .256
Starters	Terry 23-12	Herbert 20-9

	Ford 17-8	Pizarro 12-14
	Stafford 14-9	Fisher 9-5
	Bouton 7-7	Buzhardt 8-12
	Sheldon 7-8	Wynn 7-15
Relievers	Bridges 3.14	Lown 3.04
	Daley 3.59	Baumann 3.38
	Arroyo 4.81	Zanni 3.59
	Coates 4.44	Stone 3.26

1963	**NEW YORK**	**CHICAGO**
Won-lost	104-57	94-68
Finish	1st	2nd
Games behind	....	10 1/2
Home attendance	1,308,920	1,158,848
Team batting avg.	.252 (2nd-T)	.250 (5th-T)
Team slugging pct.	.403 (2nd)	.365 (7th)
Team ERA	3.07 (2nd)	2.97 (1st)
Team fielding pct.	.982 (2nd)	.979 (5th)
Total DP	162 (3rd)	163 (2nd)
Total strikeouts	965 (3rd)	932 (5th)
Total shutouts	17 (2nd)	19 (1st)
Total runs scored	714 (2nd)	683 (4th)
Total HR	188 (2nd)	114 (8th)
Total SB	42 (8th)	64 (4th)
Batting leader	Howard .287	Ward .295
HR leader	Howard 28	Ward 22
		Nicholson 22
RBI leader	Pepitone 89	Ward 84
Pitching (W)	Ford 24*	Peters 19
Pitching (ERA)	Bouton 2.53	Peters 2.33*
Left field	Lopez 14, 52, .249	Nicholson 22, 70, .229
	Blanchard 16, 45, .225	
Center field	Tresh 25, 71, .269	Landis 13, 45, .225
	Mantle 15, 35, .314	Hershberger 3, 45, .279
Right field	Maris 23, 53, .296	F. Robinson 13, 71, .283
Third base	Boyer 12, 54, .251	Ward 22, 84, .295
Shortstop	Kubek 7, 44, .257	Hansen 13, 67, .226
Second base	Richardson 3,48, .265	Fox 2, 42, .260
First base	Pepitone 27, 89, .271	Cunningham 1, 31, .286
		McCraw 6, 33, .254
Catcher	Howard 28, 85, .287	Carreon 2, 35, .274
Starters	Ford 24-7*	Peters 19-8
	Bouton 21-7	Pizarro 16-8
	Terry 17-15	Herbert 13-10
	Downing 13-5	Horlen 11-7
	S. Williams 9-8	Buzhardt 9-4
Relievers	Hamilton 2.60	Wilhelm 2.64
	Reniff 2.62	Brosnan 2.84
		Fisher 3.95

1964	**NEW YORK**	**CHICAGO**
Won-lost	99-63	98-64
Finish	1st	2nd
Games behind	....	1
Home attendance	1,305,638	1,250,083

Team batting avg.	.252 (2nd-T)	.247 (6th-T)
Team slugging pct.	.387 (4th-T)	.353 (8th)
Team ERA	3.15 (3rd)	2.72 (1st)
Team fielding pct.	.983 (2nd)	.981 (4th-T)
Total DP	158 (4th)	164 (2nd)
Total strikeouts	989 (5th)	955 (8th)
Total shutouts	18 (3rd)	20 (2nd)
Total runs scored	730 (2nd)	642 (7th)
Total HR	162 (5th)	106 (9th)
Total SB	54 (5th)	75 (3rd)
Batting leader	Howard .313	F. Robinson .301
HR leader	Mantle 35	Ward 23
RBI leader	Mantle 111	Ward 94
Pitching (W)	Bouton 18	Peters 20*
Pitching (ERA)	Ford 2.13	Horlen 1.88
Left field	Tresh 16, 73, .246	McCraw (1B) 6, 36, .261
Center field	Mantle 35, 111, .303	H'berger (RF) 2, 31, .230
		Landis 1, 18, .208
Right field	Maris 26, 71, .281	F. Rob'son (LF) 11, 59, .301
Third base	Boyer 8, 52, .218	Ward 23, 94, .282
Shortstop	Kubek 8, 31, .229	Hansen 20, 68, .261
	Linz 5, 25, .250	
Second base	Richardson 4,50, .267	Buford 4, 30, .264
		Weis 2, 23, .247
First base	Pepitone 28, 100, .251	Skowron** 4, 38, .293
Catcher	Howard 15, 84, .313	Martin 4, 22, .197
Starters	Ford 17-6	Peters 20-8
	Bouton 18-13	Pizarro 19-9
	Terry 7-11	Herbert 6-7
	Downing 13-8	Horlen 13-9
	Stottlemyre 9-3	Buzhardt 10-8
Relievers	Ramos 1.25***	Wilhelm 1.99
	Reniff 3.12	Fisher 3.02
	Hamilton 3.28	Mossi 2.93
	Mikkelsen 3.56	

Appendix C
Some Individual Statistics

How Top Yankee Hitters Fared against White Sox Pitchers

MICKEY MANTLE

Year	AB	R	H	HR	RBI	AVG
1951	52	12	17	4	15	.298
1952	92	13	24	2	10	.261
1953	73	14	20	6	16	.274
1954	78	19	25	3	12	.321
1955	80	15	20	7	15	.250
1956	83	17	30	6	16	.361
1957	86	21	36	6	20	.419
1958	72	23	17	8	12	.236
1959	83	14	23	6	13	.277
1960	73	16	26	7	14	.356
1961*	56	10	14	4	11	.250
1962	44	10	9	2	6	.205
1963	5	0	0	0	0	.000
1964	46	9	18	4	8	.391
TOTALS	923	193	279	65	168	.302

* — Beginning of 10-team league, meaning 18 games vs. each club rather than 22.

YOGI BERRA

Year	AB	R	H	HR	RBI	AVG
1951	70	11	22	4	11	.314
1952	81	10	18	5	14	.222
1953	67	10	16	3	12	.239
1954	83	15	29	5	25	.349
1955	79	11	20	2	9	.253
1956	86	11	28	4	17	.326
1957	80	12	20	3	11	.250
1958	63	9	17	3	12	.270
1959	78	11	23	2	7	.295
1960	42	3	12	0	8	.286
1961	26	6	6	2	6	.231
1962	31	3	7	0	1	.226
1963	15	2	6	0	0	.400
TOTALS	801	114	224	33	133	.280

BILL SKOWRON

Year	AB	R	H	HR	RBI	AVG
1954	31	6	9	2	5	.290
1955	52	11	21	3	8	.404
1956	76	10	20	2	11	.263
1957	66	5	17	2	15	.258
1958	74	14	26	4	17	.351
1959	35	3	10	2	5	.286
1960	80	11	30	4	14	.375
1961	61	5	13	1	4	.213
1962	53	4	19	3	7	.358
TOTALS	528	69	165	23	86	.313

ROGER MARIS

Year	AB	R	H	HR	RBI	AVG
1960	83	18	22	6	13	.265
1961	71	19	27	13	26	.380
1962	55	8	15	1	4	.273
1963	32	5	7	3	7	.219
1964	56	5	11	1	7	.196
TOTALS	297	55	82	24	57	.276

How Top White Sox Hitters Fared against Yankee Pitchers

NELLIE FOX

Year	AB	H	AVG
1951	92	32	.348
1952	83	26	.313
1953	86	24	.279
1954	94	26	.277
1955	87	27	.310
1956	94	29	.309
1957	82	24	.293
1958	88	21	.239
1959	88	32	.364
1960	86	17	.198
1961	63	14	.222
1962	69	16	.232
1963	54	10	.185
TOTALS	1066	298	.280

MINNIE MINOSO

Year	AB	H	RBI	AVG
1951	81	23	8	.284
1952	81	24	9	.296
1953	71	16	7	.225
1954	87	27	9	.310
1955	78	20	5	.256
1956	72	19	10	.264
1957	76	22	9	.289
1960	83	29	18	.349
1961	55	12	4	.218
1964	5	1	0	.200
TOTALS	689	193	79	.280

Bibliography

Boyd, Brendan C., and Harris, Fred C. *The Great American Baseball Card Flipping, Trading and Bubble Gum Book*. Boston: Little, Brown,1973.

Cairns, Bob. *Pen Men*. New York: St.Martin's Press, 1992.

Condon, David. *The Go-Go Chicago White Sox*. New York: Coward-McCann,1960.

Creamer, Robert. *Stengel: His Life and Times*. New York: Simon & Schuster, 1989.

Enright, Jim, et.al. *Trade Him! 100 Years of Baseball's Greatest Deals*. Chicago: Follett, 1976.

Ford, Whitey, with Phil Pepe. *Slick: My Life In and Around Baseball*. New York: Morrow, 1987.

Forker, Dom. *The Men of Autumn: An Oral History of the 1949-53 World Champion New York Yankees*. Dallas: Taylor, 1989.

Forker, Dom. *Sweet Seasons: Recollections of the 1955-64 New York Yankees*. Dallas: Taylor, 1990.

Gallagher, Mark. *Explosion! Mickey Mantle's Legendary Home Runs*. New York: Arbor House, 1987.

Golenbock, Peter. *Dynasty: The New York Yankees, 1949-64*. Englewood Cliffs, N.J.: Prentice-Hall, 1975.

Halberstam, David. *October 1964*. New York: Villard Books, 1994.

Houk, Ralph, with Robert Creamer. *Season of Glory*. New York: Putnam's, 1988.

Kahn, Roger. *The Era: 1947-57*. New York: Ticknor & Fields, 1993.

Kubek, Tony, with Terry Pluto. *Sixty-One: The Team, the Record, the Men.* New York: MacMillan, 1987.

Lindberg, Richard. *Who's on 3rd? The Chicago White Sox Story.* South Bend, Ind.: Icarus, 1983.

Minoso, Orestes, with Herb Fagen. *Just Call Me Minnie: My Six Decades in Baseball.* Champaign, Ill.: Sagamore, 1994.

Nemec, David, et.al. *20th Century Baseball Chronicle.* Montreal: Tormont, 1992.

Official Baseball Guide. St. Louis: The Sporting News, 1947-65.

Okrent, Daniel, and Wulf, Steve. *Baseball Anecdotes.* New York: Oxford University Press, 1989.

Peary, Danny. *We Played the Game: 65 Players Remember Baseball's Greatest Era, 1947-64.* New York: Hyperion, 1994.

Reichler, Joseph L. (ed.). *The Baseball Encyclopedia, 6th Edition.* New York: MacMillan, 1985.

Rosenthal, Harold. *The Ten Best Years of Baseball: An Informal History of the Fifties.* Chicago: Contemporary Books, 1979.

Sox: Complete Record of Chicago White Sox Baseball. New York: MacMillan, 1984.

Thompson, S.C. *All-Time Rosters of Major League Baseball Clubs.* Canbury, N.J.: Barnes, 1967, 1973.

Vanderberg, Bob. *Sox: From Lane and Fain to Zisk and Fisk.* Chicago: Chicago Review Press, 1982.

Veeck, Bill, with Ed Linn. *Veeck As In Wreck.* New York: Putnam's, 1962.

Veeck, Bill, with Ed Linn. *Hustler's Handbook.* New York: Putnam's, 1965.